ILLUSTRATED HISTORY
OF THE DODGERS

RICHARD WHITTINGHAM

TRIUMPH
BOOKS
CHICAGO

Portions of this book originally appeared in *The Los Angeles Dodgers: An Illustrated History,*
by Richard Whittingham, published by Harper & Row Publishers, New York, 1982.

Library of Congress Cataloging-in-Publication Data

Whittingham, Richard, date
        Illustrated history of the Dodgers / Richard Whittingham.
            p. cm.
        Includes index.
        ISBN 1-57243-714-6
        1. Los Angeles Dodgers (Baseball team)—History. 2. Los Angeles Doders (Baseball team)—History—
    Pictorial works. I. Title.

GV875.L6W43 2005
796.357'64'0979494—dc22

                                                                                    2004059874

This book is available in quantity at special discounts for your group or organization.
For further information, contact:

Triumph Books
601 South LaSalle Street
Suite 500
Chicago, Illinois 60605
(312) 939-3330
Fax (312) 663-3557

Printed in U.S.A.

ISBN-13: 978-1-57243-714-2
ISBN-10: 1-57243-714-6

Design by Eileen Wagner, Wagner/Donovan Design

CONTENTS

WHEN DICK WHITTINGHAM asked me to do the Foreword for his book on the history of the Dodgers, I was thrilled. I have had the honor of spending more than five decades in the Dodgers organization as a player, scout, coach, and manager, and have many wonderful memories.

The Dodgers are a class organization. They are synonymous with baseball. Somebody says "Padres," and you want to know where the priest is. Somebody says "Indians," and you want to know which reservation. Somebody says "Twins," and you want to know where the other brother is. Somebody says "Dodgers," and you know exactly what he's talking about.

I always had dreams of being an outstanding baseball player in the big leagues. Then when I got there, I wasn't. A number of times I didn't get the opportunity because I was playing with a ballclub that had outstanding players, and consequently I didn't get a chance. Because of that, I felt bad, yes; but that wasn't the end of the world for me. Being a manager in the major leagues gave me another opportunity in a different direction, for which I'm so grateful.

My minor league record as a pitcher was pretty good, but let me give you an illustration of why I never really caught on with the Dodgers:

When we were leading the league by 12 games in July 1955, and I was thinking of various ways to spend my World Series check, I was summoned into the office of our general manager, Buzzy Bavasi. He said to me, "Tom, I've got some bad news."

And I said, "What's wrong, Buzzy, one of your relatives sick?"

And he said, "No, I'm going to have to send you back to Montreal," which was our Triple A club at the time.

And I said, "Send me back to Montreal? You've got to be crazy, Buzzy. Last year when you brought me up I was 14–5 in July; in 1953 I won 21 games in the season and the playoffs. What do I have to do to prove to you and to management that I can pitch for this ballclub?"

And he said, "Tom, I've got a problem. I'm one player over the limit. I've got to get rid of one player, and you're the guy. If you were the general manager, who would you get rid of?"

I said, "Hey, I'd get rid of Koufax. Here's a guy who can't pitch, he can't hit a barn door 60 feet away with a baseball. You're telling me that I've got to go back to Triple A and this guy is going to stay?"

And he said, "Tom, the rules of baseball say that if a player receives a bonus over $4,000 he must remain on the major league club for two years. Koufax stays and you go."

So now I can walk around and honestly say that it took the greatest left-handed pitcher in baseball to knock me off that Brooklyn club.

After my playing days were over, I knew I wanted to be a manager, and the first time I put on the manager's uniform in the minors, I knew I wanted to be the Dodgers manager someday.

A manager has to be an understanding person. He has to know the strengths and weaknesses of his team, and he has to know the strengths and weaknesses of his opponents. There's a lot of strategy involved in managing. You have many players you must contend with during the course of a game. Then, of course, you may be thinking innings or even days ahead. Sometimes you manage according to the way your bullpen is set up, or because your strength is in a particular place. I will play hunches many times, because sometimes you have to throw out the book and go against the percentages or the accepted strategy of managing.

I didn't have that much to do with the ballclub's winning—that was the players' doing, plus the great deals made by the front office. They are the ones that put teams together. We had successful people running this organization, from Pete O'Malley on down. Everybody took a special interest; we were all proud to be Dodgers. It's something special and we wanted to do anything we could to make it the best organization in baseball. All I was, was a traffic cop. Maybe I helped the players believe in themselves—but nothing more. I felt like a father sitting at the dinner table feeling pride and love for his family.

I loved my players. I wanted them to play to their full potential. We had a lot of togetherness. Our guys realized that it would take teamwork for them to win. They believed they could beat anybody. That's the tremendous thing about them. When they walked out on the field, they didn't think there was a pitcher alive who could get them out. And that's a great attitude to have. I feel like the luckiest guy in the world to have managed that team. I am grateful and thankful. Every time I hug my players, it's to show them that. Many of them are the men I grew up with as a manager. They started out in the rookie leagues with me and played on up through the ranks, finally arriving in the majors. Along with those men, our newcomers blended right in, and together they made a great ballclub.

I think all people, anytime they undertake anything, should always feel confident they will be successful, whether it be in baseball or everyday life. I think if a person believes in himself, in the company he works for, and the product he represents, then he has a good chance of being a happy and successful man.

I'm very, very fortunate to have worked for Mr. and Mrs. Walter O'Malley. They and their children, Peter O'Malley and Terry Seidler, have done so much to help me, like I was really an important part of the organization—whether I was scouting, managing one of the minor league clubs, playing, coaching in the big leagues, or managing in the big leagues. They always did everything they could to help me feel like we were part of something. They always did everything they could to help make me happy here. I will be forever grateful to them. Because of them, I was fortunate to be a part of this organization for more than five decades.

No question about it—baseball is a great big part of our country. Just like all sports are. Playing in a sport teaches youngsters the art of competition at an early age. It teaches them how to follow orders. It teaches them how to get along with their fellow man. Playing professionally gives them an opportunity to travel and an opportunity to earn a good living. Baseball probably has one of the finest pension plans in this country. All of these things give the youngsters an incentive, the opportunity, and the desire to play baseball.

Baseball is all about the fans. We play for the people in the stands. When they come out to a ballpark to see us play, we always want them to go home happy and be able to say: "We had a great time at the Dodgers game."

There are four things I've never regretted: my love for God, my love for my family, my love for my country, and my love for the Dodgers. The Dodgers are the organization with a heart. Before Walter O'Malley died, he presented me with a Dodger Blue tombstone that read: "Tom Lasorda: Dodger Stadium was his address, every ballpark was his home." I couldn't ask for more.

—*Tommy Lasorda*

ACKNOWLEDGMENTS

THE AUTHOR AND PUBLISHER wish to express their appreciation to the Los Angeles Dodgers organization for the assistance and cooperation they so generously offered during the creation of the original book under this title. And special thanks are extended to Tommy Lasorda for the Foreword he so graciously provided and the in-depth interview he granted to the author.

A debt of gratitude is also owed to the National Baseball Hall of Fame in Cooperstown, New York, and to the authors, compilers, and publishers of two classic reference books on the subject of major league baseball: *The Baseball Encyclopedia,* Macmillan Publishing Company, New York, 1969, et al; and *The Sports Encyclopedia: Baseball, 2004,* David S. Neft, Richard M. Cohen, and Michael L. Neft, St. Martins Press, New York, 2004.

CHAPTER 1

A BEGINNING LONG AGO

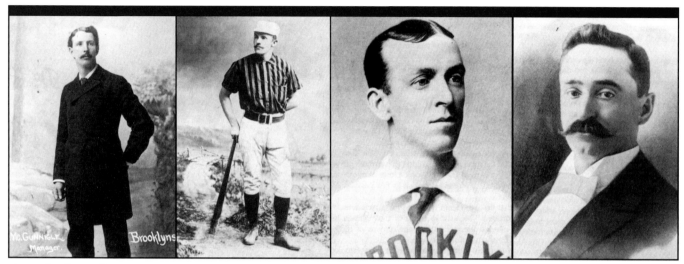

The early pilots: Bill McGunnigle (1888–1890), John M. "Monte" Ward (1891–1892), Dave Foutz (1893–1896), and Ned Hanlon (1899–1905).

THE GAME OF BASEBALL had been a major source of entertainment around Brooklyn since the days before the Civil War. An ever-changing array of amateur and semipro teams appeared and disappeared back then; they played a game in which the ball was commonly pitched underhand, batters could call for the kind of pitch they wanted (high or low), and the number of strikes or balls necessary to retire a batter or get him to first base varied with the whims of those running each game. But it was a genuinely popular sport, and it was inevitable that baseball would one day become a prosperous professional enterprise in Brooklyn.

In 1884 the Dodgers came into being, although they were known by a variety of other nicknames back in those days. The team was suggested by editor George Taylor at the *New York Herald*, and it came to fruition as a result of investments by businessman/attorney Charlie Byrne and two

gamblers, Joe Doyle and Gus Abell. The team they created, known only as the "Brooklyns" or "Brooklyners," was sent out onto the field to play in the American Association, a "major league" that had surfaced two years earlier to compete with the National League. The owners built a ballpark in south Brooklyn, a shaky arrangement of wood benches, and named it Washington Park. One of the first employees was a young man in his early twenties by the name of Charles Hercules Ebbets, who began his Dodgers career selling scorecards, peanuts, and tickets.

At the time, Brooklyn was an independent city of about nine hundred thousand people; its single umbilical connection to the city of New York on the other side of the East River was the Brooklyn Bridge, which had just been completed the year before. It was a time when New York City had a population of less than 1.5 million, when Chester A. Arthur was president of the then 38 United

1

States of America, when the automobile, airplane, and radio were still dreams of the future.

There were 12 teams in the American Association when Brooklyn joined it in 1884. The newcomer hardly made a mark its maiden year, finishing ninth. Like any other enterprise, it would take time to develop. The owners were serious about attracting talent to their fledgling team, and the most notable acquisition was manager William McGunnigle in 1888. He took a loser of a team and turned it around, winning Brooklyn its first pennant ever in 1889.

By that time, the team had acquired a nickname, the "Bridegrooms," because so many of its players had gotten married during the spring and summer of 1889. It was soon shortened to "Grooms."

The next year, the pennant winners from Brooklyn moved from the foundering American Association (it soon went out of business after the 1891 season) to the National League, which had been in existence since 1876. The admission of the Dodgers to the National League in 1890 sparked one of the greatest intercity rivalries in all sportsdom: the Dodgers versus the Giants. (They did not become "intracity" adversaries until 1898 when Brooklyn was annexed to New York.) Lee Allen, famed historian at the National Baseball Hall of Fame, described the inauguration of the rivalry in his book, *The Giants and the Dodgers: The Fabulous Story of Baseball's Fiercest Feud*:

The two teams met in a National League game for the first time at Washington Park on Saturday, May 3, 1890. The first man to go to bat was Silent Mike Tiernan. Parisian Bob Caruthers was the starting pitcher for the home team, Smiling Mickey Welch for the visiting Giants. Brooklyn scored three runs in the first inning and ran out the game, 7–3, before a crowd of only 3,774. Mickey Welch and his smile were hammered out as smoothly as a piece of glass . . . and the Brooklyns ran the bases just as if there was no one behind the bat.

The adroit William McGunnigle brought his team another pennant that first year in the National League. There were some close contests with the Giants both at Washington Park and at the Polo Grounds up by Coogan's Bluff in Harlem, but the Giants never gave the Brooklyners a run for the pennant. The team that came closest was the Chicago White Stockings, also known as the Colts and later the Cubs, piloted by Adrian "Cap" Anson. McGunnigle, however, was rewarded for his back-to-back championships by being ousted as manager, the result of some front-office politics rather than his performance as a pilot.

The new manager in 1891 was John Montgomery Ward, who had been pitching, playing the infield and outfield, and managing with various National League teams since 1878. The Brooklyn Grooms also opted for a different ballpark that year, moving their games over to a stadium called Eastern Park.

They struck a course that was unfortunately straight downhill. The Grooms, who then became known as "Ward's Wonders," dropped to sixth place under their new manager, with a dismal record of 61–76.

A shake-up in the front office followed, and Joe Doyle sold off his interests in the club. At the same time, much more responsibility for the club's operation was given to Charles Ebbets. Ward held his job as manager and turned in a much better record of 95–59 in 1892, but it was only good enough to land Brooklyn in third place. After the season, Ward left to manage the archrival Giants across the river.

The new manager was Dave Foutz, who had been a mainstay as a player for Brooklyn since 1888. With his ascension came another name for the Brooklyn team—"Foutz's Fillies." Foutz guided the club for four years, but it never once ended up higher than fifth place in the then 12-team National League. The only really notable event during his tenure was the evolution of the team's ultimate nickname. In 1893, Brooklyn was sometimes called Trolleyville, after the many trolley lines that crisscrossed the city. Nowhere were they more apparent than outside the Brooklyn ballpark. First, some writers of the day began to refer to the fans as Trolley Dodgers, after observing their efforts to get into the ballpark. The name was soon applied to the team, and by the mid-1890s it was shortened to Dodgers.

During this time, Charles Ebbets began to accumulate stock in the Brooklyn team, at first buying up small amounts. But in 1897, he was able to acquire the large block owned by Gus Abell and thus gain a controlling interest in the team. Because of his style and royal manner, he also became known as "the Squire of Flatbush," which would stay with him for the rest of his days. In 1898, Ebbets bought some land in south Brooklyn, put up a twelve thousand–seat wooden stadium and named it Washington Park. That year, coincidentally, the team turned in its worst performance since joining the NL. They finished 10th, winning only 54 of 149 games, and going through three managers during the season, the last one Ebbets himself.

The next year, 1899, however, was an important one in Brooklyn baseball history. It was the year that Ebbets and Baltimore Orioles owner Harry Von der Horst got together to do some backroom wheeling and dealing. The Orioles had been the class of the league for most of the decade, winning three consecutive pennants (1894–1896), and their roster still held a wealth of talent. Both owners exchanged half interests in each other's teams, and Von der Horst sent a troupe of his best players up to Brooklyn, including Wee Willie Keeler, Hughie Jennings, Dan McGann, Joe Kelley, and Jay Hughes. (The next year Von der Horst would "trade" Iron Man Joe McGinnity and Jimmy Sheckard to Brooklyn.) Another plum for the Dodgers was the acquisition of Orioles manager Ned Hanlon, respected as one of the finest in the game.

The change in Brooklyn's baseball fortunes was immediate. Hanlon brought them a pennant his first year, 1899, and then another the following year. He was also the indirect cause of a change, if

TRIVIA

Oscar Jones and Jack Cronin have the dubious distinction of being the first Dodgers pitchers to lose more than 20 games in a single season (Jones 17–25 and Cronin 12–23 in 1904).

Harry McIntyre has the record for most 20-game-loss seasons, three (1905: 8–25, 1906: 13–21, 1908: 11–20). The most losses in a season were charged to George Bell in 1910 when he posted a record of 10–27.

temporary, in the team's nickname. At the time, there existed a vaudeville act called "Hanlon's Superbas" (no relation to the baseball Hanlon), and soon the Dodgers were being called the "Superbas."

Things were to change after Hanlon's dual pennants, however. Just as the American Association had raided the talent troves of the National League in the 1880s, the neophyte American League did the same in 1901. The AL enticed many of the National League players into the folds of their new eight-team league, including such superstars of the day as Nap Lajoie, Cy Young, John McGraw, and Clark Griffith. The Dodgers lost their ace pitcher, Iron Man Joe McGinnity, to the new league. The year before, McGinnity had become Brooklyn's first pitcher in the 20th century to win 20 or more games (29–9). The Superbas also lost one of their best hitters, Fielder Jones, to the Chicago White Sox.

The losses were duly felt. Hanlon's Superbas dropped to third place in 1901, trailing the Pittsburgh Pirates, who were paced by the immortal Honus Wagner, and the Philadelphia Phillies, who were led by another Hall of Famer, Ed Delahanty.

The Brooklyn stars that year were Wee Willie Keeler, who batted .355, Jimmy Sheckard (.353), Tom Daly (.315), and Joe Kelley (.308). Leading the pitching staff was Wild Bill Donovan, with 25 wins against 15 losses; he also lived up to his nickname by leading the league in the number of bases on balls given up (152).

Keeler and Donovan played one more year for the Superbas; both then moved to the American

3

League for the 1903 season. There were no adequate replacements, and Brooklyn slid to fifth, sixth, and finally eighth place over the next three seasons. The latter was the team's first finish in the cellar, and the only one in their entire history. Their record that awful year was 48–104, and no Dodgers team since has ever lost more games in a season than that. They ended up 56½ games out of first place— also a record low in the club's history.

Charles Ebbets hired a new manager for 1906, Patsy Donovan, who had been a player in the majors since 1890 and a player-manager since 1897. With some strong pitching from Bill "Doc" Scanlan (18–13), consistent hitting by Harry Lumley (.324), and power from Tim Jordan (12 home runs, the most in the NL that year), the team edged back to fifth place. Their record, however, was still below .500 (66–86), and they ended up a full 50 games behind the pennant-winning Chicago Cubs, who boasted the famed Tinker-to-Evers-to-Chance double-play combination and the amazing, if unorthodox, pitching of Mordecai "Three Finger" Brown.

The Dodgers added a great pitcher of their own the following year when they signed 22-year-old rookie Nap Rucker. Rucker won 134 games for Brooklyn over the next 10 years and posted a career ERA of 2.42. Still, the Dodgers languished in the second division; in fact, they remained there until 1915, putting together a disappointing string of 12 years below the first division level. Patsy Donovan remained at the helm for only three years; that first-year finish of fifth had turned out to be his best. He was followed by the one-year appearance of Harry Lumley, who could edge Brooklyn no higher than sixth, and then the four-year term of Bill Dahlen, a shortstop who had been bouncing around the National League since 1891 (including a tour with Brooklyn from 1899 through 1903).

Although the team was not winning during those years (they would not have a winning season until 1916), it could be said that they were "building a roster," even if it was over an inordinately

Nap Rucker joined the Dodgers in 1907 and for most of the next 10 years was the club's premier pitcher. His stats never did justice to his abilities as a pitcher because he hurled for Dodgers teams that were consistently mired in the second division. Only in his last year did Rucker pitch for a team that won more games than it lost. His best year was 1911 when he won 22 and lost 18, with an ERA of 2.71.

long period of time. Two fine hitters were added in 1910—first baseman Jake Daubert and outfielder Zack Wheat. Neither would hit above .300 his rookie year with the Dodgers, but together they would develop into the best one-two hitting punch since Wee Willie Keeler and Jimmy Sheckard wore Brooklyn uniforms back at the turn of the century. In 1912 another newcomer of note made his appearance—a 21-year-old outfielder named Charles Dillon "Casey" Stengel.

Casey Stengel broke into the major leagues at age 21 with the Brooklyn Dodgers. He roamed the Dodgers outfield from 1912 through 1917, then moved on to the Pittsburgh Pirates. He would return to manage the team for three years (1934–1936), but "the Old Professor," as he would come to be called, would make his managerial mark at Yankee Stadium up in the Bronx. As a Dodger, Stengel hit .316 twice (in 1912 and 1914), but as a manager could not bring the team in higher than fifth place. Casey was elected to the Hall of Fame in 1966. Photo courtesy of the National Baseball Hall of Fame and Museum.

The following year marked the Dodgers' move to a new home. Charles Ebbets had acquired a parcel of land on Bedford Avenue near the perimeter of Flatbush in a less-than-romantic area that was then known as Pigtown. He built a stadium there for the sum of $750,000. The edifice was imposing, built solidly of brick and adorned with ornamental concrete castings, great arched windows, and a basilica-like entrance rotunda; it stood as one of the sturdiest and most impressive ballpark structures in the major leagues. At that time, its seating capacity was eighteen thousand, with standing room for perhaps another three thousand.

Another important change took place in 1914 with the arrival of Wilbert Robinson to replace Bill Dahlen as manager. Robinson, 51, had been John "Little Napoleon" McGraw's key coach with the Giants for years. He had played major league ball from 1886 through 1902 with a variety of teams in the American Association, National League, and the burgeoning American League, and was highly regarded as an astute baseball strategist. He was also known for more than that. Baseball historian Lee Allen described him this way:

> **As a young player he weighed 180 pounds. But finally the hotel menus took their toll, and one morning he awoke to discover that he was as broad as he was tall, with flesh clinging to his frame like ivy to a dormitory. Jovial, genial, and an object of mirth, he was, by the time he came to Brooklyn, one of the most popular figures in the game. Damon Runyon would soon be calling him "Your Uncle Wilbert." Others would refer to him as "The Round Robin." These would be shortened to "Uncle Robbie."**

In 1914 Robinson began what would be the longest tenure of any Brooklyn manager, 18 years, a record which stood until Walt Alston came along 40 years later. With Uncle Robbie, still another nickname for the Brooklyn ballclub emerged—no longer Grooms, Dodgers, or Superbas, they would now be called the "Robins."

Robinson felt that he had a team whose talents were capable of producing a winner his maiden year, but that they just hadn't yet learned how to do it together. He was basically correct. They came in fifth in 1914, still playing below .500, but the good signs were there: their 75 wins that year were the most since 1902. Four players hit above .300. Jake Daubert's .329 was the league's best, and it was the second year in a row he had captured the NL batting crown. (His .350

Holder of many Dodgers batting records, Zack Wheat played all but his last year in the majors with Brooklyn. During his 19-year career (1909–1927), he compiled a lifetime batting average of .317 and hit .375 in two consecutive years (1923 and 1924). He was inducted into the Hall of Fame in 1959.

WORLD SERIES LINEUPS, 1916

DODGERS
Hy Myers, cf
Jake Daubert, 1b
Casey Stengel, rf
Zack Wheat, lf
George Cutshaw, 2b
Mike Mowrey, 3b
Ivy Olson, ss
Chief Meyers, c

RED SOX
Harry Hooper, rf
Hal Janvrin, 2b
Tilly Walker, cf
Dick Hoblitzel, 1b
Duffy Lewis, lf
Larry Gardner, 3b
Everett Scott, ss
Hick Cady, c

STARTING PITCHERS
Game 1: Rube Marquard, Ernie Shore
Game 2: Sherry Smith, Babe Ruth
Game 3: Jack Coombs, Carl Mays
Game 4: Rube Marquard, Dutch Leonard
Game 5: Jeff Pfeffer, Ernie Shore

average in 1913 had won him the honor of becoming the first Brooklyn player ever to lead the league in batting, and the first to be named the National League's Most Valuable Player.) His offensive efforts were bolstered by Zack Wheat and Jack Dalton, who both hit .319, and Casey Stengel, who batted .316. On the mound, Jeff Pfeffer turned in a sterling performance, winning 23 and losing only 12.

The next year, 1915, Brooklyn broke into the first division, finally producing a record better than .500 (80–72). The third place finish was the best since 1902.

It was 1916, however, that became the year to remember at Ebbets Field. Uncle Robbie guided his Robins to their first pennant since 1900, and Brooklyn paid its first-ever visit to a World Series. It had been a close race, with the Philadelphia Phillies applying the most pressure. Pitching was the Phils' forte, with Grover "Pete" Alexander winning 33 games that year and Eppa Rixey 22. But Brooklyn prevailed by winning 94 games while losing only 60, outdistancing the Phillies by two and one-half games.

In the American League, the Boston Red Sox came up a winner, largely because of the pitching of a 21-year-old left-hander in his third major league season: Babe Ruth had won 23 and lost 12 and had posted the lowest ERA in the league, 1.75.

In 1916 the pennant winners from Brooklyn fielded pretty much the same team. The most crucial change was the addition of Rube Marquard to the regular pitching rotation. Acquired from the Giants late in the preceding season, in 1915 he went on to chalk up 13 wins for Uncle Robbie and was still considered as reliable as he had been when he was a consistent 20-game winner with the Giants earlier in the decade. Marquard was a fine complement to Jeff Pfeffer, who won 25 games that year, and Larry Cheney and Sherry Smith, who boasted 18 and 14 victories, respectively. And both Jake Daubert and Zack Wheat hit above .300.

The first game of the World Series brought Brooklyn to enemy territory. Rube Marquard was pitted against Ernie Shore, who had won 16 games for the Red Sox in the regular season. The American Leaguers battered the Robins most of the afternoon and took a 6–1 lead into the ninth inning. Then Brooklyn rallied for four runs, but could not get another to send the game into extra innings. The game ended with the bases loaded and the Robins on the short end of a 6–5 score.

Still in Boston for Game 2, Robinson selected Sherry Smith to go against Babe Ruth. The game is historic because it went 14 full innings with the same two pitchers throughout. When it was over, the Babe had given up one run and six hits and Smith two runs and seven hits. No two pitchers ever have labored so long in a World Series game.

Ebbets Field got its first taste of a World Series game the following day, and it was a relatively blissful event. With Jack Coombs on the mound, the Robins beat the Red Sox 4–3 for their first

TRIVIA

The Dodgers played in the longest game in major league history—26 innings in Boston against the Braves on May 1, 1920. The game ended with the score tied at 1–1. And both pitchers, Leon Cadore of Brooklyn and Joe Oeschger of Boston, pitched the entire 26 innings.

The Squire of Flatbush, Charles Hercules Ebbets was a part of the Dodgers from the very beginning back in 1884, starting out as an errand boy and vendor and working his way up to president by 1897. By the early 1900s he had taken over ownership of the ballclub and would lead it until his death in 1925. Dapper, dignified, and a shrewd but stuffy businessman, Ebbets guided the Dodgers organization through the financially delicate early years, built the imposing ballpark on Bedford Avenue that would take his name, curried a legendary feud with New York Giants manager John McGraw, and brought to Brooklyn some of the game's most illustrious names, such as Wilbert Robinson, Casey Stengel, Wee Willie Keeler, Jimmy Sheckard, Zack Wheat, Rube Marquard, and Dazzy Vance. Photo courtesy of the National Baseball Hall of Fame and Museum.

postseason victory ever, to bring themselves within a game of the Series leaders.

The glory was short-lived, however. Hubert "Dutch" Leonard (not to be confused with the Dutch Leonard who pitched for the Dodgers in the thirties) threw a five-hitter at the Robins the next day, and the young men from Brooklyn were decisively trounced, 6–2. Then, back in Boston, Ernie Shore of the Red Sox recorded his second victory of the Series, hurling a masterful three-hitter. The final score was 4–1, the Series was over, and Brooklyn had lost it four games to one.

The most obvious cause of their demise in the postseason festivities was the lack of hitting. Premier sluggers Zack Wheat and Jake Daubert hit .211 and .176, respectively. The team's collective

average was only .200. The one memorable performance at the plate was the one turned in by Casey Stengel, who batted .364.

Even more abrupt than Brooklyn's escalation to pennant winning was the team's plummet to ignobility the year after. With the same players and the same manager, the club nose-dived from first place to seventh, finishing 26½ games behind John McGraw's pennant-winning Giants. The Robins also lapsed back into losing more games in a season than they won, their record 70–81. The second-division syndrome would continue over the next two seasons.

World War I came and went, as did the abbreviated 1918 season (cut short by the war) and the "Black Sox" scandal—the infamous throwing of the 1919 World Series by eight members of the Chicago White Sox. Charles Ebbets got together with Wilbert Robinson, and the two dealt away Casey Stengel and George Cutshaw, who had handled the chores at second base since 1912. In return, however, Brooklyn got Burleigh "Ol' Stubblebeard" Grimes, one of the game's finest spitballers, who became their ace pitcher for the next nine years, winning more than 20 games four times, and eventually earning his way into the Hall of Fame. Another trade sent Jake Daubert to Cincinnati.

Wee Willie Keeler, one of the all-time greats to wear a Dodgers uniform, was one of the gifts Baltimore Orioles owner Harry Von der Horst bestowed on the Brooklyn ballclub when he went into partnership with Charles Ebbets in 1899. Keeler, along with such other luminaries as Iron Man Joe McGinnity, Hughie Jennings, Joe Kelley, and manager Ned Hanlon, was "transferred" to the Dodgers, giving them a team mighty enough to win two consecutive pennants. Keeler's Dodgers career batting average of .352 (1899–1902) is the best in club history. Over his 19 years in the majors, he batted .343. He was inducted into the Hall of Fame in 1939. Photo courtesy of the National Baseball Hall of Fame and Museum.

A feisty first baseman, Jake Daubert has the distinction of being the first Dodger ever to be named the National League's MVP (1913). During his Dodgers career (1910–1918), he batted above .300 seven times, leading the NL in 1913 with an average of .350 and in 1914 with .329. Daubert was traded to the Cincinnati Redlegs in 1919 and ended his 15-year major league career with a lifetime average of .303. Photo courtesy of the National Baseball Hall of Fame and Museum.

By 1920, the face of the Robins had changed, although not drastically. There were still several remnants of the 1916 pennant winners around—Zack Wheat and Hy Myers in the outfield, Ivy Olson at short, Otto Miller behind the plate, and Jeff Pfeffer on the mound. But there were also some notable newcomers—Ed Konetchy at first, Pete Kilduff at second, Tommy Griffith in right field, and Grimes, Leon Cadore, and Al Mamaux on the pitching staff.

The blend was obviously a good one. Uncle Robbie's squad of 1920 won Brooklyn its second trip to the World Series, breezing through the season on a record of 93–61, finishing seven games ahead of the Giants. Grimes won 23 games, losing only 11, his win percentage of .676 the best in the league that year. Zack Wheat led the Robins hitters with an average of .328, and Ed Konetchy and Hy Myers both hit above .300 as well. In addition, Myers contributed 22 triples, the most in the league.

Over in the American circuit, Tris Speaker's Cleveland Indians barely got by the scandal-scarred Chicago White Sox (their "fixers," including such bona fide stars as Shoeless Joe Jackson, Eddie Cicotte, Happy Felsch, and Lefty Williams, were not expelled from the game until two weeks before the season's end, when a grand jury finally made public its findings). Speaker himself batted .388 that year, and his 50 doubles were the most in either league. Five other Indians hit above .300 as well. Jim Bagby won 31 games and lost only 12, his win percentage of .721 the best in the majors.

ZACK WHEAT

Zack "Buck" Wheat was 71 years old in 1959 when he went to Cooperstown to be formally enshrined in the Baseball Hall of Fame. Fifty years earlier he had first arrived in Brooklyn. The year was 1909, the Dodgers were known as the Superbas, and they played at Washington Park because Ebbets Field was still four years away.

Part English, Irish, and Cherokee Indian, Wheat was wiry and strong—a natural athlete. He had grown up in the small farm town of Hamilton, Missouri, and had played for a minor-league team in Mobile, Alabama, in the Southern Association. He had been discovered by scout Larry Sutton and signed by the Squire of Flatbush, Charles Ebbets himself. He staked his claim to left field and homesteaded there for 18 years. But he was most fearsome at home plate, where he terrorized an endless stream of enemy pitchers. He batted left-handed and to this day still owns practically every batting honor in Dodgers record books.

No Dodger has played in more games; batted as many times; produced more hits, triples, or doubles; or chalked up more total bases than Zack Wheat. Only Duke Snider has slugged more extra-base hits; only Pee Wee Reese has scored more Dodgers runs; and only Snider and Gil Hodges have driven in more runs.

Wheat's lifetime batting average is .317, and only four Dodgers can boast higher averages: Wee Willie Keeler (.352), Babe Herman (.339), Jack Fournier (.337), and Mike Piazza (.331). Wheat's lifetime totals are truly impressive: 2,884 hits, 172 triples, 476 doubles, and 4,100 total bases. He batted over .300 14 times, and in two of those years he hit .375 consecutively.

The legendary Giants manager John McGraw once said Wheat was one of the most dangerous left-handed hitters any of his pitchers ever faced. Fellow Hall of Famer and Cleveland Indian Stan Coveleski stated it simply when he prepared to pitch against him in the 1920 World Series: "They told me, if you want to beat Brooklyn, you've got to stop Zack Wheat." Coveleski managed to do it on that occasion, and won three Series games. Few others could ever claim such a distinction.

Stan Coveleski won another 24 games and Ray Caldwell 20.

It was destined, for some reason, to be a World Series filled with anomalies. First of all, it would be decided by the best of nine, not seven, games. Second, Indians second baseman Billy Wambsganss

WORLD SERIES LINEUPS, 1920

DODGERS	INDIANS
Ivy Olson, ss	Joe Evans, lf
Jimmy Johnston, 3b	Bill Wambsganss, 2b
Tommy Griffith, rf	Tris Speaker, cf
Zack Wheat, lf	George Burns, 1b
Hy Myers, cf	Larry Gardner, 3b
Ed Konetchy, 1b	Smokey Joe Wood, rf
Pete Kilduff, 2b	Joe Sewell, ss
Ernie Krueger, c	Steve O'Neill, c

STARTING PITCHERS
Game 1: Rube Marquard, Stan Coveleski
Game 2: Burleigh Grimes, Jim Bagby
Game 3: Sherry Smith, Ray Caldwell
Game 4: Leon Cadore, Stan Coveleski
Game 5: Burleigh Grimes, Jim Bagby
Game 6: Sherry Smith, Duster Mails
Game 7: Burleigh Grimes, Stan Coveleski

would pull off the only unassisted triple play in World Series history, and third, Elmer Smith, the Indians right fielder, would become the first player ever to hit a grand-slam home run in World Series play. Finally, Stan Coveleski would rack up three wins in the Series, going the distance in each. The collective ERA of the Indians pitching staff would be a remarkable 0.89 over the seven games that the Series lasted.

Ebbets Field was the site of the first three games. Coveleski beat the Robins in Game 1 with a five-hitter, 3–1, but the Brooklyners came back—first on the arm of Burleigh Grimes, a 3–0 shutout in Game 2, and then behind Sherry Smith, who dished up a 2–1 three-hitter the next day.

Cleveland did not prove to be as hospitable, however. Coveleski was back in Game 4, and this time squelched the Robins 5–1 on another five-hitter. Jim Bagby followed the next day, holding Brooklyn to one run in an 8–1 defeat, despite the fact that the Dodgers' 13 hits were one *more* than the Indians'. This was also the game in which Smith hit his grand slammer and Wambsganss orchestrated his triple play.

The next day, it was Duster Mails' turn for the Indians. The 24-year-old left-hander, who had produced a record of 7–0 in the 1920 season, had been in the bullpen for the 1916 Brooklyn pennant winners. But now he took his former teammates to task, hurling a three-hit shutout that put the Indians up four games to two in the Series. The next day it was all over. Coveleski tossed his third five-hitter, this one a 3–0 shutout. The Indians only needed seven games to collect the five wins necessary for the 1920 world championship title.

Only Zack Wheat and Ivy Olson hit well for the Robins in the Series. In seven games, the team could only sneak eight runs across home plate. The composite team batting average was a meager .205. And, as disheartening as it was, it would have to satisfy the Brooklyn fans' postseason hunger for a long time; the club's next trip to a World Series would be more than two decades later.

Just as they had plunged downward after winning the pennant in 1916, the Brooklyners managed a repeat performance after the 1920 Series, skidding again into the second division, although not quite as deeply (fifth instead of seventh place). In fact, only once throughout the remainder of the age known as the Roaring Twenties did they slip back above the divisional border. That was in 1924. The three previous years the Robins had come in fifth then sixth twice. The highlight of that bleak period was the arrival of Clarence "Dazzy" Vance, a 31-year-old rookie, who had finally caught on in the majors. He won 18 games for Brooklyn in 1922 and stayed around for another 10 years after that, rewriting most of the pitching entries in the Brooklyn record book and blazing a midlife career that eventually landed him in the Hall of Fame. The only other pleasantries during those years were the 21–12 season in 1922 from hurler Dutch Ruether, whom the Robins had acquired from Cincinnati; Zack Wheat's batting average of .375 in 1923; the .351 recorded by first baseman Jack Fournier that year, his first with Brooklyn (it was his best year since coming up

DAZZY VANCE

His name was Clarence Arthur Vance, but he changed it to Arthur Charles Vance because, as he explained, "I'm not the Clarence type." But anyone who even remotely followed the game of baseball during the Roaring Twenties and the early thirties knew him best as "Dazzy."

His tongue was as gifted as his pitching arm, and he became one of the game's most renowned storytellers as well as one of its most admired hurlers. His repartee with manager Wilbert Robinson was legend, and his wit and behavior were essential factors in dubbing his team the "Daffy Dodgers."

Vance had played in the minor leagues for 10 years, with two brief and unsuccessful appearances in the majors, before landing with the Dodgers in 1922 at the ripe age of 31. Despite his age, he would come to be known as the Dodgers' greatest pitcher, a reputation that was not challenged until Sandy Koufax blossomed in the sixties. (Koufax would retire from the game at 30, a year younger than Vance's age at the start of his career.)

Blessed with the best breaking curveball of the day and a sizzling fastball, Vance made his presence known immediately. He led the National League in strikeouts his first seven years in a row. For 11 years (1922–1932), he was Brooklyn's premier pitcher; he returned in 1935, at the age of 44, to play out the last year of his career.

During those years, he won a total of 197 games and lost 140 (.585), and in 1924 became the second Dodger ever to be named the NL's Most Valuable Player (that year he won 28 games). He was inducted into the Hall of Fame in 1955.

As Dodgers, only Don Sutton and Don Drysdale have won more games than Vance's 190. His 1,918 strikeouts rank fourth, and his 30 shutouts sixth in Dodgers history. He appeared in 378 games, started 326, pitched 2,758 innings, and had a Dodgers career ERA of 3.17. Only Brickyard Kennedy and Adonis Terry completed more games than Vance's 212. And he is one of only three Dodgers pitchers to strike out three batters on nine pitches in one inning (the others are Sandy Koufax and Pat Ragan).

after the Dodgers took the pennant in 1920. They had taken the league crown three straight years and faced their in-town rival, the Yankees, in each of the three World Series (and they had defeated the Yankees of Miller Huggins and Babe Ruth in two of them).

But in 1924, the Robins gave the Giants a run for their money. It was the classic September horse race of an event. The Robins had edged into first place once in August, then ceded it to the Giants. But they remained close, bearing down on the confident Giants who were seeking an unprecedented fourth straight NL pennant. The race went down to the last few days of the season, but Uncle Robbie's team could not quite make that last little spurt at the wire. They got as near as one and one-half games and ended there when the season closed.

Nineteen twenty-four was a year of exceptional performances in Brooklyn. Dazzy Vance posted a record of 28 wins against only six losses (.824). In all of Dodgers history, only Iron Man Joe McGinnity had won more games in a season (29 in 1900).

Vance's 262 strikeouts in 1924 were the most in the major leagues that year and remained a Brooklyn record until the era of Sandy Koufax almost four decades later. And Vance's 15 consecutive wins that year are still an all-time Brooklyn mark. He was named the league's MVP. Along with Vance's successes that year, Burleigh Grimes won another 22 games while losing 13.

Rube Marquard was one of the game's premier left-handers when he came to the Dodgers in 1915. He had been hurling for the New York Giants in Harlem since 1908, had led the league with a record of 26–11 in 1912, and had won 24 games in 1911 and 23 in 1913. Marquard would remain with the Dodgers through the 1920 season, his best year being 1917, when he won 19 and lost 12. In his 18-year major league career, Marquard would win 201 games against 177 losses and post a lifetime ERA of 3.08. He was named to the Hall of Fame in 1971. Photo courtesy of the National Baseball Hall of Fame and Museum.

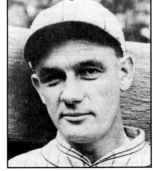

with the Chicago White Sox back in 1912); and Fournier's 22 home runs that same year, at that point the most ever clouted by a Brooklyn batter.

The New York Giants, still under the tutelage of John McGraw and now behind the bats of Frankie Frisch, Dave Bancroft, George Kelly, and Casey Stengel, had dominated the National League

TRIVIA

One item better forgotten: the only player in the history of major league baseball to hit into both a triple play and a double play in a World Series game was Clarence Mitchell of the Dodgers back in 1920. (The triple play, incidentally, is the only unassisted one in the history of the World Series— Billy Wambsganss of the Cleveland Indians caught a low liner in short right-center, raced in, tagged the Dodgers runner who had left second base, and continued to chase down and tag the runner who had left first base.)

Thirty-six-year-old Zack Wheat again hit his career high of .375, second in the league only to Rogers Hornsby's .424. Jack Fournier, hitting .334, led the league in home runs with 27, bettering by 5 his Brooklyn record set the year before. Second baseman Andy High also turned in an impressive average, .328.

That year, however, brought expectations that went unfulfilled, for Brooklyn would not be in the running for the National League pennant again until 1941, a long 17 years down the baseball path.

In 1925, Charles Ebbets, who had been ill, died at the age of 66. The presidency of the club was transferred to Ed McKeever, who owned the other 50 percent of the team's stock. Eleven days later, however, he too died. Wilbert Robinson was then named president of the ballclub, but still continued in his role as manager.

Uncle Robbie remained the team's pilot through the 1931 season, but it was a disappointing time. Only twice did his team rise above sixth place, and in both those years, 1930 and 1931, the best they did was fourth. After the 1931 season, Uncle Robbie was fired. He was 62 years old and had been manager for 18 years. When he was elected to the National Baseball Hall of Fame in 1945, he became the first member of that elite group to have spent the dominant portion of his career with the Brooklyn baseball club.

With the departure of Uncle Robbie went the nickname "Robins." Brooklyn sportswriters went back to the old "Dodgers," and shortly afterward the name was officially adopted by the club.

During the late years of Robinson's tenure, there was little to get excited about in Brooklyn. The stars that had shone earlier were subdued by age now. By 1927 Zack Wheat, Burleigh Grimes, and Jack Fournier were gone. Dazzy Vance was in his late thirties, still strong enough to win 22 games in both 1925 and 1928, but after that his career was indeed in its twilight years.

In the Brooklyn baseball sky there did appear, however, a high-magnitude star. Twenty-three-year-old Floyd Caves "Babe" Herman arrived as a rookie in 1926, and he soon became the pride and joy of Flatbush fans. He hit .319 his freshman year in the league and tied Jack Fournier for team home run honors with 11. He also led the club in RBIs (81), hits (158), triples (11), and doubles (35). Had there been a Rookie of the Year award back then, he surely would have won it.

Babe Herman played for Brooklyn through the 1931 season. Donald Honig, in his book *The Brooklyn Dodgers,* described him aptly:

> **He could hit. He hit for distance and he hit line drives that were murderous. . . . When Ted Williams first appeared on the scene, awed observers, groping for comparisons, likened the youngster's incomparable swing to Herman's. . . . Hornsby called him the hardest hitter in the major leagues, McGraw described him as one of the greatest natural hitters he had ever seen.**

In five of his six years in Brooklyn, Herman batted well over .300. His best year was 1930 when he hit .393, an all-time Dodgers record that was, amazingly, not enough to win the NL batting crown that year— the Giants' Bill Terry batted .401. Herman also hit 35 home runs that year, a Brooklyn record that remained until Gil Hodges banged out 40 in 1951. But Herman set five other single-season marks in 1930, which still stand today: most hits (241), most runs scored (143), most extra-base hits (94), most total bases (416), and highest slugging average (.678).

Manager Wilbert "Uncle Robbie" Robinson (right) chats here with one of his ace hurlers, Jack Coombs. Uncle Robbie managed the Dodgers from 1914 through 1931, bringing home two pennants (1916 and 1920). His 1,375 wins as a Dodgers manager rank third behind the 2,040 recorded by Walt Alston and the 1,599 by Tommy Lasorda. A garrulous man and an addict to the good life, the portly Robinson was one of the best-liked baseball men of his time. He was elected to the Hall of Fame in 1945. Coombs hurled for the Dodgers from 1915 through 1918, but his best years were as a Philadelphia A: in 1910 he won 31 games with only nine defeats, and in 1911 he posted a record of 28–12. Photo courtesy of the National Baseball Hall of Fame and Museum.

Babe Herman, however, was traded to the Cincinnati Reds after the 1931 season, as was back-up catcher Ernie Lombardi, a second-year man who was about to start a most impressive career. In return, Brooklyn got second baseman Tony Cuccinello, third baseman Joe Stripp, and reserve catcher Clyde Sukeforth. It was not a trade Brooklyn fans would hold near and dear to their hearts.

The new manager for 1932 was Max Carey. He had been a premier center fielder in the National League since coming up in 1910 with the Pittsburgh Pirates and had stayed with them until joining Brooklyn in 1926 for the last three years of his career. "Scoops" Carey, as he was sometimes known, was inducted into the Hall of Fame in 1961. As a manager, however, his career was much briefer and not all that illustrious. He sneaked Brooklyn into third place his first year, watched them slide to sixth the next year, and was given his walking papers in favor of Casey Stengel in 1934.

Stengel, who was still as popular with Brooklyn fans as he had been as a young player, lasted only a year longer than Carey, turning in sixth-, fifth-, and seventh-place finishes before moving on to higher managerial glories with the Boston Braves and the

Dazzy Vance was 31 years old when he joined the Dodgers in 1922 and was 44 when he won his last game for them in 1935. As a rookie, he won 18 games against 12 losses and led the league in strikeouts with 134 (he would lead the NL in that category for seven straight years). Vance's best year was 1924, when he posted a league-high 28 wins (against 6 losses), a 2.16 ERA, 30 complete games, 262 strikeouts, and was named the league's MVP. He was enshrined in the Hall of Fame in 1955.

New York Yankees. He was more than 70 years old when he spent three and a half years as manager of the hapless New York Mets.

During the last of Uncle Robbie's days at the Brooklyn helm and on through the regimes of Max Carey and Casey Stengel, the Robins/Dodgers went through a roster of great baseball names, although most were well over the hill by the time they

BABE HERMAN

He got his nickname, it is said, because as a batter he was as natural and as flawless as the "Babe" of the Yankees; the famed hitter Rogers Hornsby called him "the perfect free-swinger." Sports columnist John Lardner remembered other aspects of his career in a 1952 article in *Sport* magazine: "Floyd Caves Herman, known as Babe, did not always catch fly balls on the top of his head, but he could do it in a pinch. . . . He spent the best part of his life upholding the mighty tradition that any-thing can happen at Ebbets Field, the mother temple of daffiness in the national game."

Whether Herman was wielding a white-hot bat or flub-bing a fly ball, he was one of the most popular players ever to wear a Dodgers uniform. His career was a check-ered one, however, before he found his niche with the Dodgers. As John Lardner explained:

> **Mr. Herman worked for 18 different man-agers before he met up with Uncle Robbie (Dodgers manager Wilbert Robinson). . . . He came up from Edmonton in the Western Canada League, to Detroit, in the year 1922, and was promptly fired by Ty Cobb, the Tigers idealistic manager. . . . He was fired from the Omaha club the same year while batting .416. A pop fly hit him on the head one day, and the Omaha owner lost his temper. . . . The Babe tried baseball in Boston briefly, when Lee Fohl managed the Red Sox. He never played an inning there. Studying his form on the bench, Mr. Fohl fired him. . . . The Brooklyn club bought the Babe for $15,000 . . . [then] tried to get rid of him for nothing and failed. . . . The Dodgers wanted a Minneapolis player, of no subsequent consequence. . . . They traded Herman and eight other men to Minneapolis (who) took the eight other men but refused to take Herman.**

But, oh, could Babe Herman hit. In his first six years with the Dodgers (1926–1931), he batted over .300 five times—including an imposing .393 in 1930 (still the all-time Dodgers record), .381 in 1929, and .340 in 1928. In 1930, he also set all-time Dodgers single-season marks for hits (241), runs (143), extra-base hits (94), total bases (416), and slugging average (.678). His career batting aver-age as a Dodger was .339, and over the entire 13 years he played in the majors it was .324. Only Hall of Famer Wee Willie Keeler has a higher Dodgers career average; Keeler, however, only played four years with the Dodgers.

Babe Herman became an instant hit with Dodgers fans when he arrived in Brooklyn in 1926. The gangly, 6'4" slugger, with the large slug of chewing tobacco in his cheek and a majestic bat, played six years with the Dodgers before being traded to Cincin-nati. His batting average of .393 in 1930 is still the all-time Dodgers mark, and the year before that he hit .381. His lifetime Dodgers batting average was .339.

donned Dodgers uniforms. Among them (along with their age on arrival) were Dave Bancroft, 38; Lefty O'Doul, 34; Waite Hoyt, 32; Hack Wilson, 33; and Fred Lindstrom, 30. Only Lefty O'Doul would make any kind of mark in Brooklyn, and he did that by hitting .336 in 1931 and then copping the National League batting crown the next year with an average of .368.

The team also had an interesting array of young-sters who came up during the same period of time. There was catcher Al "Señor" Lopez, rather mediocre as a backstop but later a Hall of Famer as one of the game's most successful managers. And there was pitcher Bobo Newsom, who moved on to a fine career in the American League. There were

Burleigh "Ol' Stubblebeard" Grimes spent the better part of his 19-year major league career with the Brooklyn Dodgers. Between 1918 and 1926 the right-hander was the club's key pitcher, winning more than 20 games four times. His best year was 1920, when he won 23 while losing only 11. The following year his 22 wins were a league high. When he finally let his arm rest from the rigors of major league pitching, Grimes had won 270 games and lost 212; his lifetime ERA was 3.53. He was inducted into the Hall of Fame in 1964. Photo courtesy of the National Baseball Hall of Fame and Museum.

also pitchers who became stalwarts with the Dodgers during that period, Van Lingle Mungo and Dutch Leonard foremost among them. There was also a utility infielder by the name of Fresco Thompson who batted 181 times in 1931 for a .265 average, but, more importantly, later became an important Dodgers front office figure and a master of scouting for the Dodgers of the future.

Replacing Casey Stengel as manager of the Dodgers in 1937 was the player he had been traded for back in 1918, the future Hall of Famer Burleigh Grimes. His two years at the helm, however, proved to be as fruitless as those of his two predecessors:

WHO'S ON THIRD? EVERYONE.

One of baseball's more slapstick moments occurred in 1926 and featured the daffiest of Dodgers in a game against the Boston Braves. The story has been told countless times, but never better than by onetime Dodgers outfielder Rube Bressler (1928–1931) in *The Glory of Their Times* by Lawrence S. Ritter (MacMillan Co., 1966):

It started out with Babe Herman up at bat with none out and the bases loaded. Hank DeBerry was on third, Dazzy Vance on second and Chick Fewster on first. Babe hit a ball out to right field and it was hard to say whether it would be caught or would hit the wall. Turned out it hit the wall, and DeBerry came home from third easily. Vance held up so long on second, waiting to see if the ball would be caught, that he could only make it halfway to home, so at the last minute he decided to play it safe and scampered back to third. Chick Fewster kept on going from first and made it to third, so that as Vance came back to third Fewster was already there, standing on the base. And Babe Herman just kept on going as fast as he could, without looking up at anything. So as Vance slid back to third, and Fewster stood on the base, Babe slid into third from the second base side!

It's a wonder Fewster didn't get spiked. Anyway, there was a rather substantial amount of dust and confusion at third base. The third baseman didn't know what to do, so he tagged all three of them. And the umpire hesitated, trying to decide which two of these guys are out and which one is safe . . .

Well, while all this discussion is going on, Daz is still lying there flat on his back, feet on third and head toward home . . . "Mr. Umpire, fellow teammates, and members of the opposition," he intones, "if you carefully peruse the rules of our national pastime, you will find that there is one and only one protagonist in rightful occupancy of this hassock—namely yours truly, Arthur C. Vance."

He was right. The base always belongs to the advance runner.

One of the most volatile Dodgers of all was executive vice president and general manager Larry MacPhail, shown here with an arm around his manager of 1938, Hall of Famer Burleigh Grimes. MacPhail had made history at Cincinnati before coming to the Dodgers by introducing night baseball and the radio broadcasting of home games. He would turn the Dodgers' destinies around, bringing them into the first division in 1939 and to a pennant in 1941. He added to the Dodgers club such famous names as manager Leo Durocher (with whom MacPhail would forever feud), Babe Ruth as a first-base coach, and players like Dolph Camilli, Pete Reiser, Ducky Medwick, Pee Wee Reese, and Cookie Lavagetto. Grimes' two years as manager (1937 and 1938, sixth and seventh places respectively) were less memorable than the years he hurled for the team. Photo courtesy of the National Baseball Hall of Fame and Museum.

MacPhail. Brooklyn Dodgers historian Donald Honig referred to him as a "hurricane . . . a man in motion, aggressive, dynamic, brimming with ideas. A showman." MacPhail was all of that. He had brought many innovations to the game while serving as general manager of the Cincinnati Reds. He chose as his next challenge the Dodgers, a team that had spent 15 of the previous 20 years in the second division and had not captured a pennant since 1920.

MacPhail brought a whirlwind of change to baseball as Brooklyn knew it. First, he announced that the team's games would be broadcast on the radio, something totally new to baseball fans not only in Brooklyn, but in New York City as well (the Giants and Yankees would follow suit later). To handle the chores, he persuaded a young Cincinnati sportscaster, Red Barber, whose career he had helped start, to come to Brooklyn. His second innovation was night baseball, another phenomenon he had instigated with the Reds. He had a powerful lighting system installed in Ebbets Field. In addition, he completely renovated the rather decaying house that Charles Ebbets built. He even hired 44-year-old Babe Ruth as a coach.

His next auspicious act, in 1939, was to offer the managerial reins to his shortstop, Leo Durocher, upon the dismissal of Burleigh Grimes. And soon began a stormy relationship between general manager and manager, which has been almost unparalleled in baseball history; it produced exciting baseball in Brooklyn, however.

The effects of MacPhail's ideas and changes and Durocher's leadership were immediate. The Dodgers moved into the first division in Durocher's first year as manager, 1939—their third place finish was their best since 1932. The next year they landed in second place, although still a good 12 games behind the team MacPhail had patterned in Cincinnati.

The newcomers were filing in, having been sought out and signed by MacPhail. First was Dolph Camilli. Then came Fred "Dixie" Walker.

sixth- and seventh-place finishes and, predictably, the pink slip. A few faces of promise had shown up in Brooklyn under Grimes, however. One was a second and sometimes third baseman from the Pirates, Harry "Cookie" Lavagetto. Another was a 32-year-old shortstop, Leo Durocher, who later became a most integral part of the Dodgers story.

The real excitement came about in 1938 with the arrival of 49-year-old general manager Larry

Then Harold "Pee Wee" Reese. Then "Pistol" Pete Reiser. The stage was being set for a run at the pennant, something that had been denied the citizens of Brooklyn for more than two decades. It was the advent of a new age of baseball in Brooklyn, one that would be alternately exciting and frustrating, sometimes heartbreaking, but always eventful. It would prove to be one of the most vibrant and interesting 18-year periods of baseball that any city has ever experienced.

CHAPTER 2

THE BOYS OF SUMMER

President Dwight D. Eisenhower tosses out the ceremonial first ball of the 1955 World Series. To the right of him is Dodgers owner Walter O'Malley, and at the far left is Secretary of State John Foster Dulles. The president apparently brought the Dodgers some luck because they went on to win their first ever world championship that year.

THE TEAM THAT REPRESENTED the borough of Brooklyn in the National League for more than 70 years went through more nicknames than any other team in baseball history, from the innocuous Bridegrooms to the ill-suited Dodgers. Under Uncle Robbie in the twenties, many sportswriters enjoyed referring to them as the "Daffy Dodgers"—Westbrook Pegler dubbed them the "Daffiness Boys"—not only because so many of the players had a penchant for clowning, but also because of the team's aptitude for getting involved in ludicrous situations on the field, like triple plays, several runners mistakenly being on the

same base, and multiple player collisions. Later, they became known as the "Bums," a moniker allegedly first applied by fans expressing their opinions about the baseball prowess of various Dodgers players or the team in general, and then immortalized by the pen of sports cartoonist Willard Mullin.

More romantic, however, was the nickname "Boys of Summer," which author Roger Kahn, borrowing a phrase from a Dylan Thomas poem, gave to the Brooklyn team in the glory days of the forties and early fifties. It is especially appropriate because it evokes a warm nostalgia for the exuberant youths who grew up together into a team that became a legend on the Ebbets Field diamond. The names Durocher, Reiser, Walker, Robinson, Campanella, Reese, Snider, Furillo, Hodges, Cox, Branca, Erskine, Roe, Black, Newcombe, and Labine would become as distinct to the Dodgers as Campbell was to soup. They would bring to Brooklyn fans—whose patience with a loser through the Roaring Twenties and the Great Depression was stoic and constant—one of the most exciting eras in all baseball history. It really began in 1941, the summer before Pearl Harbor; Donald Honig described it in *The Brooklyn Dodgers* as "a glorious summer to live in Brooklyn, be a Dodger fan, and have 55 cents for a bleacher seat." Leo Durocher was in his third year as manager of the Dodgers and was still listed on the roster as a shortstop, although he started 22-year-old Pee Wee Reese ahead of himself at that position. "The Lip," as Durocher was appropriately known, feuded as much and as openly with general manager Larry MacPhail as he did with umpires on the field, but together he and MacPhail were molding a winner. MacPhail had gone to the trading table and secured the services of veterans like first baseman Dolph Camilli, outfielders Dixie Walker and Ducky Medwick, catcher Mickey Owen, and a pitching staff headed by Whit Wyatt, Kirby Higbe, and Hugh Casey. Before the season was out he would add future Hall of Famer Billy Herman at second base. And, of course, there was the blossoming of Dodgers youths: Pee Wee Reese, Pete Reiser, and Cookie Lavagetto.

Cincinnati had been the team to beat in 1939 and 1940, and no one came close to doing it. They were still considered the league's best in 1941, relying mainly on a pitching staff highlighted by Bucky Walters, Paul Derringer, and Johnny Vander Meer. They were vulnerable when it came to hitting, however, and that ultimately kept them from being a real threat that year. Instead, it was the St. Louis Cardinals whom the Dodgers would have to vanquish. The Cardinals' fortunes were guided from the front office by Branch Rickey, the "Mahatma," as he was called, and by Billy Southworth from the dugout. On the field they had Johnny Mize, Marty Marion, Enos Slaughter, Terry Moore, and late in the season, a 20-year-old outfielder named Stan Musial who, in 12 games, would bat .426.

The Dodgers wanted a pennant that year, hoping to slake the thirst caused by a 21-year drought. And it looked as if they might just get their wish. They led much of the way through the season, but the Cardinals were never far behind. There was a crucial series at Sportsman's Park in St. Louis in mid-September, and the Dodgers took two of the three games. They managed to hang on for the next two weeks of the season and beat out the Cardinals by two and one-half games. Their record was 100–54, at that point the most wins ever amassed in a single season by a Dodgers team. It was their first pennant since 1920, and the people of Brooklyn were wild with delight and pride.

The most sterling performances that year came from Dolph Camilli, who was chosen the league's MVP, and Pete Reiser. Rookie center fielder Reiser took both the NL batting and slugging crowns with respective averages of .343 and .558. He also

WORLD SERIES LINEUPS, 1941

DODGERS	YANKEES
Dixie Walker, rf	Johnny Sturm 1b
Billy Herman, 2b	Red Rolfe, 3b
Pete Reiser, cf	Tommy Henrich, rf
Dolph Camilli, 1b	Joe DiMaggio, cf
Joe Medwick, lf	King Kong Keller, lf
Cookie Lavagetto, 3b	Bill Dickey, c
Pee Wee Reese, ss	Joe Gordon, 2b
Mickey Owen, c	Phil Rizzuto, ss

STARTING PITCHERS
Game 1: Curt Davis, Red Ruffing
Game 2: Whit Wyatt, Spud Chandler
Game 3: Freddie Fitzsimmons, Marius Russo
Game 4: Kirby Higbe, Atley Donald
Game 5: Whit Wyatt, Ernie Bonham

TRIVIA

The most runs scored in a single inning in the National League since 1900 is the record 15 that crossed the plate for the Dodgers against the Cincinnati Reds on May 21, 1952. It was the first inning and here is how it happened, according to the official Dodgers media guide:

Billy Cox grounded out. Pee Wee Reese walked. Duke Snider homered to right (2). Jackie Robinson doubled to left. Andy Pafko walked. George Shuba singled Robinson home (3) and Pafko went to second. Pitcher Ewell Blackwell (Reds) was replaced by Bud Byerly. Pafko was thrown out trying to steal third and Shuba went to second. Gil Hodges walked. Rube Walker singled home Shuba (4). Chris Van Cuyk singled Hodges home (5). Cox singled home Walker (6). Reese singled home Van Cuyk (7). Byerly was replaced by Herm Wehmeier for the Reds. Snider walked to load the bases. Robinson was hit by a pitch, scoring Cox (8). Pafko singled home Reese and Snider (10). Frank Smith relieved Wehmeier. Shuba walked to load the bases again. Hodges walked to force in Robinson (11). Walker singled home Pafko and Shuba (13). Van Cuyk singled in the 14th run of the inning (Hodges). Cox was hit by a pitch to load the bases. Reese walked, forcing in run number 15 (Walker). Snider struck out.

The totals: 15 runs, 10 hits, 7 walks, 2 hit by pitch, 3 left on base.

The Dodgers' chief slugger from 1938 through 1943 was first baseman Dolph Camilli. He hit 139 career Dodgers home runs; his best year was 1941, when he clouted 34 homers (an all-time Dodgers record then) and drove in 120 runs, both NL highs that year. He was also named the NL's Most Valuable Player, only the third Dodger to earn that honor at the time.

led the league in triples (17) and doubles (39). Dolph Camilli won both the league's home-run crown with 34 (the first Dodger to win it since Jack Fournier back in 1924) and RBIs with 120. Ducky Medwick batted .318 and Dixie Walker .311, and Whit Wyatt and Kirby Higbe won 22 games each.

The 1941 postseason get-together inaugurated a legendary intracity World Series rivalry that would occur seven times over the next 15 years—the Dodgers versus the Yankees. Up in the Bronx, Joe McCarthy's "Bombers," as they were known, had

virtually danced through the season. They had posted 101 wins, and no team came within 17 games of them. The reasons were fairly obvious. First, there was center fielder Joe DiMaggio, who not only hit .357 with 30 homers, 43 doubles, and 125 RBIs, but also established his still-untouched record of hitting safely in 56 consecutive games. There were also home-run hitters like Charlie "King Kong" Keller (33), Tommy Henrich (31), and Joe Gordon (24); a masterful shortstop named Phil Rizzuto; a Hall of Fame–bound catcher, Bill Dickey; and pitchers like Lefty Gomez, Red Ruffing, and Spud Chandler.

Curt Davis, a 38-year-old right-hander the Dodgers had picked up from the Cardinals a year

Ebbets Field as it looked in the heyday of the Boys of Summer.

prior, got the call for Game 1 to go against Red Ruffing at Yankee Stadium. It was a close one— each team gave up only six hits to the other—but the Yankees, thanks to a Joe Gordon homer, managed one more run to win it 3–2. The next day it was better for Brooklyn. Whit Wyatt went the distance and got the decision for the Dodgers. It was another 3–2 game, and the Dodgers tallied the winning run when Dolph Camilli singled home Dixie Walker in the sixth inning.

The third game was at Ebbets Field. Freddie Fitzsimmons, the 40-year-old patriarch of the Dodgers staff, went after his first World Series victory. And it looked like he might just get it, having shut the Yankees out through seven innings. But a line drive that bounced off his knee on the last out of the inning ended his duties for the day. The Yankees got two runs off Hugh Casey in the eighth, enough to give them a 2–1 win and a 2–1 edge in the Series.

Game 4 was fated to be an historic one, although a rueful one for the Dodgers and for their fine catcher Mickey Owen. His ninth inning faux pas will live forever in baseball infamy. The Dodgers were leading, 4–3, in the top of the ninth. Two were out, and Tommy Henrich was at bat with two strikes on him. Hugh Casey had been hurling in relief for the Dodgers since the fifth inning. He wound up and grooved a fast-breaking pitch that Phil Rizzuto later said had to be a spitball. "Sure that's what he threw. . . . When Henrich swung [and missed], Owen didn't get near the ball. . . . It exploded by him." The umpire, seeing only Henrich's missed swing, signaled him out. Police and spectators surged out onto the field, and some of the players started for the ramps to their dressing rooms. But Henrich had glimpsed the ball rolling back toward the backstop and Owen chasing after it. Henrich raced for first, and by the time Owen retrieved his "dropped third strike there," were people between him and his first baseman, thwarting any chance of throwing the batter out. Henrich was safe, and instead of celebrating a 4–3 Dodgers victory, Casey had to face DiMaggio, Keller, Dickey, and Gordon, who among themselves brought four runs across the plate. The Yankees won, 7–4, and instead of having drawn the Series to a tie at two games apiece, the Dodgers were down three games to one.

The snake-bitten Dodgers were feeling the sting the next day, and the Yankees wrapped it up at Ebbets Field when Ernie Bonham outdueled Whit Wyatt to give the Bronx Bombers a 3–1 win and the world championship.

The Dodgers went on to win even more games in the next regular season, 104 against only 50 losses, which stands today as the second win-ningest season ever in Dodgers history (tops would be the 105–49 record of 1953). But, incredibly, the 104 wins of 1942 were not enough to win the National League flag—the Cardinals beat them out by winning 106.

The war then interrupted baseball for fans and players alike. The games went on through 1943,

Dixie Walker, also known in Brooklynese as "the People's Cherce," became one of the most popular players ever to wear a Dodgers uniform. He came to Brooklyn in 1939 after seven and a half years in the American League and stayed for eight and a half more, batting over .300 in seven of them. Always an outstanding fielder in right, his best year at the plate was 1944, when he led the NL with an average of .357. When Walker was dealt to Pittsburgh in 1948, the Dodgers received Preacher Roe and Billy Cox in return.

The irrepressible Leo Durocher managed the club from 1939 through 1946, finishing in the first division all but once. He brought Brooklyn one pennant (1941) and three runner-up seasons, as well as an unending series of feuds on and off the field, classic scenes of umpire baiting, and volumes of notable quotes and anecdotes. Durocher also played shortstop for Brooklyn in 1938 and 1939 before giving that job up to Pee Wee Reese, and was a member of Walt Alston's coaching staff from 1961 to 1964.

1944, and 1945, but most of the big names were gone, fulfilling a variety of military duties, along with many of the fans. Among the regular Brooklyn Dodgers to exchange baseball uniforms for those of the armed forces were Cookie Lavagetto, Dolph Camilli, Billy Herman, Pete Reiser, Pee Wee Reese, Hugh Casey, and Kirby Higbe. There were some newcomers, too, who made brief appearances with the Dodgers only to go off to the war—such future stalwarts as Gil Hodges, Gene Hermanski, Eddie Miksis, and Rex Barney. General manager Larry MacPhail also went to join the war effort and was replaced in the

Brooklyn front office by a rival of his from St. Louis, Branch Rickey, who had had a falling out with Cardinals ownership. MacPhail never did return to the Dodgers, but came back to haunt them years later in the World Series as an executive of the Yankees.

Their ranks depleted, the Dodgers dropped to third place in 1943, a distant 23½ games behind the Cardinals. The following year they skidded all the way to seventh, 42 games below a Cardinals team that earned its third consecutive NL pennant. The Dodgers rebounded to third the next year, ending up 11 games behind the Chicago Cubs, who had finally unseated the Cardinals from the National League throne.

During the war years there were only two notable arrivals at Ebbets Field. Arky Vaughan played third base and shortstop for two years, then temporarily retired from the game. And a little pepper pot of a second baseman, Eddie "the Brat" Stanky, was acquired from the Chicago Cubs in 1944.

Another event that occurred during the war years, one that would have a long-term effect on the Dodgers organization, was the sale of a block of stock in 1944 to a triumvirate of investors: an attorney named Walter F. O'Malley, Branch Rickey, and John Smith, president of Pfizer Chemical Company. The following year, the three purchased a controlling interest in the ballclub.

After the transition in the ownership and the conclusion of the war, just about everybody was back for the 1946 season. And there were a few new and youthful faces, among them outfielder Carl Furillo, 24, and a couple of right-handed pitchers—Ralph Branca, 20, and Rex Barney, 21. The reunion and the infusion of new blood were enough to propel the Dodgers to a season's-end tie with the Cardinals for the National League crown, both ending up with records of 96–58. The sport's first pennant playoff series was decreed: the best of three games. Unfortunately for Brooklyn, the Cardinals—spearheaded by pitchers like Howie Pollet and Harry Brecheen and by a murderer's row at the plate, which included Stan Musial, Red Schoendienst, Enos Slaughter, Marty Marion, Whitey Kurowski, and Joe Garagiola—wiped them out 4–2 and 8–4 in two straight games.

The Dodgers incurred another loss after the season. Their manager, Leo Durocher, was suspended for a year by new baseball commissioner

TRIVIA

The youngest player ever to get a base hit for the Dodgers was Tommy Brown, in 1944, at the age of 16. Brown was also the youngest player ever to hit a home run for the Dodgers, at age 17.

A. B. "Happy" Chandler. It seems Chandler was not so happy about some of the people Durocher allegedly hung around with, "gamblers and other low-lifes addicted to the high-life," or about some of the things Durocher had said in print about Larry MacPhail, his longtime adversary who was now in the Yankees front office. The nebulous phrase "actions deleterious to the game of baseball" was cited by the commissioner for Durocher's suspension. It now seems one of baseball's more unfair acts in view of the absence of any real proof that Durocher had done anything at all to detract from the game. On the contrary, he was one of the game's more colorful characters and popular draws. Sixty-three-year-old Burt Shotton, who had managed the Phillies from 1928 through 1933 and the Reds in 1934, was signed to replace the banished Durocher.

Much more historic than Durocher's departure at the start of the 1947 season was the arrival in Brooklyn of 28-year-old speedster Jackie Robinson, who, it was said, could bat and field with the very best in the major leagues. Branch Rickey had signed him the year before for the Dodgers minor league club in Montreal, thus bringing the first black player into the major league farm club system. Robinson had been a blazing success in Canada; now he was to become the first black to play major league baseball.

Since the Dodgers still had Eddie Stanky at second base that year, Jackie Robinson was stationed at first base, where the Dodgers were weak. The only other lineup change for 1947 occurred when Spider Jorgensen won the starting job at third from Cookie Lavagetto. There were also a couple of rookies of note on the bench—20-year-old Duke Snider and a catcher named Gil Hodges,

"Pistol" Pete Reiser nailed down the center-field job his second year in Brooklyn. A hurricane hustler in the field and on the base paths, he hit .343 and slugged .558 in 1941, best in the NL, and also hit the most doubles (39) and triples (17). For the next two years he would lead the league in stolen bases (20 and 34), but a fractured skull (incurred while running into an outfield wall in 1942 at St. Louis) would take a dreadful toll on what had promised to be a great major league career.

who would be reassigned the next year to first base. Ralph Branca, at 21, had been promoted to the regular rotation to join Joe Hatten, Vic Lombardi, and Harry Taylor. Hugh Casey was the mainstay of the bullpen corps.

The Dodgers' season was a pleasure cruise that year; they took first place in June and never relinquished it. When the season came to a close, they boasted a record of 94–60 and a five-game margin over the normally troublesome Cardinals. Jackie

OPENING NIGHT

The first night game in Dodgers home-game history was played at Ebbets Field on June 15, 1938. Even more historic, however, was the fact that opposing pitcher Johnny Vander Meer of the Cincinnati Reds hurled a no-hitter that night to defeat the Dodgers 6–0. Not only that, it was his second consecutive no-hitter (he had blanked the Boston Braves four days earlier), a feat no other pitcher has accomplished in the history of major league baseball.

A moment of baseball history: Branch Rickey, Dodgers president, and Jackie Robinson break the racial barrier in major league baseball with this contract signing. Rickey brought Robinson first to the Dodgers farm club in Montreal, Canada, then to Brooklyn in 1947. "The Mahatma," as Rickey was called, had an illustrious career with the St. Louis Cardinals before joining the Dodgers organization in 1942. He remained president of the Brooklyn ballclub until relinquishing that position to Walter O'Malley in 1950. Rickey was named to the Hall of Fame in 1967. Photo courtesy of the National Baseball Hall of Fame and Museum.

Ralph Branca is unfortunately more often remembered for the home-run ball he threw to Bobby Thomson of the New York Giants in the playoffs for the 1951 NL flag than for his otherwise fine Dodgers career (1944–1952). Branca's best year was 1947, when he won 21 and lost 12, and his 36 starts that year were a league high.

one award for both leagues then). He also batted a creditable .297 and tied for team honors with 12 home runs—surprisingly enough, with the diminutive Pee Wee Reese. Ralph Branca was the surprise and delight of the pitching staff, toting up 21 wins against only 12 losses. And fireman Hugh Casey's 18 saves were the most in the majors that year.

The Yankees had breezed through the American League to capture their eighth flag in 12 years. They still had DiMaggio, Rizzuto, Henrich, and Keller, and a rookie catcher of promise with the unusual name of Yogi Berra. There was a relatively new pitching staff, which included Allie Reynolds, Spec Shea, Vic Raschi, fireman Joe Page, and the old vet Spud Chandler, now 40. The Yankees were also under a new pilot, Bucky Harris, who had replaced a discontented Joe McCarthy (he couldn't get along with Larry MacPhail either).

It was the second world championship meeting of the Dodgers and the Yankees, and there was little love between them, either on the field or at the front office level. This Series would go the route, seven games, and would be filled with some especially memorable moments. It began in Yankee Stadium

Robinson was, needless to say, the game's most noticeable presence that year, cheered by some, silently accepted by others, but often scorned, taunted, maligned, and abused by spectators, hotel managers, restaurateurs, and even other ballplayers. But he was also acutely visible for qualities other than simply being black—he exhibited class that instantly put his detractors in proper perspective, for example, and proved to everyone what a gifted baseball player he was. Robinson led the league with 29 stolen bases in 1947 and was named the first major league Rookie of the Year (there was only

WORLD SERIES LINEUPS, 1947

DODGERS	YANKEES
Eddie Stanky, 2b	Snuffy Stirnweiss, 2b
Jackie Robinson, 1b	Tommy Henrich, rf
Pete Reiser, cf	Yogi Berra, c
Dixie Walker, rf	Joe DiMaggio, cf
Gene Hermanski, lf	George McQuinn, 1b
Bruce Edwards, c	Billy Johnson, 3b
Spider Jorgensen, 3b	Johnny Lindell, lf
Pee Wee Reese, ss	Phil Rizzuto, ss

STARTING PITCHERS
Game 1: Ralph Branca, Spec Shea
Game 2: Vic Lombardi, Allie Reynolds
Game 3: Joe Hatten, Bobo Newsom
Game 4: Harry Taylor, Bill Bevens
Game 5: Rex Barney, Spec Shea
Game 6: Vic Lombardi, Allie Reynolds
Game 7: Hal Gregg, Spec Shea

Jackie Robinson (No. 42) is congratulated here by St. Louis Cardinals star Stan Musial after homering in the 1952 All-Star Game. The Nationals won it 3–2 in a game that was stopped after five innings because of rain. Robinson was a representative for the Dodgers in six All-Star Games during his 10 years with the club (1947–1956).

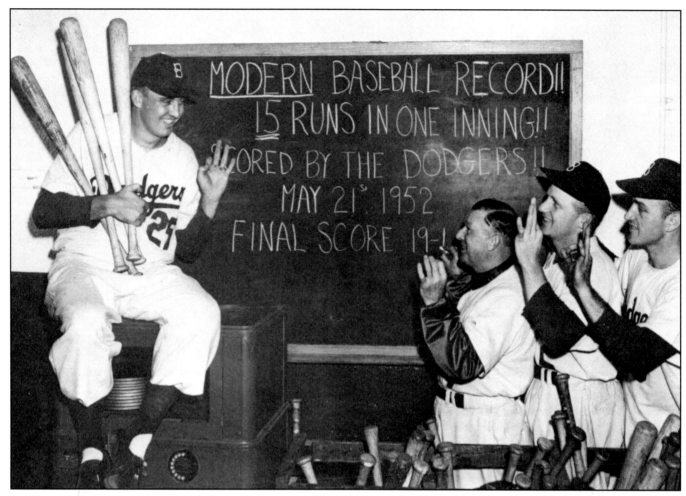

Celebrating the Dodgers' phenomenal 15-run inning (a major league record) against the hapless Cincinnati Reds in 1952 are pitcher Chris Van Cuyk (with bats) and (from left) manager Chuck Dressen, infielder Bobby Morgan, and outfielder George Shuba.

with Ralph Branca and Spec Shea as starting pitchers. The Yankees won it, 5–3, exploding with all five runs in one inning. They repeated the next day when Allie Reynolds went the distance and struck out 12 Dodgers in a 10–3 massacre.

Over at Ebbets Field, however, the Dodgers found their hitting in the second inning of Game 3, during which they chalked up six of the nine runs they would score that day, just enough to edge the Yanks by a run.

The fourth game brought the excited fans a classic ending. Bill Bevens, a 30-year-old right-hander who had a less-than-exciting 7–13 season, started for the Yankees. In the bottom of the ninth inning he was only one out away from a no-hitter (although he had walked a total of 10 batters, a World Series record that still stands today). The score was 2–1 in favor of the Yankees, and there were runners on first and second. Carl Furillo had drawn a walk; then Al Gionfriddo, pinch running for him, stole second. To the dismay of many, Bucky Harris ordered an intentional pass to Pete Reiser, putting the winning run on base. Eddie Stanky was due up, but Shotton sent out a somewhat age-worn Cookie Lavagetto to bat for him. At 34, he had been used primarily as a pinch-hitter during the year and had batted .261. Lavagetto promptly destroyed Bevens' no-hitter with a line

JACKIE ROBINSON

"It is impossible to think of Robinson except as a Dodger," the late, great sports columnist Red Smith wrote in the *New York Herald-Tribune* on the occasion of Robinson's retirement in 1956. "His arrival in Brooklyn was a turning point in the history and the character of the game; it may not be stretching things to say it was a turning point in the history of this country."

When Branch Rickey did bring Jackie Robinson to major league baseball back in 1947, it was an early and important step on the same path that would later be trod by the young school girl in Topeka, Kansas, Linda Brown; by Martin Luther King Jr.; and by the whole array of civil rights advocates that would emerge in the sixties.

It was not easy in a nation used to segregation and subordination of blacks, and despite the discrimination in hotels and restaurants, the invectives of spectators and sometimes other players, Robinson prevailed and established the blacks' place in baseball. In the words of Brooklyn Dodgers historian Donald Honig, "Playing under conditions that no athlete, before or since, has ever had to endure, Robinson transcended baseball and stepped into American history."

Robinson was a truly gifted baseball player. Born in Cairo, Georgia, he came to the Dodgers at age 28 via UCLA, the U.S. Army, a black baseball team called the Kansas City Monarchs, and the Dodgers farm club in Montreal, Canada. He was named the game's first Rookie of the Year in 1947, as a first baseman who batted .297 and led the league with 29 stolen bases.

During his 10-year Dodgers career, Robinson batted over .300 six times, and played second, third, and first bases as well as the outfield. His best year was 1949 when he led the NL with an average of .342 and 37 stolen bases (both career highs); he also drove in 124 runs, scored 122, and was named the league's Most Valuable Player.

His lifetime Dodgers batting average was .311, and he stole a total of 197 bases. Only six Dodgers have scored more runs than Robinson's 947. He ranks 10th in extra-base hits (464). Overall he hit 137 home runs, drove in 734 runs, accounted for 2,310 total bases and 1,518 hits, which included 273 doubles, and he has the dubious distinction of being the Brooklyn Dodger hit by the most pitched balls in a single season (14 in 1952).

drive that bounced off the right-field wall, bringing in both the tying and winning runs. The Series was tied at two games apiece.

Spec Shea threw a four-hitter at the Dodgers the next day, and Joe DiMaggio homered, enabling the Yanks to eke out a 2–1 win.

The Dodgers came back in the sixth game with an artillery of bats that pounded out 12 hits. But it was little-known Al Gionfriddo's miraculous catch that actually decided this game. The Dodgers were leading 8–5 in the sixth inning, with two runners on base, two outs, and Joe DiMaggio at the plate. Gionfriddo was in left when DiMaggio cannoned one that appeared headed for the bullpen out there. He raced frantically back and made a spectacular over-the-shoulder, over-the-railing catch at the 415' mark to deny DiMaggio a three-run homer and save the inning, the lead, and eventually the game. The Dodgers finally won it 8–6.

In Game 7 the next day, the Dodgers blew a 2–0 lead and then could not overcome the relief wizardry of Joe Page, who gave up only one hit and shut them out in the last five innings. The Yankees won it 5–2 and brought another world-championship cup to their already-crowded trophy case in Yankee Stadium.

Leo Durocher was back in the Dodgers dugout in 1948, but only for 73 games. And it was not a happy return. There was soon discord between the manager and his players, and between the manager and the general manager. The Dodgers had a disappointing record of 35–37 when Branch Rickey, with no hesitation, gave his approval for Durocher to take the managerial job offered by the New York Giants. Burt Shotton came out of retirement to lead the team through the remainder of the year.

The Dodgers finished third behind the Boston Braves and the St. Louis Cardinals, their final record somewhat improved to 84–70. There had been some changes for the better during the disappointing season, however. Gil Hodges had been successfully converted to a first baseman to make room behind the plate for rookie Roy Campanella. And a utility infielder, Billy Cox, broke into the

Reliever Joe Black was a sensation his rookie year with the Dodgers in 1952. He won 15 games against only four losses and was credited with 15 saves. Black was also the surprise starter in three games of that year's World Series against the Yankees and was named the NL Rookie of the Year. But his star sputtered out after that first year as decidedly as it had flared.

starting lineup at third and dazzled everyone with his fielding prowess. On the pitching staff there was the addition of a rangy left-hander, 33-year-old Preacher Roe, who had been picked up from the Pirates. And a promising 21-year-old rookie right-hander, Carl Erskine, was coming along nicely.

The following year, "Big" Don Newcombe (he was 6'4", 220 pounds) made his appearance, and the slate of the Boys of Summer was just about full. The starting lineup for 1949 was: first base, Gil Hodges; second base, Jackie Robinson; third base, Billy Cox; short stop, Pee Wee Reese; left field, Gene

Hermanski; center field, Duke Snider; right field, Carl Furillo; catcher, Roy Campanella; and Don Newcombe, Preacher Roe, Ralph Branca, Joe Hatten, Carl Erskine, and Rex Barney in the bullpen.

The fiery young Dodgers, with an abundance of talent and a deep-rooted spirit, were about to establish their supremacy in the National League—a potent presence that would remain for almost a decade until the club moved to California.

Carl Erskine chalks up the 14 strikeouts he threw for a World Series record in 1953. He achieved the then-single-game strikeout record while beating the Yankees 3–2 in Game 3 of that Series. Still, the Yankees took the Series, four games to two.

They proved themselves in 1949. It was a heated pennant race in the National League from Opening Day all the way to the last game of the season. The Dodgers were in second place behind the Cardinals almost the entire month of September, but in the closing days they moved into a tie and then won the pennant on the last day of the season.

WORLD SERIES LINEUPS, 1949

DODGERS	YANKEES
Pee Wee Reese, ss	Phil Rizzuto, ss
Spider Jorgensen, 3b	Tommy Henrich, 1b
Duke Snider, cf	Yogi Berra, c
Jackie Robinson, 2b	Joe DiMaggio, cf
Gene Hermanski, lf	Johnny Lindell, lf
Carl Furillo, rf	Billy Johnson, 3b
Gil Hodges, 1b	Cliff Mapes, rf
Roy Campanella, c	Jerry Coleman, 2b

STARTING PITCHERS
Game 1: Don Newcombe, Allie Reynolds
Game 2: Preacher Roe, Vic Raschi
Game 3: Ralph Branca, Tommy Byrne
Game 4: Don Newcombe, Eddie Lopat
Game 5: Rex Barney, Vic Raschi

A common sight in the late forties and early fifties. Duke Snider accepts congratulations after homering, this time from Jackie Robinson. Snider hit 407 home runs in his 18-year career, 389 of them for the Brooklyn and Los Angeles Dodgers—the most in the club's long history.

Their final record of 97–57 was one game better than that posted by the St. Louis Cardinals.

Again it was the Yankees who prevailed in the American League, this time under a new leader, the one-time Dodger Casey Stengel. They had just barely gotten by a powerful Boston Red Sox team, who were paced by such stars as Ted Williams, Bobby Doerr, Vern Stephens, Dom DiMaggio, Birdie Tebbetts, Mel Parnell, and Ellis Kinder. Still, the Yankees were the Yankees, and felt quite at home in the World Series.

The Dodgers, to their remorse, would find out quickly just how good the Yankees were in the clutch. Don Newcombe had a four-hit shutout going into the bottom of the ninth in Game 1 when Tommy Henrich ended it with a home run to give

the Yanks a 1–0 victory. Allie Reynolds had allowed the Dodgers only two hits all afternoon.

The next day the score was reversed, as Preacher Roe slipped a 1–0 win past the Yanks at Yankee Stadium, the winning run driven in by Gil Hodges.

Game 3 was a cliffhanger all the way. The Yankees led by a run; then Brooklyn tied it. In the top of the ninth, New York erupted with three runs to take a convincing 4–1 lead. In the bottom of the inning, Luis Olmo pinch hit a homer for the Dodgers, then Roy Campanella hit another. But they just could not get that life-saving last run and lost it 4–3.

Then the Yankees erupted like Etna, 16 runs in the next two games, which they swept easily, 6–4 and 10–6. Once again, the Dodgers' hitting had deserted them in the postseason. The team batted only .210 for the five-game Series.

But the year had been a good one, at least until the World Series collapse. Jackie Robinson had an impressive season and led the league with a .342 average. He was also named the National League's Most Valuable Player, the first black player so honored and the first Dodger since Dolph Camilli in 1941. Carl Furillo hit .322 and was reputed to be one of the most adept right fielders in the game, with an unequaled rifle arm. Gil Hodges and Duke Snider shared the team home-run honors with 23 each, and Campanella was right behind with 22. Three Dodgers hitters drove in more than 100 runs: Robinson 124, Hodges 115, and Furillo 106. Don Newcombe won the most games and posted a 17–8 record. The Dodgers closed out the forties with style and great promise, if without a world championship to their credit.

The Dodgers of 1950 were heavy preseason favorites to take the NL crown. What the handicappers failed to take fully into account, however, was an even more youthful team from Philadelphia, one which sportswriters were calling the "Whiz Kids." The Phillies had youngsters like Richie Ashburn, Del Ennis, Granny Hamner, Robin Roberts, Curt Simmons, and Bob Miller, and a few others

One of the great Dodgers double-play combinations: Pee Wee Reese (No. 1) and Junior Gilliam (No. 35) tone their act here at spring training in Dodgertown before the 1955 season. Gilliam won the right to second base on his arrival in Brooklyn in 1953, forcing Jackie Robinson to play out the last four years of his career in the outfield, at third, or at first.

Duke Snider, but Richie Ashburn threw him out at the plate with a whistling strike from center field. Jackie Robinson was then intentionally walked, which filled the bases. Waiting were two of Brooklyn's best clutch-hitters. But the first, Carl Furillo, popped one up, and the next batter lofted an easy floater to the outfield to end the threat. It gave Dick Sisler the opportunity to whack a three-run homer in the top of the tenth, and the Dodgers were through, the final score 4–1.

After the 1950 season, there was a front-office shakeup; Branch Rickey sold his share of the club (25 percent) and stepped down from his position of president and general manager. Walter O'Malley bought that block of stock and moved into the home office as club president. With the departure of Rickey came the firing of Burt Shotton, then 65. O'Malley hired Chuck Dressen to manage the team. Dressen, whose sports career was many-sided (he had once been a quarterback for the original 1920 Decatur Staleys, one of the National Football League's charter teams, later known as the Chicago Bears), had been around major league baseball since 1925 when he broke in with the Cincinnati Reds as a third baseman. He had served as a coach on various teams, including the Dodgers, and most recently had served under Leo Durocher with the Giants. Dressen had also managed the Reds from 1934 through 1937, but had never led his team to a first-division finish. O'Malley also hired Emil "Buzzy" Bavasi as general manager and Fresco Thompson to run the Dodgers' well-tuned farm system and be their head scout.

By 1951 the Dodgers were used to photo finishes at the end of the regular season. No one, however, was quite prepared for the drama that the 1951 baseball season would hold for the Dodgers.

It began, as most baseball pundits predicted, with the Dodgers dominating the National League. By mid-August the Boys of Summer were coasting along with a 13½ game lead over the second-place New York Giants. Then the unexpected began. Over at the Polo Grounds, Leo Durocher switched his

approaching 30 years of age like Eddie Waitkus, Dick Sisler, and Andy Seminick. The only over-30 member of the regulars was ace reliever Jim Konstanty, 33, whose age was hardly a hindrance en route to 22 saves for the Phillies that year (the most in either league).

The Dodgers went head-to-head with the Whiz Kids to the very last day of the 1950 season. It was a dramatic showdown with aces Don Newcombe and Robin Roberts dueling into the ninth inning with the score tied 1–1. The Dodgers needed a win to tie in the standings and send the two teams into a playoff for the pennant; a loss and it was all over for them. In the bottom of the ninth, Cal Abrams tried to score from second on a clean single by

WORLD SERIES LINEUPS, 1952

DODGERS	YANKEES
Billy Cox, 3b	Hank Bauer, rf
Pee Wee Reese, ss	Phil Rizzuto, ss
Duke Snider, cf	Mickey Mantle, cf
Jackie Robinson, 2b	Yogi Berra, c
Roy Campanella, c	Joe Collins, 1b
Andy Pafko, lf	Irv Noren, lf
Gil Hodges, 1b	Gil McDougald, 3b
Carl Furillo, rf	Billy Martin, 2b

STARTING PITCHERS
Game 1: Joe Black, Allie Reynolds
Game 2: Carl Erskine, Vic Raschi
Game 3: Preacher Roe, Eddie Lopat
Game 4: Joe Black, Allie Reynolds
Game 5: Carl Erskine, Ewell Blackwell
Game 6: Billy Loes, Vic Raschi
Game 7: Joe Black, Eddie Lopat

lineup; he brought Bobby Thomson and Whitey Lockman into the infield, sent Monte Irvin to the outfield, and changed the pitching rotation around. The Giants reeled off a 16-game winning streak as a result. And the Dodgers began losing. Suddenly, what seemed like a cakewalk was turning into a pennant race. The Giants continued to win (37 of their last 44 games) while the Dodgers ambled on, playing mediocre baseball. On the last day of the season, the two teams were wedged in a tie for first place.

The Giants won their game handily that day, but the Dodgers were having a lot of trouble with the Phillies. They could not afford the loss, but in the fourth inning at Shibe Park in Philadelphia they were trailing 6–1. Brooklyn battled back slowly but steadily; however, they were still down 8–5 in the eighth. Then, pinch-hitter Rube Walker, who had come to the Dodgers earlier in the season from the Chicago Cubs along with outfielder Andy Pafko, doubled to drive in two runs. Moments later Carl Furillo singled to bring in the tying run, sending the game into extra innings. Don Newcombe and Robin Roberts, uncharacteristically in relief roles, faced each other all the way to the fourteenth inning.

Jackie Robinson would be the hero that day—twice. In the twelfth inning, with the bases loaded and two outs, Eddie Waitkus slashed a line drive that appeared to be a sure game-winning hit. Robinson dove and made a spectacular catch to squelch the threat. Then, two innings later, with two outs, Robinson drove a Robin Roberts fastball into the left-field seats to give the Dodgers a 9–8 victory and the chance to take on the Giants in a playoff series for the National League pennant.

For the Giants, a rangy power hitter named Bobby Thomson drove in the two winning runs in Game 1 at Ebbets Field with a homer off Ralph Branca—a harbinger of things to come. The Dodgers roared back the next day at the Polo Grounds, however, and annihilated the Giants, 10–0.

The final game, certainly one of the most famous in all of baseball history, was also played at the Polo Grounds. It was, of course, the game in which Bobby Thomson hit "the shot heard 'round the world," the ninth-inning, three-run homer off ill-fated Ralph Branca. The Dodgers had been winning 4–1 in the bottom of the ninth. With one out, one run driven in by Whitey Lockman, and two men on, Thomson came to bat. Ralph Branca was brought in to relieve

WORLD SERIES LINEUPS, 1953

DODGERS	YANKEES
Junior Gilliam, 2b	Gil McDougald, 3b
Pee Wee Reese, ss	Joe Collins, 1b
Duke Snider, cf	Hank Bauer, rf
Jackie Robinson, lf	Yogi Berra, c
Roy Campanella, c	Mickey Mantle, cf
Gil Hodges, 1b	Gene Woodling, lf
Carl Furillo, rf	Billy Martin, 2b
Billy Cox, 3b	Phil Rizzuto, ss

STARTING PITCHERS
Game 1: Carl Erskine, Allie Reynolds
Game 2: Preacher Roe, Eddie Lopat
Game 3: Carl Erskine, Vic Raschi
Game 4: Billy Loes, Whitey Ford
Game 5: Johnny Podres, Jim McDonald
Game 6: Carl Erskine, Whitey Ford

Don Newcombe, who had pitched all the way to that point. Branca threw two pitches, a fastball strike, then a fastball he would rue forever. And the season came to an end for the Dodgers.

Roy Campanella was named the National League's MVP that year. He hit .325, including 33 homers and 108 RBIs. Jackie Robinson batted .338 and stole 25 bases. Gil Hodges hit 40 home runs and Duke Snider another 29. Preacher Roe won 22 games and lost only 3, his win percentage of .880 the best in Dodgers history for a 20-game winner. And Don Newcombe won 20 games against 9 losses. But none of it was enough to win the pennant, thanks to Bobby Thomson's historic stroke in the very last moment of an incredibly dramatic season.

Their revenge came the next year, 1952. The Dodgers staved off the Giants and won the NL flag by four and one-half games. They did it with the same team, except for a few personnel changes. Newcombe had been drafted into the army, and two pitchers had been added: Billy Loes and rookie reliever Joe Black

For the fourth time, they faced their cross-borough rivals, the Yankees, who had slipped by the Cleveland Indians that year. And for the fourth time they went down to defeat at the hands of the Bronx Bombers. Part of it was due to the superb pitching of Vic Raschi and Allie Reynolds, part to the .345 hitting of 20-year-old Mickey Mantle who had replaced Joe DiMaggio in center field, and part to three clutch home runs (and six RBIs) by 39-year-old Johnny Mize. The Dodgers did not go down easily, though—they pushed the Series to a full seven games.

The Series came to a climax October 7, Game 7 at Ebbets Field. Eddie Lopat was on the mound for the Yankees, Joe Black for the Dodgers. Neither lasted to the end. The score was 2–2 at the end of five. Then Mickey Mantle drove the game-winner into the seats, and Bob Kuzava, in relief, blanked the Dodgers the rest of the way.

The Dodgers had some fine hitting in the Series from Pee Wee Reese (.345) and Duke Snider

(.345, four home runs, and eight RBIs), and some strong pitching from Joe Black, who also earned Rookie of the Year honors that year. But they just could not shake the Yankees jinx.

They got another chance, however, just 12 months later, because the Dodgers again took the National League pennant easily. Their closest competition came from the Braves, who had moved that year from Boston to Milwaukee, but even they finished a distant 13 games behind. Carl Furillo took the National League batting crown that year with a career high average of .344. And Duke Snider smashed 42 home runs, at that point the most ever in a single season by a Dodger; in addition, his slugging average of .627 was the best in the league. But the premier performance was turned in by Roy Campanella, who was named National League MVP, becoming the first and only Dodger ever to win the award more than once. "Campy" drove in 142 runs that year, then an all-time Dodgers record, hit 41 homers, and batted .312. Rookie of the Year Junior Gilliam hit 17 triples, the most in the major leagues. And Carl Erskine won 20 games while losing only 6, turning in his best year up to then as a Dodger.

In the 1953 Series, it took the Yankees only six games to dispose of the Dodgers. The Boys of Summer dropped the first two at Yankee Stadium, the result of some fine relief hurling by 35-year-old Johnny Sain in the first game and a sterling nine-inning performance by Eddie Lopat in the second. But the Dodgers rallied at Ebbets Field. Carl Erskine put on one of the finest performances of his career and set a then–World Series record by striking out 14 Yankees. He was credited with the Dodgers win, 3–2. The Dodgers then tied the Series the next day by trouncing the Yanks 7–3, largely as a result of Duke Snider's four RBIs on a home run and two doubles. The next day, however, it was Mickey Mantle's turn to play hero; he contributed a grand-slam homer to boost the Yankees to an 11–7 victory. The following day at Yankee Stadium, Whitey Ford and Allie Reynolds held the Dodgers off 4–3, the winning run coming in the bottom of the ninth when Billy Martin singled Hank Bauer home.

Billy Martin had been the hitting star of the Series, batting .500, and his 12 hits were a record for a six-game World Series. He also cracked two home runs and drove in eight runs. Five Dodgers hit over .300 in the Series: Gil Hodges, Carl Furillo, Duke Snider, Billy Cox, and Jackie Robinson. And Junior Gilliam banged out two homers and three doubles.

In 1954, the Giants were back in the picture, and Leo Durocher's club unseated the Dodgers from first place by five games. They were paced by a 23-year-old batting crown winner, Willie Mays, who hit .345; by other good hitters including Alvin Dark, Whitey Lockman, Don Mueller, and Monte Irvin; and by pitchers Johnny Antonelli, Sal Maglie, and Ruben Gomez.

The year had a special significance for the Dodgers, however. It marked the first year of Walt Alston's tour of duty as manager of the team. He took over for ousted Chuck Dressen and started a managerial career that would last 23 years. Alston had managed in the minors for 13 years before coming to the Dodgers. Soft-spoken, not given to the limelight, he had the very difficult job of infusing himself into a Dodgers squad that had been playing together as a tightly knit team for six or seven years.

It would not take very long for Alston to assert his value; in fact, he did it quite convincingly the next year. Alston guided the 1955 Dodgers through

The reason for the smiles from Johnny Podres (left) and manager Walt Alston here is that just minutes earlier Podres had shut out the Yankees in Game 7 of the 1955 World Series (2–0) to give the Dodgers their first major league title. Podres was also the winner of Game 3; altogether he struck out 10 and posted a 1.00 ERA in his two complete games. It was only Alston's second year as Dodgers manager.

an unchallenged season. The team won 22 of its first 24 games that year and virtually coasted through the rest of the season, bringing Brooklyn its third pennant in four years. With a record of 98–55, the Dodgers ended up 13½ games ahead of the Milwaukee Braves, thereby gaining another chance to break the strange sort of sorcery that the Yankees seemed to exercise over them in postseason play.

After having won five World Series in a row, the Yankees the year before had lost out to the Cleveland Indians. Like the Dodgers, they had been deprived of the yearly pennant to which they had become accustomed. Now they were back, still under Casey Stengel, still led by hitters like Mantle, Berra, Gil McDougald, Bauer, and Bill Skowron, and pitchers like Ford, Bob Turley, and Don Larsen.

The only changes in the 1955 Dodgers lineup involved Sandy Amoros, who became a full-time left fielder, and Clem Labine, who proved to be the club's chief relief pitcher. It was a big year for Duke Snider, who led the league in RBIs (136) and runs scored (126), belted 42 home runs, and batted .309. Campy hit .318 and was named the National League MVP for the third time, while Carl Furillo hit .314.

Among baseball's most breathtaking moments: Jackie Robinson (No. 42) in one of his famed steals of home. Here he is doing it successfully against the Yankees in the 1955 World Series. The catcher is Yogi Berra and the Dodgers batter stepping out of the way is pinch-hitter Frank Kellert.

Don Newcombe won 20 games for the second time in his then five-year career. With only five losses, his win percentage of .800 was the best in the majors. "Newk" also batted .359 that year and hit seven home runs, the most a pitcher in the National League had ever slugged (a record that would later be tied twice by L.A. Dodger Don Drysdale).

The Series with the Yanks was destined to go seven full games in 1955, just as it had in 1947 and 1952. It was the sixth time the two teams had gone head-to-head in the after-season classic, and the Yankees had won all of the previous five encounters. After the first two games in 1955, it seemed history would repeat itself: Whitey Ford and Tommy Byrne set the Dodgers down with ease, and the Yankees were off to a 2–0 Series lead.

To start Game 3 at Ebbets Field, Walt Alston chose a 22-year-old left-hander, Johnny Podres, who had won only nine games against ten losses during the regular season. The Dodgers bats cooperated

Don Newcombe poses with the plaques he received as the National League's MVP and Cy Young Award winner for 1956. That year he won 27 games against 7 losses, his best year as a Dodger and the third time he won more than 20 games. At right is Warren Giles, NL president.

Crossing home plate here is rookie Don Drysdale (No. 53) after hitting his first major league home run in 1956. One of the more powerful hitting pitchers, Drysdale would clout 29 homers in his 14-year Dodgers career in Brooklyn and L.A., including seven in each of two seasons (1958 and 1965).

nicely with him and produced eight runs, more than they had in the two previous games combined. Podres held the Yankees to a mere three tallies, and the Dodgers trailed by only a game.

The Dodgers hitters were just as forceful the next day. Homers by Roy Campanella and Gil Hodges got them an early lead, and a three-run round tripper by Duke Snider in the fifth inning insured an 8–5 win. The Yanks were held in check with consistent pitching from Carl Erskine and relievers Don Bessent and Clem Labine, who got the win.

Game 5 was another three–home run affair for the Dodgers, two by Duke Snider and one by wispy little Sandy Amoros. Roger Craig, a 24-year-old

rookie, pitched six fine innings, giving up only two runs, and Clem Labine came on for the save. The Dodgers had swept three at home and took command of the Series, three games to two. But the next game was to be played in Yankee Stadium, that foreboding place that always seemed to harbor clouded fates and common disasters for the Dodgers.

The visit began true to form. In the very first inning of Game 6, the Yankees logged five runs, three of them on a homer by Bill "Moose" Skowron. That alone was enough. The Dodgers hitters, who had accounted for 21 runs and 34 hits in the three preceding games, could only come up with one run and four hits off a superlative performance by Whitey Ford. And the Series was again deadlocked.

The last pitch from Yankees hurler Don Larsen in the historic perfect game he threw against the Dodgers in the 1956 World Series. Striking out is Dodgers pinch-hitter Dale Mitchell, Larsen's 27th consecutive victim that day. The catcher is Yogi Berra, the third baseman Andy Carey, and the home-plate umpire Babe Pinelli.

Young Johnny Podres was Walt Alston's choice to pitch the final game; Casey Stengel chose Tommy Byrne. The Dodgers got a run in the fourth and another in the sixth, both driven in by Gil Hodges. In the bottom of the sixth, Sandy Amoros squelched a big Yankees threat. With two men on base, Yogi Berra ripped what appeared to be a sure extra-base hit, but Amoros made a spectacular catch and turned it into a clutch double play. That was the closest the Yankees got. Podres shut them

out, and the Dodgers had their first world championship ever. The doomsday jinx the Yankees had woven over them for so long was finally undone.

It was a special joy for Walt Alston in only his sophomore year as the club's manager. His somewhat surprising choices of youngsters like Podres and Craig, along with a variety of other gambles, had paid off. He had a lot of help, however, from Duke Snider, who hit four homers, drove in seven runs, and batted .320 in the Series. Sandy Amoros

Pitcher Carl Erskine (No. 17) and third baseman Charlie Neal (No. 43) have future Dodger Wally Moon caught in a rundown during this game against the Cardinals in 1957, one of the last the Dodgers would play in Ebbets Field. That's Roy Campanella backing up Neal.

hit .333, and Pee Wee Reese and Carl Furillo batted .296 each. Podres, of course, was the real hero with two wins and an ERA of 1.00. But also important were Clem Labine's four relief appearances, two of which contributed to Dodgers wins.

The world champs had a tough time of it in 1956. There was no explosive start, as there had been the year before, and the Milwaukee Braves and the Cincinnati Reds were doggedly determined to make them earn a repeat pennant. The Braves had an awesome lineup, which included Eddie Mathews, Hank Aaron, Joe Adcock, and Johnny Logan, and a devastating pitching staff headed by Warren Spahn, Lew Burdette, and Bob Buhl. The Reds were hardly lightweights either, paced by Ted Kluszewski, Frank Robinson, Johnny Temple, Wally Post, Ed Bailey, and Gus Bell, although their pitching was not especially strong.

It made for an exciting run at the pennant. The Braves dominated the second half of the season, turning the reigning champion Dodgers into chasers, while Cincinnati was never more than a few games off the pace. Milwaukee maintained the lead into the season's last week, but then began to break down. During the last weekend of play, the Braves lost two in a row, while the Dodgers knocked off the Pirates in a double header. Going into the season's final day, the Dodgers had slipped into first place by a game. The Braves won that Sunday, beating the Cardinals and making it mandatory that the Dodgers defeat the Pirates to avoid a tie for the league honors and a playoff with the Braves. The Dodgers rose to the occasion against the Pirates. Duke Snider and Sandy Amoros each slammed two home runs, and Jackie Robinson hit another one. The final score was 8–6, and the Dodgers' record of 93–61 put them a full game ahead of the Braves and two in front of the Reds. It was the Dodgers' second pennant in a row, their fourth in the last five years, and their sixth in the last ten years.

The 1956 season belonged to Don Newcombe. The huge right-hander had his best season ever, winning 27 games and losing only 7. His win percentage of .794 was the best in either league. He won both the National League MVP and the Cy Young awards that year. The Dodgers also got a fine performance from 39-year-old Sal Maglie, who in the past had tortured them during his long and distinguished career with the Giants. Maglie had been picked up on waivers by general manager Buzzy Bavasi on the astute assumption that Maglie still had another year in him. Clem Labine also turned in a stellar relief performance, picking up 19 saves, the most in either league. And in 1956, two rookies worked sparingly for the Dodgers, but offered a glimmer of hope for the future: 20-year-old Sandy Koufax (2–4) and 19-year-old Don Drysdale (5–5).

Duke Snider blasted 43 home runs that year, breaking the old Dodgers mark of 42 that he held jointly with Gil Hodges, and setting a team record that would stand until the year 2001. It was also the league high, as was his slugging average of .598. But Junior Gilliam was the only .300 hitter on the team that year.

Again waiting for them were the Yankees, who had just won their eighth pennant in 10 years, and who were aching to avenge their only World Series loss during those 10 years. Just as it had in 1955, the World Series of 1956 went the entire distance, only this time the Dodgers were the team to get off to the swift start. Sal Maglie picked up the first win, aided by a home run by Gil Hodges with two on and a solo blast by Jackie Robinson (his last major league homer, incidentally). The final was 6–3.

In the next game the Dodgers were even more volatile. They battered Yankees pitchers for 13 runs in what was the longest nine-inning game in World Series history to that point. The final was 13–8, and the Yankees had used seven pitchers, another Series record.

Whitey Ford was slated to face the Dodgers in Game 3 at Yankee Stadium. He went the distance, aided by a three-run homer by Enos Slaughter and a solo by Billy Martin, giving the Yankees a 5–3 triumph. Tom Sturdivant did the honors for the Yankees the next day, allowing the Dodgers only two runs and six hits. This time Mickey Mantle and Hank Bauer teamed for a pair of home runs. The 6–2 win brought the Series to a 2–2 tie.

Game 5 at Yankee Stadium is legend. That October 8 afternoon, Don Larsen took the mound and retired 27 consecutive Dodgers for the first and only perfect game in World Series history. It totally overshadowed another fine pitching performance that day, Sal Maglie's five-hitter. The 2–0 victory moved the Yankees ahead by a game.

Reliever Clem Labine was somewhat of a surprise choice to start the next day. But the selection was a good one because he hurled meticulously through 10 full innings to shut out the Yankees 1–0, the winning run coming when Jackie Robinson singled to drive in Junior Gilliam in the bottom of the tenth.

Again the Series came down to a climactic final game. At Ebbets Field, Don Newcombe took

WORLD SERIES LINEUPS, 1956

DODGERS	YANKEES
Junior Gilliam, 2b	Hank Bauer, rf
Pee Wee Reese, ss	Enos Slaughter, lf
Duke Snider, cf	Mickey Mantle, cf
Jackie Robinson, 3b	Yogi Berra, c
Gil Hodges, 1b	Bill Skowron, 1b
Carl Furillo, rf	Gil McDougald, ss
Roy Campanella, c	Billy Martin, 2b
Sandy Amoros, lf	Andy Carey, 3b

STARTING PITCHERS
Game 1: Sal Maglie, Whitey Ford
Game 2: Don Newcombe, Don Larsen
Game 3: Roger Craig, Whitey Ford
Game 4: Carl Erskine, Tom Sturdivant
Game 5: Sal Maglie, Don Larsen
Game 6: Clem Labine, Bob Turley
Game 7: Don Newcombe, Johnny Kucks

the mound for the Dodgers and Johnny Kucks for the Yankees. But this game was not to be a nail-biter; it was more like a migraine headache for Dodgers fans. New York built a 5–0 lead by the seventh inning and then increased it to nine when Moose Skowron clobbered a grand slammer. Kucks allowed the dispirited Dodgers only three hits all day and chalked up the Yankees' second shutout of the Series.

It was, of course, the last World Series to be played in Ebbets Field, or Brooklyn for that matter. The team played only one more season in the borough, and they fell to third place that year, never really in contention with Milwaukee, which brought the first World Series to the city that was known for its beer and brats, and after the 1957 Series, its Braves.

Jackie Robinson retired by 1957, after an outstanding career that would eventually earn him a place in the Baseball Hall of Fame. The other Boys of Summer were well into their thirties, now more like the "Middle-Aged Men of Summer." Utility infielder Charlie Neal proved to be a fine addition to the team, and Don Drysdale emerged as the pitching staff's ace performer that year (17–9).

Sandy Koufax was still apprenticing, trying to get a handle on his pitching control.

Meanwhile, Walter O'Malley was working behind the scenes on a project that would change the habitat of the Dodgers. Ebbets Field, which had been such a showcase when it was unveiled back in 1913, had become an archaic ballpark. It seated only about thirty-two thousand spectators, far fewer than Walter O'Malley would like to accommodate, and the physical plant itself was in dire need of renovation. There were just too many detracting factors to save Ebbets Field. So O'Malley looked to other sites in Brooklyn that might be suitable for building a new ballpark. But his gaze also wandered much farther—all the way across the continental United States, in fact.

It was not long until both O'Malley and Giants owner Horace Stoneham saw the efficacy of moving their franchises to the shores of the Pacific Ocean. The National League approved the dual relocations and the institution of major league baseball on the West Coast. The once-great intracity rivalry became an intercity one as the Dodgers moved to Los Angeles and the Giants to San Francisco.

The last game at Ebbets Field was played the night of September 24, 1957, and the Dodgers won it, 2–0. The memory-filled stadium would be boarded up, eventually razed. On its Bedford Avenue site today is a housing development. The next year the *B* on the Dodgers caps was replaced with *LA*, and the team took the field in an amphitheater called the Coliseum that could and would hold more than ninety-two thousand spectators for a Dodgers game.

The image of the Bums and the Daffy Dodgers was left in Brooklyn. A new era was launched, an altered image forged. Still, the excitement of Dodgers baseball would not abate. On the contrary, there lay ahead a whole series of memorable games, great individual performances, pennant races, and World Series action—enough to satisfy the most baseball-hungry West Coast fan. It was a loss for Brooklyn, but a gracious gift for Los Angeles.

CHAPTER 3

A NEW HOME

A Los Angeles welcoming committee in 1958.

UP NORTH, SNOW AND SLUSH PAVED most of the streets and the winds still carried icy daggers when the baseball teams made their traditional trek to the sun states for the 1958 spring training season. The Dodgers again went to Vero Beach, Florida, where they had been spending their early springs since 1948. Only this time,

when the Grapefruit League ended, the Dodgers did not head back north, but instead traveled the breadth of the country to settle into their new hometown in sunny Southern California.

The year 1958 was one in which great names glistened on the rosters of just about every team in the major leagues—some old and fading, others

ROY CAMPANELLA

Campy was not ready to retire when that awful automobile accident ended his playing career in January 1958. He was 36, but felt he had a couple more good years to spend with the team in Los Angeles.

Roy Campanella was brought up to the majors midway through the 1948 season, after toiling for 10 years with teams like the Nicetown Colored Athletic Club, the Baltimore Elite Giants of the Negro League, and eventually a couple of Dodgers farm clubs. He secured the starting catcher job within a matter of days and never relinquished it during his 10 years with the Dodgers.

The highest accolade of major league baseball was bestowed on him in 1969 when he was inducted into the Baseball Hall of Fame at Cooperstown, New York. Three times Campanella was named the National League's Most Valuable Player; up to then only Stan Musial had achieved the honor that many times. Seven times Campy was named to the National League All-Star Team.

Campanella is the fourth-leading home-run hitter in Dodgers history with 242 and ranks eighth in RBIs with 856. He hit more than 40 home runs in one season, more than 30 in three others, and 20 or better in another three. In each of three seasons, he drove in more than 100 runs. On one particular afternoon in August 1950, he slammed three consecutive home runs.

His best year, however, was 1953 when he batted .312, hit 41 homers, and drove in a total of 142 runs. His lifetime batting average is .276, and his slugging average stands at an even .500.

Red Smith, the dean of American sportswriters until his death in 1982, said of Campanella: "Fans watching him work were looking over the shoulder of an artist. . . . In the great social contribution which baseball has made to America since 1946, Jackie Robinson was the trailblazer, the standard-bearer, the man who broke the color line . . . Roy Campanella is the one who made friends."

Carl Furillo was 36 when he accompanied the Dodgers to Los Angeles; he was nearing the end of a fine career that had begun in Brooklyn back in 1946. He would play only one year as a regular in California and then parts of the two ensuing seasons. In 1958, his last full year, he hit .290, including 18 home runs, and there were still vestiges of his fabled rifle arm.

new and rising. It was an age that could boast of Ted Williams, Mickey Mantle, Yogi Berra, Willie Mays, Stan Musial, Warren Spahn, Hank Aaron, Roberto Clemente, Eddie Mathews, Harvey Kuenn, Al Kaline, Nellie Fox, Early Wynn, Robin Roberts, Johnny Antonelli, Bob Friend, Ernie Banks, Richie Ashburn, Frank Thomas, and Lew Burdette, to name only a select few. The Dodgers brought with them to Vero Beach a roster of equally grand baseball names. Many of them were a bit age-worn: Pee Wee Reese (39), Carl Furillo (36), Gil Hodges (34), Don Newcombe (32), and Duke Snider and Carl Erskine (both 31). But there were some youngsters, too, who had yet to establish the names for themselves that they one day would; they were Sandy Koufax, Don Drysdale, Ron Fairly, John Roseboro, and Frank Howard.

Roy Campanella, who had hoped to play another year or two, was not there, however. A tragic automobile accident in New York had left him paralyzed from the chest down and confined to a wheelchair, abruptly ending his illustrious 11-year career behind the Dodgers plate.

Some scenes from Opening Day in Los Angeles, 1958. Clockwise from upper left: comedian Joe E. Brown introduces opposing managers Bill Rigney of the Giants and the Dodgers' own Walt Alston; the Dodgers line up for the national anthem; the motorcade down Broadway from earlier in the day, with coach Chuck Dressen (left) and Walt Alston in the lead car; and the enormous, jam-packed Coliseum from an angle that gives an idea just how far a spectator could sit from the playing field action.

Major league baseball officially came to the West Coast of the United States on tax day, 1958. The Dodgers appeared in San Francisco on April 15 to face the Giants in a stadium that had formerly been the home of the minor league San Francisco Seals. A crowd of 23,448 shivered in the chilly winds that blew in from the ocean and San Francisco Bay. But no one was colder than the Dodgers were in their California debut. Ruben Gomez shut them out 8–0,

TICKET PRICES AT THE COLISEUM, 1958

Box Seats $3.50
Reserved Seats $2.50
General Admission $1.50
Bleachers $0.90
Children (General Admission) $0.75

LASORDA REMEMBERS . . .

Question: What about some of the Dodgers you played ball with? Do you have any special memories about them?

Tommy Lasorda: Pee Wee Reese to me was the greatest leader of a ball club I have ever seen. He had this magnetic ability to just lead everybody. Pee Wee had a tremendous knack for making people like him. I never heard of anybody ever saying a bad word about Pee Wee Reese. It is hard to believe. I go all my life working hard to try to get at least 50 percent of the people liking me. Jackie Robinson, I thought, was one of the finest competitors. I played with Roy Campanella; he was a tremendous ballplayer and a tremendous guy. I played with Duke Snider, who is in the Hall of Fame, who had the greatest talent of anybody who ever lived. I played with Gil Hodges, who I thought was destined to get into the Hall of Fame because of his great contribution to baseball, and he was also one of the nicest human beings that God ever put on this earth. And Sandy Koufax, who is in the Hall of Fame, who is probably one of the greatest pitchers I ever laid eyes on. And Don Drysdale who is [also in] the Hall of Fame. I played with Don Newcombe who should be in the Hall of Fame. I played with one of the greatest human beings that I could ever come across, Junior Gilliam, who later on coached with me, then became a coach under me. He was a tremendous person and I loved him very, very dearly.

---

and 21-year-old Don Drysdale, in his third year as a Dodger, got the loss.

The next night, however, behind the pitching of Johnny Podres, the Dodgers of Los Angeles posted their first major league victory. It was equally blustery in Seals Stadium that night, but much of the excitement in the air was generated by Dodgers bats. Duke Snider contributed a pair of home runs and third baseman Dick Gray another as the Dodgers hammered out a 13–1 win.

When the Dodgers arrived in L.A. for their hometown opener April 18, they were 1–2 for the season. But they were welcomed as if they were returning triumphantly from a World Series. On the morning of the game, the team, in uniform, paraded down Broadway in downtown Los Angeles, sitting atop the backs of a fleet of convertibles. Fans lined the street. Manager Walt Alston and coach Chuck Dressen were in the lead car (inauspiciously, an Edsel), and they waved like a pair of practiced politicians. The tumultuous welcome dramatically demonstrated the city's eagerness for big league baseball.

At the Coliseum that afternoon, 78,672 fans made their way through the turnstiles, at that time the largest crowd ever to attend a National League game. Sportswriters could find only superlatives to describe the crowd and its enthusiasm. But their phrases about the San Francisco weather—"arctic winds" and "deep-freeze temperatures"— gave way in Los Angeles to "sweltering heat" and "sun-bathed crowds."

The Dodgers pleased the hometown fans that day, but hardly impressed them. The Giants, in a slapstick effort, seemed to do practically everything within their power to hand the game over to the Dodgers. It started in the first inning. The Giants had runners on first and second when Daryl

One of the most famous Dodgers to make the cross-country move to L.A. was center fielder Duke Snider, bringing along the powerful bat he had used to belt 40 or more homers in the preceding five seasons. But Snider, 31 in 1958, saw his stats decline in his five California seasons. His best effort on the West Coast was in 1959, when he hit 23 home runs and batted .308.

Spencer hit a little scrub pop-up to pitcher Carl Erskine. He lost it in the sun, and the ball fell at his feet. He picked it up, looked around at second base, and was surprised to find both Giants runners standing there, neither on the bag. He threw to Charlie Neal, who tagged both and then looked at the umpire for some kind of decision. The infield fly rule was invoked, but it was also ruled a double play. In the ninth inning, with the Dodgers leading 6–5, the Giants' Willie Kirkland smashed a triple to drive in rookie Jim Davenport with the tying run. Unfortunately for the Giants, Davenport neglected to touch third base, and so when Dick Gray, with ball in hand, stepped on that base, the Giants got, instead of a run, an out. Clem Labine, apparently refreshed by the turn of events, retired the next two batters in a row, leaving Kirkland stranded on third and the Dodgers victorious in their home opener.

By the end of that three-game series, the Dodgers could claim an attendance figure of 167,204—more than 55,000 per game—a full 16 percent of what the team had drawn at Ebbets Field in the *entire* 1957 season.

In that three-game set there were also 12 home runs lofted over the screen along the short left-field fence. The new stadium appeared to be a right-handed batter's dream and a pitcher's night-

At 6'4" and 220 pounds, Big Don Newcombe had been an imposing figure on the Dodgers mound. He threw his blazing fastball for seven seasons in Brooklyn (1949–1951, 1954–1957) but the transition to L.A. proved a difficult one. He appeared in 11 games in 1958, posting a dismal record of 0–6, and was then traded to the Cincinnati Reds.

DAFFINESS TAGS ALONG

Lee Allen, long the official historian of baseball at the National Baseball Hall of Fame in Cooperstown, New York, conjectured in print whether the daffiness and eccentricities so long associated with the Dodgers would accompany the team to Los Angeles:

> **Were the Dodgers destined to find new dignity among the palms? . . . There was a reassuring hint that life in Los Angeles might be as zany as it ever had been in Brooklyn: buried in the avalanche of ticket orders was a letter from Lassie, the celebrated collie of television, requesting a season box.**

mare, as so many baseball pundits had feared. Some were even predicting that a powerhouse right-handed hitter like Gil Hodges would break Babe Ruth's home-run record of 60 with what would be nothing more than a shotgun spray of fly-ball outs in other ballparks.

After the season was underway, the Dodgers acquired power hitter Steve Bilko and pitcher Johnny Klippstein. In return for the pair, the Dodgers sent Don Newcombe to the Cincinnati Reds. He had lost six straight games and had not adjusted to the move from Brooklyn to L.A.

The crowds continued to pour into the Coliseum, even though the Dodgers were playing

This was the scene at the Coliseum for the Dodgers' debut in Los Angeles on April 18, 1958. An all-time record Opening Day crowd of 78,672 watched their new home team whip the San Francisco Giants 6–5. This photo clearly shows the lopsided scale of the Coliseum. The left-field foul line stretched a mere 251 feet, while the center-field fence at one point was 440 feet from home plate. It would have to do, Walter O'Malley said, until he could build the Dodgers their own home stadium, and although the playing conditions might not have been ideal, the crowds, on some occasions topping ninety thousand, were most gratifying.

disappointing baseball. The team that had represented the National League in the World Series two years earlier, and had ended up in third place in the preceding season with a respectable record of 84–70, had become rooted in the cellar in 1958.

In one early May game, the Dodgers gave the fans their money's worth. They hosted the Philadelphia Phillies, a team that was giving them a run for the cellar that year. The game lasted 14 innings and did not end until after midnight. It

even had to be halted temporarily in the top of the fourteenth when the umpire ran out of baseballs and a Dodgers aide had to be dispatched to the club storeroom to dig up some more. But it was the game in which Duke Snider scored his 1,000th major league run, and Don Drysdale, in a relief appearance, chalked up his first win as an L.A. Dodger (bringing his record to 1–5 for the season). Snider also saved the game both offensively and defensively, first by driving in Junior Gilliam to tie the

Don Zimmer was the Dodgers' transitional link at shortstop between Pee Wee Reese and Maury Wills; he held down the position most of the time during the 1958 and 1959 seasons. Zimmer had come up with Brooklyn back in 1954 and would be traded to the Chicago Cubs in 1960. He would end a 12-year major league career in 1965. His best year in the majors was 1958 when he hit .262 and 17 home runs as a Dodger.

Charlie Neal, a deft base runner and notorious hustler, took over the chores at second base for Junior Gilliam in 1957. Gilliam, like Jackie Robinson, whom he had replaced, moved over to third. For a small man (5'10", 165 pounds), Neal could hit the long ball; he belted 22 homers in his first year in L.A., and followed in 1959 with 19 more. He would hit two clutch ones and bat .370 in the World Series that year, then would be traded to the New York Mets in 1962.

game in the ninth, and then by making a spectacular over-the-shoulder catch of a drive by Chico Fernandez in the tenth. The Dodgers finally won the game when another vet, Carl Furillo, drove home the winning run in the early morning hours.

On July 2, the Dodgers' home attendance went over the 1 million mark. And before the All-Star Game break, it exceeded the total 1957 attendance at Ebbets Field. But still, the Dodgers languished in last place. By early August, the Dodgers managed to move into seventh place. They had only two .300 hitters at that point in the season, Norm Larker (.338) and Duke Snider (.300). Charlie Neal led the team in home runs with 19, and Duke Snider, impeded by the vast acreage in right and center fields, had hit only 14. Johnny Podres had a 10–9 record, and Sandy Koufax, having his best season yet as a Dodger, stood at 9–5. Don Drysdale, on the other hand, was saddled with a disappointing record of 5–11.

The high point of the season came on August 15. The headline on the sports page of the *Los Angeles Examiner* was DODGERS SMASH INTO 1ST DIVISION. Sportswriter Bob Hunter explained it:

DON NEWCOMBE

Big Don Newcombe had played at Montreal with Jackie Robinson and Roy Campanella in the days before the major leagues were integrated. He followed both to the Dodgers, making his first appearance in 1949 and going on to win 17 games while losing only 8 that year. He struck out 149 batters, posted an ERA of 3.17, and earned the honor of National League Rookie of the Year.

He was called "Newk" much of the time, but when his given name was used it always seemed to be prefaced with the adjective Big because he was the most physically imposing pitcher in the game.

The burly right-hander with the smoking fastball had his glory days in Brooklyn. There, he was a three-time 20-game winner, including his finest year, 1956, when he won 27 and lost only 7. He led the league in pitching, received the Cy Young Award, and was named the National League's Most Valuable Player. It was the highest point of his career, but unfortunately it was the last of his really successful years as a pitcher.

Newk did not make the transition to Los Angeles well at all. He lost his first six games in 1958 and was traded to Cincinnati. He tried a comeback at the Dodgers' 1961 training camp, but it was fruitless and he retired from the game.

Newcombe's lifetime stats include a record of 149–90, an ERA of 3.56, and a total of 1,129 strikeouts.

To add a little might to the Dodgers batting order, the burly Steve Bilko, 6'1" and 230 pounds, was acquired in 1958. But he did not work out for L.A., contributing only seven home runs and batting a weak .208. Bilko, however, did hit 20 or more home runs twice in his 10-year major league career (in 1953 and 1961).

"*Around the World in 80 Days* was fiction, but from last to fourth in 80 hours is fact. On Tuesday, when the Dodgers opened against the Cubs, they were dead last, maybe even both. Last night, after dusting off St. Louis (in both games of a double header) they busted all the way into the first division to share fourth place with the Cardinals (both with records of 54–59)."

It was not long-lived, however. The decline came soon and steadily, and when that first long season mercifully ended, the Dodgers were in seventh place with a record of 71–83, 21 games behind the pennant-winning Milwaukee Braves. The Phillies had beaten them out for the cellar by a mere two games. The Dodgers' year had been as dismal on the field as the Edsel Walt Alston rode in on Opening Day had been in the automotive marketplace.

Not nearly as many home runs had been hit in the lopsided Coliseum as had been feared. The total of 193 was less, in fact, than had been belted out of Ebbets Field in several seasons. The figure was also 26 below the major league record of 219. Of the 193 home runs in the Coliseum that year, 182 of them sailed over the left-field screen (only 8 were hit to right and 3 to center). Gil Hodges, who was supposed to have had such a field day with the short left-field fence, hit only 13 of his 22 home runs at home that season.

A grand total of 1,845,556 fans had graced the Coliseum that year, a gain of more than 800,000 in

Stalwarts of the Dodgers bullpen in 1958 were longtime Dodger Clem Labine (No. 41) and new-comer Johnny Klippstein (No. 35), acquired that year in a trade that sent Don Newcombe to the Cincinnati Reds. Labine, who had been a Dodger reliever since 1950, was the bullpen ace of 1958, with 14 saves and a record of 6–6. Klippstein saved nine games but had a record of only 3–5.

but they were far short of his 17–9 record and 2.69 ERA the year before. Sandy Koufax won the most games of his then four-year career and posted a record of 11–11 (he had won five games the year before and two in each of the preceding two seasons). Stan Williams won nine and lost seven. And Clem Labine was credited with 14 saves.

The only .300 hitter in 1958 was Duke Snider (.312). But his 15 home runs were distressingly down from the 40 or more he had hit in each of the five previous seasons. Charlie Neal and Gil Hodges led the team in that category with 22 four-baggers each. And Carl Furillo led the club in RBIs with 83.

attendance over the last year in Brooklyn, and the most ever in the franchise's long history. Walter O'Malley was more than comfortable about his decision to move the Dodgers to the City of Angels.

Johnny Podres had won the most games (13) and lost the most (15). Don Drysdale went some distance in redeeming himself after a disastrous start and ended up with a 12–13 record and a 4.16 ERA,

It had been a disappointing season, a less-than-gratifying way to launch a franchise in a new hometown. But if the fans were disillusioned, they nevertheless showed no signs of withdrawing their support as the season dragged to its conclusion. They were about to be rewarded for their constancy with one of the most remarkable one-year turnarounds in major league history.

CHAPTER 4

A WINNER FOR L.A.

A bedazzling "Roy Campanella Night" at the Coliseum in 1959, as tens of thousands of fans light matches in the otherwise darkened Coliseum to honor the former Dodgers great. Campy is wheeled out onto the playing field by his former teammate and Dodgers captain, Pee Wee Reese. The largest crowd in all of baseball history turned out that night—93,103—and an estimated 15,000 were turned away at the gates. The exhibition game was with the New York Yankees.

THE DODGERS' SOPHOMORE YEAR in Los Angeles offered a few lineup changes, but perhaps not as many as some might have expected, considering the debacle of the 1958 season.

Pee Wee Reese had retired after a season in which he had played a mere 59 games and had batted only .224, but he bequeathed his golden glove and legendary leadership forever to Dodgers lore. Don Zimmer would fill in for him between second and third before having that position taken away in early summer by a speedster named Maurice Morning Wills, who had been in the minors since 1951. Steve Bilko, whose big bat had not resounded loudly enough to satisfy Walt Alston in 1958, was sent to the Dodgers' farm team in Spokane, Washington. The Dodgers, as it would turn out, made an especially propitious trade before the season when they picked up Wally Moon from the Cardinals in exchange for Gino Cimoli. Veteran Carl Furillo, a Dodger since 1946, would spend most of his time in the dugout and his right-field haunts would be occupied transiently by Ron Fairly, Norm Larker, and Don Demeter. Roger Craig and Danny McDevitt would move into the regular pitching rotation.

A hint of the change to come was played out down in Florida in March. The Grapefruit League, a perennial proving ground, turned out to be a delightful romp for the Dodgers. From their lowly status of 1958, they suddenly blossomed in the spring of 1959 and ended up on top of the Grapefruit League with a record of 13–10. One of their games, incidentally, was down in Havana against the Cincinnati Reds. Fidel Castro threw out the ball to start the game in the last days of Cuba's friendship with the United States.

A few reporters were saying that the rejuvenated Dodgers would not be a team to be taken for granted in 1959. Others—the majority, in fact—shrugged off the Dodgers' preseason success and suggested that reality would catch up with them once the regular season was underway.

Opening day for the Dodgers was to be on April 9 in Chicago. But spring had not started on time for the Windy City, and neither would the baseball season. As Frank Finch wrote in the *Los Angeles Times:* "The Dodgers won the toss today at Wrigley Field and elected to receive, but the Cubs canceled the National League opener as a steady snowfall pelted the diamond." Besides the carpet of snow, the temperature at what would have been game time stood icily at 32 degrees Fahrenheit. The next day it rose 10 degrees and the snow was cleared from the playing field so the Dodgers and the Cubs could launch their 1959 seasons. Don Drysdale once

PEE WEE REESE

He was called "the Little Colonel" and "Pee Wee," Harold Henry Reese, and he put on his first Dodgers uniform in Brooklyn in 1940 and took his last one off in Los Angeles at the close of the 1958 season.

Reese became the first Dodgers captain in 1949, and he retained that duty and honor until he retired. His leadership was incomparable, on the field and off. Tommy Holmes, sportswriter for the *New York Herald-Tribune,* once wrote: "Pee Wee had closer and friendlier relations with Leo Durocher than any other ballplayer on the club. He had the respect and admiration of fiery Jackie Robinson. From time to time, he helped ease the way for the brooding Carl Furillo and the temperamental Duke Snider. He delighted in the homespun Arkansas philosophy of Preacher Roe and the gritty pragmatism of Campanella. Hodges and Erskine were among his closest friends, and he hadn't any enemies."

Reese was also a consummate ball player. "Pee Wee was 20 years old when I first saw him in spring training," Leo Durocher said, "and looked 12 . . . what we got here is a diamond [I said]. . . . What we got to do is polish the diamond up, and he is going to be as good a shortstop as they ever heard of in the major leagues."

Only Zack Wheat would step into the batter's box more often than Reese in Dodgers history, and only Wheat and later Bill Russell would appear in more games. No one in Dodgers history has scored more than Reese's 1,338 runs, and only Wheat got more hits than Reese's 2,170. Reese was also a superb fielder and an expert base runner who stole a total of 232 bases. Reese ranks fourth in doubles, behind Wheat, Duke Snider, and Steve Garvey, and seventh in extra-base hits and in total bases. His lifetime batting average is .269. He was inducted into the Hall of Fame in 1984.

again got the call to open the year's festivities, but he fared no better than he had during most of the year before, and the Cubs won it handily, 6–1.

Back in much warmer California for their home opener, the Dodgers apparently had not thawed out and were decisively beaten by the Cardinals, 6–2. Johnny Podres chalked up the loss. Roy Campanella was at the ballpark to watch the game; it was his first visit to the Dodgers since his auto accident. Along with Campy were 61,552 other fans.

Gil Hodges is happy enough to mess up the hair of Larry Sherry after one of the young relief pitcher's wins in the 1959 World Series. Both were Dodgers heroes of the Series, Sherry winning two games in relief and posting an ERA of 0.71, and Hodges batting .391 in the six-game championship spectacle.

Despite the unimpressive openings on the road and at home, by April 26 the Dodgers had quelled the skeptics and astonished just about everyone. That was the day they catapulted themselves into first place in the National League. And they did it with style, drubbing the Cardinals 17–11 while banging out 20 hits (Charlie Neal had 5, Carl Furillo 4, and Gil Hodges and Don Demeter 3 each). Baseball in Los Angeles had taken a decided change for the better.

Roy Campanella came back out to the Coliseum on the night of May 7. The occasion this time was a special exhibition game with the New York Yankees that had been arranged as a tribute to him. Before the game, Pee Wee Reese, his longtime teammate and fellow retiree, wheeled him onto the field before the cheers of an awesome crowd. It was, in fact, the largest number of people ever gathered to watch a major league baseball game. There were 93,103 people in the Coliseum that night and an estimated fifteen thousand had been turned away at the gates. It was a dramatic and emotional evening, and the fact that the Dodgers lost to the Yankees 6–2 was merely an aside.

May did not prove to be a great month for the Dodgers. They skidded all the way down to fourth place, four and one-half games behind the reigning pennant holders, the Milwaukee Braves.

To add some punch to the batting order, Frank Howard was brought up. The 6'6", 248-pound power hitter had been having a phenomenal year with the Dodgers' Victoria farm club in the Texas League (which was managed by Dodgers old-liner Pete Reiser). At that point in the still-young season, Howard had blasted 27 home runs, a number of them hit well over 400 feet, and was batting .365.

Sandy Koufax had yet to plant his foot firmly on the Dodgers' pitching mound. Manager Walt

CARL ERSKINE

They called him "Oisk" in Brooklyn, where he pitched for 10 years. But when Carl Erskine added another two years out in Los Angeles before retiring in 1959, the accentless Californians never picked up on the patently Flatbush nickname.

Erskine was a charter member of the Boys of Summer. A right-hander with a notorious curve ball, he started with the Dodgers in 1948 and was soon in the regular rotation, pitching alongside Don Newcombe, Preacher Roe, Ralph Branca, and Joe Black.

His best year was the pennant-winning season of 1953 when he won 20 and lost only 6. His won-lost percentage of .769 was the league high that year, and he struck out more batters (187) than in any other season. His career record is 122–78, with an ERA of 4.00. Erskine's career won-lost percentage is .610, and Oisk struck out 981 batters in his 12 seasons.

The two finest days of his career were the two no-hit games he hurled for the Dodgers: 5–0 over the Cubs in 1952, and 3–0 over the Giants in 1956. Only two other Dodgers pitchers have thrown two or more no-hitters: Sandy Koufax with four and Adonis Terry with two (back in 1886 and 1888).

The Dodgers' Don Demeter stirs up some dust and forces White Sox shortstop Luis Aparicio to drop the ball in this action shot near second base in the 1959 World Series. It was representative of the Sox's misfortunes in the championship match that year. Although they got off to a fine start, whipping a tired Dodgers team 11–0, they then collapsed and lost four of the next five games to give Los Angeles its first World Series crown.

Alston said of him earlier in the year, "He's either awfully good or awfully bad, just the way I play pool." By midsummer 1959, however, Koufax was about to prove how awfully good he really was. If Alston's pool game were to keep pace, he would soon be wielding a cue in the same league as Willie Mosconi and Minnesota Fats.

It was shortly before the All-Star Game break when Koufax took on the Philadelphia Phillies in a night game and struck out 16 of them. It was the most strikeouts ever chalked up in a major league night game, and it tied the Dodgers club record for the most strikeouts in any game. No Dodger had fanned 16 players since Nap Rucker did it back in 1909.

A singular honor was bestowed on Don Drysdale when he was chosen to start for the National League in the All-Star Game. Another Dodger, Wally Moon, on the way to having one of the best seasons of his big-league career, was out in left field. Drysdale pitched three perfect innings. Although an eighth-inning triple by Willie Mays

gave the National League a 5–4 win, the game's Most Valuable Player award still went to Drysdale.

The Dodgers moved up during July and finally regained the league lead by the end of the month. The Giants and Braves, however, were both only one-half game behind.

When the Phillies came back to town, they found that Sandy Koufax was not the only Dodgers pitcher who could throw strikes. Don Drysdale fanned 14 of them in one game, his most prodigious strike-out performance ever.

Frank Howard had boomed only one home run in 21 at-bats and was hitting a miserable .143 when it was decided to ship him back to the minors, this time to Spokane, Washington. But Wally Moon was hitting home runs. He had mastered a most unique stroke. A left-handed batter, Moon was nevertheless slicing lofty fly balls over the left-field screen to the amazement of all those who commonly viewed home runs to the opposite field as distinct phenomena.

The Giants were in a close race for the pennant with the Dodgers when they came to the Coliseum for a night game on August 31. A good hitting team with such sluggers as Willie Mays, Orlando Cepeda, and rookie sensation Willie McCovey, they were hardly prepared for what Sandy Koufax had in store for them. He struck out 18 Giants in nine innings to tie the major league record set by Bob Feller back in 1938. And he broke the all-time National League record of 17 strikeouts in a single game, which had been held by Dizzy Dean since 1933. When Bob Feller set the record, his Cleveland Indians nonetheless lost the game. The same thing almost happened to Sandy Koufax and the Dodgers on that equally historic night in 1959. Going into the ninth inning the Dodgers and Giants were tied. Koufax struck out the side on 10 pitches. Then, he singled to start a last-of-the-ninth rally, which climaxed when Wally Moon lofted a three-run homer to give the Dodgers a 5–2 win.

The National League lead was exchanged several times in September between the Dodgers, Giants, and Braves. By the 19th of the month, the

Posing at batting practice before Game 2 of the 1959 NL play-offs are Duke Snider (left) and Wally Moon. Snider missed the first game because of a painful knee injury, but he was back for Game 2 to help Moon and the other Dodgers rack up a 6–5 win over the Milwaukee Braves to take the pennant.

Chuck Essegian pinch hit three times in the 1959 World Series and whacked out two clutch home runs. He had joined the Dodgers earlier in the season, coming from the St. Louis Cardinals, and would depart after the 1960 season for the Baltimore Orioles.

Dodgers had sunk two games behind the Giants and had to go up to Seals Stadium for a crucial three-game series. It was a do-or-die situation, and the Giants had the home-field advantage. But the Dodgers were scarcely ready to expire. Behind the pitching of Roger Craig and Don Drysdale, they swept a day-night doubleheader, and they came back the following day to whip the Giants again and move into first place.

The Braves, however, were still around and thirsting for their third consecutive National League flag. By September 23, they had moved into a tie with the Dodgers for first place, with the Giants trailing two games out. The race went helter-skelter all the way to the last day of the season. On that day, it was mathematically possible that the National League race could end in a three-way tie. It didn't. The Giants lost two games to the Cardinals and were out of the running. But the season did end in a two-way tie when both the Dodgers and the Braves won and ended their seasons with identical records of 88–68. So the pennant would have to be decided by a three-game playoff series.

The Dodgers had hardly showered after that last regular-season game before they were on the team airplane headed cross-country for Milwaukee. There would be no rest period: the first game of the playoffs was scheduled for the next afternoon.

Danny McDevitt started for the Dodgers but gave up two runs and was relieved in the second inning by a young right-hander named Larry Sherry, who was about to become the Dodgers' ace fireman. The Dodgers tied it up in the third and then went ahead for good in the sixth when John Roseboro homered. The final: Dodgers 3, Braves 2. Sherry did not give up a run in a superb seven-and-two-thirds-inning relief performance.

It was back on the plane for another two thousand–mile flight to L.A. In Game 2 the following afternoon, Don Drysdale (17–13) would pitch for the Dodgers, facing the Braves' Lew Burdette (21–15).

Old reliable Carl Furillo, 37, lashes out a hit here in the seventh inning of Game 3 of the 1959 World Series to drive in two runs and break a scoreless tie. The Dodgers went on to win the game 3–1. A few days earlier, in the last game of the NL playoffs, Furillo drove home a run to tie the game in the ninth and another to win it in the twelfth. He would only play in eight games the next year and then retire to end his fine 15-year Dodgers career. The White Sox catcher is Sherm Lollar.

It appeared as if the Braves would even up the playoffs when they routed Drysdale and took a 5–2 lead into the ninth inning. But with a barrage of five hits in the bottom of the ninth, crowned with a sacrifice fly from the bat of old vet Carl Furillo, the Dodgers made up the three-run deficit and sent the game into extra innings. In the last of the twelfth, with Gil Hodges on third, Furillo came back and slashed a ground ball up the middle off Bob Rush. Felix Mantilla, the Braves' shortstop, could not make the play and Hodges trotted home with the winning run and the National League pennant. As Frank Finch aptly put it in the next day's *Times*: "With the fine Italian hand of Carl Furillo writing one of the most stirring chapters in Dodger annals, the Dodgers yesterday qualified to play the White Sox in the 1959 World Series."

In only one year, the Dodgers had rebounded from seventh place to first, a feat that had never before been accomplished in National League history. It was the Dodgers 13th pennant since 1890, and it was certainly earned in the most dramatic of ways.

Not only was the Dodgers' ascension from seventh to first place in 1959 astounding, but so was the decline of the New York Yankees in the American League. After four straight appearances in the World Series, they had dropped to the cellar in late May, an unheard-of experience in New York. They did not stay there, but made it back to only third place, a full

WORLD SERIES LINEUPS, 1959

DODGERS	WHITE SOX
Junior Gilliam, 3b	Luis Aparicio, ss
Charlie Neal, 2b	Nellie Fox, 2b
Wally Moon, lf	Jim Landis, cf
Duke Snider, cf	Ted Kluszewski, 1b
Norm Larker, rf	Sherm Lollar, c
Gil Hodges, 1b	Billy Goodman, 3b
John Roseboro, c	Al Smith, lf
Maury Wills, ss	Jim Rivera, rf

STARTING PITCHERS
Game 1: Roger Craig, Early Wynn
Game 2: Johnny Podres, Bob Shaw
Game 3: Don Drysdale, Dick Donovan
Game 4: Roger Craig, Early Wynn
Game 5: Sandy Koufax, Bob Shaw
Game 6: Johnny Podres, Early Wynn

Wally Moon came to the Dodgers in 1959 from the St. Louis Cardinals, where he had played in the outfield since 1954, and instantly found the Los Angeles Coliseum to his liking. He would gain a certain kind of fame for being able to slice looping fly balls to the opposite field that would then drop over the Coliseum's short left-field fence for home runs. Moon had a fine season that pennant-winning year, batting .302, lofting 19 home runs, and hitting a league-high 11 triples. But his best Dodgers year would be 1961, when he led the team with a batting average of .328. Over 12 years Moon had a lifetime batting average of .289.

Sandy Koufax crosses the plate with the winning run in this 1959 game against the San Francisco Giants. More significant that night, however, was the fact that he struck out 18 batters to tie the major league record held by Bob Feller of the Cleveland Indians. In the bottom of the ninth, with the score tied 2–2, Koufax singled and scored when Wally Moon homered.

15 games behind the Chicago White Sox. Not since 1919 had the White Sox played in a World Series, and that Series, of course, was cloaked in the sordid "Black Sox" scandal.

The Chicagoans in 1959 were known, however, as the "Go-Go Sox" because they ran and hustled with such gusto as to inspire the fans at Comiskey Park to a chant of "Go, go, go . . ." almost every time one of them got on base. Sox shortstop Luis Aparicio led the majors in stolen bases that year with 56, and Jim Landis was third in the American League with 20. The team total of stolen bases (113), highest in

CASEY COVERS THE SERIES

Life magazine had a special correspondent cover the 1959 World Series: Casey Stengel. Some of his observations:

> Between you and me this Series started out wacky from the beginning. . . . If you'd tell people around the world [the White Sox] would get 11 runs in one day, they wouldn't believe it unless they see it because sometimes Chicago doesn't get that many runs in two weeks.

> Being an American League manager I am naturally partial to the American League club. Besides that, the American League manager, Al Lopez, is a depositor in my bank in Glendale, California, and if he wins the Series he will have more money to put in my bank than if he lost.

The willowy Don Demeter, 6'4", 190 pounds, played only one full year (1959) with the Dodgers as a regular, and that year cracked 18 home runs. The following year he served as a key pinch-hitter and posted a .274 average. Demeter would have even better years with other teams down the road, his best, 1962, when he batted .307 and hit 29 home runs for the Philadelphia Phillies.

Roger Craig broke back into the regular rotation for the Dodgers in 1959 (he had been a regular with Brooklyn in 1956) and pitched four shutouts to tie for league honors. His record of 11–5, and the 12–11 he produced in 1956, would stand as his best Dodgers performances. Craig was sent to the New York Mets in 1962, where he would earn the undistinguished honor of posting the most losses in the NL in two consecutive seasons, 24 and 22.

the majors, was 29 more than the second-best total by the Dodgers (84). Nellie Fox, at 31, was still as dependable as ever at bat and was the game's finest fielder at second base. They had some power from veteran catcher Sherm Lollar and from mighty Ted Kluszewski, whom they had acquired from the Pittsburgh Pirates late in the season. Early Wynn, less than a year away from his 40th birthday, won 22 games for the Sox and posted an ERA of 3.16. Bob Shaw won another 18 games and Billy Pierce 14, and relievers Turk Lown and Gerry Staley saved 15 and 14 games, respectively.

The Dodgers were at a distinct disadvantage going into the Series. They had played their last game of the season at home, flown that night to Milwaukee to play the Braves, then flown back to Los Angeles for another afternoon game, and now with only a single day's rest were flying back to the Midwest—three flights of more than two thousand miles each in less than 72 hours and two pressure-cooker games within three days of the Series start. The toll was all too evident. Dodgers starter Roger Craig was knocked out of the box in the third inning as the White Sox amassed a 9–0 lead; they continued to storm to an 11–0 finale. Big Ted Kluszewski hit two home runs for the Sox, and Early Wynn was masterful on the mound.

Don Drysdale rebounded from a disappointing 12–13 season in 1958 to lead the Dodgers staff in 1959 with a record of 17–13, four shutouts, and 242 strikeouts (the most in the majors that year). He also picked up a crucial win for the Dodgers in Game 3 of the World Series that year.

Out at Comiskey Park the next day, it looked like the Dodgers might never recover from the playoffs. But then, down a run in the seventh inning, the Dodgers got a pinch-hit, game-tying home run from Chuck Essegian, who had come to the Dodgers from the Cardinals during the season. In the same inning Charlie Neal added a two-run homer, his seond homer of the game. It was enough to give the Dodgers an eventual 4–3 win. The game was saved by Larry Sherry, who relieved Johnny Podres in the seventh. Credited with the win, Podres became the first Dodger ever to win three World Series games.

From there it was back to the West Coast. The fans, as expected, jammed the Coliseum to watch their pennant-winning team. At the first game in the Coliseum, a record 92,394 fans showed up and were treated to Don Drysdale's 3–1 win over the Sox and another save by Larry Sherry. The game was won in the seventh when Carl Furillo came through with a clutch-hit to drive in Charlie Neal and Norm Larker and break a scoreless tie.

In the fourth game of the Series, 92,650 fans came out to the Coliseum. And they saw another old Brooklyner, Gil Hodges, win it for L.A. He belted an eighth-inning home run to break a 4–4 tie and provide the winning one-run margin. The win went to reliever Larry Sherry, who had replaced Roger Craig in the top half of the eighth.

Sandy Koufax started the fifth game of the Series and pitched a very creditable eight innings, but he gave up one run in the fourth inning when Nellie Fox scored on a double play hit into by

Duke Snider scores easily here after a wild pitch from the Milwaukee Braves' Bob Buhl (right) in this 1959 game. Out of the batter's box and looking toward where the errant pitch rolled is Dodger Don Demeter. The Braves and Dodgers went neck and neck all the way to the wire, but the Dodgers prevailed by winning two straight in the NL playoffs.

Sherm Lollar. The Sox got only five hits all day, but the one run was enough as Bob Shaw, Billy Pierce, and Dick Donovan teamed to shut out the Dodgers.

The sixth game pitted Early Wynn, making his third start of the series, against Johnny Podres back in Chicago. A weary Wynn was shelled in the third and the fourth, and the Sox could not get their bats to do much of anything for them. The Dodgers, however, were invincible that day. They took an early lead, 2–0. Larry Sherry came on to relieve Podres in the fourth inning after Ted Kluszewski cracked a three-run homer, and he proceeded to shut out the Sox for the next five and two-thirds innings. The final score was 9–3. The Dodgers were aided by home runs from the bats of Duke Snider, Wally Moon, and Chuck Essegian. It was the Dodgers' first world championship in Los Angeles, Walt Alston's second in three Series as the Dodgers manager, and only the second triumph for the Dodgers in 10 World Series appearances.

Larry Sherry, with two wins, two saves, and an ERA of 0.71, was certainly a premier hero in the Series. But so were a lot of other Dodgers, especially old-timers like Furillo, Hodges, and Snider, who all provided clutch hits.

A total of 420,784 people had attended the six games, the most up to that time in World Series history. The take was another record. Each Dodgers player went home with $11,231 in World Series money, and the runner-up White Sox received $7,257 each. Walter O'Malley threw a gala party for the team in Chicago, replete with champagne, caviar, and steak, to celebrate both the Dodgers' victory and his own 56th birthday.

CHAPTER 5

FORGETTABLE YEARS

Holman Stadium of Dodgertown in Vero Beach, Florida, where the Dodgers have held spring training since 1948. This ballpark, named for Bud Holman, a local Floridian who first enticed the Dodgers there, was dedicated in 1953 and could handle five thousand spectators. The Dodgers of L.A. chose to keep the same site for spring training as their predecessors from Brooklyn had used.

AFTER THE 1959 WORLD SERIES, the Dodgers returned to Los Angeles in much the same style as Caesar and his legions had returned to the Roman Forum. It had been a wonderfully exciting year, and a lucrative one. Besides the bonus income from the playoff games and the World Series, the Dodgers' take at the Coliseum gate was the largest in club annals. For the first time, they enticed more than 2 million people (2,071,045) into their home ballpark during the regular baseball season. It was

Then director of scouting Al Campanis (center) makes a few notes about two of his more promising prospects, Tommy Davis (left) and Willie Davis, in this 1960 spring training shot. The year before, Tommy hit .345 for the Dodgers farm club at Spokane, Washington, while Willie batted .365 for the Dodgers franchise in Reno, Nevada.

not a major league record, but at that time in major league history only three teams could lay claim to having drawn more in a single season—the New York Yankees, Cleveland Indians, and Milwaukee Braves.

Only two players had batted above the .300 mark: Duke Snider (.308) and Wally Moon (.302). Gil Hodges cracked the most home runs, 25, but Snider's 23 were a close second. Both Wally Moon and Charlie Neal knocked out 11 triples, which were the most in the National League that year. Neal also led the team in doubles (30), hits (177), and runs scored (103). And Junior Gilliam drew the most walks (96) of any National Leaguer.

From the pitching staff, there were some encouraging signs. Sandy Koufax was beginning to impress

people as a strikeout artist, although Don Drysdale led the team and the National League in that area with 242 that year. Drysdale had also regained his winning form and led the Dodgers staff with a record of 17–13, the second-best effort in his first four years as a Dodger. His tally of four shutouts was tied for the National League high in 1959.

After a year of baseball nirvana for the Dodgers and their followers, 1960 was truly a fall from grace. Selected by some baseball prognosticators to repeat their pennant-winning ways, the Dodgers would quickly and clearly show that that was far from forthcoming. They were a team in transition. They had depended heavily for success on the old pros who had come out west from Flatbush. In

CARL FURILLO

Carl Furillo, in the 14 years before 1960, had been an integral part of one of the most illustrious segments of Dodgers history. His throwing arm so often squelched many players' hapless attempts to stretch a hit or to tag up on a fly ball to right that it earned him legendary status and the nickname "the Reading Rifle" (he was from Reading, Pennsylvania). And he played the right-field wall in Ebbets Field with the same finesse that a concert pianist has with the ivory keys of a piano.

Furillo came to the Dodgers back in 1946 and won a starting job in the outfield alongside Dixie Walker and Pete Reiser. Roger Kahn in *The Boys of Summer* described him as:

> **A pure ball player. . . . There was a fluidity to his frame you seldom see, among such sinews. His black hair was thick and tightly curled. His face was strong and smooth. He had the look of a young indomitable centurion. . . . I cannot imagine Carl Furillo in his prime as anything other than a ball player. Right field in Brooklyn was his destiny.**

He also made his mark at the plate. In all of Dodgers history only seven players have batted in more games. Only seven have banged out more hits or driven in more runs, only three have hit more doubles.

He was the major league batting champ in 1953 with an average of .344. He batted over .300 four times, and his lifetime average is a praiseworthy .299. He hit 192 home runs—26 in 1955, his best slugging season (a slugging average of .520).

1960, the last of the Boys of Summer were deep in the winter of their careers. Carl Furillo, 38, injured, discontented, and scarcely utilized, had a feud with management early in the season and was released. It was not a pleasant parting, and Furillo ended up having to sue to collect his 1960 salary, claiming that, according to his contract, he could not be released while injured. He won the suit, but was out of baseball forever.

His longtime field mates Duke Snider and Gil Hodges also had their problems. They had slowed down considerably and would only participate in about two-thirds of the games in 1960. Hodges would bat a lowly .198 and Snider .243. Between the two of them they would account for only 22 home runs.

Gargantuan Frank Howard, whose two-year baseball career had so far been a roller-coaster ride between the majors and minors, was brought back up, this time to stay. Another rookie, Tommy Davis, landed the left-field job after spending four years in the Dodgers farm system. Later in the year, Willie Davis (unrelated) would come from Spokane, Washington, to secure the center-field position.

The Dodgers opened against the Chicago Cubs at the Coliseum in 1960. Don Drysdale was on the mound for the third consecutive season opener and—unlike the previous two years—led the Dodgers to victory. It took the Dodgers 11 innings, but they beat the Cubs 3–2. A few days later they traveled north to meet the San Francisco Giants. The Giants had settled into their new ballpark on Candlestick Point. One writer described the facility as a "wind tunnel"; hitters and fielders, after experiencing the winds that cycloned through it, spoke mostly in unprintable terms.

Still, the Dodgers must have carried some trace of envy with them into that stadium. They were still two years away from their own new stadium in Los Angeles, and the Coliseum had many demerits that made the new Candlestick Park look impressive in spite of its wind problems. It was a modern park with three levels of seats, plush

Stan Williams was 23 when he became part of the regular rotation in 1960, two years after coming up with the Dodgers. A big man (6'5", 230 pounds) with a sizzling fastball, Williams was often referred to as the "other right-hander" on the Dodgers staff, condemned to hurl in Don Drysdale's shadow. Still, he had three fine seasons pitching for the Dodgers (1960–1962: 14–10, 15–12, 14–12) before moving on to the Yankees in 1963. In his 14-year major league career, Williams won 109 games and lost 94 (.537).

locker rooms, and no beams, poles, or other obstructions to block spectators' views. Perhaps the envy worked to the Dodgers' advantage, because in their Candlestick Park debut, Johnny Podres led them in a 4–0 shutout over their old archrivals.

After that, however, the season was anything but thrilling. The Dodgers were never really in contention, and the season turned into one of prolonged disappointment. When it was over, the Pittsburgh Pirates, behind the hitting of Dick Groat and Roberto Clemente and the pitching of Vern Law and Bob Friend, had virtually sailed through the National League. The Milwaukee Braves and St. Louis Cardinals trailed them by seven and nine games, respectively. And in fourth place were last year's flag holders, the Dodgers, with a record of 82–72, a full 13 games behind the Pirates. The fans had not despaired, however. A new Dodgers home-attendance record was posted: 2,253,887 people passed through the Coliseum turnstiles in 1960.

There had been a few sparkles in Walt Alston's otherwise murky skies. Maury Wills had not merely been playing at shortstop with a blessed glove; he had become a dazzling base thief. His 50 stolen bases in the 1960 season had been the most in the National League and only 1 behind the pre-eminent speedster of the Go-Go White Sox, Luis Aparicio. Wills had also collected the most Dodgers hits (152), but the club batting crown had gone to Norm Larker—converted that year to a full-time first baseman—whose .323 had been only two percentage points behind league-leader Dick Groat of the Pirates. At the time it was the highest batting average ever recorded by a Dodger in Los Angeles.

Frank Howard had been the Dodgers' home-run king for the year with 23, and he was named National League Rookie of the Year by *The Sporting News*. It had been a year for grand-slam home runs, if not for winning games. Frank Howard had hit two, and John Roseboro, Norm Sherry, Wally Moon, and Tommy Davis had tagged one each.

Onetime slugger Duke Snider takes some bunting practice in this 1960 scene. It was the year the great center fielder, then 33, would begin to turn his job over to 21-year-old Tommy Davis.

Don Drysdale had again led the pitching staff (15–14), but Larry Sherry, Stan Williams, and Johnny Podres had chalked up 14 wins each. Sandy Koufax had his worst year ever as a Dodger, winning only 8 games and losing 13, although he did hurl a one-hit shutout over the Pirates early in the season.

Walt Alston had managed the National League teams to victories in both All-Star Games of 1960. The Dodgers were represented on those playing fields by Norm Larker, Charlie Neal, Johnny Podres, and Stan Williams.

The catching corps at spring training in 1960: (from left to right) Joe Pignatano, John Roseboro, and Norm Sherry. Roseboro became the Dodgers' frontline catcher in 1958 after Roy Campanella's career ended and would remain there through 1967. Backup catcher Norm Sherry would be instrumental in helping Sandy Koufax hone his talents to Hall of Fame caliber.

Most thought there would be some changes for 1961. After all, Los Angelenos had breathed the ambrosial air of triumph in 1959 and had enjoyed the high drama of that frenzied pennant race. Baseball in L.A. in 1960 had been such a deflating experience that Dodgers fans waited and hoped for a shake-up that would restore the team's winning ways.

The major changes in baseball in 1961, however, were in the league and its structure, not in the Dodgers ranks. Expansion came, and with it a longer baseball season. The American League added two teams that year: the Washington Senators (the original Senators franchise having been moved to the Twin Cities and renamed the Minnesota Twins) and the Los Angeles Angels. To accommodate the new teams, the schedule was extended to 162 games, 8 more than had previously been played in a regular season. (The National League did not expand until the following year, 1962, when it added the Houston Colt .45s (later renamed the Astros) and the New York Mets, and also lengthened its schedule.)

CLEM LABINE

The youngster with the crewcut came to Ebbets Field in 1950 and became Brooklyn's greatest fireman. Clem Labine had a strong curve and a dazzling slider, and it is said that Stan Musial went hitless 49 times in a row facing him. No one, at least in the Brooklyn era of the Dodgers, came close to saving as many games (83) as Labine.

The Dodgers traded him in 1960 to the Detroit Tigers, and he got in two more years of playing time after that. At the end of his career he had amassed 551 strikeouts, an overall record of 77–56, and an ERA of 3.63. He could also remember a different slice of his career: two memorable starts in crucial Dodgers games. In the 1951 playoff game, he shut out the Giants 10–0, and five years later in the 1956 World Series blanked the Yankees 1–0.

First baseman Norm Larker had the best season of his six-year major league career with the Dodgers in 1960. His .323 average was far and away the team's best, and the 78 RBIs and 26 doubles he contributed were also Dodgers highs that year.

The Angels agreed to play their first season in the smallish Wrigley Field in L.A. They would move into joint tenancy with the Dodgers in their new stadium in Chavez Ravine the next year, and then finally settle into their own new ballpark in Anaheim in 1966.

One of the more surprising developments for the 1961 Dodgers was the hiring of a new third-base coach, none other than the irrepressible Leo Durocher. He had managed the Dodgers in Brooklyn from 1939 through 1946 and then again for half a season in 1948. Speculation spread immediately that it was the first step in a plan to eventually remove Walt Alston from the managerial tower. Durocher shook his head at that idea. "I'm just here to coach," he said. Walter O'Malley vehemently denied that he was disenchanted with Alston, but nothing could stop the rumors from flitting back and forth.

Another old-time Dodger also came back on the scene. The once-stunning right-hander Don Newcombe showed up in Vero Beach, a free agent after being released by the Cleveland Indians. At 35, he hoped to latch on to the Dodgers for another season or two, but it did not work out and he retired from the game before Opening Day.

Some other changes took place down in Florida that spring of 1961. Veterans Gil Hodges and Junior Gilliam, as well as 1960 Rookie of the Year Frank Howard, were sentenced to the bench as competition from Dodgers youngsters sizzled in the Florida sun.

The Dodgers worked their way across the country after the Grapefruit League ended, playing

Dodgers ace Don Drysdale didn't just fire off fastballs in 1960. Here, in a publicity shot from the TV show The Lawman, *in which he appeared, the pitcher-turned-actor is flanked by the show's stars John Russell (left) and Peter Brown.*

exhibition games in Tucson, Phoenix, Las Vegas, and San Diego before hosting the Phillies in the league opener at the Coliseum. A crowd of more than fifty thousand was there to watch Don Drysdale in his fourth consecutive Opening Day start for the Dodgers. He went against Robin Roberts, who was hurling his 12th straight Opening Day game, a National League record he shared with Hall of Famer Grover Cleveland Alexander. The Dodgers won it 6–2 for Drysdale.

The defending champion Pittsburgh Pirates and the San Francisco Giants were allegedly the teams to beat in 1961, but also a real threat were the Milwaukee Braves, who were in their second year under former Dodgers manager Chuck Dressen. Before the season, no one had considered the unheralded Cincinnati Reds, but the oversight would be rectified quite quickly.

Wally Moon accepts a Gold Glove award for his fielding prowess during the preceding season (1960). The left fielder was only the second Dodger to be so honored; Gil Hodges had won the award three times (in 1957, 1958, and 1959). The presenter is Bill Schaeffer of Rawlings Sporting Goods.

Sandy Koufax finally asserted himself as a master pitcher in 1961 after six years of mediocrity on the mound. He had tied the major league strikeout record for a single game (18) two seasons earlier, but he had not produced a sustained successful season until he won 18 games in 1961. He also led the major leagues in strikeouts that year with 269, a feat he would accomplish three more times in the following five years.

Caught in this pensive moment are the Dodgers' slugging outfielder–turned–movie star, Frank Howard, and the old crooner himself, Bing Crosby. Howard's role in the movie High Times was less memorable than his career as a baseball player, which was really just getting started in 1960.

The Dodgers started out well but were overshadowed as the Giants established a two-game lead by May 15. The Dodgers, however, had won 18 and lost 13 and were playing very good baseball, as were the Cincinnati Reds. By June 1, the Reds and Giants shared first place, with the Dodgers a game behind.

During that period, Duke Snider clouted his 370th major league home run. Unfortunately, two innings later his elbow was broken by an errant pitch from Cardinal ace Bob Gibson. It was estimated he would be out for at least five weeks.

After June 15, however, the Reds seemed indomitable. Behind the red-hot bats of Frank Robinson and Vada Pinson and the consistently

The gargantuan Frank Howard stretches to beat out an infield grounder in this 1960 game against the Milwaukee Braves. That's pitcher Lew Burdette (No. 33) trying to get a handle on the underhand toss from first baseman Joe Adcock. Burdette bobbled the ball; Howard was safe and subsequently went on to score what became the winning run that day. This was Howard's first productive year for the Dodgers; he slugged a club-high 23 home runs.

superb pitching of Joey Jay, Jim O'Toole, Bob Purkey, and Jim Brosnan, they won 21 of 28 games and by mid-July had taken a commanding five-game lead in the National League pennant race.

The Dodgers hung in there, however, and by August 15 were back in first with a record of 69–42, a one-game advantage over the Reds. Then, in a torrent, came a 10-game losing streak, a disastrous double-header double shutout by the Reds at the Coliseum (6–0, 8–0), and a September three-game sweep by the Giants to snuff out any lingering Dodgers hope.

When it was finally over, the Dodgers were in second place, four games out of first. The Giants and the Braves trailed by eight and ten games, respectively. The Cinderella Reds had won the pennant, their first since 1940, and had earned the chance to face in the World Series one of the most explosive New York Yankees teams ever.

While all this had been going on in the National League, most baseball eyes had been focused on what was happening in the American League, principally the spectacular power hitting emanating from the New York Yankees. It was, of course, the year of Mantle and Maris, who each belted out homer after homer as they made a run at the venerated record of Babe Ruth. Roger Maris, as everyone knows, broke it with 61, but in 8 more games than the 154-game season in which Babe Ruth had stroked his 60. After 154 games in 1961, Maris had hit 59 and then added the last 2 in the elongated part of the season. Mickey Mantle's 54 that year would be the single-season high in his Hall of Fame career, and four other Yankees hit more than 20: Bill Skowron (28), Yogi Berra (22), and Elston Howard and Johnny Blanchard (21). The team total of 240 was a major league record.

It was also a year of other historic major league moments. Warren Spahn of the Braves pitched the second no-hitter of his career. And Willie Mays tied a major league record when he hit four home runs in a single game. In Baltimore, Orioles first baseman Jim Gentile tied another major league record when he smashed five grand-slam home runs during the season. (Ernie Banks of the Cubs, in 1955, was the only other player up to that time to have done that.) Whitey Ford, who led both leagues in pitching with a record of 25–4 (.862), pitched 14 scoreless innings in the World Series, extending his 18 from the preceding Series and breaking Babe Ruth's record of 29 consecutive scoreless innings pitched in a World Series. And the Dodgers' own Sandy Koufax set a National League strikeout record by fanning 269 batters.

Dodgers pitchers (from left to right) Stan Williams, Roger Craig, and Don Drysdale form zeros here to signify the three consecutive shutouts they threw July 22, 23, and 24, 1960. Drysdale would hurl a total of five shutouts that year and lead the major leagues in strikeouts with 246. Williams would post two shutouts while having his best year yet as a Dodger (14–10, 3.00 ERA), but Craig (8–3) would be hampered most of the season with an injured shoulder.

With the end of the 1961 season, the tenancy of the Dodgers at the Coliseum also came to an end. The last game played there took place on September 20. It lasted 13 innings, and Sandy Koufax endured to beat the Cubs 3–2. There was an uncommonly small crowd of 12,068 on hand to watch the closing act. The next day one sportswriter eulogized:

> **And now that the last Chinese homer has fluttered like a wounded duck over the Coliseum left-field screen we say "Aloha"—and good riddance to the diabolical barrier that all but sent Don Drysdale to the nut house and made many sluggers out of many a mouse.**

It wasn't all that true. Surely there were a lot of home runs that floated over the left-field screen that would have been fly-outs in other stadia. But home-run records were not set in the Coliseum; in fact, none of the totals came close. Certainly pitchers had to change tactics when left-field pull hitters moved into the batter's box, but none of the right-handed sluggers had shone that brightly in the Coliseum to warrant recognition either. And, no, Don Drysdale did not like the pressures it put on him, but he did produce winning seasons his last three years there and had been impressive in all of them.

Elsewhere in the league, other owners would have reveled in what the Coliseum had to offer.

Almost eight million people had attended regular-season baseball games in the four years of the Dodgers' residency there. They had seen the Dodgers win 173 games and lose 140, and win a World Series. And, as testament to the climate of sunny California, *Examiner* sportswriter Bob Hunter pointed out that not a single game in four years had been called because of rain.

For the Dodgers, the 1961 season had been an improvement of considerable proportions. They had stayed in the race almost to the wire. There had been many heartening, hopeful moments during the year. They had even been in first place on 26 different dates.

Sandy Koufax had turned in his best year yet as a Dodger, winning 18 while losing 13, along with his league strikeout record. Johnny Podres had also won 18 games, but lost only 5, to post the best won-lost percentage in the National League that year (.783). Stan Williams (15–12) and Don Drysdale (13–10) also had respectable seasons. Larry Sherry chalked up 15 saves, and a rookie reliever by the name of Ron Perranoski looked very good, posting a 7–5 record. Wally Moon hit .328, and his 17 home runs were only 1 less than team leader John Roseboro. Maury Wills stole 35 bases, tops in the NL for 1961.

Dodgers fans, as they filed out of the Coliseum for the last time, left with a lot to look forward to in 1962—a new stadium and a fresh team that appeared to be on its way back to the top.

CHAPTER 6

CHAVEZ RAVINE AND
DODGER STADIUM

A couple of fans from the neighborhood joined Leo Durocher (left) and Don Drysdale (second from left) before the first celebrity "Stars" game in 1962: Dean Martin, who handles the bat more like a microphone, and James Garner.

"IT WAS FOUR YEARS, SIX MONTHS, and two days ago that Walter O'Malley telegraphed Norris Poulson, then mayor of Los Angeles: 'GET YOUR WHEELBARROW AND SHOVEL—STOP—I'LL MEET YOU IN CHAVEZ RAVINE,'" wrote *Los Angeles Times* sports editor Paul Zimmerman on the occasion of the grand opening of Dodger Stadium in 1962. Walter O'Malley's dream, after all the haggling and litigation and referendums, was finally a reality.

It was a magnificent sight of monumental proportions, in purity white and Dodger Blue, symmetrically sculpted in tiers, encircled by vast concrete aprons, and fed by myriad roads and access ways. Sportswriters quickly dubbed it "Taj O'Malley."

A half-decade earlier, Chavez Ravine was nothing more than a dusty, parched set of hills interlaced with gulches, arroyos, and poorly paved roads, and littered with a few squatters' shacks; it was a wasteland where scraggly goats once grazed, and where raccoons and opossums rooted among the garbage dumped there. The plot of ground appeared more like what the dust-bowl Okies tried to escape rather than a municipal region a mere 10-minute drive from downtown Los Angeles. But the goats were shooed away, and the other foragers fled when the bulldozers came. Captain Emil Praeger, a New York architect, had drawn up the elaborate plans, and after $18 million and a few years, Dodger Stadium was ready for the opening of the 1962 baseball season. It was the first stadium to be built with private funds since Yankee Stadium had been erected in the Bronx back in 1923 to house the huge crowds who wanted to watch Babe Ruth play.

More than 8 million cubic yards of earth had to be moved to build the stadium, and approximately twenty-one thousand precast concrete units, weighing up to 32 tons each, were trucked in to form the stadium's structural framework. The tiers were cantilevered, supported by bracketing rather than poles or beams that could impede a spectator's view of the playing field. It was designed to seat fifty-six thousand people, and the paved terraces of land around it would be able to accommodate sixteen thousand parked automobiles. And in time, the once barren landscape of Chavez Ravine became a veritable arboretum as towering palm trees and a rich mixture of other tropical shrubbery sprang up around Dodger Stadium.

The date of its formal christening was April 10, 1962. And there was appropriate hoopla. Commissioner Ford Frick was there, as was National League president Warren Giles. Cardinal James McIntyre, the chief Roman Catholic ecclesiastic in Los Angeles, gave the invocation. There

was an army of usherettes decked out in Dodger Blue skirts with the monogram *LA* sewn on them. There were also 52,564 people in the brand-new seats to watch the Dodgers take on the Cincinnati Reds, the previous year's pennant winner.

For the first time since the Dodgers came to Los Angeles, Don Drysdale was not on the mound to open the season. Instead, nine-year Dodgers veteran Johnny Podres was given the call to face the Reds' Bob Purkey. And despite the festal day it was, it was not to be the Dodgers' day on the field, and when Wally Post blasted a three-run homer to break a 3–3 tie, the celebrated baptism turned into a bust for the Dodgers.

The following night, however, Sandy Koufax appropriately anointed Dodger Stadium by hurling a four-hitter at the Reds, and the Dodgers, aided by a Junior Gilliam home run, recorded their first win in their new home, 6–2. It launched a four-game winning streak.

The Dodgers had not had a captain since Pee Wee Reese retired at the end of the 1958 season. The club got the second in its history in 1962, when manager Walt Alston named Duke Snider to that post. It was Snider's 16th year as a Dodger and he reigned as the team's all-time home-run king, and certainly one of its most popular personages. The 1962 season was also destined to be the Duke's last as a Dodger.

His longtime teammate, Gil Hodges, at 38, had gone to the New York Mets in the expansion draft after 17 long seasons as a Dodger. Also off to the Mets were second baseman Charlie Neal and pitcher Roger Craig. The Dodgers sent Norm Larker to the other expansion team, the Houston Colt .45s. And shortly after the season got underway, Wally Moon gave up his outfield job to Frank Howard, who had knocked off 14 pounds over the winter and so weighed in at 236.

The 1962 season was Sandy Koufax's eighth in a Dodgers uniform. His only really good year so far had been the preceding one, in which he had won 18 games. It appeared that he had finally overcome

Pete Richert made an impressive debut in 1962 when he re-lieved Stan Williams and struck out the first six batters he faced. In doing so, he tied three National League records: most succes-sive strikeouts by a relief pitcher, most successive strikeouts in a first-game performance, and most strikeouts in one inning (four—one batter got on, the result of a dropped third strike). Richert worked from the Dodger bullpen for two more seasons, was traded, and then returned to play out the last 2 of his 12 years in the majors in 1972 and 1973. His best year was as a starter for the Washington Senators in 1965 (15–12, 2.60 ERA).

his control problem that year. A lot of the credit, Koufax said, had to go to catcher Norm Sherry, the brother of Dodgers reliever Larry Sherry, who had worked with him in spring training. Dodgers fans did not know it yet in 1962, but Sandy Koufax was already out of the starting blocks on his sprint to the Hall of Fame.

The season was only two weeks old when Koufax began to give hard evidence of where he was headed. He took on the Chicago Cubs and scorched them with 18 strikeouts to tie the major league record he already held jointly with Bob

Feller. Then, on May 2, again against the Cubs, he struck out Ron Santo to register his 1,000th career strikeout. At the same time, Don Drysdale was on the way to having the best year of his Dodgers career, and Johnny Podres and Stan Williams were throwing with the best of them.

Two records were set in Dodger Stadium in May 1962. The Dodgers took part in the longest game that had been played in Los Angeles, a 16-inning, five-hour-and-eight-minute contest against the Cubs that lasted all the way to 1:08 in the morning. The few who stayed to watch the ending saw the Dodgers win, 6–5. And on May 19, Stan Musial lined a Ron Perranoski pitch into the out-field for his 3,431st hit, a new National League record. The previous high of 3,430 hits, by Honus Wagner, had been in the record books since 1917.

Later in the month Koufax was at it again. This time he struck out 16 Philadelphia Phillies in a game that the Dodgers won 6–3. This turned out to be just one game in a 13-game Dodgers winning streak. But the San Francisco Giants were also white-hot that year, and even after 13 straight wins, the Dodgers still trailed them by one and one-half games.

On June 30, Sandy Koufax once again dazzled everyone, especially the New York Mets; they faced him for nine innings and came away both runless and hitless. The 5–0 victory was his first no-hitter, and it would not be his last. He struck out 13 Mets that day as well, and was credited with his 11th win of the season against 4 losses.

The Dodgers were soaring. The next day Don Drysdale won his 14th game of the season, and like Koufax, he had lost only 4 games. The following day it was Johnny Podres striking out eight Phillies in the first game of a doubleheader and giving the Dodgers an easy win; in the second game, Stan Williams tossed a 4–0 shutout. On July 4, Sandy Koufax and Joe Moeller, a rookie that year, teamed to sweep another doubleheader from the Phillies. The day after, Drysdale beat the St. Louis Cardinals for his 15th triumph of the year. It was the last win in a seven-game streak.

73

When the first All-Star Game of 1962 rolled around, Drysdale was a consensus pick to start for the National League. The Dodgers also placed on the NL squad Tommy Davis, John Roseboro, and Johnny Podres, as well as Maury Wills, who had more than 40 base thefts with the season just half over. Drysdale pitched three scoreless innings, and Wills scored two of the NL's three runs to lead a victory over the AL, 3–1. In the year's second All-Star Game, Johnny Podres got the call to start and pitched two innings, but the NL lost, 9–4.

By the end of July, the Dodgers were a full four games ahead of the Giants. It seemed nothing could stop them. The pitching could only be described as sublime: Tommy Davis was batting .350, a single percentage point behind league-leader Stan Musial, and Maury Wills was making baseball buffs wonder if Ty Cobb's base-stealing record was really as untouchable as everyone had thought.

But something happened on July 17 that would eventually levy a hefty toll on the Dodgers pennant drive. Sandy Koufax was on the mound against the Cincinnati Reds, but in the second inning he had to leave the game after developing a strange numbness in his throwing hand. Later it was diagnosed as a rare and mysterious affliction called Raynaud's Phenomenon, which required more than two months to heal.

On the brighter side, Don Drysdale posted his 20th win of the year August 3. And on his next outing he chalked up his 100th career victory.

But the ominous notes were growing louder. In August, the ever-pursuing Giants swept a three-game series and pulled to within two and one-half games of the league-leading Dodgers. Then, in

Ron Fairly broke into the starting lineup with the Dodgers in 1962, although he had played off and on for them since 1958. Covering either first base or the outfield, Fairly would remain a regular until he was traded to the Montreal Expos in 1969. His two best years in L.A. were 1962 (.278, 14 home runs) and 1966 (.288, 14 home runs).

Reliever Ed Roebuck has the unique distinction of not having suffered a single loss in 80 consecutive appearances for the Dodgers during the period from 1960 to 1962; he recorded 12 wins during that stretch. Roebuck broke into the majors in Brooklyn in 1955 and remained with the Dodgers until he was dealt to the Washington Senators in 1963. His best year was 1962 (10–2, nine saves).

early September, the Giants came down to Dodger Stadium and took three of four games, advancing to within one and one-half games.

September was also the month during which the fleet Maury Wills broke the National League base-stealing record. On September 7, he swiped his 82nd base in a game against the Pirates. The record had been held by Bob Bescher of the Cincinnati Reds since 1911. A little more than two weeks later, Wills snatched two bases in a game against the St. Louis Cardinals to tie and then break Ty Cobb's longtime major league record of 96.

Sandy Koufax came back midway through September, but was routed 11–2 by the Cardinals in his first appearance. It was quite apparent that his form was off, and he never regained it that season.

The Dodgers were faltering badly in late September. With just four games left, they still held a two-game lead over the Giants, but lost ground by dropping three games in a row, one to Houston and two to the Cardinals. The Giants, on the other hand, won one and lost two, and pulled to within a game. And so the season, which the Dodgers had once dominated, would have to be decided by the last game.

The date was September 30, and the Dodgers faced the St. Louis Cardinals, a mediocre team in sixth place, 16 games out. But the Dodgers bats were not equal to the task. They could not score a run and lost 1–0. The Giants took on the Houston Astros and did what they had to do; behind a home run by old reliable Willie Mays, they won

2–1 and earned a tie for the National League lead. It was the first time that the Dodgers had not been all alone in first place since the beginning of the second week in July.

The resultant National League playoff was the second to involve the Los Angeles franchise, and the fourth in National League history for the Dodgers (the Brooklyn team had participated in the other two and lost both—to the Cardinals in 1946 and the Giants in 1951).

Going into it, the Dodgers were clearly in a slump. They had lost six of their last seven games and had been shut out in the last two. The Giants were surging, having won 16 of their last 19 in a sensational race down the 1962 season's final stretch.

The first game was scheduled for Candlestick Park. Sandy Koufax took the mound against former White Sox ace Billy Pierce, who, at 35, had posted a remarkable 16–6 record in his first year away from Chicago. Koufax, still ailing, did not last a full two innings. And the Dodgers batters again could not produce a run. Pierce's shutout and the Giants' power—two home runs by Willie Mays, another by Orlando Cepeda, and still another by Jim Davenport—annihilated the Dodgers, 8–0. It was the third consecutive shutout handed to the Dodgers.

Down in Los Angeles the next day, it looked as if the grim reaper had come for good. The Giants took what seemed to be an insurmountable lead of 5–0, routing 25-game winner Don Drysdale. But the impotent Dodgers offense came alive in the sixth inning with a burst of seven runs. The Giants tied it up, but the Dodgers were able to pull it out in the bottom of the ninth when Ron Fairly lofted a long fly ball to center that enabled speedster Maury Wills to tag up and score the winning run.

The final game was also in Los Angeles. Johnny Podres was Walt Alston's choice; the Giants sent out their ace Juan Marichal, who had accounted for 18 wins that year.

The Dodgers seemed rejuvenated. They built a 4–2 lead and took it into the top of the ninth. Reliever Ed Roebuck was on the mound by then,

GIL HODGES

Gil Hodges left the Dodgers in 1943 for the marines and the war in the Pacific, and did not come back to Ebbets Field until 1947. In the one game he had played before leaving, he was a third baseman. When he returned, he was moved to catcher.

It was 1948 when he finally moved to first base. Roy Campanella had taken over the catching job, so manager Leo Durocher decided he ought to do something with Hodges rather than have him languish on the bench. "I put a first baseman's glove on [Hodges] and told him to have some fun. Three days later I looked up and—wow!—I was looking at the best first baseman I'd seen since Dolph Camilli."

Gil Hodges stayed there through all the Brooklyn heydays and went with the franchise to Los Angeles. He remained a Dodger until the New York Mets acquired him in the expansion draft of 1962.

His strength was fabled. Roger Kahn described it in *The Boys of Summer:*

> He had the largest hands in baseball. "Gil wears a glove at first because it's fashionable," Pee Wee Reese said. "With those hands he doesn't really need one. . . . You know what happens when big Gil squeezes the bat? . . . Instant sawdust."

Only Duke Snider has hit more home runs or driven in more runs in Dodgers history. Hodges' lifetime totals of 370 home runs and 1,274 RBIs are impressive stats, but he was also agile and fast on the playing field, an excellent fielder and a canny base runner.

Twice he hit 40 or more home runs in a season (1951 and 1954), and seven years in a row he drove in more than 100 runs (1949–1955). Hodges tied the major league record by hitting four home runs in a single game one sunny August day in 1950. That same day he set two other Dodgers single-game records: most RBIs (nine) and most total bases (17). His lifetime batting average was .273, with a slugging average of .487.

Gil Hodges was manager of the New York Mets when he suffered a fatal heart attack two days before his 48th birthday in 1972.

The heart of the Dodgers bullpen in 1962, Larry Sherry (left) and Ron Perranoski, posed together here at Dodger Stadium. Perranoski was credited with 20 saves in 1962, and Sherry, the hero of the 1959 World Series, rescued 11. The two firemen appeared in a total of 128 games that year.

and the Dodgers were a mere three outs away from the National League pennant. The Giants' Matty Alou led off with a single, but then Roebuck got Harvey Kuenn, the former Detroit Tigers great, for the first out of the inning. Then Roebuck's control failed him. He walked Willie McCovey and Felipe Alou, and the bases were loaded. As if that didn't provoke enough worry, the next batter was Willie Mays, the league's leading home-run hitter (49) that year. And the "Say Hey Kid" came through with a single to center that scored one run. That was all for Roebuck. Walt Alston called for right-hander Stan Williams, who had pitched the day before in relief and had gotten the win. He was tired, however, and he had to face a very threatening Orlando Cepeda, who had batted .306 that year

Maury Wills slides into second base here for his 104th and final base theft of 1962. Earlier in the month he had broken Ty Cobb's major league record of 96 stolen bases, which had stood since 1915. Wills' record would survive until Lou Brock swiped 118 bases in 1974. During Wills' record-setting season, he also batted .299, led the league in triples with 11, and was named the National League's MVP.

and belted 35 home runs. Williams got Cepeda on a sacrifice fly ball to right, but the tying run scored from third on the play.

Walt Alston called for an intentional pass to be given to catcher Ed Bailey to load the bases again. Jim Davenport was the batter now and he simply watched as the weary Williams tried vainly to get the ball over the plate. Williams couldn't, and the walk produced what was to be the winning run, although the Giants added another before the inning was over. The Dodgers could not get anything going in their half of the ninth, and so the Giants had the National League pennant for 1962.

Sportswriters rushed to compare the ninth-inning loss to the heartbreaker of 1951 when the Giants' Bobby Thomson hit his historic game-winning home run. But it was not quite that dramatic. Perhaps it was equally disheartening, but this game was not decided on a single pitch; it had really been decided in the last two woeful weeks of the season.

After the champagne in the Dodgers locker room was returned to the store unopened and the players and management went home to watch the World Series on television, there was much second-guessing about the Dodgers' late-season swan dive. Many agreed that if Sandy Koufax had

77

remained healthy all season the Dodgers would have breezed directly into the World Series.

Indeed, when the World Series began, it seemed unbelievable that the Dodgers were not out there on the playing field. They had ended the season with a record of 102–63 (.618), a far better record than the 88–68 of 1959 when they did win the pennant. In fact, it had been their winningest season since their pennant-taking 105–49 year of 1953 back in Brooklyn.

The Dodgers' individual statistics had also been impressive in 1962. Maury Wills had shattered Ty Cobb's record by stealing an incredible 104 bases; Sandy Koufax had struck out 18 players in one game and no-hit a team in another. Tommy Davis, in only his third year, had captured the major league batting crown with an average of .346, and had led both leagues in total hits (230) and in RBIs (153). Frank Howard had turned in his best effort yet, booming 31 home runs and driving in 119 runs. Don Drysdale had had his best season ever, winning 25 and losing only 9. His 25 wins, 232 strikeouts, and 314 innings pitched were all league highs that year. Johnny Podres, always reliable, had chalked up 15 wins for the Dodgers, and Stan Williams and Sandy Koufax had contributed 14 each. Ron Perranoski had surpassed any expectations and come up with 20 saves, second in the league to only the Pirates' Roy Face. When the 1962 season became history, the National League's Most Valuable Player award went to Maury Wills, and the Cy Young Award was presented to Don Drysdale.

But the Giants, not the Dodgers, went on to face the Yankees in the Series. It was frustrating and depressing for Dodgers fans, but it would get better, much better, the next year.

CHAPTER 7

YANKEE KILLERS

Taj O'Malley—the house that Walter O'Malley built in Chavez Ravine, more commonly known around Los Angeles as Dodger Stadium.

THE KEY QUESTION WEAVING its way through the Dodgers management, the media, and the fans when the Dodgers convened at Vero Beach for spring training in 1963 was whether Sandy Koufax had fully recuperated from his bout with Raynaud's Phenomenon. There was a gnawing memory that he had not won a game after coming back in the dying days of the 1962 season, and he had hardly looked like the same left-hander who had sizzled through 14 wins in the earlier segment of the season.

Another question arose: would the Dodgers *really* trade 36-year-old Duke Snider? General manager Buzzy Bavasi said it was a distinct possibility that

TRIVIA

After the 1963 season, Sandy Koufax was voted the National League's Most Valuable Player and received the Cy Young Award as pitcher of the year. Only once before that time had a player received both awards in the same year—another Dodger, Don Newcombe, in 1956. Koufax had also become the first pitcher ever to be selected unanimously for the Cy Young Award.

either Snider or Wally Moon would be playing baseball in another town during the coming years. The reasons were their ages and the influx of new talent that had to be given regular-season experience.

When training camp opened in Florida, manager Walt Alston did not have an answer for either of those questions, although he would before the month of March was over. Alston was beginning his 10th season as Dodgers manager. The rumors that he had been on his way out to make room for Leo Durocher had long since faded into the Los Angeles smog. Alston was eminently and deservedly secure. In the first nine years of his tenure, the Dodgers had ended up in the first division eight times. His record of two world championships against only one World Series defeat was the best in the history of the National League at that time. Only the fabled John McGraw had won three World Series, but his Giants teams had also lost six others. Alston's third Series win was in 1963.

The answer to the great Koufax question came early in the Grapefruit League season. He took the mound against the Chicago White Sox in Sarasota, Florida, and struck out 13 of them, leaving little doubt that he was again healthy. And the resolution to the Snider rumor followed shortly afterward. His 17th year in the majors would be spent back East in a New York Mets uniform. It had been an outright sale, netting the Dodgers $40,000. With the Duke's departure, all those who are now known as the Boys of Summer were gone from the Dodgers roster, and the last nostalgic link to Brooklyn was finally removed.

A few other familiar faces would also be gone that year: infielder Don Zimmer and pitcher Ed Roebuck went to the Washington Senators, and third baseman Daryl Spencer to the Cincinnati Reds. The Dodgers would make the advantageous acquisition of Bill "Moose" Skowron from the Yankees, who later learned the extent of their loss when Skowron tormented them with relish in the World Series.

Even though the Dodgers had faltered so dramatically in the last few weeks of the preceding

The Dodger Stadium scoreboard is Sandy Koufax's marquee, its lights heralding his second career no-hit game, an 8–0 devastation of the San Francisco Giants in 1963. Koufax would pitch four career no-hitters, a major league record that stood until Nolan Ryan broke it in 1981. Koufax, however, is the only pitcher ever to have thrown four of them in four consecutive years.

After Game 1 of the 1963 World Series, Sandy Koufax borrows a hand from catcher John Roseboro to illustrate the number of strikeouts he threw that day. The 15 Yankees he fanned set a World Series record, one that would stand until 1968 when the Cardinals' Bob Gibson would strike out 17 in a single Series game. The Dodgers prevailed in this game, 5–2, the win going to Koufax, who went the distance.

season, they were the preseason pick of the odds-makers to cop the National League pennant. The Yankees, the bookmakers said, were expected to repeat in the American League.

In the early going, however, there had to be a lot of second thoughts about that National League prediction. By May 1, a half-month into the season, the Dodgers were mired in sixth place, four games behind the league-leading St. Louis Cardinals. A few days later they dropped one step closer to the cellar before getting their act in order.

Certainly one of the catalysts in redirecting the Dodgers was a game on May 11. They were hosting the always-threatening San Francisco Giants in a night game before more than fifty-five thousand fans, and Sandy Koufax offered a performance

almost to perfection. The only tarnishes were two walks, one to Ed Bailey in the eighth inning and another to Willie McCovey in the ninth. Other than that, no Giant reached first base, and Sandy Koufax had recorded his second no-hit game. At that moment there were only two active pitchers in the major leagues who had accomplished that feat: 42-year-old Warren Spahn of the Braves and 37-year-old Sad Sam Jones of the Cardinals. The Dodgers obliged Koufax with eight runs in his shutout victory.

Four days later, Koufax was back on the mound, this time against the Phillies, and he won again to launch the Dodgers on what would be their longest winning streak of the season—eight games. When it ended, the Dodgers had risen to

WORLD SERIES LINEUPS, 1963

DODGERS	YANKEES
Maury Wills, ss	Tony Kubek, ss
Junior Gilliam, 3b	Bobby Richardson, 2b
Willie Davis, cf	Tommy Tresh, lf
Tommy Davis, lf	Mickey Mantle, cf
Frank Howard, rf	Roger Maris, rf
Moose Skowron, 1b	Elston Howard, c
Dick Tracewski, 2b	Joe Pepitone, 1b
John Roseboro, c	Clete Boyer, 3b

STARTING PITCHERS
Game 1: Sandy Koufax, Whitey Ford
Game 2: Johnny Podres, Al Downing
Game 3: Don Drysdale, Jim Bouton
Game 4: Sandy Koufax, Whitey Ford

second place, below first by only a game. By June 7, they had made it to the top, if only by .002 percentage points. By mid-June, Koufax had already posted his 10th win of the year against three losses, Tommy Davis was leading the National League in batting with an average of .340, and Maury Wills was hitting .330 and menacing the base paths despite an injured leg.

Both the Cardinals and the Giants put heat on the Dodgers in the National League in 1963. The Cardinals had fine pitching from Bob Gibson and Ernie Broglio, and from an older but still stalwart Curt Simmons. And they had consistent hitting from Dick Groat, Bill White, Ken Boyer, and Curt Flood. And 42-year-old Stan Musial, in his last season, was there to be called on in clutch situations. The Giants were a team of sluggers with Willie Mays, Willie McCovey, Orlando Cepeda, and Felipe Alou. They also had pitcher Juan Marichal, having his best year yet for the Giants.

By the All-Star break it was head-to-head-to-head, the makings of a sensational pennant race. Incidentally, there was only one All-Star Game that year, ending the four-year practice of having two games. Only two Dodgers saw action in that game. Don Drysdale pitched the last two innings, giving up no runs and only a single hit, and Tommy Davis started in left field and got one hit in three at-bats. (The National League won 5–3, and on their behalf Stan Musial made his 24th All-Star appearance, a major league record.)

In the seesaw battle for first place in the National League, the Dodgers once again rose to the top on July 2, following a Don Drysdale shutout over the Cardinals (1–0). The next day, Koufax blanked them again, this time by a score of 5–0. After another win the following day, the Dodgers had swept the critical series.

Koufax was having a remarkable year. On July 12 he recorded his 15th win—it was his 8th in a row and his 3rd straight shutout, and it lowered his ERA to 1.63. By September 1, he had his 20th victory.

At the same time, however, the Cardinals were white-hot, winning 19 of 20 games, and were far from being out of the race. They pulled to within a single game of the Dodgers in mid-September, and their chance was at hand. They were to host the Dodgers in a three-game series at Busch Stadium in St. Louis. Johnny Podres was the first to face the Cards, and he tossed a three-hit, 3–1, Dodgers victory. Then Sandy Koufax hurled a 4–0 shutout the next day, raising his record to 24–5. Ron Perranoski, in the midst of his best yet season as a Dodger, led the assault the following day. The Cardinals' hope for a salvaged victory was doused in the ninth inning when Dodgers rookie Dick Nen, in his second at-bat in his first major league game, cracked a home run to tie the score. The Dodgers pulled it out in the thirteenth inning and had a three-game sweep. From that point on, the Dodgers merely added to their lead and ended the season a full six games in front. Their record was 99–63.

The bookies had been right about both leagues. No one came as close as 10 games to the Yankees, even though the team had been plagued with injuries (Mickey Mantle, because of a broken foot, appeared in only 52 games, and Roger Maris' aching back limited him to 86). Still, the Yankees were *the Yankees*. Besides their walking

At Yankee Stadium, Game 2 of the 1963 World Series, the Dodgers lead 3–0 in the sixth. Starter Johnny Podres is on the mound, en route to a 4–1 victory. The catcher is John Roseboro, and the Yankees batter stepping in is second baseman Bobby Richardson.

wounded—who would be back for the Series—they had 34-year-old Whitey Ford, the dean of AL pitchers, who had led the league with 24 victories against only seven losses. In addition, sophomore right-hander Jim Bouton had developed into a 20-game winner (21–7). That year both of them were caught by the American League's Most Valuable Player, Elston Howard. Other talented young players included Joe Pepitone, Tony Kubek, Bobby Richardson, Clete Boyer, and Tom Tresh.

On the other hand, the Dodgers were hardly a team to be taken lightly. They had had an impressive year, with pitching that could only be described as fantastic. Sandy Koufax ended the season with a record of 25–5. His 306 strikeouts were the highest in National League history. No pitcher started more games (42) than Don Drysdale that year, and his ERA of 2.63 was the best so far in his eight-year Dodgers career. Ron Perranoski posted 16 wins and only 3 losses, accounted for 21 saves, and produced an ERA of 1.67. Perranoski's won-lost percentage (.842) and the number of games he appeared in (69) were also major league highs for 1963. Johnny Podres contributed another 14 wins (he had won at least 14 games for the Dodgers every year since 1959), and Bob Miller, recently acquired from the Mets, won 10 more.

Tommy Davis led the league again with a .326 batting average; there had not been a consecutive winner of the NL batting crown since Stan Musial

Maury Wills doing what he does so naturally—stealing second base. This particular theft was in Game 2 of the 1963 World Series. Bobby Richardson, in a crouch, reaches out but can't make the tag. Looking on are Yankees shortstop Tony Kubek and umpire Shag Crawford.

did it in the years 1950, 1951, and 1952. Maury Wills, hindered most of the season by his injured foot, still managed 40 stolen bases, the most in the majors (tied with Luis Aparicio who was now playing for the Baltimore Orioles). And Frank Howard led the team in home runs with 28, fifth best in the National League.

Lee Allen, in his book *The Giants and the Dodgers: The Fabulous Story of Baseball's Fiercest Feud,* describes the Dodgers' predicament as "the formidable task of winning the World Series from the Yankees, an event that had taken place in the past about as often as snowfall in the Sahara." And if anyone should have been aware of that, it was the Dodgers. Seven times previously they had met the Yankees in the World Series, and six of those times they had come out a loser. But 1963 was destined to be a different kind of year: an Arctic blizzard, so to speak, would rage across the Sahara.

The first game brought the two teams together in Yankee Stadium. The premier pitchers from each league—Sandy Koufax and Whitey Ford—were on the mound. The Dodgers got off to a good start in the second inning when they exploded with four runs, three of them a result of a booming home run by catcher John Roseboro, the other batted in by Moose Skowron. Skowron drove in another run the next inning, and that was all it took. Koufax set the Yankees down inning after inning, with the exception of Tom Tresh's two-run homer in the bottom of the eighth. En route to the 5–2 win, Koufax struck out 15 Yankees, breaking Dodger Carl Erskine's World Series record of 14 set in 1953. The Yankees got only six hits that day.

The following day at the same location, Johnny Podres, a veteran of 10 Dodgers seasons, took control of the pitcher's mound. He was equally stunning. The once-powerful Yankees came up and went down at the plate like little soldiers in a shooting gallery. They did not post a run until the last half of the ninth inning, and by then it was simply too late. Podres hung in all the way to the ninth when Ron Perranoski came in with a man on base. After allowing the Yankees their solo run, Perranoski quelled the threat and preserved the win for Podres, 4–1. Moose Skowron belted a home run for the Dodgers in that game, Willie Davis drove in two runs, and Tommy Davis contributed a pair of triples.

There was a day of rest as the two teams flew cross-country to Los Angeles and the fashionable new Dodger Stadium. Fans had camped out for two days before the box offices were officially opened so that they could secure tickets for the home games of the World Series. It would be no problem filling the fifty-six-thousand-seat Taj O'Malley.

Jim "Bulldog" Bouton was the young man Yankees manager Ralph Houk called on to alter the course of the Series. Bouton, only 24 and in his second year as a major leaguer, admitted later, "I was incredibly nervous." It was noticeable to the practiced eye; Whitey Ford even commented on it

THE DUKE

On a summer day in 1980, Duke Snider achieved the dream of every major league baseball player. He was formally inducted into the National Baseball Hall of Fame in Cooperstown, New York. Grantland Rice, the grand old man of sportswriting, had predicted it as far back as 1954: "[I] saw two perhaps three present day stars who may take their place with the immortals. Duke Snider, Willie Mays, and Mickey Mantle." He remembered Snider "climbing the center-field walls to haul in what were certain home runs . . . and breaking those same fences with his bat." A quarter of a century later, Snider and his 18-year major league career were properly venerated.

Edwin Donald Snider broke into the majors with the Dodgers in 1947. Nobody ever got to know him by that name though, and only a few referred to him by another nickname, the Silver Fox. It was almost always "the Duke," to the denizens of Flatbush and the suntanned fans of Southern California.

It took two years for the Duke to nail down a full-time job in the Dodgers outfield, but he remained there from 1949 on, and he became one of the fans' all-time favorites.

Over his 16 years with the Dodgers, Snider came to dominate the club's record book. He hit the most home runs (389); drove in the most runs (1,271); collected the most extra-base hits (814); was third in runs scored behind Pee Wee Reese and Zack Wheat; and was fourth in total hits, trailing those same two and Willie Davis.

As a Dodger, he hit 40 or more home runs in five consecutive seasons (1953–1957), led the league with 43 in 1956, and took the RBI crown three years in a row (1953–1955). The Duke batted over .300 seven times, his best year a .341 in 1954. And his lifetime batting average was .295, with a slugging average of .540.

In World Series play, Duke Snider was incomparable. In six Series he hit a total of 11 home runs, a mark then surpassed only by Mickey Mantle (18), Babe Ruth (15), and Yogi Berra (12) in the major league record books. And he was the only player to have hit four home runs in each of two different Series (1952 and 1955). And he batted over .300 four times in the postseason classic.

Junior Gilliam scores the only run necessary to give the Dodgers a 1–0 win over the Yankees in Game 3 of the 1963 Series. It was the first inning, and Gilliam was driven in by a Tommy Davis single. Welcoming him is Dodgers first baseman Ron Fairly.

after one of the early innings: "Kid, you're throwing what we call nervous-fast." Nervous or not, however, Bouton pitched extraordinarily well. He allowed the Dodgers only four hits in the seven innings he pitched. But it was not enough, because the Yankees sluggers might just as well have been wielding toothpicks at home plate. They could not produce a run off Don Drysdale and managed only a scattered three hits all day. All it took for the Dodgers was the single run they had scored in the first inning. Junior Gilliam had walked, run to second on a wild pitch, and scored on a single that bounced off the leg of Yankees second baseman Bobby Richardson. The laurels of the day were bestowed on Drysdale, who, during his three-hit shutout, had given up only one base on balls and had struck out nine Yankees.

Above: Don Drysdale hurls the first World Series pitch ever thrown in Dodger Stadium to open Game 3 of the 1963 World Series. The Yankees batter is shortstop Tony Kubek, the umpire Al Napp. Below: Nine innings later, Drysdale is mobbed by fellow Dodgers after claiming the last Yankees victim in his three-hit, 1–0 shutout that day. The congratulators are: (from left to right) coach Joe Becker, Marv Breeding, Don Drysdale, coach Leo Durocher, and manager Walt Alston. The win put the Dodgers ahead three games to none in the Series.

Bill "Moose" Skowron catches an infield pop-up here against his former teammates, the Yankees, in Game 3 of the 1963 World Series. Skowron came to the Dodgers that year after having played first base for the Yankees since 1954. He made New Yorkers aware of their loss by batting .385 in the Series and driving in three key runs.

The Yankees were in deep trouble when they arrived at Dodger Stadium the next day. Not only were they 0–3 in the Series and playing in an unfriendly ballpark before a rabid rabble of fifty-six thousand Dodgers fans, but they had to face the golden arm of Sandy Koufax once again. The Yankees went with their ace Whitey Ford, and it was a pitchers' duel all the way. The Dodgers got a run in the fifth inning when Frank Howard drove one of Ford's pitches into the second tier in left field, the first time anyone had hit a ball that far in Dodger Stadium. Koufax maintained a shutout until the seventh inning when a still-hobbled Mickey Mantle smashed one into the stands to tie the game. But the Yankees' downfall was only a few minutes away. In the bottom half of that inning, on a ground ball to third, Clete Boyer threw a strike to Joe Pepitone at first for what should have been a routine out. But Pepitone, as he later explained, lost sight of the ball in the glare of white shirts behind third base. It bounced off his wrist into foul territory, bounced off the wall, and rolled into right field. Junior Gilliam raced all the way to third on the error. It took only a sacrifice fly by Willie Davis to give the Dodgers the deciding run. Ford and reliever Hal Reniff, who came in during the eighth inning, held the Dodgers to a paltry two hits in a final 2–1 loss, and the Dodgers took the Series in four straight games. It was the first clean sweep since the Giants had drubbed the Cleveland Indians in 1954.

It had been a magnificent Series for the Dodgers. They had allowed the Yankees an average of a single run per game and a total of only 22 hits. Sandy Koufax, besides having set the World Series record for strikeouts in one game, had also set the mark for total strikeouts in one Series (23). Johnny Podres' win in the Series had been his fourth, the most in Dodgers history at that time. Tommy Davis had batted .400 in the Series, and Moose Skowron had hit .385 and driven in three crucial runs. Each player on the Dodgers team took home $12,794 in World Series money, the most earned in the baseball classic up to that time.

Two years in Dodger Stadium had produced two fine seasons, a tie for the pennant in one and a world championship in the other. Since arriving in Los Angeles, the team had won two world championships

Jubilant Dodgers engulf Sandy Koufax after he snuffed the Yankees in Game 4 of the 1963 Series to give Los Angeles a four-game sweep and their second world championship since moving to L.A. five years earlier. Three Dodgers starters—Koufax, Drysdale, and Podres—and reliever Ron Perranoski, who pitched only one inning, allowed the once-undefeatable Yankees only four runs in the Series.

in six seasons and had ended up in the first division every year except 1958.

Certainly the Dodgers had everything going for them as they left for a winter's rest. Vengeance of the most glorious kind had been wreaked upon the longtime adversary Yankees. A wealth of pitchers was just peaking—Koufax (27 years old), Drysdale (26),

and Perranoski (27). There were young, sensational hitters like Tommy Davis (24), Frank Howard (26), Willie Davis (23), and Ron Fairly (24). They enjoyed a thoroughly committed following of fans, a magnificent modern stadium, and a respected, recordsetting manager in Walt Alston. But somehow, some way, they would lose track of all that the next year.

CHAPTER 8

FROM THE PIT TO THE PENNANT

Two legendary Dodgers, Sandy Koufax and Leo Durocher, in 1964 at Vero Beach. Presumably that's a stopwatch in Durocher's hand, but knowing "the Lip," it could be anything from brass knuckles to the morning line at Hialeah racetrack. It was Leo's last year as a Dodgers coach; two seasons later he would take over the helm of the Chicago Cubs.

THE DODGERS TEAM that took the field in 1964 was ostensibly the same as the one that won the 1963 world championship. There were, however, a few new faces in the dugout. Southpaw Jim Brewer had come from the Chicago Cubs, and the Dodgers were hoping they could turn him into a reliever to replace Larry Sherry, whom they had dealt away to the Detroit Tigers. Another new face was rookie Wes Parker, who was versatile enough to play either in the outfield or at first base.

Sandy Koufax had signed a new contract guaranteeing him an annual salary of $70,000, but there

Claude Osteen came to the Dodgers in 1965 and swiftly joined the regular rotation. He had hurled for the Washington Senators during the previous four years and was just reaching his prime when he arrived as part of a deal that sent Frank Howard, Pete Richert, and Ken McMullen to the Senators. Osteen chalked up 15 wins and then tossed a five-hit shutout in the World Series his first year in Dodger Blue.

were rumors that he was discontented and had felt pressured into signing it. Frank Howard, too, was not all that happy with his role with the Dodgers, and in the days just before spring training, announced he was going to retire. The 27-year-old Howard had second thoughts, however, and by the end of March he arrived at Vero Beach and told the media that the announcement of his retirement had been "premature." He also was 15 pounds overweight, at 255.

The first hint of the troubles that would beset the Dodgers in 1964 appeared during the spring training season. The incumbent world champs were able to muster only nine wins in their 25 games, a dismal percentage of .391.

Sandy Koufax opened the season for the Dodgers in L.A. on a different note, shutting out the St. Louis Cardinals 4–0 on a six-hitter. Aiding Koufax's cause were Maury Wills, who got three hits in four at-bats, and Frank Howard, who cannoned one of his two hits into the seats. An excited, hopeful crowd of 50,451 was there, and they went home believing it was the start of another memorable year. At 1–0, however, it was the only time during the entire season that the Dodgers would be in first place.

They followed the home opener with a seven-game losing streak that left them alone in the National League cellar. At the end of April they put together a four-game winning streak, which proved to be the longest of the season. The tongue-in-cheek headline on the sports page of the *Los Angeles Times* said it all: CHARGE! DODGERS ROAR INTO 7th.

The Dodgers added two new coaches in 1965: Danny Ozark (left) and Preston Gomez. Ozark would remain through the 1972 season; in 1973 he would take over the helm of the Philadelphia Phillies and guide them for seven years. During those years he would pick up three Eastern Division championships and a second place. Ozark returned to the Dodgers coaching ranks in 1980. Gomez remained through 1967, then rejoined the club from 1977 to 1979. In between, he would serve as the manager of the San Diego Padres (1969–1972) and the Houston Astros (1974–1975). In 1980 he moved on to manage the Chicago Cubs.

As if that weren't bad enough, Koufax's elbow became painfully arthritic and caused him to miss several turns throughout the season. To make pitching matters even worse, a fastball from Warren Spahn caught Johnny Podres on the elbow of his pitching arm and chipped off a piece of the bone. He would be out for the season and had to undergo surgery later in the summer. Fastballer Phil Ortega, who had been up and down between the majors and the minors since 1960, moved into the regular rotation to replace Podres.

There was only one stellar moment during the 1964 season; predictably, it was produced by Sandy Koufax. His arm was healthy in early June when he faced the Phillies in Philadelphia and hurled his third no-hit game. Only one other pitcher in major league history, Bob Feller, had ever thrown three no-hitters, but Koufax's were the first to have been recorded in three consecutive seasons. Only a seventh-inning walk to Richie Allen stood in the way of a perfect game for

Koufax, and he struck out 12 batters in the 3–0 victory.

At the All-Star break the Dodgers were down in fifth place, 10 games out of first. Walt Alston, whose mind was occupied with his foundering ballclub, had to manage the National League in the midseason classic that year. He picked Don Drysdale to start, and Drysdale was the only Dodger to make an appearance in the All-Star Game that year.

The All-Star break didn't help the Dodgers. During the second half of the season they floundered between sixth and eighth place. Don Drysdale was hampered for a while with a hairline fracture in the thumb of his throwing hand, and Sandy Koufax was continually troubled with his strained elbow. When the season was finally over, the Dodgers wound up in a tie for sixth place with the Pittsburgh Pirates, 13 games behind the pennant-winning St. Louis Cardinals. Their disappointing record of 80–82 was their first

DID HE WIN?

On the Dodgers' dearth of hits and runs in the early sixties, John Roseboro wrote in his autobiography *Glory Days with the Dodgers:* "One time when Drysdale wasn't with the team and was told that Koufax had pitched a no-hitter, he asked, 'Did he win?'"

below .500 since 1958, and it was the first time since that same year they did not finish in the first division. The Dodgers front office was not happy. General manager Buzzy Bavasi laid it on the line when the season was over and told the press: "There are only four untouchables on this team— Koufax, Drysdale, Roseboro, and Willie Davis. The others all can be had. . . . We are going to make some changes."

When the season stats were totaled up, there was little to crow about for the Dodgers. Koufax was the only luminary. He had won 19 games and surely would have won more had he not been sidelined with arm trouble in the latter part of the season. Still, his won-lost percentage of .792 was the best in the majors (tied with Wally Bunker of the Orioles), and his ERA of 1.74 once again was the best in the National League. Don Drysdale picked up 18 wins that year; the 40 games he started and the 321 innings he pitched were league highs. Maury Wills stole more bases (53) than anyone in the NL, but was four short of Luis Aparicio's total over in Baltimore. The Dodgers did not have a .300 hitter in 1964, nor did anyone come close to batting in 100 runs. Frank Howard again hit the most home runs (24). Attendance at Dodger Stadium was down by

Sandy Koufax opens the 1964 season at Dodger Stadium, hurling here in the first inning to St. Louis Cardinals first baseman Bill White. Koufax shut the Cards out that evening, 4–0, before a crowd of 50,451.

JUNIOR GILLIAM

Jim "Junior" Gilliam, at age 36 in 1965, was hired directly from the Dodgers playing field to replace Leo Durocher in the coaching ranks. He had been a Dodgers starter ever since 1953, playing variously at second and third bases. He remained a Dodgers coach until his untimely death in 1978.

Gilliam was named the National League's Rookie of the Year after his first Brooklyn season in 1953; he had batted .278, led the league in triples (17), collected 168 hits (only Duke Snider, who hit .336, had produced more for the Dodgers that year), and stolen 21 bases (just 1 fewer than team leader Pee Wee Reese). And he had played an almost flawless second base in the field.

In the all-time Dodgers story, only four players have taken the field more often than Gilliam in his 1,956 games (Zack Wheat, Bill Russell, Pee Wee Reese, and Gil Hodges), and only three have scored more runs than his 1,163 (Wheat, Reese, and Duke Snider). Gilliam is fifth on the Dodgers list in times at bat (7,119) and seventh in hits (1,889). He also hit 304 doubles, stole 203 bases, and contributed 2,530 total bases and 440 extra-base hits. No Dodger had ever been tougher to strike out than Gilliam, and few were more adroit at drawing walks.

Junior Gilliam was the only Dodgers player to have performed in the first four World Series that the Dodgers won (1955, 1959, 1963, and 1965).

Although Gilliam took up coaching in 1964, his services on the field were required for another two years. He ended his playing career after the 1966 season with a lifetime batting average of .265.

Wes Parker, at 24, made his major league debut with the Dodgers in 1964. That first year he switched off with Ron Fairly at first base, but would take over the position full-time the following year. During his nine-year Dodgers career, Parker would prove to be one of the game's all-time great-fielding first sackers.

more than three hundred thousand from the previous year, although most other ballclubs would have reveled in the more than 2.5 million who did come out to Dodger Stadium.

The changes Buzzy Bavasi had promised came in 1965. Walt Alston was back for his 12th straight season, but his coaching staff was totally revamped. Gone were Leo Durocher, Pete Reiser, Joe Becker, and Greg Mulleavy. In their places were Junior Gilliam, who at 36 had retired from playing (but would be back on the field before the season was a month old), Danny Ozark, Preston Gomez, and Lefty Phillips.

The biggest trade in many years sent Frank Howard, utility infielder Ken McMullen, and pitchers Phil Ortega and Pete Richert to Washington for the Senators' premier pitcher Claude Osteen and utility infielder John Kennedy. First baseman Ron Fairly was moved to the outfield to make a place for Wes Parker, who was quite impressive in spring training. And rookie Jim Lefebvre did not take long to win sole possession of the job at second base.

Sandy Koufax arrived at Vero Beach with an elbow that was both swollen and stiff. He was promptly put on a plane for Los Angeles to get some serious medical treatment. Willie Davis, on the other hand, arrived with a broken nose, but it did not slow him down much.

Helmets fly as Dodgers third baseman Junior Gilliam (No. 19) and Milwaukee base runner Felipe Alou meet in this 1965 game. Alou was not only out, but he was also pinned in the encounter. Still, the Braves went on to win the game 5–2.

The changes were readily apparent. So too was the pressure from management. Job security was not a rampant feeling among the Dodgers. The front-office personnel knew they had talent out on the field. They wanted it to meld together, and they were making it abundantly clear that they were not about to settle for the kind of lackluster year the Dodgers had experienced in 1964.

And the team reacted. Compared to a 9–16 spring training the year before, the Dodgers of 1965 posted a 17–11 record; their winning percentage of .607 was the best they had had in spring workouts since coming to Los Angeles.

The Dodgers led off the season with Don Drysdale in New York City and he took apart the hapless Mets (en route to their fourth straight season of losing more than 100 games), allowing them a mere four hits in a 6–1 wipeout. Sandy Koufax did not make his first appearance until six days later, but when he did, he allayed the worries of many concerning the health of his arm. He tossed a five-hitter at the Phillies, striking out seven.

The opener at Dodger Stadium was less joyful. Newcomer Claude Osteen went up against the National League's winningest pitcher, 44-year-old Warren Spahn, who had moved that year from the Braves to the New York Mets. He set the Dodgers down 3–2 that day.

The Dodgers' hitting attack had been notoriously weak for several years now, and it was dealt a severe blow on the first of May. Tommy Davis, the strongest and most consistent hitter on the team, broke an ankle while sliding into second base and would be out for at least three months. Lou Johnson, who had seen some major league action and had kicked around in the minors ever since 1953 (he had spent the last two years in the Dodgers farm system), was brought up to fill the hole left by Davis.

The Dodgers took over first place from the high-flying Cincinnati Reds on May 4. The Reds proved to be the hottest competition for the Dodgers during the first half of the season, but they were not able to wrest first place from Los Angeles until after July

One of the most favorably lopsided deals in Dodgers history was the 1964 acquisition of pitcher Jim Brewer, who was obtained from the Chicago Cubs for a pitcher named Dick Scott. Brewer would not do much that first year, but over his 12-year Dodgers career would prove to be one of the finest relief pitchers in team history.

Lou Johnson finally found a steady job in the majors in 1965; he had bounced around the minors and made three brief appearances with other major league clubs since 1953. The 30-year-old outfielder proved to be an outstanding clutch hitter in 1965, driving in a number of game-winning runs. As the Dodgers were trying to clinch the pennant at the end of the season, he reeled off 10 hits in 18 at-bats, an average of .555. Johnson would have his best year in 1966, batting .272 and clouting 17 homers, then would be traded to the Chicago Cubs in 1968.

4, and then only for a week. The Reds had some super hitters in Pete Rose, Frank Robinson, Deron Johnson, and Vada Pinson; there were also two pitchers who would be 20-game winners that year, Sammy Ellis and Jim Maloney. But it was the archrival Giants, with Mays, Marichal, McCovey, and the two Alous, Matty and Jesus, who would take the pennant race down to the very finish.

The Dodgers remained in first place from mid-July through mid-August. There was, however, one

day during that time destined to live forever in the hearts and minds of Dodgers as a day of ignominy. They were embarrassed on August 8 at Cincinnati when the Reds beat them 18–0, the worst drubbing in all of Dodgers history. Two days later, however, most fans forgot about it when Sandy Koufax recorded his 20th victory of the season.

By Labor Day, the pennant race was truly hot. The Dodgers, the Reds, the Giants, and the Braves were all close enough to make a run at the pennant.

Al "Bull" Ferrara is welcomed home here after a pinch-hit four-bagger that drove in the winning runs in a game against the Chicago Cubs in 1965. Those greeting him include Willie Crawford (No. 43), Dick Tracewski (No. 44), and reaching in is Maury Wills. A power-hitter, Ferrara served as a key Dodgers pinch-hitter from 1963 through 1968. His best year was 1967, one in which he played regularly in the outfield. He blasted 16 home runs, the club high, and drove in 50 runs that year.

And as the competition soared, so did the tempers. A frustrated Hank Aaron of the Braves publicly called Don Drysdale "the best spitball pitcher in the league." The name didn't hurt Drysdale, but the bat Juan Marichal rapped off catcher John Roseboro's head in a game with the Giants left a gash and a nasty lump. For striking a player with his bat Marichal was fined $1,750 by NL president Warren Giles and suspended for eight days. Marichal, the Giants' key pitcher, would miss two turns in the pitching rotation at that crucial point in the season. (Roseboro also personally sued and eventually collected a $7,500 settlement from Marichal.)

The Giants surged in early September and staged a 14-game winning streak to take over first place. And by the middle of that month, the Dodgers had sunk four and one-half games behind. During that rather bleak period, however, Sandy Koufax once again lit up the Dodgers night. Before a hometown crowd he hurled his fourth no-hitter the evening of September 9 against the Chicago Cubs, becoming the first major league pitcher ever to do that. (Nolan Ryan tied Koufax's record in 1975 and broke it when he pitched his fifth no-hitter in 1981—against the Dodgers, coincidentally.) Not only was it a no-hit game, but it was a perfect one as well—not a single Chicago Cub reached first base. Koufax also struck out 14 of the 27 Cubs he faced. The Dodgers offense was less than spectacular that night and came up with only one hit themselves, but the lone, unearned run they got was just enough to give Koufax his victory.

On September 17 Don Drysdale racked up his 20th win of the year. It was the second game of what was to become the Dodgers' longest winning streak of the year—13 straight—and it would carry the Dodgers back into first place. Only three games remained after that triumphant sweep. The Dodgers dropped the first to the Braves, but then

Frank Howard (6'7", 255 pounds) was a giant on the baseball field. He would play both the outfield and first base during his 16-year major league career, but be remembered best for his awesome power at the plate. Howard came up with the Dodgers in 1958 and departed after the 1964 season for the Washington Senators. His best year in L.A. was 1962, when he blasted 31 homers and produced a slugging average of .560 (both club highs), drove in 119 runs, and batted .296. Three times he would hit more than 40 home runs for the Senators, his highest, 48 in 1969. Howard ended his career with a total of 382 home runs.

Dick Tracewski was an important utility infielder for the Dodgers from 1963 through 1965, relieving Maury Wills at shortstop, Junior Gilliam at second, and several others at third. He was better known for his fielding than hitting (lifetime average .213).

won the last two to take the National League pennant for 1965. Their final record was 97–65; the Giants ended the season two games behind them.

Over in the American League the dominance of the New York Yankees received a stunning jolt in 1965. After having won the American League pennant in nine of the preceding ten seasons, they plummeted to sixth place in 1965. They had not been in contention all year. It was the lowest a Yankees team had finished since 1925.

It had been an express ride to the top for the Minnesota Twins through the 1965 season, winning 102 games and losing just 60. The Twins had finished in sixth place the year before and had not been expected to dislodge the Yankees in 1965. But their fine team was paced by the pitching of Mudcat Grant (21–7), Jim Kaat (18–11), and reliever Al Worthington, who saved 21 games. Hitting, however, was the Twins' real forte. Outfielder Tony Oliva led the AL with a .321 average that year, catcher Earl Battey was a consistent hitter, and shortstop Zoilo Versalles, the AL's MVP for 1965, led the league in triples (12), doubles (45), and runs scored (126). There was also an awesome assortment

Sandy Koufax has just pitched his fourth no-hitter. This one, a 1–0 win over the Cubs at Dodger Stadium in 1965, was special because it was a perfect game—not a single Cub reached first base. Koufax also struck out 14 batters that evening.

Sandy Koufax leaves the field happily after his 25th win and eighth shutout (4–0) of the 1965 season. Koufax would win one more game that year and end up with a record of 26–8 (only two other left-handers in NL history at that time had won 26 games in a season: Rube Marquard in 1912 and Carl Hubbell in 1936). His number of wins, won-lost percentage (.765), ERA (2.04), strikeouts (382), completed games (27), and innings pitched (335.2) were all major league highs. Koufax's 382 strikeouts set a major league record. Shaking hands with him is coach Lefty Phillips; No. 11 is third baseman John Kennedy.

of power in Harmon Killebrew, Bob Allison, Jimmie Hall, and Don Mincher, who had collectively hit 90 home runs that year.

The Dodgers, on the other hand, were strongest in pitching. Sandy Koufax (26–8) led both leagues in total wins, won-lost percentage (.765), strikeouts (382), and innings pitched (336). He set four major league records that year: most no-hit games (four), most consecutive years pitching no-hit games (four), most strikeouts in a season (382), most games with 10 or more strikeouts, lifetime (82). He tied two others by pitching a perfect game and leading the league in ERA for the fourth consecutive year. Don Drysdale also came up with one of the finest years of his pitching career, winning 23, losing only 12,

fanning 210 batters, and even hitting seven home runs. Claude Osteen accounted for another 15 wins, and Ron Perranoski had 17 saves.

Maury Wills stole 94 bases that year, by far the most in both leagues. He was also the leading Dodgers hitter, but his average was only .286. Newcomers Lou Johnson and Jim Lefebvre led the team in homers with 12 each.

The obvious question among sportswriters and fans alike was which would prevail in the 1965 World Series: Dodgers pitching or Twins hitting? The bookmakers favored the Dodgers, but not by much. Buzzy Bavasi was less restrained in his pre-Series assessment. He told the press that Dodger Blue would take it in four straight.

Junior Gilliam slides across home plate to break a scoreless tie in a late September game in 1965 as the Dodgers surged toward the NL pennant. The Cincinnati Reds catcher bobbling the ball is Don Pavletich, and looking on is Dodgers second baseman Jim Lefebvre. The Dodgers won the game 4–0, a Sandy Koufax shutout that put the Dodgers two games ahead of the Giants in that year's pennant race (the same margin by which they would win it four days later).

That tune changed quickly, however, after the first two games. In the first meeting at Metropolitan Stadium in Bloomington, Minnesota, Don Drysdale did not last three full innings. With the score 1–1, the Twins erupted with six runs in the third, and then won decisively, 8–2.

The next day the Dodgers sent Sandy Koufax to face the Twins. He engaged in a scoreless duel with the Twins' Jim Kaat for five innings. But then the Twins got two runs in the sixth and another in the seventh, and Ron Perranoski replaced Koufax. The Twins added another pair in the eighth, enough to give them a 5–1 win and a home sweep of the first two games.

Two days later the teams resumed at Dodger Stadium. Claude Osteen got the call for the Dodgers and he was superb. Allowing the Twins only five hits, he shut them out to put the Dodgers back in Series contention. The Dodgers bats, which had produced only three runs in Minnesota, came to life and drove in four, the key hit being John Roseboro's single that brought in two runs.

The following day Drysdale was just as effective as Osteen. He gave up only five hits. And the Twins' two runs proved meaningless against the Dodgers' seven. The often-homerless Dodgers box score showed two four-baggers that day, one each by Lou Johnson and Wes Parker.

Maury Wills steals second easily in this 1965 World Series game against the Minnesota Twins. The Twins looking on helplessly are second baseman Frank Quilici (left) and shortstop Zoilo Versalles. During the regular season, Wills stole 94 bases, far and away the best in either league, and the second most prolific effort in his career.

The fifth game brought Sandy Koufax back to the mound. The Twins were helpless before the blazing fastballs and magical curves he served them that day. Koufax whitewashed the Twins on four hits, and the Dodgers took the Series lead. In the three games in Los Angeles, the Dodgers' masterful pitching had allowed only two runs on 14 hits. If the Twins, after routing Drysdale and Koufax in the first two games, started to doubt the reputation of Dodgers pitching, they would surely not carry such rash thoughts on the plane with them back to Minnesota.

Mudcat Grant, the Twins' pitcher selected for Game 6, truly must have wanted that win. He pitched almost flawless baseball, allowed only one run on six hits, and clouted a three-run homer to aid his cause. The final was 5–1, and the Twins had sent the Series to a dramatic seventh-game showdown. And they would have the home-field advantage, which clearly had been a factor in the first six games.

Sandy Koufax had only two full days of rest when he went into the Series decider, and his elbow was sore and overworked. In the bullpen were Drysdale and fireman Ron Perranoski. Walt Alston was worried about how effective Koufax would be, or at least how long he could remain effective with the tender arm and the short rest. And although he was prepared to yank him at the

Hero of Game 4 of the 1965 World Series, Don Drysdale, who went the distance in the 7–2 triumph, headlocks Lou Johnson (left), who contributed two hits, including a home run, and Wes Parker, who also homered and scored two runs. The victory evened the Series at two games apiece.

WORLD SERIES LINEUPS, 1965

DODGERS	TWINS
Maury Wills, ss	Zoilo Versalles, ss
Junior Gilliam, 3b	Sandy Valdespino, lf
Willie Davis, cf	Tony Oliva, rf
Ron Fairly, rf	Harmon Killebrew, 3b
Lou Johnson, lf	Jimmie Hall, cf
Jim Lefebvre, 2b	Don Mincher, 1b
Wes Parker, 1b	Earl Battey, c
John Roseboro, c	Frank Quilici, 2b

STARTING PITCHERS
Game 1: Don Drysdale, Mudcat Grant
Game 2: Sandy Koufax, Jim Kaat
Game 3: Claude Osteen, Camilo Pascual
Game 4: Don Drysdale, Mudcat Grant
Game 5: Sandy Koufax, Jim Kaat
Game 6: Claude Osteen, Mudcat Grant
Game 7: Sandy Koufax, Jim Kaat

first sign of faltering, Alston, nevertheless, felt that he needed to go with his best shot.

Koufax was magnificent. He pitched a shutout, his second in three days, and gave up only three hits. In fact, in his last 18 innings against the Twins, he had allowed just seven hits. Lou Johnson homered in the fourth for Los Angeles, and later in the same inning Wes Parker singled to drive in Ron Fairly from second. That was the extent of the scoring in the 2–0 game. The World Series title went to the Dodgers for the third time in their eight-year stay in L.A. It was Walt Alston's fourth World Series crown, a National League record for managers. Koufax's win that day was his fourth in World Series play, tying the Dodgers record held by Johnny Podres. An ocean of champagne was sloshed around the Dodgers locker room at the end of that day in Bloomington, Minnesota.

The World Series stats told the story. Sandy Koufax had an ERA of 0.38 for the 24 innings he pitched, and he struck out 29 batters while walking only five. Claude Osteen was almost as effective, with an ERA of 0.64 for his 14 innings. The Dodgers shut the Twins out three times and allowed an average of just over four hits per game in their four victories.

The weak-stick Dodgers of that long summer had exploded in the postseason with a torrent of hitting. Jim Lefebvre batted .400, Ron Fairly .379 with two home runs and six RBIs, Maury Wills .367, Wes Parker .304, and Lou Johnson .296 with

Dodgers outfielder Lou Johnson is greeted joyously after hitting a home run in the fourth inning of Game 7 of the 1965 World Series. It put the Dodgers ahead 1–0; they went on to score another, but it was unnecessary that day because Sandy Koufax hurled a shutout at the Twins. Awaiting him: (from the top left corner down) Walt Alston, John Roseboro, and Sandy Koufax and (on the ledge, from the top down) Maury Wills, Dick Tracewski, and the L.A. batboy.

two crucial home runs and four RBIs. Maury Wills got four of his hits in one game, tying a World Series record. And Willie Davis shared another Series record when he stole three bases in the same game.

It had been just the turnaround Buzzy Bavasi had hoped for; the changes had indeed had their desired effect. Attendance was back up over 2.5 million at Dodger Stadium; in fact, the 2,553,577 fans who turned out that year were the second highest at that point in Dodgers history.

There was little surprise when the Cy Young Award was announced. In accepting it, Sandy Koufax became the first pitcher in history to win it twice, and, as before, he was a unanimous selection. Another major award, the National League Rookie of the Year, went to second baseman Jim Lefebvre.

The 1965 season had been a heart-stopper, with come-from-behind efforts to win both the pennant and the World Series. Frank-Merriwell finishes were not about to come to an end in Los Angeles; 1966 would be almost as breathless a baseball year as 1965.

CHAPTER 9

AND ANOTHER PENNANT

One-time Dodgers player and manager, and a baseball legend, Casey Stengel throws out the ceremonial first ball before a game in the 1966 World Series. "The Old Professor" would not bring the Dodgers much luck in what became one of their worst postseason showings ever.

THE TREMORS THAT RUMBLED through Los Angeles in early 1966 were not caused by a shifting of the San Andreas Fault, or by any other seismic activity, for that matter. Rather, they resulted from the announcement that the Dodgers' sterling pitching duet, Sandy Koufax and Don Drysdale, had not signed contracts for the 1966 baseball season. They were adamant, they said, wanting not just more money, but also three-year contracts—unheard of in those days. At the same time, the Dodgers' only other certified superstar, Maury Wills, whom one sportswriter referred to as "baseball's best banjoist and base stealer," said that he, too, was holding out for additional money.

When the Dodgers opened camp at Vero Beach, Koufax, Drysdale, and Wills were not there. Also disturbing was the fact that outfielder Tommy Davis, who was there, was still noticeably hobbled by the broken ankle he had suffered the year before.

The question of money with Koufax and Drysdale, according to management, was not the overriding issue. Yet it was reported that the two stars were seeking contracts that would guarantee them $500,000 each, paid out over a three-year period. Frank Finch of the *Los Angeles Times* wrote: "Revived after fainting, Buzzy Bavasi offered them $120,000 apiece for the 1966 season,"

The salaries they actually asked for, and Bavasi's real reaction, are sheer conjecture. The fact was, however, that the two were not at Vero Beach, and at a team meeting Bavasi told the other players: "You players are entitled to all you can get. That's the history of baseball. But I'm going to stick to our club's policy of one-year contracts."

As the end of March approached, the two pitchers and the Dodgers were still at an impasse. Bavasi had said, "We have offered them the biggest contracts any two players on the team ever received." And he made it clear that it was his final offer, and under no circumstances was he going to set the precedent of offering them more than a year's contract. He added disenchantingly, "I don't think Koufax and Drysdale will play for the Dodgers in '66." Drysdale answered for both, "I think he is right because we are not accepting the Dodgers' current offer."

Maury Wills had turned down the Dodgers' latest offer of a one-year contract for $75,000. A few days later, however, he had a change of heart and arrived in Vero Beach with pen in hand.

Meanwhile, Koufax and Drysdale, still in Los Angeles, signed a contract of a different kind. It was with Paramount Studios to play featured roles in what turned out to be a less-than-memorable

Don Sutton was 21 years old when he came up with the Dodgers in 1966, after only one year in the club's farm system. He won 12 and lost 12 that rookie year and firmly established himself in the regular pitching rotation. He would, over a 15-year career in L.A., rewrite much of the Dodgers pitching record book.

movie titled *Warning Shot*. Koufax also contracted for his official biography for a reported $110,000 advance against royalties from Viking Press and for a guaranteed $40,000 for serial rights from *Look* magazine.

Finally, however, on the last day of March, Koufax and Drysdale came to terms with Mr. Bavasi, signed their contracts, and boarded a plane for spring training camp. The particulars were: a one-year contract for each, $120,000 for Koufax, and $105,000 for Drysdale. With the Dodgers family back intact in Florida, the earth seemed considerably more stable in Los Angeles.

Eleven days later, the Dodgers opened in Los Angeles against the Houston Astros. Claude Osteen

Before the 1966 All-Star Game, Dodgers second baseman Jim Lefebvre poses with Yankees slugger Mickey Mantle. Lefebvre accompanied manager Walt Alston, Sandy Koufax, Maury Wills, and Phil Regan to the midsummer classic that year. It would prove to be Lefebvre's best year with the Dodgers during a career that ran from 1965 though 1972. He hit .274 and led the club in home runs (24) and RBIs (74).

Phil "the Vulture" Regan came to the Dodgers from the Detroit Tigers in exchange for utility infielder Dick Tracewski just before the start of the 1966 season. Although Regan was a starting pitcher, Walt Alston converted him to a spectacular reliever. He saved 21 games, the most in the NL in 1966, and produced a record of 14–1 and an ERA of 1.62. He won the NL Comeback Player of the Year award, but would be traded to the Chicago Cubs after the start of the 1968 season.

was on the mound that day before a disappointingly small crowd of 34,520. Ron Fairly drove in all three runs in a 3–2 Dodgers victory.

The only new face in 1966 that would eventually become quite familiar was a rookie right-hander brought up from the Dodgers farm club in Albuquerque, New Mexico, 21-year-old Don Sutton. Because of an impressive record of 23–5 in his only season of minor league play, he came to the Dodgers with the moniker "Sutton Death."

At the other end of the Dodgers age scale, 37-year-old Junior Gilliam was entering his second year as a coach, but his listing in the 1966 Dodgers media guide, under the section containing biographies of manager and coaches, stated simply:

"You'll find Jim listed among the player blurbs in his proper alphabetic spot." And indeed he would play one more year, alternating at third base with John Kennedy and, occasionally, with Jim Lefebvre at second.

In mid-May, Johnny Podres was sold to the Detroit Tigers. The Dodgers brass felt that after chipping the bone in his elbow two years earlier, he had never fully regained his pitching form. So, after four years in Brooklyn and eight in Los Angeles, and appearances in four Dodgers World Series, he left. Newcomer Don Sutton replaced him in the starting rotation. Phil Regan, acquired the year before from Detroit in exchange for utility infielder Dick Tracewski, joined the bullpen corps.

JOHNNY PODRES

The Dodgers career of Johnny Podres, for most practical purposes, came to its conclusion in 1964 when, while batting, his elbow was the recipient of one of Warren Spahn's fastballs. He never fully recovered from the bone chip and the ensuing operation, although he was back in uniform until a trade sent him to Detroit in 1966.

For 10 years, Podres had been an integral and reliable part of the Dodgers starting rotation. And when he left he took with him some outstanding Dodgers memories. He pitched two complete-game victories in the 1955 World Series, including a shutout in the last of the seven games that gave the Dodgers their first world championship. He spearheaded the Dodgers' drive to the pennant during 1963 by posting a six-game winning streak, pitching a one-hitter over Houston, and providing the win that spoiled the Cardinals' 10-game winning streak. In 1957 he led the league with a 2.66 ERA and six shutouts. And in 1961 his percentage of .783 (18–5) was another league high.

Podres is the Dodgers' ninth-winningest pitcher (136) and ranks seventh in strikeouts (1,331). He started 310 games and he pitched a total of 2,030 innings, including 23 shutouts. His Dodgers career ERA is 3.66, and he was named to the National League All-Star Team three times.

Sandy Koufax's bothersome elbow had not hampered his pitching effectiveness—by June 1 he had won nine games. Members of the media suggested that he might become the first 30-game winner since Dizzy Dean 32 years earlier. Borrowing from Ian Fleming and James Bond, the press now dubbed Koufax "Goldflinger."

Before the All-Star Game break, Koufax was halfway to a 30-win season. He was also chosen by Walt Alston to start for the National League in the All-Star Game that year against Detroit's Denny McLain, who two years later, ironically, would become the first 30-game winner since 1934. Also on the National League squad from the Dodgers were Jim Lefebvre and Phil Regan, as well as Maury Wills, who drove in the winning run in the tenth inning of what had to be one of the most uncomfortable All-Star Games ever played (it was a smotheringly hot and humid 105-degree afternoon in St. Louis).

By the end of July, Koufax was still soaring. He struck out 16 Phillies in one game and continued to pile up the wins. The Dodgers finally edged their way into first place in what was a three-way, neck-and-neck race. The Dodgers (59–42) were .001 ahead of the Pirates (60–43) and .003 ahead of the Giants (61–44). The entire month of August was one of sustained excitement in the National League as the three teams slipped in and out of first place by percentage points. On the 21st of the month, Koufax posted his 20th win, and two days later the Dodgers surpassed the 2-million mark in home attendance. (On September 4 they went over the 2-million mark on the road and became the first baseball team in history to draw that many people both at home and away in the same season.) They also participated in the longest doubleheader played at Dodger Stadium up to that time—nine hours against the Cubs in a day-night twin bill. The Dodgers won the first contest 4–3 in 14 innings, but dropped the second, 12–10, in 10.

On Labor Day the Giants held sway in first place, a week later it was the Pirates. But on September 11 Koufax beat the Astros, and the Dodgers took the lead en route to an eight-game winning streak that lifted them three and one-half games ahead over the next five days. Then, however, they dropped two of a three-game series to the Pirates in L.A. and their lead was reduced to one and one-half games. But as the season headed into its last week, the Pirates could not keep pace and finally dropped from contention.

The Giants, however, were still hanging in, and the pennant race was not to be decided until the last day of the season. The Dodgers were at Philadelphia, in first place, and needed only to split the doubleheader there to clinch the pennant. A double loss, however, would thrust them into a tie with the Giants and necessitate a playoff series for the 1966 NL flag.

Don Drysdale, ending up with the worst season of his career (13–16), started the first game. He was routed early, but the Dodgers managed to come back and take a 3–2 lead into the eighth inning

SANDY KOUFAX

Leo Durocher called him the best left-handed pitcher he had ever seen in the major leagues. His catcher, John Roseboro, said of him, "He was probably the straightest guy I ever knew. And one of the nicest . . . and as a pitcher he was incomparable." And the baseball community named him the Player of the Decade (sixties).

Sandy Koufax was Al Campanis' greatest find. The southpaw was only 19 years old when Campanis lured him to the Dodgers and Buzzy Bavasi signed him to a contract in 1955. His appearance, however, forced the Dodgers to send another left-hander of promise, Tommy Lasorda, back to the minors.

Despite all Koufax's potential, his first six years with the club were lackluster. He won only 36 games against 40 defeats, his worst year being 1960 when his record was 8–13. But in 1961, his seventh year in the majors, Koufax finally mastered his control, and with a blazing fastball and crackerjack curve, he became a modern baseball legend.

From 1961 through 1966, Koufax won 129 games and lost only 47, a phenomenal won-lost percentage of .733. And during that time he practically rewrote the National League pitching record book. He hurled a no-hitter in each of four consecutive years, set the major league record for strikeouts in a single season (382) and the NL record for most wins in a season by a left-hander (27, which was tied in 1972 by the Phillies' Steve Carlton), and tied Bob Feller's then–major league record of 18 strikeouts in a nine-inning game. For five consecutive years (1962–1966), he led the NL in ERA; his best year was 1966 when he earned a 1.73 while posting a record of 27–9. Four times he claimed the league strikeout crown. He also owns the Dodgers record for the most shutouts in a single season (11 in 1963), and he twice struck out three batters on nine pitches in one inning. Koufax was the league's MVP in 1963, and won the Cy Young Award three times (in 1963, 1965, and 1966).

In his 12 years as a Dodger, Koufax won 165 games (fifth in Dodgers history) while losing only 87, for a career won-lost percentage of .655, an all-time Dodgers mark. His career ERA is 2.76. He ranks third in strikeouts (2,396) and shutouts (40).

Koufax, at 36 in 1972, became the youngest person ever to be elected to the National Baseball Hall of Fame.

(the result of Ron Fairly's three-run homer in the sixth). But reliever Bob Miller could not contain the Phils, and they pulled it out, 4–3.

The Dodgers then *had* to win the second game. Manager Walt Alston called on Koufax even though the Dodgers ace had had only two days of rest. The Phillies, apparently enjoying the role of potential spoilers, sent their ace Jim Bunning at the Dodgers. But Koufax, despite fatigue and a searingly painful elbow, was again indomitable. He blanked the Phillies 6–0 through eight innings, but faltered in the ninth by giving up three runs. At that point, many focused their eyes on the Dodgers bullpen. But not Walt Alston. Koufax stayed in, regained his composure, and retired three batters in a row to stanch the rally. It was his 27th win of the season, the most any left-hander had recorded in the National League in the 20th century. No Los Angeles Dodger has ever won that many games in one season; only two Brooklyn Dodgers exceeded it—Joe McGinnity (29 in 1900) and Dazzy Vance (28 in 1924)—and one tied it (Don Newcombe in 1956). And although Dodgers fans did not know it, they had just witnessed the last win of Sandy Koufax's distinguished baseball career.

The Los Angeles newspapers heralded Koufax the next day: "Sandy Koufax, baseball's most underpaid pitcher, has whirled the Dodgers into big money for the third time in four storybook seasons, including back-to-back pennants." They searched for names to describe him and his pitching wizardry: "Golden Arm," "Goldflinger," and "the Wand Wielder of Dodger Magic."

The World Series was a transcontinental affair in 1966. The Baltimore Orioles, managed by one-time Yankee great Hank Bauer, had won the American League flag with ease, ending up nine games in front of the Minnesota Twins. The Yankees gave undisputed testimony that year to their total demise by ending up in 10th place, 26½ games out of first—only the third time they had ever ended up in the cellar in their then 64-year history (the others: 1908 and 1912).

Again, the Series promised to be a confrontation between American League hitting and National League pitching—a notion confirmed by that year's

WORLD SERIES LINEUPS, 1966

DODGERS	ORIOLES
Maury Wills, ss	Luis Aparicio ss
Willie Davis, cf	Russ Snyder, cf
Lou Johnson, rf	Frank Robinson, rf
Tommy Davis, lf	Brooks Robinson, 3b
Jim Lefebvre, 2b	Boog Powell, 1b
Wes Parker, 1b	Curt Blefary, lf
Junior Gilliam, 3b	Dave Johnson, 2b
John Roseboro, c	Andy Etchebarren, c

STARTING PITCHERS
Game 1: Don Drysdale, Dave McNally
Game 2: Sandy Koufax, Jim Palmer
Game 3: Claude Osteen, Wally Bunker
Game 4: Don Drysdale, Dave McNally

Dodgers fans would not see the high-flying, hard-hitting Tommy Davis in a Los Angeles uniform after the 1966 season because he was traded to the New York Mets. In his seven years as a regular, Davis hit over .300 three times, but a badly broken ankle in 1965 hindered him to such an extent that his career would never regain its luster. He would play a total of 18 years in the majors and retire with a career average of .294.

regular-season stats. Pitching was hardly the Orioles' forte. Baltimore's winningest pitcher, second-year man Jim Palmer, posted only 15 wins. Dave McNally had accounted for 13, and Steve Barber and Wally Bunker added another 10 each. But in the hitting department, the Orioles were another act altogether. Frank Robinson, whom they had acquired from the Reds before the season's start, took the American League's triple crown, batting .316, whacking 49 homers, and driving in 122 runs. The Orioles also had hitters like Brooks Robinson, Boog Powell, Russ Snyder, Luis Aparicio, and Curt Blefary to round out an intimidating offense. To counteract Orioles power the Dodgers, of course, had Koufax, Drysdale, and Osteen, augmented by relievers Regan, Perranoski, and Brewer.

As in 1965, pitching prevailed in 1966, but this time, not the Dodgers' pitching. It did not start out as a pitcher's fiesta, however. In the first game, Don Drysdale was knocked out early after giving up three runs, including home runs by Brooks and Frank Robinson. The Orioles' Dave McNally was similarly banished to the showers in the third inning after allowing two runs. From that moment on, unfortunately, the Dodgers bats were as silent as the forest from which they had come. Moe Drabowsky relieved McNally for the Orioles and pitched six and two-thirds innings of shutout baseball. The Dodgers got only one hit off Drabowsky, and the boys from Baltimore won, 5–2. His 11 strikeouts in relief, 6 of them in a row, set two World Series records.

The next day at Dodger Stadium Sandy Koufax failed to get it together, too, and left the game after the Orioles had sent four runs across the plate. Jim Palmer, still only 20 years old, did not find the going nearly so rough. He held the Dodgers scoreless on a four-hitter, becoming the youngest pitcher ever to hurl a World Series shutout. Another record was logged that day as well, albeit an unprized one, when Dodgers center fielder Willie Davis made three errors in a single inning. The final score that day was 6–0.

Two days later in Baltimore it was Wally Bunker's turn. He whitewashed the Dodgers with a

A meeting of two of the game's greatest base runners, Maury Wills and Luis Aparicio. In this 1966 World Series game between the Dodgers and the Baltimore Orioles, Wills moves in to put the tag on Aparicio. Actually, Aparicio had been caught off first by Sandy Koufax, then made a desperate but unsuccessful race for second. Wills stole 586 bases during his career; Aparicio's thefts totaled 506.

three-hit performance. The only run needed by the Orioles for their third Series win was a home run by outfielder Paul Blair in the fifth inning. Dave McNally was back for the fourth game of the Series, and he tossed still another shutout, this one on four hits. Frank Robinson provided a 415-foot round-tripper in this game to give the Orioles their second straight 1–0 win, and, of course, the World Series crown.

It had been a Series of despair for the reigning world champion Dodgers. Their bleak showing set a bevy of what one writer called "records for impo-

tency": most consecutive shutouts ever suffered in a World Series (three), most consecutive scoreless innings (33), fewest runs (two), fewest hits (17), fewest total bases (23), and lowest team batting average (.142). Only three Dodgers regulars had hit over .200 in the Series; Lou Johnson's .267 was the club high. The team produced only four extra-base hits in four games. And the Orioles pitching staff's overall ERA for the Series was an incredible 0.50.

Certainly the glory of having won the National League pennant was shaded by the Dodgers' woeful showing in the World Series, but the team had indeed provided their fans with lofty levels of excitement as the pennant race barreled down to the last day of the season. And, after all, it was the Dodgers' fourth pennant in eight years in Los Angeles.

Sandy Koufax had had his finest year, 27–9. His number of wins, starts (41), strikeouts (317), innings pitched (323), and shutouts (five), and his ERA (1.73), were all major league bests for 1966. For the third time in four years he had been the unanimous choice for the Cy Young Award as the major league's most outstanding pitcher. Reliever Phil Regan's 21 saves were the most in the National League.

Tommy Davis was the club's only .300 hitter (.313), but he played in only 100 games because of his injured ankle. Jim Lefebvre led the team in home runs with 24 and in RBIs with 74. Maury Wills stole 38 bases, but that was considerably fewer than the Cardinals speedster Lou Brock's 74.

Back in Los Angeles, the Dodgers front office and managerial staff knew that something had to be done about the team's powder-puff hitting. A shake-up was sure to come in that department. What they did not know, however, was that the pitching staff would need refurbishing as well, after being dealt a monumental blow not much more than a month after the Dodgers left inhospitable Baltimore.

Game 2 of the 1966 World Series found the premier pitchers of each team's staff opposing each other: Sandy Koufax (left) and Jim Palmer, here shaking hands before going out to warm up. Koufax had won 27 games during the regular season, his career high and an NL record for a left-hander, while Palmer won 15 in the AL. But Palmer would prevail that day, hurling a 6–0 shutout and putting the Orioles two games up in the Series.

This sequence of photos all too clearly illustrates the Dodgers' misfortunes in the 1966 World Series. Here, in Game 2, center fielder Willie Davis (left) and right fielder Ron Fairly go after a deep fly from the bat of Orioles slugger Frank Robinson. They hesitate, it falls between them, then bounces over them to the wall for a triple. The Orioles won the game 6–0.

The throw to third baseman Junior Gilliam (No. 19) from Ron Fairly in right field is wide, and the massive Boog Powell thunders safely to third for the Orioles in Game 2 of the 1966 Series. The Series was Gilliam's final appearance as a player for the Dodgers, and it was memorable for Powell because he was the leading batter of the Series, with a .357 average.

Only a part of Willie Davis' personal inning of infamy. Here, in the 1966 World Series, he loses a pop fly in the sun. Only moments before he had done the same thing with the previous batter's fly ball. But to compound this particular gaffe, Davis threw wildly to third base for his third error of the inning, a new World Series record. It was uncharacteristic because Davis was an accomplished fielder and would go on to win Gold Glove awards twice. The team as a whole perpetrated six errors on this day they hoped to forget, tying a Series record for the most boners in a single game.

CHAPTER 10

ROUNDING OUT THE SIXTIES

Among the more animated—if slower—base runners at Dodger Stadium, Jackie Gleason finishes in a dead heat with the first baseman in a race for the bag in the "Stars" game of 1968. The umpire, after conferring with the first-base coach, ruled him safe.

THE TWO-YEAR PERIOD THAT BEGAN on New Year's Day 1967 was hardly a pleasant one for anyone in the United States, an era pervaded by war, assassinations, civil unrest, massive demonstrations, and riots. For the Dodgers it was also a disillusioning time. Their troubles began with the announcement from Sandy Koufax that he and his beleaguered pitching arm would not be around for the 1967 baseball season. At the age of 31, he had decided to heed the pain and the doctors' advice and retire from the game. It was a surprise jolt that would stun both the Dodgers team as

Lined up are the members of the 1968 Dodgers' good-fielding, weak-hitting infield: Bob Bailey (third base), Zoilo Versalles (shortstop), Jim Lefebvre (second base), and Wes Parker (first base). Lefebvre, who was hurt much of the season, posted the best batting average that year, .241. The others: Parker, .239; Bailey, .227; Versalles, .196. As a whole, the team only hit .230, just two percentage points above the notoriously sterile New York Mets that year.

well as Koufax's legion of fans, even though it was common knowledge that he had suffered tremendously with his arthritic elbow. Perhaps the marvelous season to which he had just treated everyone was still too fresh in their minds. It seemed hard to accept that this brilliant young career simply could not stand the rigors of another season.

After the 1966 World Series debacle, the Dodgers took their show on the road for an exhibition tour of Japan. One player, team captain Maury Wills, was not happy with the postseason activities, and while most of the other players went off to tour Ginza, the pagodas, and the public baths, Wills decided to take an unauthorized leave of absence and return to the United States. It so infuriated the Dodgers hierarchy that he was summarily peddled to the Pittsburgh Pirates.

Wills was not the only Dodger to leave the lineup before the 1967 spring-training session. Tommy Davis, still slowed by an ankle that had never fully regained its strength, was traded to the New York Mets. And Junior Gilliam, 38, would devote all his efforts in 1967 to work as a Dodgers coach.

As a result, many new Dodgers faces emerged. Ron Hunt, acquired from the Mets in the Tommy Davis trade, took over at second base. In left field was Bob "Beetle" Bailey who came from the Pirates as part of the exchange for Maury Wills. Gene Michael replaced Wills at shortstop, and Bob Miller had the awesome job of filling Sandy Koufax's spot in the regular pitching rotation.

The regular season would also bring a raft of injuries to devastate the club. Lou Johnson would break an ankle. Al "Bull" Ferrara, whom the Dodgers had brought up from their Spokane farm club late the year before, would be bothered by a bruised rib cage for much of the season. And Don Drysdale would lose two weeks with a back sprain. As if all that were not enough, Drysdale began dropping some disconcerting hints that 1967 just might be his last season before retirement.

All of these circumstances took their toll on the Dodgers. It became evident from the very beginning that 1967 was to be a long and frustrating year for them. They lost their first four games of the regular season on the road and arrived in Los Angeles for their home debut as the only team in the majors who had yet to win a ballgame. Perhaps to set the mood for the season, it was a cold, overcast day with intermittent rain, which at one point delayed the home opener for more than an hour. Fewer than eighteen thousand fans showed up, the fewest ever for a Dodgers home opener. And by the time the game ended not many

A tall, rangy right-hander, Bill Singer (6'4", 185 pounds) moved into the regular rotation in 1967, joining Don Drysdale, Claude Osteen, and Don Sutton. Singer, who was only 20 when he came up with the Dodgers in 1964, won 12 and lost 8 in 1967. His best year, however, would be 1969 when he would win 20, lose only 12, and post a career-best ERA of 2.34. Singer wore Dodger Blue for nine years, then was traded to the California Angels in 1973.

of them were still around to witness the Dodgers' first 1967 victory.

The win was a scant respite, however. Three days later, the Dodgers languished in ninth place in the 10-team National League. As if a sign of abandonment from the gods, an April 22 Dodgers-Cardinals game was rained out in Dodger Stadium—for the first time in the Dodgers' 10 years (and 737 games) there, the weather caused a game to be cancelled.

In mid-May the pennant winners of the year before still had not risen higher in the NL standings

Zoilo Versalles was nearing the end of his 12-year major league career when the Dodgers acquired him from the Minnesota Twins. The Dodgers were in dire need of a shortstop since the departure of Maury Wills, but Versalles would not prove to be the answer. He hit only .196 in 1968. Versalles, however, had had some fine years with the Twins; his best was 1965, when he led the AL in doubles (45), runs scored (126), triples (12), and batted a respectable .273.

Two of the game's all-time great sluggers: Rocky Colavito (left) and Willie Mays. The 34-year-old Colavito made a cameo appearance with the Dodgers in 1968, his last year in the majors. He was used principally as a pinch-hitter, but clouted only three home runs and batted a paltry .204. In his 14-year major league career, however, Colavito belted 374 homers.

than eighth place. Buzzy Bavasi blasted the entire team, claiming that they were "not going all-out on the field." A month later, Bob Hunter wrote in the *Los Angeles Herald Examiner:* "The Dodgers are tail-spinning to their worst season in more than 50 years, or since they finished eighth in 1905." He wrote that prediction while the Dodgers were in the midst of an eight-game losing streak, their longest in six years. Hunter would prove to be a true clairvoyant. By the All-Star break in early July, the Dodgers were still in eighth place, a full 15 games behind the St. Louis Cardinals. Their record was an embarrassing 34–47.

Walt Alston managed the National League All-Stars again in 1967 and came up with a 2–1, 15-inning win. His winning pitcher was Don Drysdale, the only Dodger to see action in the game—a surprising statistic for a team that had won two consecutive NL pennants. Alston's heart and mind, however, were not really focused on the All-Star classic. They were wrapped up with the sudden dreadful decline of his ballclub. As the

second half of the season got underway, he cracked the proverbial whip—he levied fines, berated and benched errant players, and experimented with the lineup and the batting order. Nothing seemed to help. The latter half of the season was as dismal as the first. It was a metronomic routine: win a few, lose a few, but always dwell deep in the second division. When it was over, the Dodgers were in eighth place, the lowly berth where they had remained since June 17. In fact, only once during the entire season had the Dodgers been higher than seventh place, and that was only on one day, May 24. They had won only 73 games while losing 89 (.451) and finished 28½ games behind the league-champion Cardinals.

The once-dazzling Dodgers pitching battalion had proved to be a skeleton of its former self. Claude Osteen won the most games (17), but lost as many, and gave up the most hits in the league that year (298). Don Drysdale matched his uninspired record of the year before, 13–15. Bill Singer, a right-hander who took the job in the starting rotation from Bob Miller, won 12 and lost 8, while Don Sutton won 11 games but lost 15. Ron Perranoski, in his last year as a Dodger, made appearances in 70 games, an NL high that year, and was credited with 16 saves while posting a 6–7 record.

The only hint of strength in the batting order had been back-up outfielder and pinch-hitter Al Ferrara, who, despite his injured side, had led the team with a .277 batting average and a .467 slugging average, and also hit the most home runs (16). The team batting average of .236, however, was the lowest in the National League that year, as was the Dodgers' total number of hits (1,285).

As Bob Hunter of the *Herald Examiner* had predicted in June, the Dodgers had their worst showing since 1905. The 89 losses were, at the time, the most ever in Los Angeles (a total that would not be topped until 1992) and the most since they had dropped 91 games under Leo Durocher back in Brooklyn in 1944.

Dodgers second baseman Ron Hunt and Philadelphia Phillies base runner Johnny Briggs meet at second base in this 1967 game. Hunt came to the Dodgers that year after four seasons with the New York Mets, and Jim Lefebvre was moved to third to make room for him in the starting lineup. Plagued off and on by injuries, he batted .263 in 1961, almost 20 points below the career average he brought with him to L.A. Hunt departed the following year for the San Francisco Giants.

As one writer put it, "the tune the chorus of Walter O'Malley, Buzzy Bavasi, and Walter Alston hummed into the winter of 1967 was 'There'll be some changes made.'" And there certainly were.

Walt Alston, with the traces of a smile, confronted a press conference of sportswriters and broadcasters at Dodger Stadium, during which he ceremoniously signed his 15th one-year contract as Dodgers manager. He told the gathering: "We can bounce back from our eighth-place finish in 1967 to a pennant in 1968." Pupils in the eyes of many of the media members dilated and there were some throat-clearings and arched eyebrows. "It's a great challenge," Alston continued, "and there are a lot of 'ifs.' To begin with, we've got to come up with a top-flight shortstop." He was making clear his first priority—roster changes—and he soon precipitated the largest player personnel shake-up in the Dodgers' then 11-year history in Los Angeles.

Shortly thereafter, general manager Buzzy Bavasi acquired the shortstop Alston wanted. He was Zoilo Versalles, and he came from the Minnesota Twins, along with pitcher Mudcat Grant, in exchange for Dodgers veteran catcher John Roseboro and pitchers Ron Perranoski and Bob Miller. Versalles, the American League's MVP in 1965 and a two-time Gold Glove award winner, had been with the Twins since 1961. Mudcat Grant had spent the last four years with the Twins and seven years before that in a Cleveland Indians uniform. Grant was best, if unlovingly, remembered in Los Angeles as the pitcher who twice beat the Dodgers in the 1965 World Series.

The Dodgers soon acquired veteran sluggers Rocky Colavito and Ken Boyer. They were both from the Chicago White Sox, although their most prosperous years had been spent elsewhere (Colavito with the Cleveland Indians and Detroit Tigers and Boyer with the St. Louis Cardinals). Colavito, approaching 35, would play out the last year of his career in 1968, the first half with the Dodgers and the second with the New York Yankees. Boyer, at 37, also in the twilight of his career, would play the full season and stick around Los Angeles as a pinch-hitter in 1969.

In addition, second baseman Paul Popovich was obtained from the Chicago Cubs and catcher Tom Haller was brought over from the San Francisco Giants. Twenty-one-year-old outfielder Willie Crawford again donned a Dodgers uniform; ever since he was 17 he had fairly regularly "commuted" between the Dodgers and their minor league franchise in Albuquerque, New Mexico.

Paul Popovich, at bat here, came to the Dodgers from the Chicago Cubs in 1968 and landed a regular job in the infield after the departure of Ron Hunt and an injury to Jim Lefebvre. But he only hit .232 and was returned to the Cubs the following year.

The coaching staff was also looking closely at a young catcher from Albuquerque by the name of Ted Sizemore. But Tom Haller nailed down that job, and Jeff Torborg (John Roseboro's backup since 1964) also stayed on while Sizemore went back to the minors for another year of seasoning.

Gone from the Dodgers starting lineup in 1968 were Lou Johnson, infielder Ron Hunt, and shortstop Gene Michael. And before the season would be out of its embryonic stage, Al Ferrara, on whom the Dodgers had pinned so much of their hitting hopes, would be out of the lineup with a broken ankle. Reliever Phil Regan would be sent to the Chicago Cubs for outfielder Ted Savage. (Regan would go on to save 25 games for the Cubs, the most in the major leagues that year.) Don Drysdale had decided to stay, although a rainfall of rumors that he would retire persisted.

The pitching staff, despite its lusterless performance the year before, would remain relatively the same. Drysdale, Osteen, Singer, and Sutton would rotate—Mudcat Grant, at 32, would fill in occasionally, but would not become a regular. And with the departure of Ron Perranoski and Phil Regan, Jim Brewer would assume the role of chief fireman.

When the season opened, Walt Alston's familiar face was not in the Dodgers dugout for the first time in 15 years. He was recovering from an operation to remove a kidney stone.

The ominous tone of the season was set Opening Day when Claude Osteen suffered a 2–0 loss at Dodger Stadium. It said something about the kind of year Osteen was to have, and about the way the Dodgers were to perform at the plate.

Although it was not destined to be a great season for the Dodgers, it became a memorable one for Don Drysdale. First, he rewrote the Dodgers record books April 13, the third game of the season, when he hurled the Dodgers to a 1–0 win over the New York Mets. It was his 191st Dodgers victory, an all-time club record, displacing the 190 wins that Dazzy Vance had compiled in his Dodgers career in the twenties and early thirties. (It is interesting to note that Vance recorded his first Dodgers win at the age of 31, the same age that Drysdale racked up his 191st.) It was also Drysdale's 41st career shutout, moving him one ahead of Sandy Koufax for the Dodgers record. And that was just the beginning.

On May 14 Drysdale pitched another shutout, blanking the Cubs, 1–0. Then, in his next five consecutive appearances, Drysdale shut out the Houston Astros, the St. Louis Cardinals, the Astros again, the San Francisco Giants, and the Pittsburgh Pirates. His six straight shutouts were a new major league record, eclipsing the one held by Doc White of the Chicago White Sox since 1904. In his next appearance on June 8, Drysdale faced the Philadelphia Phillies and, after holding them scoreless for the first two and one-third innings,

THAT'S FIRST RUN OFF BIG-D
SINCE MAY 10...

DON WENT INTO TONITE'S GAME
WITH SIX STRAIGHT SHUTOUTS
BEHIND HIM....AN ALL-TIME
MAJOR LEAGUE BASEBALL RECORD
TREA

The end of one of Don Drysdale's most memorable efforts came this June night in 1968. The Dodger Stadium scoreboard tells part of the story. The other portion is that Drysdale had pitched 58⅔ scoreless innings, which broke the major league record Walter Johnson of the Washington Senators had held since 1913.

broke Hall of Famer Walter Johnson's major league record of 56 consecutive scoreless innings; that record had stood since 1913. Drysdale extended his runless string to 58⅔ innings before the Phillies finally moved a run across home plate (a sacrifice fly by Howie Bedell scoring Tony Taylor from third).

Unlike Drysdale, however, the Dodgers as a team were hardly setting anything on fire. Most of the month of May they were deep in the second division, and on June 1 they had a won-lost percentage of .500. In early June, the juices began to flow as they surged all the way up to second place,

as close as two games behind the Cardinals. But by midmonth an irreversible decline set in, and the Dodgers would never pose even a minute threat during the rest of the year.

Drysdale was given the honor of starting the All-Star Game for the Nationals. He pitched a scoreless three innings and was credited with a win for the second year in a row, this one by a score of 1–0. The only other Dodger to suit up for the All-Star Game that year was catcher Tom Haller.

From the All-Star break onward, it simply got more and more depressing for the Dodgers and their fans. The team was buried in the second division, sinking into ninth place by mid-July and to the league's cellar by mid-August. The Dodgers, in fact, remained in last place in the National League from August 17 through September 8.

The season ended for the Dodgers on September 29 with a loss to the Atlanta Braves and their ace Phil Niekro. It thrust them into a tie for seventh place with the Philadelphia Phillies. The Dodgers' record of 76–86 left them 21 games behind the pennant-winning St. Louis Cardinals. It was the first time the Dodgers had had back-to-back losing seasons since 1937 and 1938.

During the season, the Dodgers had posted one eight-game and three four-game losing streaks. The team batting average of .230 bettered only the .228 hit by the New York Mets. And the Dodgers' total runs for the year (470) were the least scored in the National League.

Despite his record-setting streak of runless innings and shutout games, Don Drysdale did not win the Cy Young Award for 1968. He lost it to the Cardinals' Bob Gibson, who had posted a record of 22–9 and had led the league in strikeouts with 268 and ERA at 1.12. Drysdale's record for the year had been only 14–12.

Claude Osteen had experienced his first losing year as a Dodger—against 12 wins he had 18 losses, the most in the NL that year. Both Don Sutton and Bill Singer had losing years as well (11–15 and 13–17, respectively).

Don Drysdale fires one past Pittsburgh Pirates batter Willie Stargell in this 1968 game at Dodger Stadium. Drysdale, the winner that night, 5–0, posted his sixth consecutive shutout of the season to break a major league record that had stood since Doc White of the White Sox hurled five straight back in 1904. The Dodgers catcher is Tom Haller.

Willie Davis was the only legitimate speedster on the base paths, with 36 thefts. The team's leading home-run hitter was outfielder Len Gabrielson who knocked 10 out of the park. Catcher Tom Haller hit .285 and Gabrielson .270, but they were the only two Dodgers to bat over .250.

The fans were not happy. Only 1,581,093 had come out to Dodger Stadium that year, a record low.

There would be a lot of changes in the major leagues in 1969. There would also be a number of them within the cheerless Dodgers organization. The team, the front office, and the fans all hoped that the Dodgers could spring back to end the decade of the sixties as they had the decade of the fifties.

Seven years before the United States would celebrate its bicentennial, the sport of baseball marked its first centennial anniversary. And it would celebrate the occasion with the broadest change in its structure since the American League became a major league back in 1901.

The historic changes of 1969 included the admission of four new teams into the majors (the Montreal Expos and the San Diego Padres in the National League and the Kansas City Royals and the Seattle Pilots in the American League), the

Fresco Thompson, along with Buzzy Bavasi, was made a vice president of the Dodgers back in 1950, the year Walter O'Malley took control of the ballclub in Brooklyn. Thompson ran the Dodgers farm system through 1968. In 1969 he was slated to take over the positions of executive vice president and general manager vacated by Bavasi, who had left to head the new expansion team in San Diego. Thompson died that year, however, speeding up the promotions of Peter O'Malley and Al Campanis.

separation of each league into two divisions, and an annual postseason playoff series between the divisional winners in each league. And to bring a little life to the offensive part of the game, the pitcher's mound was lowered and the strike zone reduced.

For the Dodgers, the front office took on a new look that year. Buzzy Bavasi, the Dodgers general manager since 1951, resigned to head the new expansion team down in San Diego. Fresco Thompson, longtime Dodgers associate and director of the club's minor league operations, had been slated to take over his responsibilities, but it was clear that Walter O'Malley was grooming his son, Peter (then a team vice president in stadium operations), to take charge of the organization in the near future.

Fresco Thompson died before the 1969 season began, and O'Malley had to quickly readjust his administrative plans. Son Peter was installed as executive vice president, the chief operating officer of the organization. (The following year he assumed the title of president when Walter O'Malley stepped up to become chairman of the board.) Moved up to vice president of player personnel and scouting, assuming all Bavasi's duties as general manager, was Al Campanis, who had headed the Dodgers scouting organization since 1957. Among those Campanis had discovered and signed in his scouting days were Sandy Koufax (whom Campanis stood behind firmly during the

lean years of Koufax's early career), Roberto Clemente, Tommy Davis, Bob Aspromonte, Sandy Amoros, Al Ferrara, and Pete Richert. The alliance between Peter O'Malley and Al Campanis, and the dissemination of duties as it was set up in 1969, would carry over virtually intact into the eighties.

Elsewhere in the Dodgers ranks, there were more changes. After two awful seasons, the emphasis was on acquiring youth—the team simply needed to be rebuilt. The Dodgers were taking a long, hard look at such youngsters from their farm system as Bill "Ropes" Russell, 20, then an outfielder who had slugged away impressively with the Bakersfield, California, farm club the year before; another 20-year-old, Steve Garvey, who had hit .373 in 1968 in Albuquerque; and 19-year-old

Maury Wills is back in 1969, again adding some excitement to Dodgers base paths. He makes it safely to first while former Dodger Ron Fairly, here a Montreal Expo, tries vainly to grab the ball. Fairly had gone to the Expos earlier in the year in the trade that brought Wills back to L.A.

Manny Mota came to the Dodgers midseason in 1969 after tours with several other teams since coming to the majors in 1962. One of the game's most adept hitters, he batted as high as .332 with the Pirates in 1966 and would bat .323 in his 85 games for the Dodgers in 1969. It began a fine Dodgers playing career that would carry all the way through 1980, during which time he would establish himself as the then–most productive and consistent pinch-hitter in major league history.

Bill Buckner, who had hit .344 in Ogden, Utah. Only Russell would make more than a token appearance in 1969, but as it was for the Dodgers management, the groundwork for the future of the team was being laid.

Ted Sizemore, 24, was recalled from Spokane. Under the tutelage of his minor league manager, Tommy Lasorda, and Dodgers scout Monty Basgall, Sizemore had been converted from a catcher to a second baseman. Manager Walt Alston now wanted to see how the metamorphosis had turned

out. Bill "Suds" Sudakis, 23, who had been brought up in September 1968, was expected to fight it out with Jim Lefebvre for the job at third base. And Al Campanis negotiated with the Yankees to get some power in the lineup, acquiring outfielder Andy Kosco. Youthful Willie Crawford, 22, was also expected to win a job in the outfield.

While the fountain of youth was being tested and scrutinized down at Vero Beach, some of the veterans were sitting out spring training in defiance of the contracts offered them. Unsigned hold-outs included Don Drysdale (asking for $125,000 for 1969), Claude Osteen, Paul Popovich, and Len Gabrielson. By Opening Day, however, all were signed and in uniform. (Drysdale accepted $10,000 less than he was asking.)

There was some hope and some dubiousness about the Dodgers as they took the playing field in Cincinnati for the opening of the 1969 season. Old reliable Don Drysdale was on the mound, his seventh opening-game start in the Dodgers' 12 Los Angeles seasons, but the rest of the lineup was so sprinkled with youth that sportswriters quickly dubbed the team the "Mod Squad." The lineup

THE NEW MAJOR LEAGUE LINEUP, 1969

AMERICAN LEAGUE EAST
Baltimore Orioles
Boston Red Sox
Cleveland Indians
Detroit Tigers
New York Yankees
Washington Senators

AMERICAN LEAGUE WEST
California Angels
Chicago White Sox
Kansas City Royals
Minnesota Twins
Oakland A's
Seattle Pilots

NATIONAL LEAGUE EAST
Chicago Cubs
Montreal Expos
New York Mets
Philadelphia Phillies
Pittsburgh Pirates
St. Louis Cardinals

NATIONAL LEAGUE WEST
Atlanta Braves
Cincinnati Reds
Houston Astros
Los Angeles Dodgers
San Diego Padres
San Francisco Giants

Umpires do not always agree, a fact vividly illustrated here. The umpire at the right calls Dodgers base runner Bill "Suds" Sudakis safe, but his colleague to the left thinks that Cardinals shortstop Dal Maxvill has successfully put the tag on Sudakis.

was, in fact, so drastically altered that it included only two players who had started the opener in 1968. Catcher Tom Haller was back, and so was Ron Fairly, but he had been moved to a different position. A right fielder the year before, Fairly started at first base in place of Wes Parker, who was ill. Jim Lefebvre replaced Paul Popovich at second. Ted Sizemore, the catcher cum second baseman, was moved to shortstop in place of Zoilo Versalles, who had been taken by the San Diego Padres in the expansion draft, and subsequently traded to the Cleveland Indians. Suds Sudakis had won the slot at third. Outfielder Willie Davis was benched temporarily because of a hairline fracture

in his arm, and in his place at center on Opening Day was Willie Crawford. Andy Kosco was in left instead of Al Ferrara, who had departed for the Padres and Len Gabrielson took over Ron Fairly's right-field spot.

The refurbished Dodgers got off on the right foot with a 3–2 win over the Reds, and by the time they came home they were 3–3, tied for second place in the National League West. The new faces on the field and the mounting evidence that they could, in fact, hit the ball did not, however, trigger a rush into Dodger Stadium for the home opener. A crowd of 22,200 was on hand, about 4,000 more than the previous year, but still the second lowest

TWO GOOD DAYS
AT THE PLATE

In three games played over July 8 and 9, 1969, Dodgers outfielder Manny Mota collected 11 hits in 14 at-bats, a two-day average of .786. The eight hits he got in the doubleheader against the Atlanta Braves were one short of the all-time major league record.

Willie Crawford was a newcomer to the Dodgers roster in 1964, but over his first five years he would regularly commute between the Dodgers and their farm clubs. He did not land a full-time job in the Dodgers outfield until 1969, but once he did he maintained it for seven years.

attendance for a Los Angeles Dodgers home opener in the club's history. The loyal fans who were there, however, received a rare treat. The Dodgers annihilated the San Diego Padres, 14–0. The next day, they clubbed them again, this time 9–1. In the latter contest, for the first time in eight years, Dodgers hitters belted four home runs in a single game—contributed by Andy Kosco, Tom Haller, Wes Parker, and Willie Crawford. They extended their winning streak to six. By late April they finally moved into a tie for first place in the NL West with the Atlanta Braves, a team that sported one of the most awesome hitting ensembles in baseball: Hank Aaron, Orlando Cepeda, Rico Carty, Felipe Alou, and Clete Boyer, among others. It was the first time the Dodgers had been on top (excluding Opening Day) since they won the pennant in 1966. Even more astounding was the fact that in their first 15 games they had scored 80 runs, an average of more than 5 per game, almost double their average output the year before.

A sour note in the Dodgers' sudden success story was a shoulder problem (a strained muscle that was not responding well to treatment) that had troubled Don Drysdale since Opening Day. By late April it was severe enough to cost the Dodgers a month of his services in the regular rotation. A different problem arose at shortstop. The more Walt Alston looked at that position, the more he felt that Ted Sizemore should be playing on the other side of second base, the position for which he had been trained the year before. In early June that problem was rectified. Maury Wills, apparently forgiven his 1966 postseason transgression in Japan, was brought back to the Dodgers from the Montreal Expos. He was accompanied by the sharp-hitting Manny Mota in a deal that sent Ron Fairly and Paul Popovich to the new Canadian franchise. With Wills at short, Sizemore took command at second.

By mid-June Don Drysdale rejoined the regular rotation, and late that month he led the Dodgers in a 19–0 shellacking of the San Diego Padres, mak-

Don Drysdale

Don Drysdale shattered just about every Dodgers career pitching record in his 14 years with the club (1956–1969). His accomplishments stood until Don Sutton displaced them after his 15 years with the Dodgers in 1980.

Drysdale, a rangy 6'6", 190-pounder, was 19 when he joined the Dodgers in 1956. He had apprenticed in Bakersfield and Montreal before making it to the majors, and Walt Alston predicted that the big right-hander "had the potential to one day dominate the league." And he did, as part of the awesome tandem of Koufax and Drysdale.

Drysdale's best year was 1962 when he won 25 games, lost only 9 (.735), and led the league in wins, strikeouts (232), starts (41), and innings pitched (314⅓). He walked off with the Cy Young Award that year, only the second Dodger at that point to be so honored (the other was Don Newcombe). In 1968, his next to last year as a Dodger, he set two major league records when he hurled six straight shutouts and a grand total of 58⅔ consecutive scoreless innings.

Three times "Big D" (as he was sometimes called) led the league in strikeouts and four times in number of starts. He could hit the long ball as well, and shared the National League record for most home runs by a pitcher in one season: seven, which he hit twice, once in 1958 and again in 1965. (The other slugging pitcher was Dodger Don Newcombe, who belted his seven in 1955.)

When Drysdale ended his career after the 1969 season, he owned all the following Dodgers all-time records: most wins (209), most strikeouts (2,486), most shutouts (49), most starts (465), most games (518), and most innings pitched (3,482).

Big D stayed a part of the game, serving as a color commentator in baseball broadcasting. He was honored with election to the Hall of Fame in 1984.

Hitting Streak

Willie Davis established an all-time Dodgers hitting streak in 1969 when he hit safely in 31 consecutive games. At the time, it was the third-longest hitting streak in National League history. The previous Dodgers record was 29, set by Zack Wheat back in 1916.

season, he announced his retirement. Drysdale had been the only player remaining on the club who had played in Brooklyn, and when he finally put his pitching arm to rest he owned practically every Dodgers career pitching record.

The Dodgers actually did not play badly during the second half of the year. They continued to hit relatively well; there was still reliable, strong pitching from Osteen, Singer, and Sutton; and Jim Brewer was proving to be a true bullpen ace. The problem was that they just weren't playing as well as most of the other teams in their division. As a result, the Dodgers slid downhill and finally ended up in fourth place, ahead of the Astros and Padres, but eight games behind the division champion Braves. Their record of 85–77 was encouraging; it brought them back above the .500 mark for the first time since 1966. The Mod Squad had performed respectably, most sportswriters agreed, especially considering their ages and limited experience in the big league. The year proved to be, as it had been heralded from the outset, one of rebuilding, of polishing new talent.

The most notable improvement had been in the Dodgers' production at home plate. The Dodgers of 1969 hit 30 more home runs and collected 171 more hits than the Dodgers of 1968. The team's collective batting average was .254, 24 percentage points more than the year before. (Only three teams in the entire 12-team NL had higher batting averages that year.) The slugging average was up another 40 percentage points, from .319 to .359. And their total of 52 triples was even a National League high.

ing the 14–0 home Opening Day rout seem mild by comparison. The barrage included a 10-run third inning that featured six singles, six walks, and four wild pitches.

For some reason, after the All-Star break the Dodgers could not regain their momentum from the season's first half. Perhaps one factor was Drysdale's continually troublesome shoulder. In fact, Drysdale finally accepted the inevitable in early August: at 33, he felt he simply could not overcome the injury. So, in his 13th major league

For the first time since 1963, the Dodgers had two .300 hitters in the lineup. Manny Mota had come through for them and hit .323 and had coached Willie Davis as well, enabling him to have his best season yet, batting .311. Andy Kosco had shown more than a little power and led the team with 19 home runs and 74 RBIs. Maury Wills once again had stolen the most bases (25) for the Dodgers, and Willie Davis had trailed him by only 1 base.

The Dodgers had two 20-game winners in 1969—Claude Osteen (20–12) and Bill Singer (20–15)—for the first time since Koufax and Drysdale had combined to do it in 1965. Jim Brewer had 20 saves to his credit. And Ted Sizemore walked off with the NL Rookie of the Year award; he batted .271 and had a fielding average at second base of .979.

The Dodgers fans had apparently noted the improvement and showed their appreciation at the box office. Attendance picked up by almost three hundred thousand over the previous year. It did not turn out to be the Cinderella year 1959 had been, but there was a lot of hope for the seventies because the Dodgers were a young team, one that definitely appeared to be on the rise. "We are building," Al Campanis said. "And we are still looking."

It was "Don Drysdale Day" at Dodger Stadium in 1969, and the illustrious right-hander posed with his wife, daughter, and then–governor of California Ronald Reagan. It was Drysdale's last year in the majors—all 14 years of his career were spent with the Dodgers.

CHAPTER 11

RUNNERS-UP, BACK-TO-BACK

Wes Parker displays four of his Gold Glove awards. During his nine-year Dodgers career, Parker won the award six consecutive times (1967–1972). As a Dodger he set the major league record for the highest career fielding average for a first baseman (1,000 or more games), .996 (later tied by Dodger Steve Garvey and Yankee Don Mattingly). His lifetime batting average is .267, and his best year at the plate was 1970, when he hit .319, drove in 111 runs, and led the majors in doubles with 47.

IN THE 1970 SEASON Walt Alston entered his 30th year as pilot of a professional baseball team. And that year he would be working for a new boss, one who was a mere two years old in 1940 when Alston first managed a baseball team in Portsmouth, Ohio, and who was only a teenager when Alston took command of the field for the Dodgers in 1954. In 1970, 32-year-old Peter O'Malley officially became the youngest team president of any club in the major leagues.

There were several other youngsters down at spring training whose talents everyone was talking about, such as third baseman Steve Garvey and outfielder Bill Russell, both 21, and outfielder/first baseman Bill Buckner, 20. They fit in nicely with the Mod Squad image, although it would be a year or two before they would find the right positions and earn starting berths on the Dodgers team.

The anticipation and hope generated by the past season's notable improvement quickly soured when the regular season began. The Dodgers were shut out at home on Opening Day, and that began a five-game losing streak at Dodger Stadium. During those first five clashes, the Dodgers were shut out three times, scored a total of only four runs, and sank to sixth place in the NL West. To add to those woes, before the season was two weeks old, key pitcher Bill Singer was taken to the hospital with a case of hepatitis that would keep him out of action for a full two months. Sandy Vance, a 23-year-old right-hander, would move into Singer's place in the regular rotation, joining Claude Osteen, Don Sutton, and Alan Foster.

Things began to pick up in May, however, and by midmonth the Dodgers edged up to third place. They even beat Juan Marichal, the Giants' ace, whom they had been able to defeat only four times in 11 years. The winner that day was Sandy Vance, on his way to four consecutive wins. And if overcoming Marichal wasn't enough, the Dodgers went up to San Francisco at the end of the month, pasted the Giants 19–3, and tied the then-Dodgers record for most runs scored in a single game. Claude Osteen got that win, and he also contributed a home run, a double, two singles, and four RBIs. All told, the Dodgers collected 20 hits that night.

The Dodgers managed to climb into second place for a while in the latter half of May. What they had not counted on, however, was the team

Utility infielder Billy Grabarkewitz, on the ground here, became a regular in 1970, his second year in the big leagues, playing mostly at third, but filling in at shortstop and second as well. It would prove to be his best year in the majors; he hit .289, clouted 17 home runs (the club high), and drove in 84 runs. Grabarkewitz would injure his shoulder the next year and never regain his form. He was traded to the Angels after the 1972 season. The Cub is Juan Pizarro.

from Cincinnati whom sportswriters were now calling the "Big Red Machine." Under Sparky Anderson, the Reds were on their way to their first National League pennant since 1961. They were paced by such superstars as catcher Johnny Bench, who hit 45 homers, drove in 148 runs, and was voted the league's MVP; Pete Rose, then an outfielder, whose 205 hits were the most in the majors that year; Tony Perez (40 home runs and 129 RBIs); Bernie Carbo (.310); and Bobby Tolan (.316 and a major league high of 57 stolen bases). The Reds were out of first place only one day the entire season, and that was in the first week.

The Dodgers, although they spent most of the season's second half in second place, were never

Dixie Walker, beloved in Brooklyn as a Dodgers player, rejoined the club as a coach in 1970. He would be a member of the staff through the 1974 season.

really in contention. The Reds maintained a 10-game-or-better lead throughout that period and ended up 14½ games ahead of the Dodgers.

There were some exceptional highlights for the Dodgers during the 1970 season, however. Bill Singer came back from his bout with hepatitis and pitched a one-hitter, a two-hitter, and finally a no-hitter (5–0 over the Phillies). It was the first no-hit, no-run game pitched by a Dodger since Sandy Koufax had done it in 1965. After his return, Singer also won seven of eight games before fracturing a finger on his pitching hand, which benched him for the remainder of the year.

Another performance of note was the batting of Wes Parker. He was still the game's stellar fielder at first base, winning his fourth consecutive Gold Glove award. And he also produced his first .300 year; in fact, he led the team with an average of .319 (his career high). Parker drove in 111 runs, the first time a Dodger had broken the 100-RBI mark since Tommy Davis' 153 and Frank Howard's 119 in 1962. And Parker's 47 doubles were by far the most in either league that year.

Dodgers hitting as a whole was roundly improved in 1970. The team average of .270 tied the Reds and the Braves for the best in the major leagues that year and was a full 16 percentage points higher than their average the preceding year. During one four-day stretch in early August, the Dodgers collected 67 hits in four games and batted a sizzling .416 as a team. Rookie third baseman Billy Grabarkewitz (or "Grbkwtz" as it appeared in most box scores), hit as high as .356 after the first month and a half of the season, ended up with a .289 average, and led the team in home runs with 17. Other Dodgers who con-

One of the game's most graceful and powerful hitters, Richie Allen came to the Dodgers in 1971 in a trade that sent Ted Sizemore and Bob Stinson to the St. Louis Cardinals. Since landing a starting berth in the majors in 1964, Allen had hit at least 20 home runs each season and had accounted for 40 in 1966 for the Phillies. In 1971 he would belt 23 for the Dodgers, drive in 90 runs, and produce a slugging average of .468, all club highs. But discontented and difficult to deal with, Allen would be traded the following year to the Chicago White Sox for ace left-hander Tommy John.

tributed some offensive spark were Ted Sizemore (.306), Willie Davis (.305), and Manny Mota (.305). And Davis' 16 triples were the most in the majors that year.

In the pitching department, Claude Osteen (16–14) and Don Sutton (15–13) turned in the year's most noteworthy performances. Jim Brewer racked up 24 saves, an all-time Dodgers record at the time, while compiling seven wins against six losses. The youngsters of promise, at least Steve Garvey and Bill Buckner, had spent much of the year at the Dodgers' farm club in Spokane. During their brief stints in Los Angeles, Garvey batted 93 times for a .269 average, including one home run, but Buckner

Steve Garvey hit his first home run in the majors for the Dodgers in 1970, and this sight would soon become a familiar one to Dodgers fans over the next decade and into the eighties. Garvey began as a third baseman and would not take permanent possession of first base until 1974.

hit a weak .191 in his 68 appearances at the plate. No one in the Dodgers organization, however, was giving up on either of them, nor on Bill Russell, who had participated in 81 games for the Dodgers, batted 278 times, and recorded an average of .259.

The 1970 finish was the best for the Dodgers since their pennant-winning year of 1966. And their final record of 87–74 brought them into the

first division for the first time since that same memorable year.

But the biggest news, perhaps, came just after the season ended. The Dodgers front office announced that Ted Sizemore and backup catcher Bob Stinson had been dealt to the St. Louis Cardinals for notorious slugger Richie Allen. The powerful Allen, who could play in the outfield and at first or third base, had hit 20 or more home runs every year since becoming a starter with the Phillies in 1964 (he played with them through 1969). His career bests at that time were the 40 homers and 110 RBIs he had accounted for in 1966. Besides that, he had hit above .300 three times and had brought with him to the Dodgers a career batting average of .297. He also had a reputation for being difficult to get along with, an image confirmed by a variety of front office administrators, coaches, players, and sportswriters.

The Dodgers also acquired another power hitter, catcher Duke Sims, who had hit 23 home runs for the Cleveland Indians the year before. The Dodgers would go into 1971 with not only the spirit and speed of youth, but also, thanks to the trades, a healthy helping of power, a commodity they had been short on for quite some time.

There were two nonroster players who arrived in 1971 from opposite ends of the country: 23-year-old Ron Cey from Tacoma, Washington, who had hit .331 for the Dodgers Albuquerque farm club the year before, and 24-year-old Davey Lopes from Providence, Rhode Island, who had played in Spokane in 1970. There was also a catcher named Steve Yeager, who had impressed many people in Albuquerque the year before. None of them would make the team in 1971, but it would not be long before they would earn their way into Dodgers uniforms.

The veterans and other members of the organization who left Los Angeles for spring training that year went aboard the new company plane, a $3-million 720B fan jet that both added to the team's fanciful image and helped satisfy its

Dodgers catcher Tom Haller (No. 15) arrives home after smashing one into the Dodger Stadium seats in a 1970 game against the Montreal Expos. Haller took over the regular backstop chores in 1968 after John Roseboro was traded to Minnesota, and would serve there until he himself would be traded to the Detroit Tigers in 1972. Haller is welcomed here by Jim Lefebvre (No. 5), Steve Garvey (No. 6), and Willie Crawford (No. 27). The Expos catcher is John Bateman.

logistical requirements. It was, at the time, the largest corporate-owned jet in the world, seating 70, all in first-class seats, and replete with four lounges and two galleys. The Dodgers were the first major league team ever to own its own airplane. Back in the Brooklyn days, Walter O'Malley bought a Cessna, which was sequentially replaced by a Beechcraft, a DC-3, a Convair 440, a DC-6, and an Electra II before the new 720B.

The Dodgers had a pleasant blend of experience and youth on their roster. Maury Wills, at 38, was the team's patriarchal figure, but he could still hit and steal bases. At the other end, there was a raft of youngsters who were still awaiting their 25th birthdays. And the meld was working well. In fact, they looked so good down in Florida that it prompted Los Angeles sportswriter Bob Hunter to write an article headlined: DODGERS SO GOOD IT'S SCARY.

Bill Buckner (No. 22) returns triumphantly to the dugout after hitting one of his first major league home runs, in a 1971 game against the Pirates. Buckner debuted with the Dodgers in 1969 at age 19, but only appeared in one game. In 1971 he was there to stay, playing mostly in the outfield, but also spelling Wes Parker at first. Buckner hit .277 that first year, including five homers and 41 RBIs. The welcoming committee consists of (from left) Jim Lefebvre (No. 5), Wes Parker, Walt Alston (No. 24), and Tom Hutton (No. 34). No. 8 is Duke Sims.

The Dodgers did have a good spring training, ending up with a 13–9 record. But the use of spring training as a barometer is questionable at best. After all, back in 1966, the year the team won its last pennant, they had won only 10 preseason games and lost 16.

The home opener in Los Angeles was a special one that year because it marked the Dodgers' 10th season in Dodger Stadium. And 31,413 people came out to watch them take on the San Diego Padres, indifferent to the facts that the Dodgers had lost two of their first three games in Houston before coming home and that they were then in fourth place in the NL West. The crowd totaled almost ten thousand more than the previous year's home-opener crowd. Part of the reason, of course, was that fans were expecting big things from the Dodgers after their second-place finish in 1970 and the good vibrations that were being sent out by reporters during spring training.

In 1971, however, it would not be just the Cincinnati Reds whom the Dodgers would have to contend with, although the Big Red Machine, on paper anyway, still seemed to be the division's blue-ribbon franchise. There was also the Dodgers' ever-present nemesis, the Giants. With veteran pitchers like Juan Marichal and Gaylord Perry and such hitters as Willie McCovey, Bobby Bonds, Ken Henderson, and 40-year-old Willie Mays, they had to be considered a very real threat. Elsewhere in the division, the Atlanta Braves also had an

At 38, Maury Wills (No. 30) is still hell on the base paths. Here he eludes Chicago Cubs second baseman Glenn Beckert in a 1970 game. This was not a base theft, however; it was merely an advance on a passed ball, but Wills did steal 15 bases that year, second on the club only to Willie Davis' 20.

impressive roster, including Hank Aaron, Ralph Garr, Orlando Cepeda, and Phil Niekro.

Things did not go well for the Dodgers in the early weeks of the season, and it took them 16 games before they could claim a .500 record. One three-game series against the Pirates in early May exemplified the Dodgers' starting troubles: they whacked out a total of 35 hits but still could not win one of the three games.

By late May, however, the Dodgers had worked themselves into second place behind the Giants, who were surprising everybody (especially the Cincinnati Reds) by dominating the NL West since the season's start. But even though the Dodgers were in second place, they were 10½ games behind. At that time, Willie Davis was the leading hitter in both major leagues with an average of .386. Davis was also in the middle of an eventual 25-game hitting streak, exceeded in the Dodgers record log only by his own 31-game streak in 1969. Also around that time, Maury Wills reached a batting milestone when he whacked his 2,000[th] career hit. It came off Giants hurler Gaylord Perry, and it marked a hitting achievement equaled or surpassed by only 140 other major leaguers at that point in the game's history.

The pitcher of note in June was young Don Sutton, now well established as one of the Dodgers' premier hurlers; he threw a one-hit 4–0 shutout against the Houston Astros at Dodger Stadium. It was the first one-hitter by a Dodger since Sutton hurled his first one in 1969.

When the Dodgers moved into second place on June 2—their 27–25 record trailing the Giants by nine and one-half games—they established themselves there until the end of the season. The Giants, on the other hand, never gave up first place since they first moved there after the second game of the season on April 6. Nevertheless, there was excitement throughout the season in both Los Angeles and San Francisco, because the National League pennant would not be decided until the very last game.

Utility infielder Bobby Valentine successfully puts the tag on Jose Cardenal of the St. Louis Cardinals in a 1971 game at Dodger Stadium. Valentine was 20 years old and one of the Dodgers' hottest prospects. He had come up in 1969, gone back to the farm club in Spokane, and returned in 1971. He would bat .274 in 1972, then be traded to the California Angels the following year.

Through June, the Dodgers had remained somewhere between five and nine games behind the Giants. During July it was much the same. In August they came as close as four games, but then lapsed back to eight by month's end. September was the month, however, when things got very hot. The Dodgers, eight games out, chipped away at the San Francisco lead until it was down to a single game by September 14—the result of a Dodgers eight-game winning streak coupled with seven Giants losses during the same period.

By September 23, the Dodgers were three games behind with six games remaining in the season. The first three were with the Braves in Atlanta, and then there would be a three-game wrap-up back home against the Houston Astros. With wins from Al Downing and Don Sutton, the Dodgers narrowed the Giants lead to a single game. Claude Osteen then won the last game, but the Giants also won to maintain their single-game lead.

Bill Singer kept the Dodgers' hopes alive in the first game at Los Angeles, setting the Astros down 2–1. But the next day disaster struck as the otherwise unheralded hitters from Houston humiliated the Dodgers 11–0. There was good news, though: the Giants lost too. That left only one game. The

Duke Sims dives futilely for third base as Chicago Cub Ron Santo prepares to grab the throw and put a sweeping tag on him in a 1971 game at Dodger Stadium. Sims, after coming to the Dodgers from the Cleveland Indians, traded off that year with Tom Haller behind the plate. He hit .274, then was traded to Detroit the next year.

Al Downing (No. 44) shakes hands with manager Walt Alston after shutting out the Atlanta Braves 12–0 in a crucial late September game in 1971. It was Downing's 18th win of the year on his way to a 20–9 season. The game was the first of a double shutout that day; Don Sutton would blank the Braves 4–0 in game two of the doubleheader. But the Dodgers would still lose the pennant to the San Francisco Giants by a single game that year.

L.A. DODGER RECORDS

By the end of the 1970 season, these stood as the best performances in a single season by the Dodgers since the team moved to Los Angeles in 1958:

BATTING
Batting Average: Tommy Davis, .346, 1962
Hits: Tommy Davis, 230, 1962
Home Runs: Frank Howard, 31, 1962
Triples: Willie Davis, 16, 1970
Doubles: Wes Parker, 47, 1970
Singles: Maury Wills, 179, 1962
RBIs: Tommy Davis, 153, 1962
Runs Scored: Maury Wills, 130, 1962
Total Bases: Tommy Davis, 356, 1962
Walks: Junior Gilliam, 96, 1959 and 1960
Slugging Average: Duke Snider, .562, 1961
Stolen Bases: Maury Wills, 104, 1962

PITCHING
Wins: Sandy Koufax, 27, 1966
ERA: Sandy Koufax, 1.73, 1966
Strikeouts: Sandy Koufax, 382, 1965
Shutouts: Sandy Koufax, 11, 1963
Completed Games: Sandy Koufax, 27, 1965 and 1966
Starts: Don Drysdale, 42, 1963 and 1965
Innings Pitched: Sandy Koufax, 335.7, 1965
Won-Lost Percentage: Phil Regan, .933, 1966
Saves: Jim Brewer, 24, 1970

Dodgers had to win it, and the Giants had to lose theirs, to bring the NL West race to a dead heat and send the two teams into a divisional playoff. Manager Walt Alston sent Don Sutton up against the Astros, and he eked out a 2–1 win. But elsewhere in the state, the Giants rose to the occasion and defeated the San Diego Padres, thereby squelching the Dodgers' hopes.

With that cliffhanger over, the Giants went on to face the Pittsburgh Pirates, who, behind the bats of Roberto Clemente, Willie Stargell, and Manny Sanguillen, and the pitching of Dock Ellis, strode through the NL East (they would also stride through the NL playoffs and the World Series that year). The Dodgers, however, had offered their fans the most exciting season since 1966, producing their best record (89–73) and enticing the most fans to Dodger Stadium since that pennant-winning year. The 1971 season marked the eighth time in Dodgers history that more than 2 million spectators had passed through the Dodger Stadium turnstiles. With more than 1.5 million in attendance at their road games, the Dodgers could boast a total attendance of 3,677,047 for their 162 games.

Among the heroes that year was pitcher Al Downing, who became only the third left-handed Dodgers pitcher to win 20 games since the team had come to Los Angeles (the others were Sandy Koufax and Claude Osteen). His 20–9 record (.690), 2.68 ERA, and five shutouts (a league high) were enough to earn him *The Sporting News* award for Comeback Player of the Year (his previous year's record with Oakland and Milwaukee had been 5–13). Downing also came in third in the balloting for the National League Cy Young Award, which went that year to Ferguson Jenkins of the Chicago Cubs who had led the league in wins (24), innings pitched (325), completed games (30), and starts (39).

Don Sutton turned in his best year thus far as a Dodger, 17–12, with an ERA of 2.55, at that time his career best. And he pitched three clutch wins during the last 10 games of the season to keep the Dodgers in the pennant race. Jim Brewer was again excellent in relief, saving 22 games and posting an ERA of 1.89. Bill Singer, beset by more injuries in 1971, could not get going and ended up with his worst season as a Dodgers hurler (10–17).

The Dodgers team batting average (.266) was the best in the NL West. Richie Allen led the team with 23 home runs and 90 RBIs, although it was his leanest season in those categories since 1967. He also batted a respectable .295, and his slugging average of .468 was the highest on the team. Batting honors once again went to Willie Davis, whose phenomenal hitting in the first half of the season tapered off, but only enough to lower his average to .309. Manny Mota appeared in only 91 games, often as a pinch-hitter, but hit .312.

And the dean of major league managers, Walt Alston, after his 18th year at the Dodgers helm, was named National League Manager of the Year for the fifth time.

Walt Alston, 1954–1976.

Jim Brewer (far right), 1964–1975. Also, from left: Ken McMullen, Joe Ferguson, and Don Sutton.

Don Drysdale, 1956–1969.

Manny Mota, 1969–1982,
coach 1980–present.

Willie Davis, 1960–1973.

Maury Wills, 1959–1966, 1969–1972.

Maury Wills, 1959–1966, 1969–1972.

Claude Osteen, 1965–1973.

Tommy Davis, 1960–1966.

Wes Parker, 1964–1972.

Don Sutton, 1966–1980, 1988.

Bill Russell, 1969–1986.

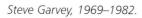
Jerry Reuss, 1979–1987.

Ron Cey, 1971–1982.

Steve Garvey, 1969–1982.

Fernando Valenzuela, 1980–1990.

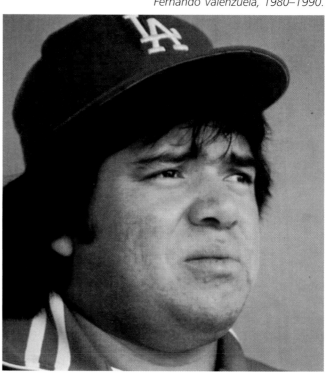

Dusty Baker, 1976–1983.

Bill Russell and Davey Lopes in the 1974 National League championship series against the Pirates.

Roy Campanella and Tommy Lasorda at the 1978 World Series.

Tommy John and catcher Steve Yeager in the 1978 World Series.

Tommy Lasorda and Pedro Guerrero (No. 28) in 1981.

Steve Garvey in the 1981 National League playoffs versus the Montreal Expos.

Orel Hershiser (1983–1994, 2000) in the 1988 NLCS versus the New York Mets. Photo courtesy of AP/Wide World Photos.

Kirk Gibson (1988–1990) after his game-winning home run versus the Oakland A's in the 1988 World Series. Photo courtesy of AP/Wide World Photos.

Orel Hershiser with the 1988 World Series Most Valuable Player trophy. Photo courtesy of AP/Wide World Photos.

Five straight Rookies of the Year (from left): Eric Karros (1992), Mike Piazza (1993), Raul Mondesi (1994), Hideo Nomo (1995), and Todd Hollandsworth (1996). Photo courtesy of AP/Wide World Photos.

Eric Gagne (1999–present) en route to the 2003 Cy Young Award.
Photo courtesy of AP/Wide World Photos.

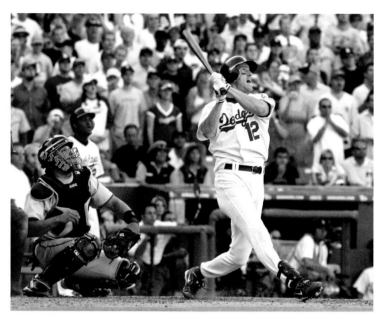

Steve Finley (2004) hits the National League
West Division–clinching grand slam versus the
San Francisco Giants on October 2, 2004.
Photos courtesy of AP/Wide World Photos.

CHAPTER 12

STILL STRUGGLING

Tommy John joined the Dodgers staff in 1972 after seven years with the Chicago White Sox. He was immediately integrated into the regular rotation, joining Claude Osteen, Don Sutton, and Al Downing. John won 11 and dropped 5 his first year in L.A., would win 16 the next year, and 13 in 1974 before injuring his elbow. Here he is pitching to Randy Elliott of the San Diego Padres.

FROM THE POINT OF VIEW of major league baseball's legion of devoted fans, the 1972 season hardly got off on the appropriate foot. The year was marked by the game's first players strike: it lasted 13 days and postponed the opening games until April 15. Although it was minimal in com-parison to the lengthy strike that awaited baseball fans eight years later, it did serve as a warning of the sport's changing face. The emerging emphasis on salaries, fringe benefits, pension plans, and other business concerns was to become as preemi-nent in baseball as it had been at the United Auto

The first three Dodgers numbers to be formally retired—those once worn by Jackie Robinson, Roy Campanella, and Sandy Koufax—were presented in a ceremony at Dodger Stadium in 1972.

Workers/automotive industry bargaining table. Nineteen seventy-two was also a year filled with tragedy, especially for Dodgers followers. Gil Hodges, 47, died shortly before the start of the season, as did Jackie Robinson, 53, shortly after the season; both were victims of heart attacks. And before the year's end Pittsburgh Pirates great Roberto Clemente would be killed in an airplane crash while trying to bring food and medical supplies to victims of an earthquake in Nicaragua.

On a brighter note, 36-year-old Sandy Koufax became the youngest player ever elected to the National Baseball Hall of Fame. Only seven other Dodgers had preceded Koufax into the Cooperstown shrine—Wee Willie Keeler, Dazzy Vance, Zack Wheat, Jackie Robinson, Burleigh Grimes, Branch Rickey, and Roy Campanella.

There were some major arrivals and departures in the 1972 Dodgers ranks. The most suprising was the trading away of Richie Allen. Perhaps the

Bill Singer (No. 40) is mobbed after shutting out the San Diego Padres in this early 1972 game. It was his second win in the first week of that season, which would be his last season as a Dodger and his worst as a major league pitcher. He ended the year with a dismal record of 6–16. Singer had only one really good season with the Dodgers (1969, 20–12), but he would be rejuvenated and win 20 for the California Angels in 1973.

Famous for his knuckleball, the great fireman Hoyt Wilhelm came to Los Angeles to play out the last 2 of his 21 years in the majors. He only picked up four saves, however, and retired in 1972 at the age of 49. At the time, Wilhelm held practically every major league relief pitching record: most saves (227), most wins as a reliever (123), and most games appeared in (1,070). His career ERA was 2.52.

Dodgers front office felt that despite his relatively productive year he was not worth the grief, and they traded him to the White Sox for left-handed pitcher Tommy John, who had been a mainstay in Chicago since 1965. Also gone were catchers Tom Haller and, shortly after the season started, Duke Sims. New to Dodger Blue that year was 48-year-old fireman Hoyt Wilhelm, who could still throw a nifty knuckleball. Not quite as old, but perhaps more famous, was the incomparable Frank Robinson, now 36, whom the Dodgers acquired from the Baltimore Orioles. To fill the rather gaping hole at catcher, the Dodgers picked up on waivers Chris Cannizzaro, who had played with both the San Diego Padres and the Chicago Cubs the year before. And before the season would progress very far, Bill Russell would take the starting job at shortstop from an aging Maury Wills.

Don Sutton got the call to start both the season opener and the home opener for the Dodgers of

1972. And he won both, defeating the Reds, 3–1, at Cincinnati and shutting out the Atlanta Braves, 4–0, at Dodger Stadium. Not only did Sutton start strong, but so did all the Dodgers that year. The team won seven of their first eight games and put together a six-game winning streak in the process, which unfortunately would prove to be the longest of the year.

Don Sutton actually got off to the best start of his career, en route to his finest year so far as a Dodgers pitcher. He won his first eight games that year, three short of the Los Angeles record of eleven shared by Sandy Koufax and Don Drysdale. As a team, however, the Dodgers could not keep up with him, although they managed to exchange the NL West lead with the Houston Astros several times during May and early June. But when the Cincinnati Reds took over first place on June 2, it heralded the Dodgers' doom. They dropped to second that day and sunk to third a week later, where they would remain for the next three and a half months. It was a gradual, steady decline, and the Dodgers were never in contention for the pennant after they had taken possession of third place. By the end of the season in early October, the Dodgers were a distant 10½ games behind the division champion Cincinnati Reds.

Here are some highlights that came along the way: Don Sutton pitched two two-hitters that year, shutting out the Atlanta Braves, 4–0, and the Houston Astros, 5–0. He also hurled two fine innings for the National League in the All-Star Game, although he was the only Dodger to attend that year. And he picked up his 100th career victory in September when he shut out the Giants, 1–0, at Dodger Stadium. Al Downing also threw a two-hitter, blanking the Astros, 2–0, and chalked up his 100th major league win. Manny Mota was consistently among the NL's top 10 in batting, ascending as high as third (.332 in mid-August). Bill Buckner joined him there in September when his average rose to .312, and he remained there for the rest of the season. Willie Davis drove in 26 runs in 26 games during one stretch of the season. Willie Crawford hit a home run in each of four consecutive games, and Billy Grabarkewitz had a three-game home-run hitting streak. On the other hand, the season's low point was reached August 7, when the Dodgers lost a 19-inning marathon to the Cincinnati Reds, 2–1, during which the Dodgers struck out 22 times. Only once before in National League history had a team fanned that many times in a single game, and that was the New York Mets in 23 innings against the San Francisco Giants in 1964.

Despite the fact that it seemed to be Don Sutton's year, the team's winningest pitcher was Claude Osteen, who won 20 and lost 11. It was Osteen's second 20-game year with the Dodgers,

Sandy Koufax was enshrined in the Baseball Hall of Fame in 1972. At 36, he was the youngest person ever to be so honored.

and it would prove to be his best year ever in the majors; his 2.64 ERA was also a career best. Sutton settled for a record of 19–9, but nine of the wins were shutouts—the most ever for a Dodgers right-hander—and he tied Nolan Ryan of the California Angels for the most in the majors that year. (Southpaw Sandy Koufax had pitched the most Dodgers shutouts, 11 in 1963.) Tommy John, in his first year as a Dodger, won 11 while losing 5, and Jim Brewer was again the club's key fireman, this time saving 17 games and posting a distinguished 1.27 ERA.

Manny Mota was the Dodgers' most consistent hitter, ending the season with an average of .323. Bill Buckner was close behind with .319. Willie Davis dropped to .289, but led the club in hits (178), doubles (22), triples (7), RBIs (79), runs

Frank Robinson (No. 36) is congratulated after blasting one of the 19 home runs he hit as a Dodger in 1972. He shared team honors in that category with Willie Davis, who is welcoming Robinson here at the left. To the right is Wes Parker. But Robinson, whose age in 1972 matched the number on his jersey, was past his prime, and should perhaps more appropriately be remembered for his mighty hitting against the Dodgers as a Cincinnati Red (1956–1965) and as a Baltimore Oriole in 1966, when he hit two key homers off Dodgers pitchers in the World Series. Robinson remained in L.A. just one year, then moved to the California Angels.

scored (81), and stolen bases (20). He also won the Gold Glove award for the second year in a row.

Frank Robinson, plagued by injuries, had one of the most disappointing seasons of his then 17-year major league career. Although he tied Willie Davis for team home-run honors, his total of 19 was disappointing, and his 59 RBIs were 20 less than what Davis produced for the Dodgers. His lean production and hefty salary were two of the reasons Robinson was put on the trading block after the 1972 season. But he was not alone. There would be a lot of reshuffling in the Dodgers ranks

for the 1973 season as the name of the game in Los Angeles became "youth."

The 1973 season was a unique one, filled with remarkable performances and strange happenings. Nolan Ryan set a new modern major league record for strikeouts (383, one more than Sandy Koufax had fanned back in 1965), and pitched two no-hitters in the same season. Thirty-nine-year-old Hank Aaron belted out 40 homers to bring his career total to within one of the immortal Babe Ruth's record of 714. Superstars Reggie Jackson (then an Oakland A) and Pete Rose won the MVP

Second baseman Lee Lacy was a rookie of promise in 1972, frozen here in the act of completing a double play against the New York Mets in a 1972 game. A knee injury would hobble him later, but he would be back to serve as a dependable pinch-hitter and backup to Davey Lopes. Lacy's best year at the plate was 1975, when he hit .314, second on the club to only Steve Garvey's .319. He would be traded to Atlanta the next year, but was retrieved in another deal the year after that. In 1979 he was sent to the Pittsburgh Pirates.

Dodger Chris Cannizzaro tries gamely to reach third base, but Atlanta Braves third baseman Darrell Evans already has the ball in his glove, ready to apply it here. Cannizzaro was the Dodgers' primary catcher in 1972, but would lose the job to Joe Ferguson the next year.

awards in the American and National Leagues, respectively. The year also brought the initiation of the designated hitter in the AL; ominous threats of another strike; Oakland owner Charley Finley's intervention in the field management of the club, which outraged baseball fans everywhere; and the ever-surprising New York Mets, who rose again from the ashes to go to another World Series, as they had done in 1969.

For the Dodgers it was a time of major transition. Many familiar faces disappeared. Danny Ozark, a coach since 1965, departed to become the manager of the foundering Philadelphia Phillies. Ozark, who had been affiliated with the Dodgers since 1942 as a player, minor league manager, and coach, was replaced by another Dodger, Tommy

Lasorda, whose life had also been continually intertwined with the organization. Drafted as a pitcher by the Dodgers in 1948, he too had served as player and minor league manager. And no one in the history of the franchise had ever been more vociferously devoted to the Dodgers than Lasorda, who explained to Los Angeles sportswriters on his arrival: "You know what I bleed when I bleed? Dodger Blue."

Players left in droves. Frank Robinson, pitcher Bill Singer, and infielder Billy Grabarkewitz were among the first, sent to the California Angels for right-handed pitcher Andy Messersmith, who had had a poor year there in 1972, but had won 20 games the year before that. He brought with him an overall major league record of 73–57 and an ERA of 2.76. Forty-year-old Maury Wills, after having been with the Dodgers for 12 of his 14 years in the major leagues, retired. So did Wes Parker, a mere 33. He left the game with the major league record as the best fielding first baseman ever, a career average of .996. Jim Lefebvre, who had worn a Los Angeles uniform for eight years, shipped out to play baseball in Japan.

The lineup for 1973 was for the most part an array of young faces. Two were rookies—Ron Cey at third base and Davey Lopes at second. Bill Russell remained at shortstop, and Steve Garvey and Bill Buckner traded off at first base. Joe Ferguson, up from the farm club in Albuquerque, took over as front-line catcher, backed up by young Steve Yeager. The only relative old-timers were Manny Mota, 35, and Willie Davis, 33, who both covered the outfield along with the younger Willie Crawford, 26. With the exclusion of Mota and Davis, the average age of the Dodgers starters was 25.

For the fourth straight year the Dodgers came out on the winning end of their season in spring training. The talk had been that this was to be a year of building for the future, of giving youth a

chance to gather some major league experience. However, from the way the Dodgers were playing, a lot of sportswriters were already predicting that the older and allegedly wiser teams in the National League might do well to be on their guard in 1973.

The season began poorly for the Dodgers, with Don Sutton going down to defeat on Opening Day, 4–2, at the hands of the San Diego Padres, the NL West's weakest team (they would win only 60 of 162 games that year). The Dodgers lost to them again the following day. By the end of the season's first week, Los Angeles had a record of 1–6 and held the lease on the division cellar. It would not be until early May that they would reach .500 (13–13). And during that rather dismal period of time, San Francisco Giant Juan Marichal, the longtime Dodgers bedeviler, beat them for the 37th time of his career.

Relief ace Jim Brewer (No. 21) became a common sight walking off the mound after rescuing a game for the Dodgers. Here, he shakes hands with Tommy John and gets a slap on the back from Steve Garvey; the catcher is Joe Ferguson. Brewer was credited with 125 saves in his 12 years with the club (1964–1975).

Jim Lefebvre, completing a double play here, retired from American baseball after the 1972 season. He had been a regular for most of the preceding seven years, at either second or third base. Occasionally he played at first or in the outfield. His career batting average was .251.

The most heralded addition to the Dodgers lineup in 1973 was the hard-throwing Andy Messersmith, who came from the Angels. He would win 14 and lose 10 that first year with the Dodgers, as well as hurl three shutouts to justify his role as a member of the regular rotation.

MURRAY ON LASORDA

When Tommy Lasorda came to Los Angeles in 1973 to join the Dodgers coaching staff, Jim Murray of the *Los Angeles Times* described him this way: "Tom Lasorda is as noisy as a bowling alley, about as self-effacing as the Gabor sisters, and as truculent as a tomcat."

Hitting could not necessarily be blamed. By May 20 the Dodgers had two batters in the NL's top 10, rookie Davey Lopes at .370 and Manny Mota at .363. Don Sutton was pitching well, but he had completed only two games and had an uninspiring record of 4–3, exactly the same statistics as Andy Messersmith at that point in the season. Tommy

John had a record of 3–2, and Claude Osteen 3–3. The team was in fourth place with a record of 23–17, but they were only four games behind the San Francisco Giants.

The Dodgers hung in for the next month and then in the middle of June made their move. They took over first place June 17, putting together a seven-game winning streak. From June 16 to the All-Star break July 23, the Dodgers won 26 of 38 games and had another seven-game winning streak. By July 1 they were six and one-half games ahead of the next-closest contender. Then the everpowerful Cincinnati Reds, who were paced by Pete Rose, Johnny Bench, Tony Perez, Joe Morgan, and Dave Concepcion, beat them three in a row, followed by similarly disastrous treatment from the weakling San Diego Padres. The six-game losing streak was the Dodgers' worst period since the first week of the season, but they rebounded to win ten of the next eleven games and post their third seven-game winning streak of the year. They built their lead in the NL West back up to a hefty eight and one-half games. Too bad the season could not have ended there, or even at the All-Star break a few days later, when they were still five and one-half games in front.

The Dodgers were soaring. In June, Willie Crawford joined Mota and Lopes in the NL batter's top 10 with an average of .321, and Willie Davis collected his 2,000th career hit (a two-run homer). Don Sutton had improved his record to 12–6, and Claude Osteen had lifted his to 11–5. Andy Messersmith was at 9–6, and he had also tied a major league record when he struck out the first

WILLIE DAVIS

Willie Davis was 21 years old when the Dodgers brought him up from their farm club in Spokane. He was being groomed, he was told, for a very large job: filling the center-field slot that had been handled so magnificently for 14 years by Duke Snider.

A speedster on the base paths, a sometimes dazzling fielder, and a consistent hitter capable of an occasional long ball, Davis played an integral role in the Dodgers' story for 14 years.

As a base runner, he often sprinted in the shadow of Maury Wills, but managed to steal double-digit amounts of bases every year but his first as a Dodger. His best effort was 42 thefts in 1964. As a fielder, his image was tarnished by the three errors he made in an uncharacteristic inning in the 1966 World Series, but he did win the Gold Glove for fielding excellence twice (1972 and 1973) and brought Dodgers fans to their feet countless times as he raced down a fly ball in center or made spectacular diving catches.

As a hitter, Davis batted .279 in his Dodgers career. His best year was 1969 when he hit .311, and his most prodigious year as a power hitter was 1962 when he belted 21 homers and drove in 103 runs. Twice he led the league in triples (1962 with 10 and 1970 with 16, the latter a Los Angeles Dodgers record at the time). His 31-game hitting streak in 1969 still ranks as the all-time Dodgers best. Davis also tied the Dodgers mark for most hits in a single game when he knocked out six singles in a 19-inning affair in 1973.

Only Zack Wheat and Pee Wee Reese have collected more hits with the Dodgers than Davis' 2,091, and only Maury Wills and Davey Lopes have stolen more bases than his 335. Davis ranks second in triples (110), trailing only Hall of Famer Zack Wheat; fourth in extra-base hits (585) and total bases (3,094); and sixth in doubles (321). He hit 154 home runs and drove in 849 runs as a Dodger. Davis was traded to the Montreal Expos in 1974 for relief pitcher Mike Marshall, then went on to play for the Texas Rangers, St. Louis Cardinals, San Diego Padres, the Japanese League, and finally ended his career in 1979 with the California Angels.

six of Danny Ozark's Phillies to face him in a game at Philadelphia.

For the All-Star Game that year, the Dodgers were represented by six players—Don Sutton, Claude Osteen, Jim Brewer, Manny Mota, Willie Davis, and Bill Russell—the most since 1954 when the Brooklyners contributed Jackie Robinson, Duke Snider, Pee Wee Reese, Roy Campanella, Gil Hodges, and Carl Erskine. (Incidentally, that 1954 NL All-Star squad was managed by Walt Alston, then in his very first year as Dodgers manager.)

But alas, after the All-Star break, the Dodgers' fortunes went into a dreadful decline. Their lead gradually shrank through the rest of July and August, then rose to four games just before September to rekindle a little hope, but it turned out to be a last gasp. After that the Dodgers launched a losing streak that began on the last day of August and carried through nine games. It was a mortal blow to their divisional aspirations. The Cincinnati Reds took over first place on September 4 and did not give it up for the remainder of the season. The Dodgers dropped as far as six and one-half games behind them and finally rose to three and one-half by season's end.

When it was all over, the Dodgers had a record of 95–66, by far their best performance since their pennant-winning year in 1966. Although they had faded after the All-Star break, during that period they had still won 32 games while losing only 29. Walt Alston summed it up best after the season: "We didn't blow it. We didn't even play what you could call bad ball. You have to remember the Reds put on some kind of a show, they won 60 of their

In 1973 Ron "Penguin" Cey took over third base, the most transient position in L.A. Dodgers history. Before Cey nailed it down, 4 different players had at one time or another played the keystone sack for the Dodgers since they moved to L.A. in 1958. His first full year he also established himself as a competent power-hitter, belting 15 homers, but he batted only .245.

MAURY WILLS:
BASE THIEF
EXTRAORDINAIRE

It had been said for years in baseball circles that Ty Cobb's record of 96 base thefts in a single season was one of those "unbreakable" records, a mark that would stand forever. Someone must have forgotten to tell Maury Wills because he astonished everyone in 1962 when he demolished the mark by stealing 104 bases. That same year he was named the National League's Most Valuable Player.

It was an amazing feat for a ballplayer who did not make it to the major leagues until he was 26, a veteran of eight years in the minor leagues. Wills came to the majors in 1959, and the very next year took over the starting shortstop position and stole 50 bases, the most in the National League. He led the league in base thefts for six straight years (1960–1965).

Wills went to six All-Star Games in his 11 years with the Dodgers, and twice won the Gold Glove award for fielding prowess. During his 14 years in the major leagues, he played 1,942 games and posted a career batting average of .281. His best years at the plate were 1963 and 1967; he hit .302 in each.

Maury Wills, however, will best be remembered for his daring and dazzling feats on the base paths. Besides capturing Cobbs' 47-year-old single-season record, Wills stole a career total of 586 bases. Only seven players in the history of the game at that time could claim more thefts. John Lardner in *Newsweek* magazine called him a "base runner with style," with "grace and method and a sudden acceleration that was breathtaking." He was indeed like a thoroughbred racing the base paths, and he will always be remembered right along with Lou Brock, Ty Cobb, Eddie Collins, and Honus Wagner.

As a Los Angeles Dodger, he is the all-time top base stealer. But he also ranks second in runs scored (876), hits (1,739), and triples (56), bested only by Willie Davis in each of those categories. Wills ranks third in total bases with 2,045. His Los Angeles Dodgers lifetime batting average is .281.

A new double-play combination takes over in 1973: second baseman Davey Lopes (No. 15) and shortstop Bill Russell (No. 18).

last 86 games." The Reds had indeed played at a level just a few percentage points below .700 and had simply overwhelmed all other teams for the 1973 division crown.

The Dodgers pitching staff had performed well. Their collective ERA of 3.00 was the best in the major leagues that year. Tommy John's won-lost percentage of .696 (16–7) was tops in the National League, but it was Don Sutton who led the corps with a record of 18–10. His ERA of 2.42 was second only to the Mets' Tom Seaver (2.08) for pitchers who had worked 150 innings or more. And the Newspaper Enterprise Association, which took a poll among major league players after the season, named Sutton as one of the five best pitchers in the major leagues. Claude Osteen also had a respectable record of 16–11, and Andy Messersmith won 14 while losing 10. Jim Brewer

Charlie Hough found work in the Dodgers bullpen in 1973 and would become one of the team's steadiest relievers over the next seven seasons. His best years would be 1976 and 1977, when he would be credited with 18 and 22 saves, respectively. (In 1976 he also posted a 12–8 record, the best of his career.)

Willie Crawford makes a spectacular backhanded catch of a fast-falling fly ball in a 1973 game. Also racing for it is Steve Garvey, who had just broken into the Dodgers' regular lineup. Crawford played through the 1975 season, ending a 12-year Dodgers career when he went to the St. Louis Cardinals. His best years at bat were 1973 and 1974; he hit .295 both years.

saved 20 games, apparently not hampered by the arm surgery he underwent before the season. In five years, Brewer had averaged more than 20 saves a season.

In the hitting department, the 1973 Dodgers were up in every category. Compared to 1972, the team batting average improved by 7 percentage points and the slugging average by 11. The club produced 91 more runs and 124 more hits and increased its home-run total from 98 to 110.

There were only two .300 hitters, however—the always-consistent Manny Mota (.314) and the young Steve Garvey (.304). In his 30 appearances as a pinch-hitter, Garvey had come through with a .400 average. Catcher Joe Ferguson led the team in homers with 25 and in RBIs with 88, despite missing 18 days of the season with a fractured thumb. Davey Lopes was the team's most productive base thief with 36 steals.

It had been a good year. The inexperienced players had picked up some valuable experience. There was every reason to look forward to the 1974 season. And no one was more optimistic than Walt Alston. Looking back over 20 years as mentor of the Dodgers, all the way to Brooklyn and Ebbets Field, he said as he stowed his uniform away until the next year: "This team has it. They have great potential. With just a little help here and there they may become the single best Dodger team I've ever had."

Willie Davis dives head-first for home plate here to score his 1,000th run in the major leagues. The catcher in this 1973 game is the Montreal Expos' Bob Stinson. It was Davis' last year with the Dodgers, marking the end of a 14-year career in L.A. There were some memorable achievements during that period: the 21 homers and 103 runs scored in 1962, the .311 he hit in 1969, the 38 bases he stole and 16 triples he hit in 1970, and the Gold Gloves he won in 1972 and 1973.

CHAPTER 13

THE BABES OF SUMMER

This is the scene of one of baseball's most historic blasts. At Atlanta Stadium April 8, 1974, Hank Aaron strokes his 715th career home run to break the career record of Babe Ruth. Dodgers pitcher Al Downing has the unprized distinction of serving up the pitch that Aaron drove into the left-field bullpen. A crowd of 53,775 had gathered that day in expectation of Aaron's moment of glory—and this is it.

FOR THOSE WHO WANTED A RESPITE from Watergate and the manifold dilemmas of Richard Nixon in 1974, the baseball season would offer many diversions and a few historic moments of its own. Californians would be especially blessed. They would be treated to an intrastate World Series for the first time ever. The Golden State would produce two pennant winners, one from Los Angeles and the other from Oakland. And for the Angels in Anaheim, Nolan Ryan would hurl his third no-hitter and in another nine-inning game, strike out 19 batters to tie the modern major league record held jointly by Steve Carlton and Tom Seaver. In each of two other extra-inning games, he would also fan 19 batters. Up north, Oakland owner Charley Finley would continue to enrage players and fans alike by refusing to leave the management of his team to his manager, prompting sportswriters to describe him as Svengalian and megalomaniacal.

Elsewhere, Hank Aaron of the Braves would take a fastball from the Dodgers' Al Downing and drive it into the seats of Atlanta Stadium to break Babe Ruth's career home-run record of 714. Al Kaline, in his 22nd and last year as a Detroit Tiger, would become the 15th major league player in history to collect 3,000 hits. Lou Brock of the St. Louis Cardinals would race off with 118 stolen bases, breaking the previous single-season base-theft record of 104 held by Maury Wills since 1962. Frank Robinson, after the season, would be hired by the Cleveland Indians to become the first black manager in the history of major league baseball. And former Yankees Mickey Mantle and Whitey Ford would be inducted into the Hall of Fame at Cooperstown.

The "Babes of Summer," as Frank Finch of the *Los Angeles Times* had dubbed them—adapting Roger Kahn's title for another Dodgers team of another time—arrived at Vero Beach full of hope and confidence. Their announced goal for the year: to wreak vengeance on the Big Red Machine, that smoothly oiled, consistently brilliant group of ballplayers from Cincinnati who had dominated their division for three of the previous four years and had so unpleasantly wrested what seemed like a sure division crown from the Dodgers in the last half of the 1973 season.

To strengthen the young team, the Dodgers front office made two especially lucrative trades in the winter. First, they acquired ace relief pitcher Mike Marshall from the Montreal Expos for 34-year-old Willie Davis. Marshall had led the league in 1973 with 31 saves and had appeared in a record 92 games. The plan was for him to join Jim Brewer in the bullpen to provide one of the most potent relief tandems in the game. The next day, to replace Davis in the outfield, the Dodgers sent veteran pitcher

Power-hitter Jimmy Wynn came to the Dodgers in 1974 after 11 years with the Houston Astros. To obtain him, the Dodgers had to give up pitcher Claude Osteen. But Wynn justified the cost the very first year by cracking 32 home runs, the most any Dodger had hit since the franchise was moved to L.A. He also drove in 108 runs and scored 104 himself, both club highs. This hit is one of those 32 round-trippers of 1974. The catcher is the Cincinnati Reds' legendary Johnny Bench, who hit 33 home runs himself that year.

Claude Osteen to the Houston Astros for slugging outfielder Jimmy "Toy Cannon" Wynn. In his 11 years down in Texas, Wynn had blasted 223 home runs, including a memorable 1967 season when he whacked 37 four-baggers and drove in 107 runs.

With such a strong bullpen corps, the Dodgers were not as worried about using only three principal starters as they might otherwise have been. The regular rotation was to be entrusted to Don Sutton, Tommy John, and Andy Messersmith, with Al Downing, Doug Rau, and Geoff Zahn making sporadic appearances to ease their burden.

Doug Rau moved into the regular rotation in 1974 after having toiled sparingly on the staff for the two previous seasons. He won 13 games in 1974 and would win in double figures each subsequent year through 1978, after which he injured his shoulder. His winningest year was 1976, when he racked up 16 against 12 defeats.

Bill Buckner had his best year on the base paths in 1974, swiping 31 bases. This is one of them, lifted against the San Diego Padres. Leaping above him is shortstop Enzo Hernandez. Buckner also hit .314 that year, highest on the team, and his second best effort as a Dodger.

The infield that had played together much of the season before would cement itself in 1974 so solidly that it would remain intact all the way into the eighties. Steve Garvey took full-time possession of first base, and his partner there from the year before, Bill Buckner, shifted all his efforts to the outfield. Davey Lopes now handled second base and Bill Russell took shortstop. And Ron Cey staked a claim at third base.

Along with Buckner and Wynn in the outfield was Willie Crawford and occasionally Tom Paciorek. The catching chores were to be divided almost equally between Joe Ferguson and Steve Yeager. Manny Mota, now 36, served chiefly as a pinch-hitter.

Perhaps as a harbinger of what was to come, the Dodgers turned in their best spring-training

record since moving to Los Angeles, winning 17 of 24 encounters.

They carried that kind of play right along into the regular season. Opening at home, the "Big Three"—Sutton, John, and Messersmith—set the San Diego Padres down one after the other on three consecutive days. Each Dodger pitcher completed his game, backed by some awesome hitting. The scores: 8–0, 8–0, 9–2.

The Dodgers' first loss of the year came with the game in which Hank Aaron delivered his record-setting 715th career home run. But their losses were few. By the end of April, the Dodgers had compiled a record of 17–6, which included a seven-game winning streak, and they were comfortably in first place by four and one-half games. They had met the Big Red Machine twice in Cincinnati, eking out a 5–3 extra-inning win in the first game and then humiliating their now archrivals 14–1 the next day. Tommy John built a record of 5–0, and Don Sutton was at 4–1. Mike

One player who had an immediate and far-reaching impact on the Dodgers of 1974 was reliever Mike Marshall. He had come from the Montreal Expos in exchange for Willie Davis and not only became the club's ace fireman, but set four major league season records in the process—most appearances (106), most innings pitched in relief (208.1), most games finished (83), and consecutive games pitched (13). He was credited with 21 saves (the most in the NL), a record of 15–12, and an ERA of 2.42—and Marshall became the first relief pitcher ever to win the Cy Young Award. He was also named NL pitcher of the year by The Sporting News.

Marshall was proving to be every bit the fireman he was cracked up to be, and equally outstanding was Jim Brewer, who had toted up a record of 4–1 by May 1 and had yielded only one earned run in his first four games.

The Dodgers continued to roar through May. By midmonth they had put together a nine-game winning streak that would prove to be the longest of the year. By June 1 they were a full eight games ahead of the nearest contender and had an outstanding record of 37–14. They were playing at a .725 clip, and the former champion Cincinnati Reds were rubbing Dodgers dust out of their amazed eyes.

Just about everybody was hitting well. Jimmy Wynn had hit three home runs in one game during May to tie the Los Angeles all-time record. And by the 20th of the month, Wynn was leading both leagues in home runs (12) and RBIs (37). Steve Garvey was also among the NL top 10 in homers with eight. On the first day of June, Ron Cey set another club record when he drove in seven runs in a single game (a record he would break before the season was out), as the Dodgers annihilated the Chicago Cubs 10–0.

Some troubles were developing in the pitching ranks, however. Jim Brewer was having back problems,

Davey Lopes, beating a throw to third here, quickly established himself as one of the game's most devastating base bandits. In 1974 he stole 59 bases, second that year to Lou Brock, who set the all-time standard by snatching 118.

which unfortunately were destined to get much worse as the season progressed. And Don Sutton had somehow lost his usual picture-perfect control during the month of May; he was now losing start after start. On the other hand, Tommy John had blossomed into the league's leading pitcher by June 1, boasting a record of 8–1.

Sportswriters began calling Mike Marshall "Iron Mike" in June because of the numerous relief appearances he was making for the Dodgers. By the end of the month, he managed to establish a major league record by pitching in 13 consecutive Dodgers games, smashing the old record of 8.

The Dodgers also dominated most of the hitting statistics in June. Both Steve Garvey and Bill Buckner were among the league's top 10 hitters with averages above .320. Wynn was the game's leading home-run hitter, and he and Garvey headed the NL's RBI list.

The Dodgers continued to play impressive baseball all the way to the All-Star break. Their record of 63–34 (.649) was fine, but more astounding was the fact that in the nine games that they had faced the reigning division champions, the Reds, they had won eight of them. But several jolts to their pitching staff just before the midseason intermission

The present meets the past: at the "Old Timers" game in 1974 at Dodger Stadium, L.A. pitcher Andy Messersmith (left) jokes with one-time Brooklyn hurler Ralph Branca.

threatened the team to its very core. Tommy John, who had compiled the best record in the league (13–3), ruptured a ligament in the elbow of his throwing arm and was out for the rest of the season. This was especially dire in view of the fact that Don Sutton was still in a game-killing slump and in the process of completing a six-game losing streak. Doug Rau, a 25-year-old left-hander who had come up from the Dodgers farm system two years earlier, was chosen to fill John's slot in the regular rotation. At the same time, Jim Brewer's back grew worse and the Dodgers were to lose his services from July 15 through mid-September.

The Dodgers sent five players to the All-Star Game that year, and one of them, Steve Garvey, was a write-in candidate. The others were Ron Cey, Jimmy Wynn, Mike Marshall, and Andy Messersmith. (Messersmith had improved his record to 11–2 just before the All-Star Game.) As it turned out, Garvey, snubbed by the slaters but appreciated by the voting fans, was the only National Leaguer to play all nine innings. He rapped out two hits in four at-bats and was named the game's Most Valuable Player.

The loss of Tommy John, as it turned out, would not be as disastrous as most Dodgers observers feared, because Don Sutton regained his pitching poise after the All-Star break as suddenly and as thoroughly as he had lost it two months earlier. He won four straight, then dropped one at Pittsburgh to the Pirates. From there, he won nine in a row as the Dodgers barreled toward the division championship.

Throughout the second half of the season, manager Walt Alston urged the team to remember what had happened the year before in the stretch run: the Reds had come on like a California brush fire, scorching everything in their path, including a high-flying Dodgers team. He told them that their destiny was flatly in their own hands. If they kept winning, especially those crucial games against the Reds, they would go to the NL playoffs. If they did not, they would undoubtedly suffer the same fate they had when the season resumed after the All-Star break of 1973. The Dodgers took their manager's words to heart, at least during the first two weeks of the season's second half. They won 10 of their first 13 games, including 8 consecutive wins, their second longest streak of the year. In one of those games, when the Dodgers were stomping the San Diego Padres 15–4, Ron Cey broke his own two-month-old club record for RBIs in a single game by driving in eight runs.

At the end of that streak, the Dodgers had extended their lead to seven and one-half games. The eighth victory was especially nice; they beat the Reds in the first of a three-game series at Dodger Stadium. But then they faltered; the Reds won the next two. The Dodgers went on to drop seven of their next nine games, and their hold on first place was reduced to two and one-half games. The six-game losing streak they experienced in that period was the longest of the year, although they had managed to post an 18–8 win over the Cubs at Wrigley Field in Chicago, a game in which Davey Lopes hit three home runs. The Dodgers got a total of 24 hits that day (including six home

The 1973 Dodgers staff: (from left) standing, Red Adams, Walt Alston, and Junior Gilliam; kneeling, Monty Basgall and Tommy Lasorda.

runs), and the 48 total bases they accounted for was a Los Angeles Dodgers record.

As dim as that section of the season was, the nadir did not come until midway through September, when the Dodgers lost the first two of three games to the Reds, again at Dodger Stadium, and saw their lead cut to a mere one and one-half games. Walt Alston's worst fears seemed to be rapidly becoming reality. But they were ill-founded; 1974 was not to be a repeat of 1973. Don Sutton faced the Reds the next day and held them to a run, while the "Big *Blue* Machine" sent seven runs across the plate. The Dodgers then wound their way through the last 17 games of the season, winning 10 and gradually building their division

lead back to 4 games, where it stood at the end of the regular season on October 2.

The Dodgers' record for 1974, 102–60 (.630), was the best since the Brooklyners of 1953 won 105 games and lost 49 (.682). In fact, there were only two other years since 1890 when a Dodgers team had won as many or more games (104 in 1942 and 102 in 1962).

The Babes of Summer had done just about everything right in that delightful year of 1974. The 798 runs they scored were the most in either league, as were their 139 home runs, their 744 RBIs, and their slugging average of .401. The same sort of impressive statistics were recorded by the Dodgers pitching staff. Their collective ERA of 2.97 was the league's best and was only two percentage points short of the American League standard registered by the pennant-winning Oakland A's pitchers. And Dodgers hurlers also struck out 943 batters, the most in the NL that year.

Young Steve Garvey, 25, was named the league's Most Valuable Player for 1974, the first time a Dodger had been awarded that honor since Sandy Koufax in 1963. Garvey earned it with a batting average of .312, 200 hits, 21 home runs, and 111 RBIs. Since the club had come to Los Angeles only two other Dodgers had rapped out more than 200 hits (Tommy Davis, 230, and Maury Wills, 208, both in 1962). Garvey also led the team in doubles with 32 and posted a slugging average of .469. His near-flawless fielding won him the NL Gold Glove award that year as well.

But perhaps the most staggering of the year's performances was the one turned in by Iron Mike Marshall. He shattered the major league record for most appearances in relief by pitching in 106 games, 14 more than the record 92 he had appeared in the year before. His 21 saves were the most in the National League, his ERA of 2.42 was among the very best posted that year, and his record was 15–12. He became the first Dodger to win the NL Cy Young Award since Sandy Koufax in 1966.

Bill Buckner gets a few words of advice in the Dodgers dugout from longtime fan Jack Benny.

Steve Garvey joyfully crosses home plate after driving one out of the park—one of two he hit that day—in the last game of the 1974 NL championship series. Jimmy Wynn is ready to give him a double-five as Pittsburgh Pirates catcher Manny Sanguillen looks away. The Dodgers decimated the Pirates that day, 12–1, earning their way to the World Series by defeating the Pirates in three of four games.

Davey Lopes easily cuts down Pirate Rennie Stennett and throws to first for a double play in the 1974 NL championship series.

Dodgers third baseman Ron Cey simply waits for another Pirates base runner, Al Oliver, to slide into his tag. These plays were indicative of the Pirates' destiny in the NL pennant playoffs; the Dodgers won easily, three games out of four.

Other Dodgers also offered a bounty of fine performances. Jimmy Wynn had contributed the power Walt Alston had so much wanted and turned in one of the best seasons of his career. His 32 home runs, 104 runs scored, .497 slugging average, and 108 walks were all club highs, and his 108 RBIs were second only to Steve Garvey's 111. Bill Buckner took the team's batting crown with an average of .314.

Andy Messersmith ended the season with the best record (20–6) for the Dodgers and an ERA of 2.59, his finest year so far in the majors (he had won 20 for the Angels in 1971, but had lost 13 and posted an ERA .24 higher). Don Sutton redeemed himself with a spirited 13 wins in his last 14 decisions and closed out the year at 19–9. Tommy John's won-lost percentage of .813 (13–3) was the best in the majors, and there was a lot of Monday-morning speculation as to how good a season he might have had, had he not been sidelined in mid-July. Doug Rau had pitched exceptionally well in the early season but had run into some trouble later on, winning only one of his last twelve starts. Still, he came up with a respectable 13–11 in his first season as a regular starter.

Between the Dodgers and the National League pennant, however, still stood the Pittsburgh Pirates. Under the tutelage of Danny Murtaugh, the Pirates had won 88 games and lost 74, just barely beating out the St. Louis Cardinals for the NL East crown by one and one-half games. The Pirates lineup was stacked with power. Foremost, of course, was Willie Stargell, the only batter at that time ever to hit a ball *out* of Dodger Stadium. But there were also Richie Zisk, Al Oliver, Richie Hebner, and Bob Robertson. The pitching staff that year was headed by Dodger-to-be Jerry Reuss (16–11) and Jim Rooker (15–11), but other Pirates stalwarts, Dock Ellis and Ken Brett, had been hampered by injuries much of the year.

The playoff opened at Three Rivers Stadium in the famous city of steel mills, with Don Sutton on the mound for the Dodgers and Jerry Reuss for the

Two of the game's great base runners have a fleeting confrontation here in the 1974 World Series. Dodgers second baseman Davey Lopes tries unsuccessfully to put a tag on the Oakland A's Billy North. North led the AL in base thefts that year with 54. Lopes stole 59 himself in the NL. North would join the Dodgers in 1978 and steal 27 bases for them before moving on to the San Francisco Giants.

Pirates. Sutton was obviously ready, allowing a paltry four hits and shutting Pittsburgh out 3–0. The Dodgers made it a pair the next day. This time Andy Messersmith held the Pirates to two runs through seven innings, and Mike Marshall blanked them in the last two. Ron Cey whacked four hits, including a home run, to give the Dodgers a 5–2 victory.

Back in Los Angeles, however, the Dodgers seemed unaware of their home-field advantage. Young Pirates right-hander Bruce Kison gave up only four hits and denied the Dodgers a single run. The revived Pirates offense, with homers from Willie Stargell and Richie Hebner, scored five runs in the first and two more in the third for the 7–0 rout.

But Game 4 was not even a contest. Don Sutton made his second appearance of the series for Los Angeles, and once again he turned in a remarkable performance. He went the distance and gave up only three hits and a solitary run. The explosive Dodgers bats produced a total of 12 hits and 12 runs that day. The most outstanding batter among so many was Steve Garvey, who contributed two home runs as part of his four-hit day. And so the Dodgers gave Los Angeles its fifth National League pennant, Walt Alston his seventh as club manager, and the organization the fourteenth in its 85-year history.

The Oakland A's, that notorious congregation dressed in green-and-gold and mothered autocratically by Charles O. Finley, had won the American League West for the fourth consecutive year and the AL pennant for the third time in those four years. They had also claimed the world championship for the past two years in a row. Finley had hired a new manager in 1974 after Dick Williams had quit at the end of the preceding World Series because of Finley's interference with the team's operation on the field. Alvin Dark, the onetime great shortstop for the New York Giants, had taken over and led the A's to a relatively easy division

Joe Ferguson has just finished a trip around the bases after blasting a 400-foot homer in Game 2 of the 1974 World Series. The two-run shot made the difference in the Dodgers' 3–2 victory, and it enabled them to tie the Series at a game apiece. Congratulating Ferguson is Steve Garvey, who scored ahead of him, and looking on disconsolately is Oakland A's catcher Ray Fosse.

WORLD SERIES LINEUPS, 1974

DODGERS	A'S
Davey Lopes, 2b	Bert Campaneris, ss
Bill Buckner, lf	Bill North, cf
Jimmy Wynn, cf	Sal Bando, 3b
Steve Garvey, 1b	Reggie Jackson, rf
Joe Ferguson, rf	Joe Rudi, lf
Ron Cey, 3b	Gene Tenace, 1b
Bill Russell, ss	Ray Fosse, c
Steve Yeager, c	Dick Green, 2b

STARTING PITCHERS
Game 1: Andy Messersmith, Ken Holtzman
Game 2: Don Sutton, Vida Blue
Game 3: Al Downing, Catfish Hunter
Game 4: Andy Messersmith, Ken Holtzman
Game 5: Don Sutton, Vida Blue

crown (90–72, five games ahead of the Texas Rangers) and then through a four-game playoff victory over the Baltimore Orioles.

The A's had a jewel box lineup. There were sluggers like Reggie Jackson, Gene Tenace, Joe Rudi, Sal Bando, and Deron Johnson. They had base-running speedsters Billy North, Bert Campaneris, and Herb Washington, who was not originally a baseball player but a world-class sprinter whom Charley Finley had brought to the big leagues as, in his words, a "designated base runner." They had three of the league's most consistently good starting pitchers—Catfish Hunter (25–12), Ken Holtzman (19–17), and Vida Blue (17–15)—and Rollie Fingers in the bullpen (18 saves in 76 appearances).

The bookmakers gave the Dodgers a hairbreadth edge over the A's, perhaps because of the turmoil that had seethed within the Oakland team and its front office. Not everyone agreed with the oddsmakers, however. Ron Fimrite suggested just the opposite in *Sports Illustrated*: "This [Oakland] is a team nourished by adversity." And adversity they had—two highly publicized locker room fights, the first between outfielders Reggie Jackson

BANTER AT THE WORLD SERIES, 1974

Ron Fimrite in *Sports Illustrated*: So now the game, long criticized as a slave to tradition, gives us its first all-California World Series. . . . Tradition will hardly suffer from the encounter between the Los Angeles Dodgers and the Oakland A's, for Northern and Southern California have a long and honorable history of mutual animosity.

Bill Buckner: I definitely think we have a better ballclub. The A's have only a couple of players who could make our club. (The statement incited Oakland fans to bombard him in left field during Game 5 with an assortment of artillery that ranged from beer cans and garbage to Frisbees.)

A's Pitcher Ken Holtzman: Team spirit doesn't apply here. This isn't the college world series. With twenty-seven thousand bucks on the line, I hate everybody.

Roger Angell in *The New Yorker*: Charles O. Finley, it must be added, did not fail to intrude himself into the proceedings. During that third game, we could all watch him leading the hometown hordes in banner-waving, or, up on his feet, joining in the fervent singing of "God Bless America" during the seventh-inning stretch. Then, too, the public address system announced that Mr. Finley himself could be observed in his box, next to the Oakland dugout, in the very act of placing a call to President Ford, in which he invited him to come and throw out the first ball at one of the remaining Series games. The President said sorry, he was busy but thanks anyway, and moments later we watched Charley calling up ex-President Nixon in San Clemente—with the same result.

and Bill North, the second between pitchers Rollie Fingers and Blue Moon Odom. Charley Finley was battling a $2.5-million lawsuit from former A's infielder Mike Andrews, whom Finley had declared physically unfit to play in the preceding World Series. Catfish Hunter was hinting that he might desert the team because Finley had not paid half of his $100,000 salary that year. First baseman Gene Tenace was asking to be traded and would declare to the press that his team owner used manager Alvin Dark as "nothing more than a puppet." And third baseman Sal Bando would publicly say

to his manager, "You couldn't manage a meat market." Things were far from stable in Oakland.

At the other end of the baseball spectrum were the Dodgers—youthful, clean-cut, with what *Time* magazine called "a Jack Armstrong image," they were a team tightly bound together. There was no public squabbling, no rantings of discontent, just a lot of college-boy spirit and high-five hand slapping.

The Dodgers played host for the first two games. Almost fifty-six thousand spectators, including such celebrities as Cary Grant, Liza Minnelli, and Walter Matthau, set a Dodger Stadium record for the Series opener when they came to watch Andy Messersmith duel with the A's Ken Holtzman.

Messersmith gave up a solo home run to Reggie Jackson in the second inning. Then Holtzman helped his own cause by lacing a double to left in the fifth inning, racing to third on a Messersmith wild pitch, and then scoring on a suicide squeeze bunt by Bert Campaneris.

The Dodgers countered in the bottom of that inning, during which Rollie Fingers replaced Holtzman. Davey Lopes got on when Campaneris couldn't handle his ground ball. Bill Buckner followed with a single to right, which Reggie Jackson then muffed, allowing the fleet Lopes to sprint all the way home. That, however, was the extent of their scoring until the ninth inning.

In the eighth, Campaneris got on for the A's with a single, went to second on a sacrifice, and scored when Ron Cey threw a routine ground-out beyond the reach of Steve Garvey. In the bottom of the ninth, with two outs, Jimmy Wynn belted one out of the park to bring the Dodgers within a run of the A's. Steve Garvey followed with a single to right, and that was all for Rollie Fingers. But Catfish Hunter came in to face Joe Ferguson and struck him out to preserve the A's 3–2 win.

The score was reversed the next afternoon. Don Sutton allowed only five hits and was rescued in the ninth by Mike Marshall. The Dodgers led all the way through their 3–2 triumph. Ron Cey scored the first run in the second inning after working starter Vida

Despite his lack of baseball experience, former world-class sprinter Herb Washington was hired by Charley Finley as a "designated runner." His most inglorious moment in the majors is shown here in a scene from the 1974 World Series. Brought in to pinch run in the top of the ninth with the A's down a run, Washington represented the tying run. But Dodgers pitcher Mike Marshall deftly picked him off. Steve Garvey is shown here putting the tag on an embarrassed Washington. The Dodgers won 3–2.

A bone-jarring collision in the 1974 World Series: Sal Bando of the Oakland A's tries to run over Dodgers catcher Steve Yeager, who loses his mask and helmet but somehow manages to hold on to the ball for the out. The Dodgers were able to win only one game in the Series of 1974.

Blue for a base on balls, which was followed by two successive singles from Bill Russell and Steve Yeager. Joe Ferguson clinched it in the sixth when he sent a towering home run over the center-field wall that scored Steve Garvey ahead of him. Don Sutton held the A's scoreless into the eighth inning. But suddenly the A's threatened—the bases were loaded with one out, and the good-hitting, swift-running Bill North came to bat. He hit a hard grounder to Bill Russell, who stepped on second for the force out, then fired it into the dirt; Garvey rescued the double play and preserved Sutton's shutout by making a spectacular scoop-up.

In the ninth, Sutton ran into some more trouble, however. First, he hit Sal Bando with a pitch, then gave up a double to Reggie Jackson. Old faithful Mike Marshall replaced him on the Dodgers mound. But this time Marshall's magic was less than mystifying, at least to Joe Rudi, who promptly singled, scoring both Bando and Jackson. Marshall struck out the next batter, Gene Tenace. Herb Washington was sent in to run for Rudi, and Marshall, to the delight of Dodgers fans and the horror of Oakland followers, promptly picked him off first base for the second out. Then Marshall struck out Angel Mangual to preserve the narrow 3–2 Dodgers victory.

Up in Oakland, Al Downing got the call from Dodgers manager Walt Alston, primarily because young Doug Rau had been such a disappointment in the second half of the season. Catfish Hunter was the choice of A's manager Alvin Dark.

The A's, who had collected only 12 hits in the first two games (as opposed to the Dodgers' 17), had scored most of their runs on advantages that Los Angeles had given them. That special charm continued when the two teams moved up to San Francisco Bay. In the third inning of the first game there, Joe Ferguson made an error with two outs that would have retired the side but instead resulted in the A's first two runs. The A's added a run in the fourth inning on a walk, a sacrifice, and a single. The Dodgers came back in the eighth and the ninth with solo home runs from Bill Buckner and Willie Crawford, but the two runs were not enough.

For the third straight game, the final was 3–2, and now the fuming, feuding veterans from Oakland led the Series two games to one.

Andy Messersmith was back on the mound for the Dodgers in Game 4, and Ken Holtzman returned for the A's. Oakland took the lead in the third, 1–0, on a homer by Holtzman (he would bat .500 for the Series), but the Dodgers replied with two runs the following inning. But in the sixth inning disaster struck the Dodgers. Bill North worked Messersmith for a walk, then went to second when the Dodgers hurler threw the ball toward the Dodgers dugout in a pickoff attempt. Sal Bando singled North home and moved to second when Reggie Jackson got the inning's second base on balls. Joe Rudi sacrificed them to second and third. Pinch-hitter Jim Holt then singled the two runners in. The A's added another run before the inning was over—the four runs would prove to be the biggest inning of the Series. Mike Marshall replaced Messersmith and held the A's scoreless for the remainder of the game. Unfortunately for the Dodgers, Ken Holtzman, who went the distance, was equally stingy in the remaining three innings, and the final score was 5–2.

The Dodgers had to be disheartened by the string of mistakes and whims of fate that were dealing them out of the Series. And they couldn't change the course of events. As Roger Angell described it in *The New Yorker*:

> **The pattern continued right to the end—a pattern of little Dodger mistakes, nearly forgivable errors or youthful lapses in judgment, and deadly, coldly retributive winning play by the old and now doubly renewed champions. Rarely had any World Series offered so many plain lessons in winning baseball, or such an instructive moral drama about the uses of baseball luck and the precision with which experienced, opportunistic veterans can pry open a tough, gnarled closed-up game and extract from it the stuff of victory.**

And that is just how the Oakland A's did it in Game 5. In the first inning, Bill North, who had stolen 54 bases that year, got on base and, not unpredictably, broke for second. Dodgers catcher Steve Yeager threw the ball into center field and North circled on to third. Moments later he scored on Sal Bando's sacrifice fly to left field. The next inning Don Sutton fired a fastball he wished he hadn't to Ray Fosse, who sent it whistling into the left-field seats.

The Dodgers got both runs back in the sixth inning. Pinch-hitter Tom Paciorek tagged a double, moved to third, and scored on a sacrifice fly from the bat of Jimmy Wynn. Then, with a runner on second, Steve Garvey singled to drive in the tying run.

Mike Marshall came on for the Dodgers in the bottom of the sixth inning and suffered the terminal blow of the Series one inning later. There was an interruption in play when Oakland fans decided to rain garbage and other throwable items on Bill Buckner in left field, presumably because earlier in the Series he had made some disparaging remarks about their favorite ballclub. The groundskeepers had to be called out to clean up the mess. Baseball pundits everywhere have since wondered why Marshall did not throw any warm-up pitches during the extended interlude to keep his arm comfortably primed. Instead, he took to the rubber to face Joe Rudi with a "cold arm." And because of it, he hurled a fastball that was not all that fast. Rudi responded by hitting it square into the group of rowdy fans who had just peppered left field with their trash. The run gave the A's a 3–2 lead going into the eighth inning.

A flicker of hope flared for the Dodgers in the top of the eighth, but doused itself almost as quickly as it had appeared. Bill Buckner led off with a sharp single to center and the ball got away from Bill North. Buckner, representing the tying run, raced to second and into scoring position—but instead of holding up, he continued right on toward third. Meanwhile, Reggie Jackson had picked up the ball, and he rifled it to relay man Dick Green, who threw a perfect strike to Sal Bando. Buckner dove headfirst into third base, but Bando had the ball and put an easy tag on him. It was the final faux pas of the Series for the Dodgers. The A's won the game and the world championship, 3–2, the fourth such score in five games.

It was the A's third consecutive World Championship—only the New York Yankees had ever done that in the more than seven decades of the autumn spectacle. The result was surprising, however, in view of the Series stats. Oakland had a team batting average for the Series of only .211, 17 percentage points less than the Dodgers had. In five games, they had produced only 16 runs, 30 hits, and four home runs. Indeed, it seemed that the Dodgers, fallible and flawed after a spectacular year, had virtually made a gift of the Series to them.

The Dodgers totals were also dismaying. The six errors committed in the five games had all been crucial ones. The team hit a full 44 percentage points less than they had in the regular season. There were only two hitters who made their presence felt—Steve Garvey's .381 batting average and eight hits were tops for either team in the Series, and Steve Yeager got four hits in 11 trips to the plate for an average of .364. Mike Marshall appeared in all five games and produced an ERA of 1.00, the Series best, but he would not soon forget that lone earned run he gave to Joe Rudi in the seventh inning of Game 5.

It was the first World Series for the youthful starters of the 1974 Dodgers, but most of them would be back in Dodger Blue for other World Series just a few years down the line.

CHAPTER 14

THEN CAME THE REDS

Dodgers pitcher Don Sutton mugs before the 1975 All-Star Game in Milwaukee with Nancy and Henry Kissinger and baseball commissioner Bowie Kuhn. Sutton was one of seven Dodgers selected for the midseason classic, the largest contingent to represent the club since the famous Brooklyn Dodgers of 1954. The other six were manager Walt Alston, Ron Cey, Steve Garvey, Mike Marshall, Andy Messersmith, and Jimmy Wynn.

THE DODGERS OF 1975 had the prestige of possessing the National League pennant from the year before, which they had won with explosive hitting and consistently good pitching. Still, few of the game's closest observers predicted that the youngsters from Los Angeles would repeat. Many,

in fact, felt strongly that they would not be able to hold off the Big Red Machine, although no one suspected just how awesome Sparky Anderson's Cincinnati Reds would be that year.

In 1975 Walt Alston was planning to field a team practically identical to the one that he had in

163

1974. Tommy John, however, was still unable to pitch because of his injured elbow and would not be around at all that season. So Al Campanis brought on board a big right-hander who was a surprise to everybody—the old Dodgers destroyer, Juan Marichal, then 37 and remembered joylessly in Los Angeles as the Giant who so often defeated the Dodgers (37 times in his 14 years with San Francisco) and who once ignobly smashed his bat into the head of Dodgers catcher John Roseboro. But Marichal's effective pitching days were really over. He would start two games for the Dodgers that year, be credited with the loss of one, register an ERA of 13.50, and then retire before the season was two weeks old.

The Dodgers got a little taste of what the season was going to be like with the opening series of the year. They dropped each of their first three games at Cincinnati by a single run. By the end of April, though, the Dodgers had fought their way back and moved into first place, mostly behind the hitting of Steve Garvey (.374 and 17 RBIs in April) and Ron Cey (six home runs, the most in the majors at that point), and the mound performances of Andy Messersmith (4–0) and Don Sutton (4–1).

The Dodgers soon acquired a much-needed starter from the Chicago Cubs—25-year-old right-hander Burt Hooton. The Cubs were willing to give him up for two Dodgers minor league pitchers, Eddie Solomon and Geoff Zahn. One newspaper sports headline read: THE GREAT ARM ROBBERY— which certainly proved, over the years, to be prophetic.

If the month of May was any barometer, then the predictors of Cincinnati domination seemed to have cockeyed crystal balls. The Dodgers maintained control of the division lead throughout the month and were ahead by as much as five and one-half games at one point. By the end of the month they had a record of 30–20.

But it was also the month when fate began to take some nasty swipes at the Dodgers. First, ace reliever Mike Marshall was sidelined with a rib

injury. Then Bill Russell was forced to the dugout with a broken bone in his hand and would come back later only to hurt his knee. Bill Buckner injured his ankle, and Jimmy Wynn would miss a number of games with a variety of minor injuries. All the while the Big Red Machine was edging closer, relentlessly chipping away at the Dodgers' lead. They would take it over at the end of the first week of June.

On June 3, Don Sutton racked up his 10th win of the season, the most in either league, and both Garvey and Cey continued to hit with power (both were among the NL top 10 in home runs and RBIs). Cincinnati, however, just kept winning—at one point in midseason they had won 41 of 50 games. By the All-Star break in July, the Reds had built a 12½ game lead over the Dodgers.

In 1975 Walt Alston managed the National League team in the All-Star Game for the eighth time. The Dodgers players selected were Ron Cey, Steve Garvey, Don Sutton, Andy Messersmith, Jimmy Wynn, and Mike Marshall. During the game, Steve Garvey and Jimmy Wynn became the first National Leaguers in the history of that contest to hit back-to-back home runs; their feat helped Walt Alston to a 6–3 win over the American League.

A week later at Dodger Stadium against the St. Louis Cardinals, Dodgers batters Willie Crawford and Lee Lacy combined for a similar act, with an added twist—their back-to-back round-trippers were both pinch-hits.

After the All-Star break, the Reds continued their inexorable drive toward the division championship. Although the Dodgers were never really in the pennant race since they had dropped into second place in early June, there were some memorable performances along the way. Davey Lopes was the league's most exciting base runner. On August 9, in a game against the Mets in New York, he broke the major league record for consecutive successful stolen bases when he purloined his 32nd. Lopes continued the string of thieveries through 38

A new major league record is logged August 9, 1975, as Davey Lopes dives into third to successfully steal his 32nd consecutive base, breaking the mark of 31 set by Max Carey of the Pirates back in 1922. Lopes would extend his streak to 38 that year and end the season with a grand total of 77 base thefts, the most in the majors and his career high. The New York Met is third baseman Wayne Garrett.

and racked up a total of 77 for the year, the most in either league.

Burt Hooton became the first Los Angeles starting pitcher in history to win 12 straight games, breaking the record of 11 held jointly by Sandy Koufax and Don Drysdale. The record for any Dodgers pitcher—starter or reliever, Brooklyn or Los Angeles—is the 15 straight wins produced by Dazzy Vance in 1924; and the record then for any Los Angeles pitcher was 13, set by fireman Phil Regan in 1966.

When the season finally ended, the Reds were a full 20 games ahead of the second-place Dodgers. Not since 1906, when the Chicago Cubs won the pennant by a 20-game margin over the New York Giants, had a major league baseball team won by so many games. The Big Red Machine's 108 victories in 1975 were the most won in the National League since the 1906 Cubs won 116. And only four teams in the American League had ever won more: Miller Huggins' Yankees, 110 in 1927 (the year Babe Ruth hit 60 home runs and 164 RBIs, and Lou Gehrig 47 and 175); Al Lopez's Cleveland Indians, 111 in

1954; Ralph Houk's Yankees, 109 in 1961; and Earl Weaver's Baltimore Orioles, 109 in 1969.

The Reds of 1975 had four .300 hitters—Joe Morgan, .327; Pete Rose, .317; Ken Griffey Sr., .305; and George Foster, .300. Morgan also stole 67 bases, led the major leagues in walks with 132, and was the National League's MVP. The Cincinnati pitching staff had six starters with 10 or more wins, all with winning records. In the bullpen they had Rawly Eastwick, who led the league in saves with 22, and Will McEnaney, who saved another 15. This near-perfect Cincinnati team went on to destroy the NL East champion Pittsburgh Pirates in three straight playoff games, and then take the best of seven from the Boston Red Sox to win the 1975 World Series.

The Dodgers, despite trailing so distantly behind the Reds, had put together some fancy statistics themselves. The Dodgers pitchers' collective ERA of 2.92 was the best in either league that year, and their 18 shutouts were the most in the National League. Andy Messersmith was the team's leader with 19 wins and 14 losses. He started more games than anyone else in the league (40) and completed more (19); he also

Burt Hooton joined the Dodgers staff in 1975; he was obtained from the Chicago Cubs for two second-line pitchers. Hooton had had four losing years in Chicago before coming to Los Angeles, where he promptly enjoyed a dramatic turnaround, winning 18 games and losing only 7. He easily established himself as a rotation regular, joining Andy Messersmith, Don Sutton, and Doug Rau.

Andy Messersmith and Steve Garvey, 1974 Gold Glove winners, display their trophies before a 1975 game at Dodger Stadium. They would both be repeat winners in 1975, and Garvey would go on to win the award the next two years as well.

Andy Messersmith (just the 4 of his No. 47 showing) has just shut out the Atlanta Braves 8–0 for his fourth consecutive win of 1975. He went on to extend the streak to a record of 7–0 before losing a game and ending the year with a record of 19–14 and an ERA of 2.29. Messersmith would also lead the league in shutouts (seven), complete games (29), games started (40), and innings pitched (322). It was his last year as a Dodger, however. He moved as a free agent the next year to the Atlanta Braves. The greeters here are (from left) Rick Auerbach, Steve Yeager, Lee Lacy, Ron Cey, and Steve Garvey (shaking hands with Messersmith).

pitched the most number of innings (322). All the other Dodgers starters had a good year too: Burt Hooton (18–7), Don Sutton (16–13), and Doug Rau (15–9). But their bullpen had failed them—Mike Marshall, hampered by his rib injury, had come up with only 13 saves and a disappointing record of 9–14. Jim Brewer, at 37, had not been producing and was traded to the California Angels during the season. But the Dodgers had a lot of faith in Charlie Hough, a knuckleballer who had gotten his chance late in the season after having lived in the shadows of Marshall and Brewer for the previous few years.

Steve Garvey's batting average of .319 and slugging percentage of .476 were the club's best, and for the second year in a row he broke the 200-hit

mark, this time with 210. Ron Cey did justice to his growing reputation as a long-ball hitter by bagging 25 homers and 101 RBIs, and Garvey and Jimmy Wynn each contributed 18 home runs. Lee Lacy, utility infielder, outfielder, and pinch-hitter, batted a hefty .314 and slugged at a .451 clip in his 306 trips to the plate that year, adding dimension to the Dodgers bench strength.

Several of the hitters of 1975 would be gone from the team, however, before they had a chance to eat their Thanksgiving turkeys. Jimmy Wynn, Lee Lacy, and Tom Paciorek were sent to Atlanta as part of a trade that brought outfielder Dusty Baker to the Dodgers. At 26, Baker had already logged four years as a starter in the big leagues, with a career batting average of .278. He had hit .321 in 1972 and cracked 21 homers and drove in 99 runs in 1973; he was, in the words of Al Campanis, a player who could "run, throw, field, and hit with power, and it is our feeling that he is yet to reach his peak." Outfielder Willie Crawford was dealt to the St. Louis Cardinals for second baseman Ted Sizemore, who had worn Dodger Blue in 1969 and 1970 and had earned Rookie of the Year honors in it.

There were two other departures of note, both from the pitching corps. Andy Messersmith, the club's premier hurler, was at the end of his con-tract; he soon became one of the first of the major free agents to seek and find the highest bidder for his services. He was hired by the Atlanta Braves—a three-year contract reportedly close to $2 million. At the other end of the financial spectrum, the Dodgers sold 33-year-old reliever Mike Marshall to Atlanta during the next season for the waiver price of $20,000.

With free agents becoming a reality and the structure of major league baseball in transition because of it, the 1976 season got off on shaky legs. Spring training was delayed by the threat of another all-out strike. When it finally got underway,

That's Bill Buckner on all fours, scoring an unorthodox run in this preseason game against the California Angels, part of the 1976 "Freeway Series." And that's Angels catcher Andy Etchebarren shouting something to the effect that he was sure he had the ball right there in his glove.

167

A classic fracas, this one in 1975, demonstrating the lack of love between the Dodgers and their intrastate rivals, the San Diego Padres.

the Dodgers won 10 games and lost only 3, their won-lost percent of .769 the highest since the team came to Los Angeles in 1958.

The regular season kicked off on schedule in early April. For the first time in Los Angeles Dodgers history their home opener was rained out. Actually, that turned out to be the Dodgers' best day of the week—they lost their first five games of the season.

By late April, however, the Dodgers began to roll, and launched a 12-game winning streak that moved them into first place ahead of the mighty Cincinnati Reds. It was one game short of the Los Angeles record of 13 consecutive wins, rung up in 1962 and in 1965. Don Sutton (2–3) and Burt Hooton (1–2) were having less-than-exciting starts

that year, but Doug Rau won his fourth game against no defeats shortly after the first of the month, and Charlie Hough was performing very well in relief. And to everyone's joy, Tommy John was back in uniform, and it looked as if the surgery on his injured elbow might have corrected all his arm problems.

There would be more lineup changes for the Dodgers after the season got started. A major one was the trade of Joe Ferguson to the Cardinals for switch-hitting outfielder Reggie Smith. An 11-year veteran, Smith had played 8 years with the Boston Red Sox, 3 with St. Louis, and had played in the All-Star Game four times. Five times he had hit over .300, his best having been .309 in both 1969 and 1974. He had hit more than 20 home runs in

Walt Alston collected his 2,000th win as a Dodgers manager on July 17, 1976, and here congratulates his winning pitcher that day, Rick Rhoden. Only five other managers in the history of the game had won two thousand or more games: Connie Mack, John McGraw, Bucky Harris, Joe McCarthy, and Leo Durocher.

stood at six games by the All-Star break. The Dodgers were hanging in, but their record of 47–39 was, nevertheless, woefully short.

Rick Rhoden, the 23-year-old right-hander who had gotten his chance as a frontline starter after the departure of Andy Messersmith, was suddenly the brightest light in the Dodgers pitching department. He was invited to the All-Star Game on the basis of a spectacular performance up until that point in the season: an 8–0 record, including a three-hit shutout over the Cincinnati Reds. Elsewhere in the pitching corps, Don Sutton had been steady if unexciting through the season's first half, winning nine while dropping eight.

Rick Rhoden's ninth consecutive win of the year came only three days after the All-Star break, but it was considerably underplayed because of another milestone: Walt Alston's 2,000th win as a major league manager. Only five others in the history of the game had achieved that landmark: Connie Mack (3,776), John McGraw (2,840), Bucky Harris (2,159), Joe McCarthy (2,126), and Leo Durocher (2,019).

But that was to be the highlight of Walt Alston's last year at the Dodgers' helm. As they had done in 1975, the Reds continued to batter down every obstacle in their path in the season's second half. They went ahead by as many as 13½ games in early August and never dropped below a 7-game lead during the remaining two months of the season.

Once again the Dodgers were runners-up in the NL West at season's end. This time their 92–70 record put them 10 games behind the Reds. And once again the Big Red Machine, which won 102 games during the season, took all the chips. First they wiped out the NL East champs, Danny Ozark's Philadelphia Phillies, in three consecutive games, and then decimated Billy Martin's New York Yankees in four straight in the World Series.

Rick Rhoden's remarkable year was interrupted around Labor Day when he injured his elbow. Rhoden made one more appearance a week and a

six separate seasons—including 30 in 1971, his best effort—and he was only one short of 200 career home runs. Lee Lacy was also brought back into the Dodgers fold, his contract an outright purchase by the Los Angeles front office.

The Dodgers were the division leaders for most of the month of May. From April 24 through May 23, they won 23 games and lost only 4. But the Big Red Machine stayed right along with them, and the Dodgers could never pull more than two games ahead of them. As the month ran out, the Reds muscled their way into first place. Just as they had in 1975, the Reds steadily built their lead, and it half later, reinjured his arm, and had to sit out the rest of the season. His 12–3 record, however, yielded a won-lost percentage of .800, which was the highest in either league.

Don Sutton had as outstanding a second half of the year as Rhoden had in the first segment. He won 12 games and lost only 2, including 9 straight. It was enough to accord him his first 20-game season in the majors (21–10). In so doing, he racked up his 176th victory for Los Angeles and had moved well ahead of Sandy Koufax in total number of Dodgers wins. With 176, Sutton was tied with Brickyard Kennedy for third place in Dodgers history; only Don Drysdale, who won 209, and Dazzy Vance, 180, had won more games than Don Sutton at the end of the 1976 season. He had also recorded his 2,000th strikeout, placing him third behind Drysdale (2,486) and Koufax (2,396).

Doug Rau won 16 and lost 12, and Tommy John, the comeback kid at 33, won 10 and lost an equal number. Burt Hooton had a big comedown from his 18–7 record of the year before and posted only 11 wins against 15 defeats. But reliever Charlie Hough had come up with his best year yet in the majors, winning 12, losing 8, and saving 18 others.

The hitting stats were similar to the year before. Steve Garvey was again the top batsman, this time hitting .317. He also became the first Dodger in history to collect 200 or more hits in three consecutive seasons. Only one other Dodger produced 200 hits in each of three years, Zack Wheat (1922, 1924, and 1925). Garvey's 85 runs scored and 37 doubles were also club highs that year, and he shared the RBI title (80) with Ron Cey. Cey hit the most homers (23), and Davey Lopes stole the most bases (63, which was also the most in the National League). Steve Garvey also earned his third consecutive Gold Glove award as the best fielding first baseman in the National League.

The team and the organization lost an old veteran in late September of the 1976 season. Sixty-five-year-old Walt Alston, just a few days before the season's end, told the press that he was retir-

Bill Buckner's last year with the Dodgers was 1976, after which he was traded to the Chicago Cubs for outfielder Rick Monday and relief pitcher Mike Garman. Buckner became a regular in 1971 and hit above .300 three times. His best year was 1972, when he led the club with a .319 average.

ing. Although not unexpected, it was difficult to imagine the Dodgers without him—no one but Alston had piloted the team in the 23 years since his takeover in 1954. His career had been one of the finest and most productive in all of major league annals, and his place in the Dodgers story was forever entrenched.

No time was wasted in announcing his replacement. Besides, almost everyone knew who it would be—Tommy Lasorda, the man of Dodger Blue blood with devotion to the club as steadfast as General George S. Patton's had been to the U.S. Third Army. Lasorda's style and presence were certainly very different from Alston's, and more than a few people wondered what effect the transition would have on a Dodgers team that was passing from youth to middle age.

CHAPTER 15

ENTER TOMMY LASORDA

Super Dodgers fan Don Rickles (right) has a few words for television announcer Joe Garagiola as Tommy Lasorda looks on before Game 1 of the 1977 NL championship series.

TOMMY LASORDA'S PRESENCE—on a baseball field, in the clubhouse, or on the street—will never go unnoticed. Ebullient, ever ready with a quip or a story, bursting with Dodgers spirit and devotion, his personality is a unique amalgam of Casey Stengel, Knute Rockne, Toots Shor, and Billy Sunday.

Did he want the job? Before ever being assured of his ascendancy upon Walt Alston's eventual retirement, Lasorda turned down three solid offers to manage other National League clubs and remained a coach in waiting. When he was finally given the Dodgers reins he said, "I told the Dodgers I loved them for 27 years, and when they

To obtain the services of veteran outfielder Dusty Baker in 1976, the Dodgers had to send Jimmy Wynn, Lee Lacy, and Tom Paciorek to the Atlanta Braves. Baker played center field his first year with the Dodgers, then moved to left after the departure of Bill Buckner. A solid hitter whose best average had been .321 in 1972, he was also capable of power-hitting. Atlanta Braves teammate Hank Aaron described him as having "more potential than any outfielder I've seen in all my seasons."

Ted Sizemore was back as a catcher for the Dodgers in 1976. He had been weaned from that position by the Dodgers in the late sixties and turned into a second baseman, but in his one-year return to L.A., he caught two games. Sizemore also played second in 71 games and then moved on to the Philadelphia Phillies.

winter leagues, incited more Latin American brawls than anyone since Che Guevara." His leaps for joy and lavish hugs in triumphant moments were as animated as his explosive reactions to questionable calls by umpires. But he also brought experience and a shrewd sense of baseball strategy. As a minor league manager for seven years, Tommy had produced five pennants and had been honored as Minor League Manager of the Year. That along with five years as a key Dodgers coach under Walt Alston were the core credentials he brought to his new job.

After the 1975 and 1976 seasons, the Dodgers had become known around the league as an also-ran. Lasorda's goal was the immediate alteration of that image. He felt he had the manpower of a winning team, that his players were now seasoned and had become a cohesive unit over several years of play.

Al Campanis had made two trades that would change the lineup somewhat. First he sent Ted Sizemore to the Phillies for catcher Johnny Oates. Then Bill Buckner and reserve shortstop Ivan DeJesus went to the Chicago Cubs in a trade for outfielder Rick Monday and reliever Mike Garman. (Sizemore had not been able to find a place in the Dodgers starting lineup in 1976 and had therefore become expendable. And the plan for the outfield was to switch the positions around so that Dusty Baker could move to left and Reggie Smith to right, hence the acquisition of veteran center fielder Monday.)

The Dodgers, under their new pilot, had a fine spring training, winning 17 of their 24 games with other major league teams. Tommy John looked better than ever, his elbow not bothering him at all, and seemed to be proving that his award as 1976 National League Comeback Player of the Year was not a fluke. It was all a fitting overture to the symphony the Dodgers would create out of the regular season.

Don Sutton pitched them to a win in the season opener against the Giants at Dodger Stadium. And then, for the entire first month of the season, the Dodgers proved to be as explosive as their new manager was effervescent. By May 6, their record

named me manager, they said they loved me. It was like being presented the Hope diamond."

The new manager brought a considerably different temperament and style to the corner of the Dodgers dugout that Walt Alston had inhabited for the preceding 23 years. He was volatile. As Larry Keith observed in *Sports Illustrated,* "Lasorda, as a player and manager in the Puerto Rican, Cuban, Panamanian, Dominican Republic, and Venezuelan

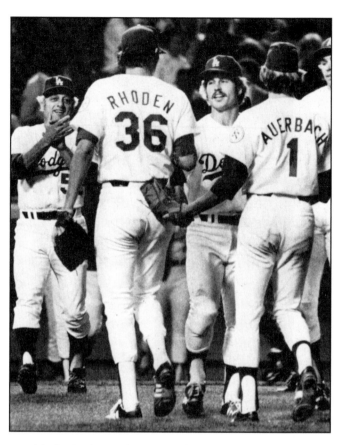

Rick Rhoden earned a place in the regular rotation in 1976, his third year with the Dodgers. The congratulations here are for shutting out the Cincinnati Reds 5–0, his third straight win of the year. Rhoden would win nine consecutive games that year before suffering his first loss, but an injured elbow would keep his season record down to 12–3. His .800 won-lost percentage, however, was the best in the majors. Those sharing the joy of the moment (from the left) are coach Tommy Lasorda, Ron Cey, Rick Auerbach, and Bill Russell.

stood at 22–4, a win rate of .846, and they were 10½ games ahead of their closest competitor, the Houston Astros. Included in the month's output were winning streaks of eight, seven, and five games, and such blockbuster scores as 16–6 and 14–10 (both over the Atlanta Braves). It was the best start for a Dodgers team since the fabulous Brooklyn club of 1955 won 24 of their first 26 games.

At that point in the season, Ron Cey led both leagues in home runs with nine and RBIs with 29, and Steve Garvey was not far behind with six homers and 22 runs driven in. Three Dodgers were among the NL's top 10 batters: Steve Yeager, .362; Ron Cey, .360; and Reggie Smith, .347. As Cey explained, "With Garvey behind me and Reggie

Smith in front, I see more good pitches in a night than I used to in a month." As for pitching, Rick Rhoden was 5–0, Don Sutton and Doug Rau 4–0 each, and Burt Hooton 3–1.

The Big Red Machine was nowhere in sight of the streaking Dodgers, although they were heard from. Manager Sparky Anderson reminded the press that "the Dodgers lack a finishing kick." He and other Reds were quoted as saying such things as: "The Dodgers are playing over their heads. . . . They're not that good. . . . They'll fade just as they did before. . . . Time will tell, the Reds will prevail." Steve Brener, the Dodgers publicity chief, duly collected the quotes and posted them on the clubhouse wall as inspiration to the players.

Charlie Hough gets a slap on the back from coach Tommy Lasorda after one of his 18 saves during the 1976 season. Hough, the Dodgers' chief reliever that year, was also credited with 12 wins, his career high. The next year he would save 22 games; only Dodgers Jim Brewer and Jim Hughes had ever saved more in a single season (each had 24, in 1970 and 1954 respectively).

Tommy Lasorda, as everyone would have expected, did not remain silent on the subject. He admonished the doubters from Cincinnati with a simple declarative sentence about his beloved Dodgers: "They're winning because they're outstanding." And then he added for color, "I call them 'the Octopus'—if you hold one of the eight tentacles down, another will get you." Around the same time, comedian Don Rickles, an off-field pal of Lasorda's, sent him a telegram: "You're winning so far Lasorda, but if things get lousy, remember we never met."

The Reds did not rebound after the season's first month as they had in the two previous years. And the Dodgers showed no sign at all of fading. Between early May and the All-Star break in mid-July, the Dodgers were in first place by no less than 7 games—and as many as 13—at any one time. Their record was 59–33 (.641).

Tommy Lasorda went to the All-Star Game as a coach in his maiden year, along with four Dodgers players: Ron Cey, Steve Garvey, Reggie Smith, and Don Sutton.

After the season resumed, the threat from the Big Red Machine never occurred. It was all Dodger Blue in the NL West for 1977—a juggernaut of resounding bats and intimidating pitching, spurred on by an evangelistic manager.

Along the way, there were indeed some moments to remember. Ron Cey set a Los Angeles Dodgers record when he rapped out nine consecutive hits in a three-day period in July; the only Dodger who ever produced a longer streak was Ed Konetchy, who hit safely 10 straight times in 1919. Don Sutton allowed the Giants only one hit and shut them out 7–0, his fifth career one-hitter. No pitcher in Los Angeles Dodgers annals had ever come close to pitching as many one-hitters as Sutton; in fact, only Sandy Koufax hurled more than one, and he had only two to his credit.

In August Steve Garvey set an all-time Dodgers record by collecting five extra-base hits in five at-bats in a single game—two home runs and three doubles. The five runs he scored in that game were also an all-time Dodgers mark, breaking the record of four scored by Cookie Lavagetto at Ebbets Field 38 years earlier. One of the homers was his second grand slammer of the year, a Dodgers record previously held by only Frank Howard (who set it in 1960) but matched one more time by Ron Cey later in the 1977 season. Two weeks after Garvey's slugfest, Dusty Baker set another all-time Dodgers record by driving in five runs during a single inning in an 18–4 massacre of the San Diego Padres.

When the season was over, the Dodgers could claim a real-live blitzkrieg. They had been alone in first place since April 15. The nearest any club came to them in the season's second half was eight and one-half games. Their final record was 98–64 (.605). When the season ended, Sparky Anderson, whose Reds were a full 10 games behind in second place, admitted that his early season comments were perhaps ill-conceived.

Not only did the Dodgers have a divisional crown, they had a box office bonanza as well. The team set a new major league attendance record by luring 2,955,087 fans into Dodger Stadium that year. That was almost two hundred thousand more than the previous record that they had set back in 1962. Adding in their total road-game attendance, a grand total of 4,929,385 spectators watched the Dodgers in person, another all-time major league mark.

The fans had been entertained royally. Four Dodgers hit 30 or more home runs each, the first time that had ever been accomplished by a major league team. Steve Garvey hit 33, Reggie Smith 32, and Ron Cey and Dusty Baker 30 each. Previously, 18 teams had had three players in the 30-home-run category in a season. Two of those were Brooklyn Dodgers teams, 1950 and 1953, and the three sluggers were the same in each year: Gil Hodges, Duke Snider, and Roy Campanella.

Both Garvey and Cey broke the 100-RBI barrier, with 115 and 110, respectively. And Reggie Smith's slugging average of .576 was a Los Angeles Dodgers record, although it was short of the all-time club record of .678 set by Babe Herman back in 1930. Garvey's 33 homers as a right-handed batter and Smith's 27 as a left-handed batter were also Los Angeles records (Smith hit five as a right-hander to account for his total of 32). Reggie Smith's 63 extra-base hits tied Tommy Davis' Dodgers mark set in 1962.

Tommy John won 20 games while losing only 7, his first 20-game year. He also posted an impressive ERA of 2.78, bettered only by Burt Hooton's 2.62. Rick Rhoden won 16 games and dropped 10 for the second-best performance from the Dodgers mound. And Don Sutton and Doug Rau each had records of 14–8. From the bullpen, Charlie Hough came on to save 22 games and Mike Garman another 12.

Now the Dodgers would have to play host to Danny Ozark's Philadelphia Phillies, who had beaten out the Pirates for the NL East title. The Phillies had won 101 games that year and, like the Dodgers, had exhibited awesome power. Greg "the

Catcher Steve Yeager hit a career-high 16 home runs in 1977, including this one. Yeager had come up with the Dodgers in 1972 and had been the club's primary backstop since 1974. His best year at the plate was 1974, when he batted .266. Awaiting him here are Dusty Baker and Yeager's battery-mate that day, Don Sutton.

LASORDA'S VIEW

Question: What were the most memorable or interesting moments that first year?

Tommy Lasorda: Well, there were a lot of things. Seeing Reggie Smith perform the way he did—that was a tremendous satisfaction. Having four guys hitting 30 home runs or more, which had never been done in the history of major league baseball. Of course winning the playoffs was a great, great satisfaction against the Philadelphia Phillies. And the idea of bringing a kind of new philosophy into baseball. I was a manager who believed in togetherness, knowing all of the players, being close to the players. No manager had come in with that philosophy before.

Question: Was that difficult to do the first year?

Tommy Lasorda: Yeah, a lot of people criticized me. I think Sparky Anderson made the statement, "If that is what it is going to take to win the game, I guess we all better start hugging players," saying it in a mocking or sarcastic way. I was the first guy to make the eight players run together before the game. Sparky said: "Look at them. Look at them out there running. It won't be long before they'll be running in eight different directions." In the World Series I said, "Yes, Sparky was right. They were running in eight different directions, but to eight different banks."

Ron Cey beats the throw to second in this 1977 NL pennant playoff game against the Phillies. Cey hit .308 and drove in four runs during the series. Waiting for the ball is former Dodger Ted Sizemore.

Bull" Luzinski had clobbered 39 homers, and Mike Schmidt, 38. Richie Hebner had hit another 18, Jay Johnstone, 15, and Garry Maddox, 14. They also had one of the league's premier pitchers, Steve Carlton, who won 23 games that year (and would win the Cy Young Award), as well as Larry Christenson, a 19-game winner, and two fine relievers, Gene Garber and Ron Reed. Another bullpen ace, Tug McGraw, had been hampered by an injured elbow during the season but would see action in the playoffs.

The Phillies traveled west for the first NL playoff game. Danny Ozark decided to send Carlton after the Dodgers in the first meeting. Tommy John was Tommy Lasorda's choice, and, as things turned out, it was not a good one. "The Bull" Luzinski, who looked more like he should be playing for the Philadelphia Eagles than the Phillies,

broke the ice in the first inning with a towering homer into the center-field seats, scoring Mike Schmidt ahead of him. In the fifth, the Phillies had runners on second and third when reserve first baseman Dave Johnson came up to face Tommy John. He lashed a single to score both runners, giving the Phils a 4–0 lead and sending John to the Dodgers showers. Mike Garman came on in relief.

The Dodgers scored their first run in the bottom of that inning, gave up another to the Phillies in the seventh, and then electrified the hometown crowd by removing the four-run deficit with a single swipe of the bat—Ron Cey's grand-slam home run in the bottom of the seventh. But then in the ninth Mike Schmidt drove in a Phillies run and Dodgers reliever Elias Sosa forced in another on a balk. The Dodgers could get nothing going in the bottom of the inning, and the Phillies took Game 1 by a score of 7–5.

In the second matchup Don Sutton went against the Phillies' Jim Lonborg, who had been troubled by shoulder problems during much of the 1977 season. Dusty Baker blew this game open in the fourth inning by smashing the team's second grand-slam homer in two days. Sutton went the distance, scattered nine hits, and gave up only one run. The Dodgers added three runs to Baker's four-spot and had an easy 7–1 win.

The pressure was still on the Dodgers, however. The Philadelphia fans at Veterans Stadium were notorious for being a thunderous horde, bent on unnerving any alien team who had the temerity to venture into their domain. And almost sixty-four thousand of them were there for the third game of the playoffs.

But it was the Dodgers who drew first blood, again sparked by Dusty Baker. He doubled in the second inning to drive in Steve Garvey, and by the end of the inning the Dodgers had a 2–0 lead. But the Phillies came back, and with them was the roar of a crowd that was raucous and unnerving. Perhaps jangled by the noise, Dodgers starter Burt Hooton loaded the bases in the bottom of the second. The decibel count rose as Phillies pitcher Larry Christenson came to bat. On a 3–2 count, Hooton walked the pitcher and allowed the Phillies to score their first run of the game. The cacophony continued, louder and more bizarre with each pitch, and Hooton walked in two more runs before being pulled by Tommy Lasorda for Rick Rhoden. It was, in fact, a combination of the fans' bedlam and some disputable calls by the home-plate umpire that discombobulated Hooton. The pitcher later explained, "I lost my head there, and let my team down . . . I lost confidence in myself."

Dusty Baker drove another run across in the fourth to tie it up for the Dodgers, at least until the bottom of the eighth. The Phillies scored two runs and took a 5–3 lead into the ninth inning.

It appeared to be all over when, with two outs, Tommy Lasorda sent up pinch-hitter Vic Davalillo, a 40-year-old who had been around the majors for

Vic Davalillo, scoring a run here, was 40 years old in 1977 when Tommy Lasorda went to the Mexican League to bring him back to the majors. Davalillo had played for the Indians, Angels, Cardinals, Pirates, and A's from 1963 to 1974, then drifted back to the minors south of the border. He proved to be just the pinch-hitter Lasorda needed, batting .313 in that capacity in 1977 and .312 in 1978. He would remain with the club into 1980 and then retire from the game.

most of his career since 1963, but had spent the last three years in the Mexican League. The Dodgers had brought him up during the pennant drive that year. With nobody on base, he surprised everybody, especially the right side of the Phillies infield, when he laid down a perfect bunt and beat it out. That brought up another pinch-hitter, Manny Mota, also a baseball "senior citizen" just a year younger than Davalillo. He whacked one to deep left that Greg Luzinski could not handle. The Bull eventually threw to relay man Ted Sizemore, who dropped the throw; Davalillo scored and Mota reached third. Lead-off batter Davey Lopes then beat out a grounder that Mike Schmidt bobbled,

WORLD SERIES LINEUPS, 1977

DODGERS	YANKEES
Davey Lopes, 2b	Mickey Rivers, cf
Bill Russell, ss	Willie Randolph, 2b
Reggie Smith, rf	Thurman Munson, c
Ron Cey, 3b	Reggie Jackson, rf
Steve Garvey, 1b	Chris Chambliss, 1b
Dusty Baker, lf	Graig Nettles, 3b
Rick Monday, cf	Lou Piniella, lf
Steve Yeager, c	Bucky Dent, ss

STARTING PITCHERS
Game 1: Don Sutton, Don Gullett
Game 2: Burt Hooton, Catfish Hunter
Game 3: Tommy John, Mike Torrez
Game 4: Doug Rau, Ron Guidry
Game 5: Don Sutton, Don Gullett
Game 6: Burt Hooton, Mike Torrez

and Mota scored to tie the game. The contest that had looked like such a certain Phillies victory moments before was suddenly disintegrating, and the hometown crowd was uncharacteristically quiet. They were soon to be sobered even more. Reliever Gene Garber, trying to keep notorious base thief Davey Lopes close to first, threw the ball instead into the Dodgers dugout. Moments later Bill Russell sliced a single to center and the Dodgers had the lead, which reliever Mike Garman managed to hold on to. He kept the Phils scoreless in the bottom of the ninth and gave the Dodgers a win and a 2–1 advantage in the playoffs.

The next day Tommy John once again opposed Steve Carlton. It was a misty, often rainy night in Philadelphia, and the contest would have been canceled if it weren't a playoff game. But it was, and the Dodgers were the ultimate beneficiary of that decision. Dusty Baker hit a two-run homer in the second inning, and that really was all that was necessary. The Phillies could only come up with a solitary run and seven hits in nine innings against a strong, slider-throwing Tommy John. The Dodgers, adding two insurance runs in the fifth, won 4–1.

Tommy Lasorda got his chance to prance and leap and hug and kiss before a national television audience, and his team had the pennant to take back to Los Angeles. The ecstatic Lasorda was only the 19th pilot ever to win a pennant in his novice year managing in the majors.

While that was going on in the National League, the New York Yankees, managed by the wild one, Billy Martin, were disposing of the Kansas City Royals. Like the Dodgers, they won the last two games on foreign turf, but it had taken five games to win their series instead of four.

The Yankees had had a fine season, winning 100 and losing only 62, but they had had a difficult time fending off Earl Weaver's Baltimore Orioles and Don Zimmer's Boston Red Sox, both of whom finished only two and one-half games out. Still, the Yankees were a powerhouse team collected from all over the majors by free-spending owner George Steinbrenner. That year alone he had bought free agents like Reggie Jackson (from the Baltimore Orioles) and pitcher Don Gullett (from the Cincinnati Reds) and had acquired first-rate shortstop Bucky Dent from an impoverished Chicago White Sox team. In addition, the Yankees had Thurman Munson, one of the game's most celebrated catchers, as well as such other stars as third baseman Graig Nettles, first baseman Chris Chambliss, second baseman Willie Randolph, and outfielders Mickey Rivers and Lou Piniella. Their pitching staff was headed by Ron Guidry, Gullett, and right-hander Mike Torrez, who

A collector's item: the souvenir ticket for Opening Day 1977, marking the Dodgers' 20th season in Los Angeles.

Rick Monday, shown welcoming Dusty Baker (No. 12), came to the Dodgers in 1977 in the trade that sent Bill Buckner and Ivan DeJesus to the Chicago Cubs. Coming off his best year as a slugger (in 1976 he hit 32 homers and drove in 77 runs), Monday brought a variety of assets to the Dodgers. A third arm, however, was not one of them. The "Popeye" forearm actually belongs to Steve Garvey.

had been brought over from Oakland during the pennant drive. They also had one of the game's best firemen in Sparky Lyle, as well as longtime pitching stalwarts Catfish Hunter, Dick Tidrow, and Ken Holtzman.

Yankee Stadium was the setting for the first encounter between the longtime rivals. It was the first time the two teams had met in the postseason since the Dodgers humiliated the New Yorkers in four straight games back in 1963. It was only the second time the two teams had faced each other in a World Series since the Dodgers had abandoned Brooklyn after the 1957 season. In those earlier days of intracity rivalry, however, the Yankees had won all but one of the seven World Series with the Dodgers.

In 1977, the Dodgers were the betting-line favorite before the Series. They had good, strong,

healthy pitchers, while most of the Yankees staff was ailing. The Dodgers were a tightly knit team, awash with spirit and respect for each other; the Yankees were a cauldron of turmoil and discontent, perhaps best characterized by the fractious relationship between million-dollar baby Reggie Jackson and his manager, Billy Martin. The team's long litany of rivalries, petty jealousies, and conspiracies could have filled a historical romance novel.

The Dodgers moved out quickly in the very first inning at Yankee Stadium. Bill Russell drove in Davey Lopes with the first run by tripling off Yankees starter Don Gullett; he then scored the second run when Ron Cey lofted a sacrifice fly deep to the outfield.

The Yankees got a run back off Don Sutton in their half of the inning, when Chris Chambliss singled Thurman Munson home. Both pitchers then took control of the game, however, and it moved to the bottom of the sixth. Then Don Sutton delivered a little mistake to Willie Randolph, who sent it reeling into the left-field seats to tie the game. Randolph crossed the plate again in the eighth inning, driven in by Munson's double, and the

New manager Tommy Lasorda watches warm-ups from the dugout he had inhabited as a coach since 1973. Now, in 1977, his lifelong dream had come true—he had the reins of the team he had been serving in one capacity or another since the late forties. Also looking on are (from left) Steve Brener, director of publicity; Fred Claire, vice president of public relations and promotions; and coach Preston Gomez.

Dodgers outfielder Reggie Smith (No. 8) scores easily in this 1977 game. Smith came from the Cardinals the year before in exchange for catcher Joe Ferguson and before that had played for the Red Sox for eight years (1966–1973). Smith had hit above .300 five times, and in his first year in L.A. he hit .280. In 1977 he had one of his best seasons, batting .307, cracking 32 homers, and leading the club in runs scored with 104.

But the strategy backfired when the next batter, Paul Blair, got what would prove to be his only hit of the Series, and Randolph raced home with a Yankees victory in Game 1. For trivia buffs, the game tied the record for most innings played in a World Series night game.

Burt Hooton was Lasorda's choice to try to redeem the Dodgers the following night. And the rambunctious manager spent most of the time before the game exhorting his batters to get their well-publicized bats in working order. It must have helped, because the Dodgers stormed Yankees starter Catfish Hunter with two runs in the first on a Reggie Smith double and a Ron Cey home run. They

Tommy Lasorda quickly proved that he could debate a call with as much intensity, verve, and colorful speech as anybody who ever managed the game, including Leo "the Lip" Durocher.

Yankees had the lead. Sutton was replaced by Lance Rautzhan.

In the ninth, Dusty Baker got on with a single for the Dodgers, Steve Yeager worked Gullett for a base on balls, and that was all for the Yankees starter. Billy Martin brought in Sparky Lyle to face pinch-hitter Lee Lacy, who promptly slapped a single to bring Baker home with the tying run and send the game into extra innings.

In the twelfth inning the Dodgers house collapsed. And again it was Willie Randolph who precipitated the disaster by leading off with a double into the left-field corner. Tommy Lasorda decided to take no chances with clutch-hitter Thurman Munson and had him walked intentionally.

Here, Dodgers catcher Jerry Grote tries to put a tag on the Cincinnati Reds' legendary hustler Pete Rose, but he fails, as can be seen in Rose's smirking expression. The smirk was wiped away, however, at season's end, when the Dodgers wound up on top of the NL West, 10 games ahead of the Reds. Grote served as a backup catcher to Steve Yeager during the 1977 and 1978 seasons.

scored another in the second when Steve Yeager homered, and two more in the third when Reggie Smith clobbered a homer with Bill Russell on.

The 5–0 lead was a mountain the Yankees could not conquer. Burt Hooton went on to pitch a fine game; he gave up only one run and five hits. The final score was 6–1, and the Series was tied at a game apiece. And now the Dodgers were able to happily depart the South Bronx for the much more enticing climes of Los Angeles.

There were 55,992 fans in Dodger Stadium for Game 3. The hope was for a Dodgers feast, but instead it was a delicatessen of Yankees treats in the first inning—four hits and three runs driven in by Thurman Munson, Reggie Jackson, and Lou Piniella. Tommy John did not get the hook, however, and remained around for the third when

QUOTE OF NOTE

Tommy Lasorda: Managing is like holding a dove in your hand. If you hold it too tightly, you kill it. If you hold it too loosely, you lose it.

Dusty Baker put him and the Dodgers right back in the ballgame with a three-run homer.

The tie did not last long. Graig Nettles scored the go-ahead run in the top of the fourth, and the Yankees added an insurance run in the following frame when Chris Chambliss drove in Reggie Jackson.

After Baker's home run, the Dodgers were unable to get to Yankees right-hander Mike Torrez at all. He went the distance, holding them scoreless in the last six innings.

Three more people showed up the next day for Game 4 to set a new Dodger Stadium attendance record of 55,995. Among them was the president's mother, Miss Lillian Carter, who was tabbed to throw out the ceremonial first ball. She said to Tommy Lasorda that she was a lifetime Dodgers fan and hoped that maybe she could bring them a little luck. She couldn't. For the second game in a row, the Yankees leaped to a 3–0 lead, although this time it took them two innings to do it. As a result, Dodgers starter Doug Rau was routed and replaced by Rick Rhoden. The Dodgers got on the scoreboard the following inning when Rhoden aided his own effort with a double and then scored

The many faces of Tommy John. Unorthodox expressions or not, he had his best year thus far in the majors in 1977, winning 20, losing only 7, and posting an ERA of 2.59. The year before he had been named Comeback Player of the Year, turning in a sterling performance after recovering from a serious elbow injury. John would pitch only one more year in L.A. before departing as a free agent for the New York Yankees. As a Dodger, he won 87 games in six seasons while losing only 42.

ahead of Davey Lopes, who tagged Ron Guidry for a home run. Unfortunately, that was pretty much the extent of the Dodgers offense that day. Guidry allowed them only four hits in nine innings, and no further runs. Reggie Jackson contributed an additional run to the Yankees victory with a homer in the sixth, and the final was 4–2.

The two Dons—Sutton and Gullett—who had launched the Series back in New York, took the mound for Game 5, the last to be played in Los Angeles. The Dodgers were in a desperate situation— they were down three games to one, and if they got by Game 5 they would still have to return to Yankee Stadium and the rabid New York fans. "If we're going back to New York," Tommy Lasorda told his team in a pregame pep talk, "you're going to have to put a mess of runs on the scoreboard against this Yankee team." He was absolutely cor-

rect because the Yankees got four runs that day. But they did not come until the seventh and eighth innings, long after the game was out of the Yankees' reach.

It proved to be a day when the Dodgers could do little wrong. They answered Lasorda's admonition with 10 runs on 13 hits. Davey Lopes tripled in the first inning and was driven in by Bill Russell's single. Four runs scored in the fourth when Dusty Baker drove in Steve Garvey, and Steve Yeager followed with a three-run homer. The Dodgers added three more in the fifth and two in the sixth on a Reggie Smith home run. The final score was 10–4, and Sutton, who pitched all nine innings, got the win for the Dodgers.

But the game two days later at Yankee Stadium belonged to Reggie Jackson. His day at the plate is now history, and it forged his long-standing reputation

BEHIND THE SCENES AT THE WORLD SERIES, 1977

Pete Axthelm in *Newsweek* (on the unending Yankees soap opera): Joe DiMaggio was not at the World Series last week. Because of a front office blunder, DiMaggio's tickets were not ready when he showed up at Yankee Stadium. . . . He was kept waiting an hour, then left in a huff. . . . Thurman Munson came on as the most valuable player ever to ask to be traded to Cleveland. Volatile Billy Martin was awaiting his first world championship as a manager or his fourth firing—quite possibly both. And Reggie Jackson created chaos with his mercurial moods, locker room rhetoric, and criticisms of Martin.

Ron Fimrite in *Sports Illustrated*: A World Series record is set even before the first pitch is thrown as Pearl Bailey, snatching the microphone from its cradle and turning this way and that so the 56,668 Yankee Stadium spectators can observe every nuance of her performance, requires 2 minutes and 21 seconds to sing the national anthem, breaking the old record of 2:13 set by The New Christy Minstrels in 1973. Jose Feliciano's famous rock version in 1968 was clocked at 1:50, though for patriots and music traditionalists it seemed an eternity.

Reggie Jackson: I represent the overdog, and the underdog. My story is not really an athlete's story. It is a human story.

Billy Martin: Trouble follows me.

Ron Fimrite in *Sports Illustrated* (on the occasion of Tommy Lasorda, Billy Martin, and Frank Sinatra dining together the night before the Series' final game): "Frank just wanted to show us that he was proud of both of us," Lasorda says, speaking of the singer as if he were a Don. "Think of it—two Italian boys in the World Series."

"You had dinner with Martin and Sinatra?" a newsman inquires.

"No," Lasorda replies, "I had dinner with Sinatra and Martin."

Tommy Lasorda: "God delays; He does not deny."

Don Sutton is congratulated after destroying the Philadelphia Phillies, 7–1, in Game 2 of the 1977 NL championship series. Ron Cey and catcher Steve Yeager are the congratulators. The win evened the series at a game apiece.

as a World Series superstar. The Dodgers had moved quickly to a 2–0 lead in the first and were still ahead 3–2 in the fourth when Jackson came up to face Dodgers starter Burt Hooton. He took a fastball down the middle and stroked it into the right-field seats, a two-run homer to give the lead to the Yankees.

An inning later, he was back at the plate, this time glaring out at reliever Elias Sosa, again with a man on base. And again he blasted the Dodgers pitch into the right-field stands to raise the score to 7–3. Charlie Hough was on the mound in the bottom of the eighth for the Dodgers when Jackson strode to the plate. The crowd was chanting "Reggie . . . Reggie . . . Reggie." Hough, cautious because of what had transpired earlier in the game with the October slugger, tried to slip a low knuckleball past Jackson. But Jackson cannoned it out of the park, this time into the center-field bleachers. No one since the immortal Babe Ruth in the 1926 Series had ever connected with three home runs in a World Series game. Added to the two Jackson

Before Game 4 of the 1977 World Series, Miss Lillian Carter throws the ceremonial first ball to Dodgers catcher Steve Yeager. She did not bring the hometown boys any luck, however; Ron Guidry of the Yankees set them down 4–2 on a four-hitter later that day.

had hit in earlier games, he became the only batter ever to hit five home runs in a single World Series.

The final score was Yankees 8, Dodgers 4. Mike Torrez had gone all the way for the New Yorkers, and the Dodgers had never really been in the game after Jackson powered his first homer that day. With the overwhelming victory, of course, went the 1977 world championship to the Yankees, four games to two.

Reggie Jackson's total Series stats were indeed impressive: five home runs, eight RBIs, 10 runs scored, nine hits, and a .450 batting average. He was the obvious choice for the Series MVP, and before long even had a candy bar named after him.

For the Dodgers, the biggest sticks were wielded by Dusty Baker (.399), Steve Garvey (.375), and Steve Yeager (.316). Reggie Smith hit the most Dodgers home runs (three, one more than Yeager). And Smith, Yeager, and Garvey shared honors for most RBIs, five each. Pinch-hitter Lee Lacy did a fine job, batting .429 in his seven trips to the plate. The pitching, however, could not contain the Yankees, whom so many had thought were far too troubled to triumph over a Dodgers team that seemed to have everything in such perfect order. But no one ever said that baseball was predictable, or that nice guys necessarily win.

CHAPTER 16

NETTLED AND JACKSONED

Dodgers catcher Jerry Grote is in perfect position to put the tag on Garry Maddox of the Phillies in this August 1978 game. Maddox was out, but the Phillies won 3–1. The hostilities between the two teams would be rekindled after each won its respective division that year and battled in the postseason for the pennant, as they had done in 1977.

THE 1978 DODGERS TEAM was virtually the same as the year before. There was only one important newcomer at the start of the season. Terry Forster had been plucked from the free-agent pool, somewhat contrary to usual Dodgers acquisitive practices. Forster was a strong left-hander who had been the bullpen ace for the Chicago White Sox through 1976 (he was AL Fireman of the Year in 1974 when he led the majors with 24 saves), but had had a mediocre season with the Pittsburgh Pirates in 1977. Al Campanis and Tommy Lasorda hoped that he would return to form and provide the perfect counterpart to right-handed reliever Charlie Hough in the Dodgers bullpen.

The Dodgers hardly looked like the pennant winners of 1977 as they loped around the field at spring training. They ended up with their worst preseason since 1967, the second worst since the team had moved to Los Angeles. They won only 10 of 24 games (.417). Fortunately, it did not carry over into the regular season.

Once again, the threat that loomed most menacingly in the NL West was the Red Machine from Cincinnati—no longer referred to as "Big" by many in the media since the Reds' demise the year before. Yet their lineup was still such a fearsome array of talent that many bettors were investing money in them. In 1977 George Foster had hit 52 homers and driven in 149 runs (the first to break the 50 mark in home runs since Willie Mays did it in 1965). And, of course, Cincinnati still had such peaking players as Pete Rose, Johnny Bench, Joe Morgan, Ken Griffey, Dan Driessen, Dave Concepcion, and Tom Seaver.

The San Francisco Giants, under Joe Altobelli (who took over the managerial reins in 1977), were also expected to be a strong contender. The preeminent reason was their top-notch pitching: they had added Vida Blue to a staff that already included Bob Knepper, John Montefusco, Gary Lavelle, and reliever Randy Moffitt. They also had reliable hitters like Bill Madlock, Jack Clark, Terry Whitfield, and 40-year-old Willie McCovey.

To say the fans were ready to welcome the Dodgers to Los Angeles for the 1978 season is a true understatement. They turned out in what would be record-breaking droves, and the area newspapers flooded them with stories about every aspect of the team; the words, thoughts, and exploits of their manager; and practically every nuance of personality among the players. In

Lindsay, California (the "Olive Capital of the World"), they even renamed a school Steve Garvey Junior High.

The Dodgers put together a four-game winning streak to launch the 1978 season, exploding in the opener at Atlanta with 13 runs behind Don Sutton. In that game, Rick Monday, who had been hampered considerably the year before by a pinched nerve in his neck, gave sharp evidence that he was back in form by collecting four hits (including a homer) and driving in four runs. During that first week, Steve Garvey embarked on a hitting streak that extended through 21 games, at that time the fourth longest in Los Angeles Dodgers history. (At the end of the season, he compiled another streak of 20 games.)

Still, the Dodgers were not able to move into first ahead of the Cincinnati Reds until the season's third week, when their record rose to 11–5. They held it for only two weeks until suddenly— in a great splash of déjà vu—they saw the lead wrested from them by their old nemesis, the San Francisco Giants. West Coast baseball fans began to relive memories of the desperate, exciting confrontations between the two displaced teams from New York during the sixties. By June 1 the NL West had turned into a foot race, with the Giants and the Reds neck and neck and the Dodgers running in their dust, and that is the way it went until the All-Star break.

The Dodgers finally extricated themselves from third place by July 1 with a six-game winning streak; the last three were key victories over the Reds, who had had control of second place. Yet the Dodgers remained three full games behind the Giants.

Tommy Lasorda went to that year's All-Star Game as manager, a step up from his appearance as coach the year before. Six Dodgers players were selected: Steve Garvey, Ron Cey, Davey Lopes, Reggie Smith, Rick Monday, and Tommy John. And the Nationals gave Lasorda his first All-Star victory, 7–3. Steve Garvey, in his fifth consecutive All-Star Game start, paced his team with two hits and was named the game's MVP.

Billy North, one of the game's more able base runners, joined the Dodgers in 1978. Here, he takes off for second after a pick-off attempt at first went awry for the Montreal Expos. The error became costly moments later when Steve Garvey singled North home from second to give the Dodgers a come-from-behind 4–3 victory. The Expos first baseman is Tom Hutton. North stole 27 bases for the Dodgers that year but batted only .234.

During the next month of the regular season, San Francisco continued to hold the edge in the NL West, but never by more than a game or two. The Dodgers traveled up to the Giants' Candlestick Park August 3 for a four-game series that was being billed as the battle for West Coast baseball supremacy. It was in fact a crucial series for both teams, and it began woefully for the Dodgers. The Giants won the first game 5–4, with a run in the bottom of the ninth. The next night Vida Blue pitched a nearly flawless game to give them another one-run victory, 2–1.

The third game of the series was nationally tele-vised on a Saturday afternoon, and Tommy Lasorda went with the youngest member of his pitching staff, 21-year-old Bob Welch, who had been brought up in mid-June from the Dodgers farm club in Albuquerque, New Mexico. Welch had won his first two decisions (one a shutout) and had also collected a save. The look of the tall, strong right-hander prompted manager Lasorda to say, "I see a lot of Don Drysdale in him."

Before the game the Dodgers were four and one-half games behind, and they had lost their last six straight. But Welch was able to turn it around for them with a 2–0 shutout. The next day Burt Hooton guided them past the Giants 5–1, and the Dodgers were able to leave town with a split in the series and a loud sigh of relief. They would get another crack at the first-place Giants in just four days, this time down on their own natural grass turf.

Bob Welch got the call for the Dodgers in the first game of that series. After his win in San Francisco, he was sporting an impressive ERA of 1.71, and his fastball was being compared to the zingers of Tom Seaver and Jerry Koosman. Welch would oppose the Giants' ace, Vida Blue, whose

Lee Lacy slides into second here in a 1978 game against the Chicago Cubs. Cubs second baseman Manny Trillo leaps for the throw from the outfield, but it went that-a-way. It was Lacy's last year with the Dodgers but his foremost as a slugger—13 home runs and 40 RBIs.

189

Bill Russell slides safely into second in a game against the Phillies in 1978. Bud Harrelson handles the high throw but has no chance to tag Russell. Nineteen seventy-eight was Russell's best year at bat in the majors: his average was .286, and his 179 hits were topped only by Steve Garvey's 202, which were the most in the NL.

record of 16–4 was, at that point, the best in the major leagues.

Between the two Dodgers-Giants series, the Dodgers had swept three games from the San Diego Padres. They were now only a single game behind the Giants, and they were rolling. They exploded with 12 runs in the first game, as Bob Welch held the Giants to 2 and racked up his fourth win of the year against no defeats. The Dodgers moved into a tie for first place, the first time they had been there since May. They slipped by the Giants the next day, 4–3, to take sole possession of first, but the Giants came back to win the next two, the last by one run in 11 innings. But the Giants were never the same after that series and fell from contention.

After a day of rest, the Dodgers regained first place in the NL West by sweeping a three-game series with the powerhouse of the NL East, the Phillies. The Dodgers never gave up the top spot

again, moving ahead of the Reds and the Giants by as many as nine games in mid-September. It was not a cakewalk, however, because they were forced to hold off a surge by the Red Machine in the last half of the month. Still, they finished two and one-half games ahead of Cincinnati, while the Giants ended a distant six games out.

The Dodgers' record of 1978 (95–67) was not quite as good as it had been the year before, and the competition for the division title was much more heated. It was a very exciting year, and it kept everybody's interest high. As a result, the Dodgers managed to set two major league attendance records. First, they became the only team ever to draw more than 3 million fans into their ballpark (3,347,845). Combining that attendance figure with that of their road games, they became the first team to play for more than 5 million spectators (5,494,168) in a single season. They were both major league records.

Davey Lopes completes the throw for a double play in one game of the 1978 playoffs between the Phillies and the Dodgers. Jose Cardenal's dust-storm slide does not deter Lopes. The Dodgers won the first two games in Philadelphia, on the way to their second consecutive NL flag.

Relief pitcher Charlie Hough beats the Phillies' Larry Bowa to first base in Game 3 of the 1978 NL playoffs. But the Dodgers went down to defeat that day, 9–4, after having won the first two games of the series.

There were no 20-game winners, but Burt Hooton came close with a record of 19–10. The other rotaters also produced enviable records—Tommy John (17–10), Doug Rau (15–9), Don Sutton (15–11), Rick Rhoden (10–8), and rookie Bob Welch (7–4, with the team's best ERA for a starter, 2.03). Terry Forster was the premier fireman, saving 22 games and producing the best ERA of his career, 1.94.

The playoffs for the National League pennant would involve the same two teams as the year before. Once again the Phillies, under Danny Ozark, beat out the Pirates, but this time by only one and one-half games. It was the Phillies' third consecutive division title.

Game 1 involved another trip to raucous Veterans Stadium. It was even more uninviting this year in light of the fact that the Phillies had won

As a team, the Dodgers had the best slugging average in the National League (.402) and accounted for the most home runs (149), the most RBIs (686), and the most runs scored (727). Their pitchers also produced the finest collective ERA (3.12) in either league that year.

Steve Garvey became the first Dodger in history to collect 200 or more hits in four separate seasons, and his 202 were the league high. Garvey was the only .300 hitter that year (.316), but other Dodgers batters hit respectably and consistently—Reggie Smith (.295), Bill Russell (.286), and Davey Lopes (.278), among others. Reggie Smith whacked the most home runs (29), Ron Cey had 23, Steve Garvey, 21, Rick Monday, 19, and Davey Lopes, 17. Garvey led the team in RBIs with 113 and in doubles with 32.

Davey Lopes tries for a spectacular grab here in Game 4 of the 1978 championship series, but he is unable to snatch the liner hit by Phillie Larry Bowa. The Dodgers won anyway, 4–3. Lopes had an exceptional series, batting .389, including two homers, five RBIs, and seven runs scored.

Dusty Baker makes a dazzling catch in Game 4 of the 1978 championship series, robbing Phillies catcher Bob Boone of an extra-base hit. It proved to be one of the crucial plays that day and helped the Dodgers eke out a 4–3, tenth-inning win to clinch the NL pennant.

After winning the 1978 National League pennant, the Dodgers' second in a row, Tommy Lasorda gets duly drenched with champagne and beer in the Dodgers locker room. Just as they had the year before, the Dodgers whipped the Phillies three games out of four.

54 of their 82 regular-season games there. Tommy Lasorda decided to give Burt Hooton a chance to redeem himself in front of the enemy fans whose taunts had attacked him so mercilessly and effectively the year before. Larry Christenson was Danny Ozark's choice as starting pitcher.

The Dodgers bats, however, prevailed that day. Steve Garvey led the attack with a pair of home runs and a triple, and both Davey Lopes and Steve

Yeager added four-baggers as well. The Dodgers toted up nine runs on 13 hits. Hooton got into trouble in the bottom of the fifth, and Bob Welch came to his rescue. The Dodgers were leading 7–4 at the time, and Welch gave up only one run and two hits in the remaining four and one-third innings. The final was Dodgers 9, Phillies 5.

The next day, gusty and cool in Philadelphia, brought a much different game. There was no

Dodgers slugfest; instead, it was a pitcher's showcase. Tommy John shut out the Phils with a masterful four-hitter. Davey Lopes carried the Dodgers offense, driving in three of the Dodgers' four runs with a homer, a triple, and a single.

The show then moved to Los Angeles for Game 3, and the Phillies were very much aware that they were in deep trouble. Still, they had saved their ace, Steve Carlton, for this game. He had had his least productive year since 1975, winning only 16 while losing 13, but the Dodgers knew Carlton was always a major threat. And Carlton showed his determination not only with his pitching arm but with his bat. He drove in four runs, three of them on a homer, and went the distance on the mound, holding the Dodgers to four runs and eight hits. All told, the Phillies came up with nine runs that day and moved to within a game of the Dodgers.

Despite that brief resurgence, the fates were not to smile on the Phillies in 1978, just as they had not in the two previous NL playoffs. Just when things seemed ready to go right for them, the

Davey Lopes accepts some well-earned plaudits after belting out his second home run in Game 1 of the 1978 World Series. This one also brought in both Rick Monday (left) and Steve Yeager and increased the Dodgers' lead to 6–0. They went on to annihilate the Yankees that day, 11–5, at Dodger Stadium. Lopes hit three homers in all during the Series, drove in seven runs, scored eight, and hit .308.

Before the opening of the 1978 World Series, two old friends, Tommy Lasorda and Yankees coach Yogi Berra, get together for some friendly mugging in front of the media cameras.

Phillies dropped the fourth and final game of the 1978 playoffs. The Dodgers struck first with a run in the second inning, but the Phillies came right back. Greg Luzinski did what he did best and skyrocketed a two-run homer deep into the left-field seats in the third. Ron Cey tied it up with a homer of his own the following inning, and then Steve Garvey sent the Dodgers ahead in the sixth with a solo blast, his fourth home run of the playoffs. Still, the Phillies were tenacious, and Bake McBride tied it up with a homer in the seventh.

By that time both starters, Doug Rau of the Dodgers and Randy Lerch of the Phillies, had departed. A bevy of relievers had combined to keep the game scoreless and send it into extra innings. Tug McGraw was now pitching for the Phillies, and he gave up a walk to Ron Cey in the bottom of the tenth, after two outs. And Dusty Baker's high line drive to center fielder Garry

Burt Hooton hurls here against the Yankees in Game 2 of the 1978 World Series. He pitched into the seventh inning, when he was relieved by Terry Forster, but he still got the win that day, 4–3. The victory put the Dodgers out in front of the Yanks, two games to none. Hooton had his best year ever in 1978—a record of 19–10 and an ERA of 2.71.

Maddox appeared to be the end of the inning. Maddox, a three-time Gold Glove center fielder, positioned himself in order to take it and retire the side. But to the astonishment and delight of the more than fifty-five thousand fans in Dodger Stadium, the ball popped out of his glove and fell to the ground for an error. Instead of having to take the field for the eleventh inning, the Dodgers suddenly had runners on first and second. Moments later, Bill Russell took ultimate advantage of the

gaffe when he tagged McGraw for a single to center, sending Ron Cey home with the winning run and the National League pennant. The Dodgers had their second flag in a row and their seventh since moving to the West Coast. Tommy Lasorda became only the second National League manager to win back-to-back pennants in his first two years managing a club (the other was Gabby Street of the St. Louis Cardinals in 1930 and 1931).

Just as the Dodgers' opposing team in the play-offs had been a repeat from the previous year, so were their rivals in the World Series. In the American League East, the Yankees had edged out the Boston Red Sox in one of the most exciting races in baseball history. Their 100–63 record topped the Bosox by only one game, the result of a special single-game playoff in Boston—the Yankees broke the tie for the division title by surmounting a 2–0 deficit in the seventh to win it 5–4. Then, as they had the year before, they snuffed out the Kansas City Royals, this time in four games.

The Yankees of 1978 were just as combustible as they had been the year before. Billy Martin and Reggie Jackson feuded openly; Jackson was relegated to the role of designated hitter and was eventually suspended for five games by Martin. Then Martin got into a verbal gun battle with owner George Steinbrenner and was fired, for the fourth time in his managerial career. Bob Lemon, a Hall of Fame pitcher with the Cleveland Indians who had been manager of the Chicago White Sox earlier in the 1978 season, was brought to the Bronx to replace Martin.

But for all the neuroses, all the personality clashes, all the delicate egos and fierce prides, the Yankees were still a veteran team of diverse talents and implacable ambitions on the playing field. Their climb to the division title was one of the most remarkable comebacks in the history of the game—their dramatic victory over the Red Sox climaxed a Yankees drive from a 14-game deficit. Starter Ron Guidry posted a fantastic record of 25–3 (.893), and new reliever Goose Gossage saved

194

27 games with a bullet-like fastball. They had another 20-game winner, Ed Figueroa (20–9), and a plethora of seasoned pitching talent in Catfish Hunter, Dick Tidrow, and Sparky Lyle. Reggie Jackson and Graig Nettles led the team in home runs with 27 apiece, and Lou Piniella hit .314. Other returnees from the world champs of 1977, albeit with less impressive stats than usual, were Thurman Munson, Mickey Rivers, Chris Chambliss, and Bucky Dent.

The Series began under a cloud of deep-felt sadness in Los Angeles, however, because of the death of longtime Dodger Jim "Junior" Gilliam. He had played for the Dodgers in Brooklyn and Los Angeles from 1953 through 1966, and he had been the Dodgers first-base coach from 1965 to 1978. At 49, Gilliam had suffered a cerebral hemorrhage and had died only two days before the World Series was to open. As an honor to him, the

Dodgers players wore a black-bordered patch with his No. 19 on their uniform sleeves.

The Dodgers were truly thirsting for revenge. They harbored little love for the Yankees and the fans who jeered them in Yankee Stadium. In addition, the Dodgers team had played together for several years, and many of the starters had played in both the 1974 and 1977 World Series only to come up on the short end each time. "This is the one we want," Davey Lopes said. "This is our third chance. You're lucky to get into just one. We just can't keep wasting these chances." Tommy Lasorda had a variety of things to say on the subject, to his team, to the media, and to anyone else in earshot— all to the effect that the great Dodger in the Sky wanted them to win this one badly and they should not let Him down.

It did not look as if they would, at least at the beginning. The Dodgers had the advantage of

Rick Monday slides safely into second for a double in Game 1 of the 1978 World Series. Leaping to avoid him is Yankees shortstop Bucky Dent. It would prove to be one of only two hits Monday could muster during the five games he played; his average was a disappointing .154.

opening the Series in their own backyard under the familiar sun, smog, and fluttering palm trees. They would have two games in the comfort of Dodger Stadium before heading east for the next three. Lasorda chose Tommy John to go for the Dodgers in the opener, and Bob Lemon sent out Ed Figueroa.

Dusty Baker got it started in the bottom of the second with a solo home run. Rick Monday followed with a double, and then Davey Lopes sent one out of the ballpark. And Figueroa headed for the Yankees showers. In the fourth, Lopes smashed another homer into the left-field seats, this time with two runners on base. The Dodgers had a convincing lead of 6–0. They added another run in the fifth, while Tommy John was shutting the Yankees down without a run—until the top of the seventh. Then their old postseason nemesis Reggie Jackson broke up John's shutout with a 460-foot blast to left, his eighth career World Series homer. It extended his Series home-run string to four games, counting the last three of 1977. The Yankees got two more runs that inning, but the Dodgers countered with three of their own in the bottom half. It was simply the Dodgers' day, and the final was 11–5. The Dodgers had amassed 15 hits, and the adrenalin was flowing.

The second game was a different show, a nail-biter all the way down to the ninth inning. It was highlighted by two of the Yankees' most destructive assets, the power of Reggie Jackson and the fielding of Graig Nettles. Both would hang like doom over the Dodgers for the rest of the Series. During the course of this game, Dodgers batters sent three hot liners down the third-base line, which Nettles and his darting glove prevented from becoming extra-base hits. Reggie Jackson drove in all three of the Yankees runs that day, and Goose Gossage came on in relief to shut the Dodgers out in the last two innings. Although these were all portents of what was to come, they did not stop the Dodgers from prevailing that day. Ron Cey drove in a run in the fourth and then

three more in the sixth with a home run to give Los Angeles a 4–3 win.

The Yankees had threatened in the ninth, however, to give the game a high-drama showdown. There were two outs, and the batter was none other than Reggie Jackson, looking for his fourth RBI of the day and another moment of October glory. On the mound was Bob Welch. Welch was a 21-year-old rookie with a blazing fastball, Jackson was a consummate veteran of the game with a penchant for destroying fastball pitches, especially at that time of the year when most other athletes were tossing footballs around. The confrontation lasted almost seven minutes, as the count ran to 3–2. Dodgers center fielder Bill North later recalled: "It was like the 15th round of a heavyweight championship fight, and you knew both guys had won seven rounds. Bob [Welch] just aired it out and said, 'Hey, Reggie, here it comes. If you can handle it, you deserve it.' It had to end in a home run or a strikeout." This time it ended in a strikeout. A collective sigh wafted through Dodger Stadium. Then the feeling of jubilation took over. The Dodgers were ahead two games to none, and rarely had any team lost a World Series after amassing such a lead.

QUOTES FROM THE WORLD SERIES, 1978

Davey Lopes: "Jimmy's spirit is still here. They will have to beat 50 of us, all 25 men on the roster and then the part of Jim Gilliam that is in all of us."

Ron Fimrite in *Sports Illustrated*: "[It was] a World Series notable for the absence of any intervention from the Big Dodger in the Sky."

George Steinbrenner: "This team is like New York. This is a city of scufflers. Everybody has had a kick in the butt somewhere along the way."

Rick Monday: "I don't like Yankee Stadium and I don't like the town. I don't understand their way of life here."

Bill Russell: "The [New York] writers are the worst, the fans are the worst, and the city is the worst."

The principal reason the Dodgers won Game 2 of the 1978 World Series was this particular hit by Ron Cey, a three-run homer that soared over the left-field wall to change the score from 2–1 Yankees to 4–2 Dodgers. The catcher is Thurman Munson.

The Yankees had saved the crown prince of their 1978 pitching corps for Game 3, which would be played back in the grayer, chillier confines of Yankee Stadium. Ron Guidry had dazzled the entire league in 1978 with a sizzling fastball and a mystifying slider, and had posted one of the finest pitching records in decades.

The Dodgers were well aware of what they would have to face from Guidry. But they could hardly have predicted what Graig Nettles would do to them in the short span of two and a half hours. The third baseman, who afterward was described in *Time* magazine as possessing "millisecond reflexes and a cannon arm" would perpetrate a series of "sprawling, crawling, flying, levitating plays" that would almost single-handedly destroy the Dodgers that day.

It began as early as the second inning. An apparent hit down the third-base line by Lee Lacy was turned into a double play when Nettles

stabbed it and threw with marksmanlike perfection to second. The next inning he stole two extra-base hits from Davey Lopes and Reggie Smith with spectacular diving catches. He robbed Smith of another in the fifth inning. But the ultimate gilding on his gold glove came on two ensuing occasions, both with the bases full of Dodgers who were trailing the Yankees each time and obviously threatening. The first was a sure-hit hard grounder from Steve Garvey's bat, which Nettles dove for, speared, and turned into a force-out to save the inning. The next inning Davey Lopes came up and sent a rocket-shot line drive down toward third, and again Nettles responded with a dive, a slap to knock it down, and a perfect throw to destroy that Dodgers rally.

Nettles' performance was summed up later by Larry Keith in *Sports Illustrated*. "His show became a nationwide hit as he put on the best World Series performance by a fielder since

An intense Davey Lopes fires a shot over a sliding Yankee, the ball headed for the glove of Steve Garvey to complete a nifty double play at Yankee Stadium. But the Dodgers lost all three games in the Bronx that year, turning their 2–0 Series lead into a 3–2 deficit.

With this swipe Reggie Smith drove one into the right-field seats at Yankee Stadium to account for all three of the Dodgers runs in Game 4 of the 1978 World Series. The Yankees, however, brought four across the plate that day. The Yankees battery here is pitcher Ed Figueroa and catcher Thurman Munson.

Baltimore third baseman Brooks Robinson shut off Cincinnati in 1970." The Yankees had come up with five runs on 10 hits, and Guidry had held the Dodgers to a single run and 8 scattered hits to get the win. Manager Bob Lemon added, "Nettles should have been credited with the save."

Game 4 was Reggie's turn. This time, however, his powerful presence was felt in a very different way. It was an important game for the Dodgers; a win and they would have a commanding 3–1 edge in the Series, a loss and they would be tied and

faced with the go-ahead game to be played in New York. Back on the mound with four days' rest were Tommy John and Ed Figueroa.

It was a pitchers' duel, at least through the first four innings. Reggie Smith changed the game's complexion in the top of the fifth, however, by blasting one of Figueroa's breaking pitches right out of the park. Two Dodgers scored ahead of him.

In the following inning Reggie Jackson added his unique touch. With one out, Roy White singled. Thurman Munson then worked Tommy John

LASORDA'S VIEW

Question: Would you describe your feelings after the 1978 Series?

Tommy Lasorda: Very, very despondent. Very down. Flying back from there on the airplane, very, very remorseful. I was sad because I thought after winning the first two games, we had it made. It was a thing that escaped me, which I wanted so badly. I thought we were good enough to win it, that we had won it. I think the Reggie Jackson play [getting in the way of the throw to thwart a double play] changed the complexion of the whole Series because Tommy John was winning that ball game. It would have been the third out, we would have left the field ahead. Instead we left trailing. It was a very, very disheartening call. I also thought that Nettles really killed us. I said this: "If God can make Nettles sick before the Series starts, we would have no trouble winning it because he always seems to do it to us."

for a base on balls. Then, the clutch-hitting Jackson came up and slashed a single between first and second bases. One run scored, but the Dodgers still had a 3–1 lead. Lou Piniella was the next batter, and he too hit Tommy John hard, a line drive headed toward left-center. Shortstop Bill Russell appeared to be in a position to grab it, and the base runners froze. But Russell succeeded only in knocking it down. His reaction was instantaneous. He snatched the ball from the ground, raced to second, stepped on the bag to force Reggie Jackson, then fired to first in hopes of completing the double play and getting the Dodgers out of the inning. But there was a problem. Standing in the base path about 15 feet off first was Jackson. Russell's throw glanced off Jackson's thigh, and instead of continuing into Steve Garvey's waiting glove, it rolled off into foul territory. The umpire signaled Piniella safe, while Thurman Munson scored. Tommy Lasorda raced from the dugout to protest. In a rage that would have done Leo Durocher, Billy Martin, and Earl Weaver proud, Lasorda argued that Jackson had interfered with the throw: he was already out, and far removed from the play. According to official rules, he could not hinder or impede the play made on another runner. The umpire retorted that he did not feel Jackson intentionally interfered with the play. Steve Garvey, who was as close as anyone to the play, including the umpire, disagreed: "The throw was right at him. But his instinct had to tell him to get out of the way of the ball. Instead, he moved his leg just enough to deflect it. It was quick thinking, but dirty pool." It was, of course, a judgment call, and in baseball all such decisions stand. (Jackson, asked later about it, would admit to no wrongdoing, nor voice an opinion on the umpire's decision. But some reported that his smile in response to the inquiry could have put the Cheshire Cat to shame.) That run and another that the Yankees added in the eighth were enough to send the game into extra innings.

In the bottom of the tenth, the alliance of Jackson and Piniella again produced the game-winning run. Jackson singled, moving Roy White into scoring position. Piniella, the next batter, drove him in and the Series was tied at two games each. Perhaps more important, the momentum had changed hands. Roger Angell aptly described it

WORLD SERIES LINEUPS, 1978

DODGERS	YANKEES
Davey Lopes, 2b	Mickey Rivers, cf
Bill Russell, ss	Roy White, lf
Reggie Smith, rf	Thurman Munson, c
Steve Garvey, 1b	Reggie Jackson, dh
Ron Cey, 3b	Lou Piniella, rf
Dusty Baker, lf	Graig Nettles, 3b
Rick Monday, cf	Chris Chambliss, 1b
Lee Lacy, dh	Fred Stanley, 2b
Steve Yeager, c	Bucky Dent, ss

STARTING PITCHERS
Game 1: Tommy John, Ed Figueroa
Game 2: Burt Hooton, Catfish Hunter
Game 3: Don Sutton, Ron Guidry
Game 4: Tommy John, Ed Figueroa
Game 5: Burt Hooton, Jim Beattie
Game 6: Don Sutton, Catfish Hunter

later in *The New Yorker:* "Game 4 was the fulcrum; when it was over the weight of this strange World Series had shifted irreversibly."

That became strikingly evident the next day. Burt Hooton could not hold the Dodgers' two-run lead in the third and was shelled out of the game in an eruption of hits that continued throughout the game. The Yankees banged out 18 hits and 12 runs, and the Dodgers contributed three errors, a passed ball, and two wild pitches to the New Yorkers' cause. Jim Beattie, a 23-year-old right-hander, went the distance for the first time in his one-year major league career. The final score was 12–2, and a disheartened and unnerved Dodgers team climbed aboard the company plane for the long flight back to Los Angeles.

There was talk from some of the players about the advantages of going back home, where they had emerged triumphant in their two meetings with the Yankees a week earlier. But there was also discontent and a rather uncharacteristic outpouring of their dissatisfactions to the public—especially about the New York fans and the members of the Manhattan media.

After a full day of rest, the two teams took the field at Dodger Stadium. Don Sutton was pegged to go for the Dodgers and Catfish Hunter for the Yankees. As they had in the game before, the Dodgers moved out to a one-run lead; and as the Yankees had in the game before, they then systematically slaughtered the Dodgers with their bats—11 hits and seven runs. The Dodgers could only move two runs across the plate. While the champagne flowed in the Yankees clubhouse to celebrate their second world championship in a row, the Dodgers were left with nothing but the nightmarish memories of Graig Nettles' dazzling plays at third, of

Reggie Jackson's little maneuver in the base path between first and second, of Goose Gossage's fastball delivered at 95-plus miles per hour during the late innings of three games, and of the surprise hitting by two youngsters named Bucky Dent and Brian Doyle. The two had batted .243 and .192 respectively in the regular season, but had come on in the Series like Ty Cobb and Rogers Hornsby. Dent batted .417 (10 for 24) and Doyle .438 (7 for 16). As a result of his batting average, his seven RBIs, and his hit-stealing fielding, Dent was named the Series MVP. Doyle, who, according to Ron Fimrite in *Sports Illustrated,* "last year at Series time . . . was selling clothes at the Golden-Farley haberdashery in Bowling Green, Kentucky," had to settle for the Series batting crown. And Reggie Jackson, omnipresent as ever, batted .391 and led the team with two homers and eight RBIs.

There were some surprises in the Dodgers ranks as well. Steve Garvey, who normally was so scintillating in postseason play, slumped through this Series with a meager .208 average, no home runs, and no RBIs. Bill Russell, on the other hand, batted .423 (11 for 26). Davey Lopes hit the most home runs (3) on either team, and his seven RBIs were the most by any Dodger. There was deep disappointment throughout the Dodgers ranks, along with many ex post facto attempts to figure out how they had managed to blow a 2–0 edge in the Series over the four games that had followed. No one was more disappointed than Tommy Lasorda. The two pennants he had won in his first two years were not enough consolation for the back-to-back losses to the men in pinstripes, whom he so much wanted to humble. There would be time, however. As Lasorda himself said, the Great Dodger in the Sky does not deny, only delays.

CHAPTER 17

BETWEEN PENNANTS

Tommy Lasorda and friend in the manager's office at Dodger Stadium. Or, in Lasorda's words, "Just a couple of nice Italian boys."

SANDY KOUFAX RETURNED to the Dodgers in 1979, this time as a pitching coach. So did Andy Messersmith, still active as a pitcher but now struggling with a troublesome shoulder; he had been released by the New York Yankees. There was a new left-hander, Jerry Reuss, whom Al

Campanis had obtained in exchange for Rick Rhoden. The 30-year-old Reuss had been in the big leagues since 1969, the year he came up with the St. Louis Cardinals. His most productive year had been 1975 when he won 18 and lost 11 for the Pittsburgh Pirates. There was also speculation that a rookie right-hander by the name of Rick Sutcliffe might make the team; he had pitched two innings for the Dodgers in 1978 and then had spent the rest of his time honing skills at the Dodgers farm club in Albuquerque.

Besides pitchers, there was only one other addition of note. Outfielder and utility infielder Derrel Thomas, who played for the San Diego Padres in 1978, was signed as a free agent. Thomas had hit only .227 the year before, but he had batted as high as .276 with the Giants in 1975. His versatility, however, would prove an important element for the Dodgers in 1979 because of the raft of injuries that would beset the club. The most notable departure was that of Tommy John, who became a free agent and found a contract with his old taunters, the New York Yankees.

It would indeed be a year of misfortunes for the Dodgers—Tommy Lasorda's Great Dodger in the Sky was obviously attending to other matters. Reggie Smith was the first casualty, a knee injury in the sixth game of the season that kept him out of action for a month. Before the season was two weeks old, Rick Monday injured his Achilles tendon and had to undergo surgery, and that kept him out of uniform for the remainder of the year. Smith returned to the lineup in May for four days then was sidelined with a pinched nerve in his neck. In July he hurt his ankle badly enough to end his play for the year. Bob Welch, the right-hander who had shown so much promise as a rookie the year before, suffered through most of the season with a sore arm. Doug Rau was plagued with a bad shoulder and departed for corrective surgery midway through the season. Reliever Terry Forster, who had undergone elbow surgery in the off-season, made only a few brief appearances early in the year, still far from recovered. And Andy Messersmith proved to be a negligible acquisition because his throwing arm remained weakened and prevented him from appearing in more than just a few games.

After losing the opener to the San Diego Padres, the Dodgers won four straight and moved

into first place by half a game. It would be the only time that year that they would hold the lead in the NL West. After that brief visit to the top, it was a relentless decline for the Dodgers; they dropped as far back as fifth place by early May. Tommy Lasorda, in his curious way with words, told his players, "You're rusting on your laurels." There was a glimmer of hope shortly thereafter, when the Dodgers put together an eight-game winning streak that would prove to be the longest of the season. Then, near the end of the month, they entertained the hometown crowd at Dodger Stadium by decimating the division-leading Cincinnati Reds, 17–6. The Dodgers collected 20 hits that memorable day and tied a single-game club record by totaling seven home runs. That was, however, a fleeting respite from a disappointing season. The Dodgers continued to lose more often than they won and steadily dropped farther behind. By early July the astonished Dodgers were 18 games behind the Houston Astros. By the All-Star break, their record was a lowly 36–57 (.387), the worst showing at that point in the season since the team's Brooklyn days.

A dejected Tommy Lasorda went to manage the National League All-Stars for the second year in a row. Once again, Steve Garvey, Ron Cey, and Davey Lopes represented the Dodgers in the game. And once again Lasorda's team won, this time by a score of 7–6.

For the second half of the season the Dodgers played respectable baseball. They won 43 games while losing only 26, a pace of .623, the best, in fact, in the NL West. But still they were never in contention. Houston and Cincinnati staged a battle royal all the way, and the Dodgers, who had been so far behind, could only make up a little ground while the others vied for the division spoils. The Reds finally won the division, finishing one and one-half games ahead of the Astros. The Dodgers were third, 11½ games behind; their record of 79–83 represented their first losing season since 1968.

The most somber note of the season was the passing of Dodgers owner and chairman of the board Walter O'Malley. He had been president of the Dodgers from the time he succeeded Branch Rickey in 1950 until he stepped down in favor of his son in 1970. After a career that included moving the team from Brooklyn to Los Angeles, building Dodger Stadium, and molding one of the finest and most successful organizations in major league baseball, he died in August at the age of 75. The ownership of the organization now passed into the hands of Peter O'Malley.

In that otherwise bleak season, there were some distinct highlights. Perhaps the most gratifying was the performance of rookie Rick Sutcliffe. The hard-throwing right-hander began the season as a reliever, broke into the starting rotation in early May, and then went on to lead the entire pitching staff. Sutcliffe's 17 victories set a new Los Angeles Dodgers record for a rookie, far surpassing the old mark of 12 set by Don Sutton in 1966 and tied the following year by Bill Singer. Only four pitchers in Brooklyn Dodgers history had won more games in their rookie year than Sutcliffe (Jeff Pfeffer, 23 in 1914; Henry Schmidt, 21 in 1903; Oscar Jones, 20 in 1903; and Dazzy Vance, 18 in 1922). Sutcliffe pitched three two-hitters, lost only 10 games, and had a won-lost percentage of .630. He also batted .247, with 21 hits and 17 RBIs. It was enough to earn him the National League Rookie of the Year award, the first Dodger so honored since Ted Sizemore in 1969.

Dodgers highlights did not only belong to the young, however. Don Sutton, then 34 and completing his 14th year as a Dodger, became the club's all-

A unique kind of honor: having a street named after you at Dodgertown in Vero Beach, Florida, where the Dodgers have trained since 1948. Duke Snider (second from left) is the honoree here. The others are Al Campanis (left) and (from left to right after Snider) Sandy Koufax, Don Drysdale, and Peter O'Malley.

time winningest pitcher, his 217 career wins surpassing Don Drysdale's 209. He also captured Drysdale's records for most career strikeouts (2,524) and shutouts (50). In addition, Sutton now held the all-time Dodgers marks for games started (486), innings pitched (3,516), and—alas—most losses (170). His record for 1979 (12 wins and 15 losses), however, was his most disappointing since 1968, when he was 11–15.

Steve Garvey once again collected more than 200 hits (204). It was the fifth time in six years that he had gone over 200, an all-time Dodgers record. His average of .315 was the team high, and was fourth best in the National League. He also ranked fourth in the league in three other categories—total hits (204), RBIs (110), and total bases (322). Garvey hit 28 home runs, tying for team honors with Ron Cey and Davey Lopes, and he led the club with 32 doubles.

Davey Lopes scored the most Dodgers runs (109). That run total and his 44 stolen bases each

In 1979 the Dodgers acquired Jerry Reuss from the Pirates for Rick Rhoden. Reuss had been hurling in the majors for 10 years by that time, and his best year had been back in 1975, when he won 18, lost 11, and produced an ERA of 2.54. He would have an awful first year with the Dodgers (7–14), but turn it around in 1980 by winning 18 while losing only 6. His victories included a no-hitter against the Giants, and his six shutouts were tied for the major league high. In 1981 he was instrumental in getting the Dodgers into the World Series and in their subsequent victory.

ranked third highest in the league. Then there was 41-year-old Manny Mota, elevated to pinch-hitting king of the majors, whose hitting once prompted *Los Angeles Times* columnist Jim Murray to write: "He could get wood on a bullet." His 1979 output of 15 pinch-hits tied the team record he had originally set in 1974, which had been tied once already by Ed Goodson in 1976. In fact, Mota had established himself as the most productive pinch-hitter in the history of the game. His 147 career pinch hits broke the old major league record of 144 held by Smoky Burgess. Mota retired from active

duty at the end of the year and signed on as a Dodgers coach for 1980. However, he would also be activated that year and add three more pinch-hits for a grand total of 150.

Except for those moments of quasi-splendor, the Dodger's year had been a long and disenchanting one. Neither Tommy Lasorda nor any of his players had expected that they would close out the seventies in such a lackluster fashion, especially in the wake of the two consecutive pennants they had won. It was time for a little regrouping, everyone agreed.

The decade of the eighties was not 10 days old before the legendary Dodgers center fielder Duke Snider was elected to the National Baseball Hall of Fame. He joined, in the game's highest honor, such other Dodgers superstars as Sandy Koufax, Roy Campanella, Jackie Robinson, Dazzy Vance, and Zack Wheat.

There were some new faces in the Dodgers dugout when the 1980 season got underway. The most notable was relief pitcher Don Stanhouse, a right-hander who had been an essential element in the Baltimore Oriole's pennant drive of 1979 (he had 21 saves and a 2.84 ERA). The 29-year-old was a free agent, and the Dodgers signed him to a five-year contract reportedly worth $2.1 million. Another reliever, Steve Howe, was brought up from San Antonio, Texas. The 22-year-old left-hander had a fastball clocked at 94 miles per hour. He and Stanhouse, it was hoped, would more than fill the void left by the still-injured Terry Forster.

Another rookie from whom a lot was expected was outfielder Rudy Law, who had apprenticed in Albuquerque the two previous seasons. A steady hitter and a speedster on the base paths, Law was

TRIVIA

A record for most consecutive errorless games by a Dodgers team was set in 1979: 11 games between May 5 and 16. The old Brooklyn Dodgers went 10 games without an error in 1942.

Ron Cey makes a spectacular diving catch of a line drive in this 1979 game. Cey, who could make big plays at third, was better known for his bat by this time in his Dodgers career. He had hit homers in double figures ever since earning a starting berth on the club in 1973, more than 20 every year since 1975. Cey's best year was 1977, when he clobbered 30 round-trippers and drove in 110 runs. In 1979 he batted .281, second in his career only to the .288 he hit in 1981. That's shortstop Bill Russell in the background.

expected to fill in for Rick Monday and/or Reggie Smith, depending on how the two would come back from their injuries of the previous year. Another outfielder of promise was Pedro Guerrero from the Dominican Republic, who had been shuttling between the Dodgers and their farm team in Albuquerque for the previous two years. He had hit .337 in 1978 and .333 in 1979 in the minors and was considered a deft base thief. There was also Mike Scioscia, who was expected to give both Steve Yeager and his backup Joe Ferguson a run for the job of catcher. Scioscia, only 21, had batted .336 the year before in Albuquerque. Another new

face was Jay Johnstone, although he was hardly a novice to the game. He had been around the majors since 1966 when he came up with the California Angels. Since then he had played with the Chicago White Sox, the Oakland A's, the Philadelphia Phillies, the New York Yankees, and the San Diego Padres. At age 34, Johnstone was signed as a free agent, to be used principally as a pinch-hitter, a role for which he had earned a fine reputation. He was also known as one of the game's most irrepressible practical jokers.

There was also an addition to the management. Danny Ozark rejoined the Dodgers coaching staff

A utility player if there ever was one, Derrel Thomas played the outfield, third, short, and second for the Dodgers in 1979, his first year with the club. The 28-year-old Thomas was only the second free agent ever signed by the Dodgers; he had played variously with the Padres and the Giants since 1972. Thomas hit .256 for the Dodgers in 1979 and stole 18 bases. He would improve his average by 10 percentage points the next year.

after his stint as manager of the Philadelphia Phillies (with whom he had won three division championships).

The Dodgers both opened and closed the 1980 season with Bill Virdon's Houston Astros. In between, it proved to be an exciting, rollicking, lead-changing race between those two teams as well as the division's defending champs, the Cincinnati Reds.

The Dodgers did not get off to a good start. Houston beat them the first two games and then took the series, three of four. Some began to speculate that the woeful 1979 season was *not* just a fluke;

perhaps the Dodgers were simply not a threat anymore. Those thoughts were put to rest later in April when the Dodgers put together a 10-game winning streak, improving a dismal 3–7 record to 13–7 and moving them to within a single game of the division-leading Astros. Eight of those ten games were won at home; after their next road trip they added two more consecutive home victories to bring their home-game winning streak to ten, displacing the previous Dodgers record of nine set in 1962.

The Cincinnati Reds, under manager John McNamara, were also in hot contention for the division lead from the very start, and they overtook

Houston in early May. But the Reds held first for only three days until the Dodgers, with a 20–13 record, pulled ahead of them. At that point in the season, Don Sutton and Jerry Reuss were setting the pitching standards for the team, both with records of 4–0. And emerging from the bullpen in fine style was rookie Steve Howe, dispelling Tommy Lasorda's concern about his relief corps. A disappointment, however, was Rick Sutcliffe, 1979's Rookie of the Year. He appeared to be a victim of that unexplainable malady called the sophomore jinx; with an 0–2 record and an astronomical ERA, he had lost his place in the regular rotation.

The Dodgers controlled the lead in the NL West for the next three weeks, but by only three games at most. Then it was Houston's turn to take over again, and they maintained predominance until two days before the All-Star break, when the Dodgers, on the strength of Bob Welch's ninth win of the season and a team record of 46–33 (.582), moved back into the lead.

The most sparkling performance of the year was the one staged in late June by Jerry Reuss. Against the Giants at Candlestick Park he gave up neither a run, a hit, nor a base on balls. It would have been a perfect game except that one runner got on base as a result of an error by Bill Russell. It was the first Dodgers no-hitter since Bill Singer's a decade earlier and the sixth since the team relocated to Los Angeles. It brought Reuss' record to 9–1 for the season.

Six Dodgers went to the All-Star Game, played at Dodger Stadium in 1980—Steve Garvey, Davey Lopes, Reggie Smith, Bill Russell, Bob Welch, and Jerry Reuss. And Reuss, in relief, was credited with the win that year. Houston took the lead back from the Dodgers four days after the All-Star Game, lost it back to them five days later, and then retook it four days after that.

The Astros were relying strongly on their pitching staff, and it was a remarkable one—starters Nolan Ryan, Joe Niekro, and Vern Ruhle, and relievers Joe Sambito, Frank LaCorte, and Dave

Smith. They also had some productive hitters—Cesar Cedeno, Terry Puhl, Jose Cruz, and Art Howe.

The Dodgers managed to grab the lead for three days in August, only to have it taken away by the Reds this time. The Reds, in turn, remained in first an equally short period of time before the Astros once again claimed it.

The Dodgers and the Astros exchanged the lead several times in September, but in the last week of the season Houston built their lead to three full games. However, with three games left,

The irrepressible Jay Johnstone became a Dodger in 1980, and besides a box full of baseballs he brought along a bag full of practical jokes. Johnstone was signed as a free agent after having played with a variety of teams since 1966. His best years had been 1975 and 1976, when he hit .329 and .318 for the Phillies. In 1980, used principally as a backup outfielder and pinch-hitter, he batted .307. In 1981 he would drop to .205, although he would come up with two clutch-hits in the World Series, one of which was a crucial home run.

Pedro Guerrero came to stay with the Dodgers in 1980 after two years of commuting between L.A. and their farm club in Albuquerque, New Mexico. That first year he played in the out-field and at second, third, and first bases, batting an impressive .322 in 253 at-bats.

The Dodgers symbol for success in the eighties, the high-five. Here, Dusty Baker, after a 1980 home run, gets a double ver-sion from Derrel Thomas and Reggie Smith. Baker hit 29 four-baggers in 1980 and batted .294.

the Dodgers still had a mathematical chance. The remaining games were against Houston at Dodger Stadium, and the Dodgers needed a sweep. A sports page headline in the *Los Angeles Times* read: DO YOU BELIEVE IN MIRACLES?

It was Friday, October 3, the first of the three games. Don Sutton, the staff's most seasoned vet-

eran and most rested starter, was Tommy Lasorda's choice to start. He rose to the occasion, going eight innings and giving up a mere two runs and seven scattered hits. But in the ninth, the Dodgers were losing 2–1, and two were out. Rudy Law was on second base, and Ron Cey was at bat. He lashed a single, and Law, racing at the first hint of Cey's bat-swing, scored easily—the Dodgers' hopes were still alive. Sutton's reliever, who had set the Astros down in the ninth, came back to the mound for the top of the tenth. He was a portly 19-year-old from Sonora, Mexico, named Fernando Valenzuela, in only his third relief appearance in the major leagues. Once again he stymied the Astros. In the bottom of the tenth, the Dodgers' first batter was catcher Joe Ferguson, and he drilled Ken Forsch's first pitch over the left-center-field wall, a 385-foot homer for a 3–2 Dodgers win.

The next day Tommy Lasorda selected Jerry Reuss, who was completing his best season ever as

Relief pitcher Don Stanhouse, shaking hands here with Ron Cey, came to the Dodgers in 1980 as a free agent, bringing with him some strong credentials. He had saved 24 and 21 games, respectively, in the preceding two seasons for the Baltimore Orioles. But back and shoulder problems hampered him throughout 1980, and he fell far short of expectations. Dodgers management agreed to honor the remainder of his five-year ($1.36 million) contract in 1981, then released him.

Don Sutton's last year as a Dodger was 1980, a season in which he won 13 games, one of which he is being congratulated for here by Steve Garvey. He lost only five games, and his ERA of 2.21 was the best in the major leagues that year. Sutton had been pitching for the Dodgers since 1966, but in 1981, he followed the free agent trail to the Houston Astros. Sutton owns practically every career pitching mark in the Dodgers record book.

DON SUTTON

For 15 years Don Sutton toiled in a Dodgers uniform and became the most productive pitcher in the club's history. No one has won more games for the Dodgers (230), thrown more strikeouts (2,652) or shutouts (52), appeared in (534) or started (517) more games as a pitcher, or hurled more innings (3,728). He also has the ignominious distinctions of having racked up the most losses (175) and given up the most hits (3,200) and the most bases on balls (966). His Dodgers career ERA is 3.07.

Only once did Sutton win more than 20 games (21–10 in 1976), but he won 11 or more games in every one of his 15 years on the Dodgers staff. He holds the club record for the most shutouts in a single season by a right-hander (nine in 1972), and—on the negative side—the most home runs given up in a season (38 in 1970).

Sutton pitched in four All-Star Games. In the 1977 classic he both started the game and walked off with the game's MVP honors. He left the Dodgers as a free agent in 1981 and signed with the Houston Astros.

LASORDA'S OFF-SEASON

Question: Everybody knows what you do during the season, but what do you do in the off-season?

Tommy Lasorda: I do a lot of speaking, I go visit the instructional league team, and I go visit the Winter Leagues. I go all over the country speaking. I speak to a lot of people on motivation, to schools, churches, civic organizations. In doing so, I have never taken a dime from schools or churches or civic organizations or Little League programs because I feel that this is my way of giving something back to the game of baseball and to the Dodgers. I want to be known as an ambassador for the Dodgers in baseball. Baseball has been great to me, and the Dodgers have been super to me. This is my way of saying to both of them, "Thank you; I want to go out and talk about you because I believe in you and I think you are the greatest product in the world and I love you very much."

The annual "Stars" game at Dodger Stadium brings together people of all sizes and professions, from actor Billy Barty to L.A. Lakers basketball star Kareem Abdul-Jabbar.

Steve Garvey drives one out of the park in this 1979 game, one of 28 homers he hit that year. Since becoming a regular in 1973, Garvey hit over .300 every year except two: in 1977 he batted .297, and in the abbreviated 1981 season he dropped to .283. In 1979 he hit .315, but his best year was 1975, when he batted .319. Garvey collected 200 or more hits in six of seven seasons between 1974 and 1980. Four times he has gotten five hits and ten times a pair of homers in a single game.

a major league pitcher. Bill Virdon sent up fast-baller Nolan Ryan. The Dodgers tallied a run in the second after Steve Garvey got a hit and was subsequently driven in on Derrel Thomas' single. Garvey accounted for the Dodgers' second run of the day two innings later with a bases-empty home run. That was all Jerry Reuss needed. He allowed only one run and seven hits, went the distance,

The youngster stepping into the Dodgers dugout here is 19-year-old Fernando Valenzuela, from Navajoa, Sonora, Mexico; Tommy Lasorda brought him up late in the 1980 season from the Dodgers farm club in San Antonio, Texas. Blessed with a dancing screwball and a fiery fastball, he made his debut September 15 at Atlanta and went on to win two games in relief before the 1980 season ended. He was not scored against in the 17⅔ innings he pitched. Tommy Lasorda said after the maiden performance, "We have great hopes for the youngster."

and logged his 18th win of the season. Suddenly Dodgers followers were beginning to believe in miracles. Perhaps Tommy Lasorda had been right about the Dodger in the Sky.

It was the bottom of the eighth in Game 3 of the series, and the Dodgers were trailing the Astros 3–2. Ron Cey came to bat with a man on and blasted a home run. The score was 4–3, and the Dodgers held on until the end. They had done it: three straight over the Astros—three one-run, nail-biting, heart-palpitating, nerve-jangling victories.

The season was over, and the Dodgers were in a tie with the Astros for the NL West title, each with records of 92–70. The divisional crown and the passport to the NL pennant playoffs with the East-division champ, the Philadelphia Phillies, would be decided the next day in a one-game, winner-take-all playoff at Dodger Stadium.

There was, however, a limit to the Dodgers' composure under the protracted tensions. The next day the miracle seekers were brought resoundingly back to the mortal world. Astros starter Joe Niekro pitched with hardly a flaw and conceded only one run to the Dodgers. His compatriots joined forces to knock in seven runs.

It had been a year of extraordinary entertainment in the National League West. No one knew that better than Dodgers supporters, who, for the second time in major league history, had broken the 3-million mark in home attendance and the 5-million mark in total home and road attendance.

Terry Forster's brilliant career as a relief pitcher suffered a setback before the 1979 season when he underwent elbow surgery. He had come to the Dodgers a year earlier as a free agent and promptly became the club's bullpen ace. Forster saved 22 games that year (the most a Dodgers reliever had racked up since Jim Brewer rescued 24 in 1971), while posting a career-high ERA of 1.94. Forster's best year in the majors, however, was with the Chicago White Sox in 1974, when he saved 24 games, the most in the AL that year.

As a team, the Dodgers had improved considerably over the previous season's spectacle. Only four teams in the major leagues had produced better records than their 92–71 (the New York Yankees, Baltimore Orioles, Kansas City Royals, and, of course, the Houston Astros). Their sluggers led the National League in home runs (148) for the fourth consecutive year. Their pitchers hurled more shutouts (19) than any team in either league.

Jerry Reuss, with a no-hitter and a record of 18–6, was the club's premier pitcher, recipient of the National League Comeback Player of the Year award, and a runner-up to Steve Carlton for the Cy Young Award. His six shutouts were tied with Tommy John's total for the most in either league; John, the former Dodger, won 22 games for the Yankees that year. Steve Howe set an all-time Dodgers record for a rookie with 17 saves, erasing the mark of 15 set by Joe Black in 1952. That and his 2.65 ERA were enough to earn him the National League's Rookie of the Year award. Bob Welch produced a record of 14–9 and led the team in strikeouts with 141. Don Sutton added to his all-time Dodgers records with 13 wins and 5 losses. His ERA of 2.21 was the best in the major leagues that year.

As far as hitting went, the story was much the same as the year before. Steve Garvey again led the club in hits with 200, a total he had then attained in six of his previous seven seasons. It was also the seventh time he had batted better than .300 (.304) for the Dodgers. The highest batting averages of the year were registered by Reggie Smith (.322), although he played in only 92 games because of his shoulder problems, and pinch-hitter/backup outfielder Jay Johnstone (.307).

Dusty Baker led the team in homers with 29, but Ron Cey was right behind with 28. Steve Garvey had 26 and Reggie Smith added 15. Garvey again drove in the most runs (106). On the base paths, Rudy Law stole 40 to set a Dodgers record for a rookie. Davey Lopes pilfered another 23, Bill Russell had 13, and Dusty Baker 12.

It had been a thrilling start to the eighties, but, although no one knew it at the time, it was a mere prelude to the excitement, drama, and jubilation that was in store for Los Angeles in the season to come.

CHAPTER 18

A YEAR TO REMEMBER

Steve Yeager cracks a pinch-hit double off reliever Joe Sambito in this regular-season game at the Astrodome in Houston. The Dodgers lost five of eight games there during 1981 and would come back for two playoff drubbings before getting their postseason act together.

IT WAS DESTINED TO BECOME known in baseball circles as the year of the strike and the year of fanciful comebacks, which seemed more appropriate to a Frank Merriwell story than the Los Angeles Dodgers. The season came to a halt when the players walked off the job in June, leaving a gaping two-month hole in the normal summer baseball schedule. Never before in the history of the game—through two world wars, the Great Depression, and other assorted disasters—had such

Hall of Fame pitcher Sandy Koufax poses with rookie Fernando Valenzuela during spring training at Dodgertown. Koufax was back on special assignment to help coach the Dodgers pitchers, and Valenzuela was in the process of revving himself up for a scintillating season.

a disruption occurred. Still, the shortened season had disproportionate excitement: a set of impromptu playoffs, some decided ironies, and a redeeming ending for all baseball fans, especially those of the Los Angeles Dodgers.

There was talk of an impending strike all through the winter of 1980–1981 and spring training. But the baseball year kicked off as scheduled April 9. The Dodgers had lost their longtime stalwart Don Sutton, owner of practically every Dodgers career pitching record, to the lure of free agency, and he had found a fat contract with the Houston Astros. The dubious financial windfall from not having to pay Sutton's salary was completely offset by the departure of Don Stanhouse. He had suffered shoulder problems midway

through the 1980 season, had shown little improvement in spring training, and was released, costing the Dodgers the $1.36 million still remaining in his five-year contract. "There is a time when you have to bite the bullet," Al Campanis said, and Peter O'Malley agreed.

Outfielder Ken Landreaux was acquired from the Minnesota Twins. He had hit .281 up in the Northland and was reputed to cover center field with deft precision. And by Opening Day, rookie Mike Scioscia had taken the starting catcher's job from Steve Yeager.

The infield remained the same—from left to right, Cey, Russell, Lopes, and Garvey. It was their eighth year in a row together, the longest any infield combination had stayed intact in the history of major league baseball. Dusty Baker and Pedro Guerrero flanked Landreaux in the outfield, and Rick Monday (whose injury seemed healed) and Jay Johnstone were available as backups.

The prominent starting pitchers would be Jerry Reuss and Burt Hooton. There was also Bob Welch, and there was a bit of a contest at Vero Beach between a troubled Rick Sutcliffe and young Fernando Valenzuela for the fourth slot in the starting rotation. In the bullpen the chief duties would fall to a group of youngsters: Steve Howe, Bobby Castillo, Dave Stewart, and Tom Niedenfuer. The relief corps was Tommy Lasorda's biggest worry for 1981.

For years, perhaps, the story will be told of how Lasorda arrived at his mound choice to open this particular season. For the previous two years, the honor had gone to Burt Hooton. The choice for 1981, however, was Jerry Reuss, who had turned in the finest pitching performance of 1980. But Reuss managed to pull a leg muscle just before the opener and was therefore relegated to the bench. Hooton, on the other hand, was not fully rested and was also bothered by an ingrown toenail. Bob Welch had a sore arm. So Tommy Lasorda decided to go with rookie Fernando Valenzuela, veteran of only a few relief appearances the year before but a stellar performer during the early spring preseason.

It was indeed an auspicious choice. Within two months, Valenzuela would be the most celebrated player in the game. Photos of him were taken at the White House with President Ronald Reagan, a biography of his brief 20 years was published in both English and Spanish, and a new word, *Fernandomania*, crept into the vocabulary of base-ball fans, even though Valenzuela himself could not speak a word of the language.

It all came about because of the way he could throw a baseball, especially a screwball, and the way he could continually render opposing teams impotent. The first sign of what was in store for Dodgers fans came that Opening Day. The Dodgers faced the Astros, the team that had thwarted the

FORTUNE TELLER

On January 22, 1981, Davey Lopes, speaking to a gathering of Dodgers fans: "Because of your loyal support, we owe you a championship, and this is the season we're going to give it to you."

Dodgers' pennant hopes the year before. Valenzuela zapped them 2–0, giving up only five hits.

The Dodgers continued what Valenzuela had started, winning their first six games in a row that year, including Valenzuela's second win, an easy decision over the Giants in which he only gave up one run. On April 22 he racked up his third straight victory, shutting out the San Diego Padres 2–0. In each of the latter two wins Valenzuela struck out 10 batters. The Dodgers, with a record of 10–2, had a firm hold on first place in the NL West.

Word was, however, that the chubby rookie and his streaking team would both get their come-uppance in Valenzuela's next appearance. He was slated to go against the Astros in their home court, the Astrodome, a stadium always hostile to the Dodgers. Manager Bill Virdon sent former Dodger Don Sutton against them, and Sutton pitched a beautiful game, giving up only a single run. But Valenzuela went one better—he pitched another shutout and even singled to drive in Pedro Guerrero with the game's winning run.

By this time, Fernando Valenzuela was a true baseball celebrity. The rookie had thrown three shutouts in four games, was leading the majors in strikeouts, possessed a screwball that nobody seemed able to hit, and had the complacency and control of a hurler who had been around the league for 10 years.

By May 3, the Dodgers were two and one-half games in front of the Cincinnati Reds, and six ahead of the previous year's divisional champs, the Astros, who were floundering in fifth place. The Dodgers had won 14 and lost 6, a winning pace of .700. Valenzuela had picked up another shutout

By 1981 the Dodgers infield had been together for eight straight years, a major league record for longevity. The four familiar faces (from left) are Ron Cey, Bill Russell, Davey Lopes, and Steve Garvey.

victory, 5–0, and his ERA for the five wins was an incredible 0.20. Burt Hooton was also having a fine time, with a record of 3–0, and although Jerry Reuss had a record of only 1–1, his ERA was just 1.59. Rick Sutcliffe stood at 2–1, and he had an ERA of 1.98. Dusty Baker was hitting .351 and Mike Scioscia, .304, but the rest of the Dodgers hitters were slumping (Steve Garvey was hitting an astonishing low of .226).

Two weeks later, the Dodgers claimed a mark of 26–9 (.743). And Valenzuela's record had soared to 8–0. By this time, Valenzuela's trips to the mound in Dodger Stadium had become cause for sellout crowds and, as the *Los Angeles Herald Examiner*

reported, scalpers were getting as much as $50 a seat to watch him weave his pitching tapestry. On the road, his presence gave rise to massive press conferences that would have been more appropriate to presidents or popes, and he smilingly fielded the questions fed to him through an interpreter.

It took the world champion Philadelphia Phillies to burst Valenzuela's bubble. They got to Fernando for four runs and relegated the Dodgers to the losing end of a shutout for a change.

It would be unfair to imply that the team was all Fernando Valenzuela, although he seemed to be kindling a superstar status. The truth is, the entire Dodgers pitching staff carried the team through

A LASORDA INSIGHT

Question: What about the behind-the-scenes operations during the season? The fans know what you do on the field, but they don't know all the other things that you have to do.

Tommy Lasorda: Well, I confer with Campanis almost on a daily basis. I am in here [the Dodgers offices] a lot in the wintertime. We go to the Winter League meetings. We negotiate trades. Al will ask my opinion; he will ask the opinion of all the people involved. He is the one who makes the final decision. Al has been like a big brother to me, the guy who taught me more baseball than anybody alive. He is the guy who took me under his wing many years ago and primed me, taught me how to scout, was responsible for me becoming a minor league manager. When I did become a minor league manager, he tried to transfer all of his knowledge to me. Since then we've always worked together for the ballclub.

May of the 1981 season. Burt Hooton had a record of 7–0, and Jerry Reuss was devastating, obviously on his way to another superb season. But the Dodgers bats were strangely silent.

After May 18 the lack of hitting began to take its toll on the Dodgers. They had been ahead by as many as six and one-half games, but suddenly they skidded, and the pitching alone could not sustain them. In the last 13 games before the season was interrupted, they won only 5.

On June 12 the strike came, and the ballparks emptied. No one knew how long it would last. The preseason interruptions of the past had always been relatively short, more symbolic than anything else. Many expected this hiatus to be similar; after all, the players were losing salaries and the owners large revenues, and the baseball season was not long enough to make up for substantial lost time. Still it went on and on, and as June passed into July and through that month, it appeared that maybe the entire season would have to be scrapped.

It was not. Differences were temporarily resolved and the season reopened. Some considered the season rescued; others had harsher terms. Baseball commissioner Bowie Kuhn and the club

owners then agreed to alter the traditions. They would consider the season to have been divided into two halves, the first before the strike and the second after. The teams would each begin the second half anew with a 0–0 record. In a special playoff, the team on top of its division at the end of the first half would face the team with the best second-half record in that division. The Dodgers, who had ended the first half in first place, a mere one-half game ahead of the Cincinnati Reds, were suddenly assured of a berth in the postseason playoffs.

Play resumed in the major leagues on August 9. Fernando Valenzuela led both leagues in strikeouts when the second part of the season got underway,

Mike Scioscia took over the starting job at catcher in 1981, displacing longtime tenant behind the plate Steve Yeager. Scioscia was brought up the year before from Albuquerque. In 1981 he batted .276, then watched as Steve Yeager took back the catching duties for the World Series.

Dave Stewart was a rookie in 1981, even though he had made a brief two-inning appearance on the mound for the Dodgers back in 1978. Brought up from Albuquerque, where he had won 15 games the year before, Stewart became a regular reliever for the Dodgers of 1981. During the strike-interrupted season, he managed six saves and produced a record of 4–3 and an ERA of 2.55. He had problems in the 1981 playoffs, most notably his serving up of the game-winning home run in the first game against Houston at the Astrodome, but he pitched a crucial, scoreless one and two-thirds innings in the World Series.

but he had been struggling on the mound ever since his first loss. His first two starts in the second half were shaky, and many observers began to wonder if he was really as good as they had thought. But Fernandomania regenerated in late August when Valenzuela struck out 12 Cardinals in a Dodgers victory. Then he pitched a 6–0, four-hit shutout over the Chicago Cubs. By early September Valenzuela was back in full form. On September 6 he followed with another shutout, his seventh of

the year, to tie the all-time National League record for shutouts by a rookie. It was also his 12th win of the year, tops in the majors at that point, and he led all other pitchers in both shutouts and strikeouts.

As a team, the Dodgers remained in contention during the season's second half, but because of the strangely structured playoffs, they didn't really have to. Even if they won both of the season's two segments, they would still have to face the second-ranked team in the NL West at the end of the season. The Dodgers were merely priming themselves for the playoffs for which they were already slated. By September 9 they were only a game behind the Houston Astros, a team that had turned its dismal season around dramatically in the second portion.

Ron Cey, one of the mainstays in the Dodgers' otherwise ineffective batting order, became a major casualty around that time. He suffered a broken bone in his forearm and would not play again until the postseason.

The Dodgers did not top their division in the second half of the season. Valenzuela's performance was the highlight of this otherwise anticlimactic period. But there were two pitching performances of special note that became part of the major league record books. The first was a positive one for the Dodgers; Fernando Valenzuela hurled his eighth shutout to tie the all-time major league record for a rookie set by Ewell "Reb" Russell back in 1913. The second occurred at the Dodgers' expense. Astros fastballer Nolan Ryan became the first pitcher in major league history to throw five no-hit games when he blanked the Dodgers in the Astrodome. Ryan had shared the record of four no-hitters with the Dodgers' own Sandy Koufax.

When the second half of the season came to a close, the Dodgers found themselves in fourth place, six games behind the Houston Astros. Their record was 27–26; added to the season's first half (36–21), their overall record was 63–47 (.573). Only the Oakland A's and the Cincinnati Reds won more games than the Dodgers. (The Reds, having ended up in second in both the season segments, would not participate in postseason play because of the weird playoff setup.)

The Dodgers record had largely been due to pitching. Not just that of Fernando Valenzuela, who had earned the most wins (13 against 7 losses), but that of the entire staff. Valenzuela had led both leagues in strikeouts with 180, the first time a rookie had done that since Herb Score led the majors with 245 in 1955 for the Cleveland Indians. His eight shutouts were also a major league high. Jerry Reuss, however, had the best won-lost percentage (.714), a result of his 10–4 record. Burt Hooton also had a fine year with 11 wins and 6 losses, and his ERA of 2.28 was the best on the club, and the second best in the National League. Jerry Reuss' 2.29 was third in the league. Steve Howe had picked up eight saves and

The clubhouse gastronome, Tommy Lasorda. Here he is pampered in the St. Louis clubhouse after having published a scathing review of the Cardinals' postgame repasts. Looking on is Dusty Baker.

THE LEAGUE GOURMAND

As well known perhaps as the fact that his blood is Dodger Blue are Tommy Lasorda's Epicurean escapades. Because of this, he was asked to rate the food served in the clubhouses around the league. Journalist Scott Ostler wrote about the interviews in the *Los Angeles Times:*

> Each major league clubhouse attendant provides a postgame meal for the team. It's known as The Spread because it is usually spread out buffet-style on a table in the center of the clubhouse. Many postgame interviews are conducted thusly: A group of sweaty, hungry reporters crowd around a sweaty, semidressed athlete who answers their questions while wolfing down a chili dog or chicken leg.

Ostler recorded gourmand Lasorda's individual comments for posterity. In Lasorda's "Michelin Guide to Clubhouse Dining" only two teams outside Los Angeles received the coveted four stars:

San Francisco Giants: "I like Murph [the clubhouse man]. He has steak sandwiches, hamburger steaks, chicken, plus tomatoes and all the stuff that comes with it."

New York Mets: "The reason it's good is his mom cooks the food, and she's Italian. He has rigatoni, meat loaf, ham and cheese, chicken, mostaccioli. The mostaccioli is delicious. That's probably the best meal on the road."

The losers, relegated to only one star:

San Diego Padres: "The only good thing is the eating room, it's separate from the clubhouse. The guy [has] . . . skinny chickens. He must get chickens that are smuggled out of Tijuana."

Montreal Expos: "The worst in the business is Montreal. He puts out chicken. I think the way they were killed was he starved 'em to death."

Pittsburgh Pirates: "It's in a class with Montreal. The guy figures he's not gonna give you good food, so he can make a profit. One day out of three or four he has something hot. I think he had a relative who was killed in a supermarket, and he doesn't want to get it the same way, so he buys everything off the streets. Whatever he's serving, it's imitation."

But the very best? "My office has gotta be four-star. We always have egg rolls and pork, sent over from a Chinese restaurant. Joe [a friend who works for a food company] brings bologna, burritos, pepperonis, and stuff like that for the office. A local deli sends hero sandwiches, and an Italian restaurant sends some stuff over sometimes when they feel generous."

And a special Lasorda recommendation: "With egg roll—chenin blanc wine."

recorded an ERA of 2.50; Dave Stewart, a rookie, had six saves, and Bobby Castillo another five.

Dusty Baker had his best season at bat since 1972; his .320 was the third highest in the National League. But he was the club's only .300 hitter for 1981. Steve Garvey was down to .283, his lowest in nine years. Ron Cey, despite missing a large part of the season with his injured arm, hit the most home runs (13). Pedro Guerrero added 12, Rick Monday cracked 11, and Garvey had 10. Davey Lopes led with 20 stolen bases, but Ken Landreaux picked up 18. Tommy Lasorda was named the National League's Manager of the Year,

Reliever Steve Howe was the National League's Rookie of the Year in 1980, and in 1981 was the Dodgers' most reliable fireman in both the regular season and the postseason. He was credited with 17 saves and a 2.65 ERA his rookie year and followed that with 8 saves and a 2.50 ERA in 1981. He would also earn his first World Series victory in 1981.

and Fernando Valenzuela won both Rookie of the Year and the Cy Young Award.

Act I of the postseason got under way October 6. It was a comfortable, air-conditioned 76 degrees inside the Astrodome that night, while outside the sprawling city of Houston was bathed in an unseasonable humidity as sweltering as an Amazon rain forest. A boisterous crowd of 44,836 and a press box packed with writers and sportscasters were gathered there to watch what certainly promised to be a classic confrontation. Nolan Ryan, at 34 one of the game's master moundsmen, who in September had pitched his fifth career no-hitter, would hurl for the Astros; toiling from the Dodgers rubber would be rookie sensation Fernando Valenzuela, a mere 20 years old, who had pitched eight shutouts that year to tie a major league record for rookies and had led both leagues in strikeouts with 180.

As the night moved on, it proved to be just what everyone expected, two virtuosos orchestrating their own brands of symphony from a podium centered in the Astrodome infield. Nolan Ryan's fastball seemed to have a special zing on it that night, and the broadcasters—with the help of some equipment that measured velocity—were telling the fans that this pitch was clocked at 95 miles per hour and that one at 97. At the same time, Valenzuela exhibited his special wizardry and sent Astro after Astro back to the dugout.

It was not until two outs in the bottom of the sixth that the shutout was broken. Astros center fielder Tony Scott blooped a Texas-leaguer to short right just barely beyond the glove of Dodgers second baseman Davey Lopes, scoring Terry Puhl, who had raced from second at the crack of the bat. But in the Dodgers half of the seventh, the run was redeemed when Steve Garvey drove one of Nolan Ryan's fastballs into the center-field seats.

As the game entered the ninth inning, Ryan had given up only two hits and Valenzuela a well-scattered six. But Valenzuela was pulled for pinch-hitter Jay Johnstone in the ninth, and Tommy Lasorda had to bring in rookie reliever Dave

L.A. ALLY: DODGER STADIUM

That is how the headline read above sportswriter Bill Gleason's column in the *Chicago Sun-Times:*

On the floor of Chavez Ravine there is this poem of a ballpark, this esthetically delightful place that has taken on a life of its own. It is as though the home of the Los Angeles Dodgers is the Los Angeles Dodgers. The stadium has become a living thing, an opponent. . . . The Dodgers are the beneficiaries of something rare in major league baseball. Their playing field has become a psychological weapon. . . . Could it be that this spacious park with its balanced dimensions, its clean architectural lines, its real, green grass sends visiting players into the blind staggers?

Bob Welch held down a slot in the regular rotation in 1981, along with Fernando Valenzuela, Jerry Reuss, and Burt Hooton. The Dodgers brought Welch up from their Albuquerque farm club in 1978 and installed him in the regular rotation later that season.

Stewart to face the Astros in the bottom of the inning. The strategy backfired. After the first two Astros were set down, manager Bill Virdon sent Craig Reynolds up to pinch hit for Kiko Garcia, and he rapped a single to center. Then catcher Alan Ashby stepped into the batter's box and created a storybook ending by driving a home run over the Astrodome wall. The final score was 3–1, and the Astros led the miniplayoffs by a game.

The next day offered another premier pitcher's duel. Knuckleballer Joe Niekro worked for the Astros, and the Dodgers pitted against him another of their aces, Jerry Reuss, whose 10–4 record (.714) was fourth best in the National League that year. Again protected from the damp tropics of Houston by the Astrodome, both pitchers worked with consummate precision. Reuss did not give up a hit until the fifth inning and did not let a run cross home plate in the nine innings he pitched. Niekro, concentrating on his dancing knuckleball, hurled eight scoreless innings before stepping aside for a pinch-hitter.

The game was still 0–0 in the bottom of the eleventh when the Dodgers' youthful bullpen corps failed again. Dave Stewart, who less than 18

hours earlier had served up Alan Ashby's home-run pitch, allowed two consecutive singles before being pulled by Lasorda. Two outs later the bases were full as a result of an intentional walk given to Cesar Cedeno. Dennis Walling, a back-up outfielder and sometimes first baseman, came to bat. Walling, who had hit only .100 against the Dodgers during the regular season, faced 22-year-old reliever Tom Niedenfuer. The fates, however, had decreed that it was Walling's night to be a hero. He lined a hit to right-center to score Phil Garner and give the Astros a 1–0 victory and a mountainous two-game lead in the playoffs. And so, as San Antonio writer Clifford Broyles put it: "The

Mike Scioscia blocks home plate more in the fashion of an L.A. Ram than a Dodger in Game 2 of the split-season playoff of 1981. He is also putting the tag on Cesar Cedeno of the Astros. Still, the Astros won it in 11 innings, 1–0. No. 28 on the Dodgers is Pedro Guerrero.

Houston Astros headed west needing one win while the Los Angeles Dodgers went home in search of their offense and a three-game sweep."

Home was, of course, Dodger Stadium, where the fabled "10th player" lurks. The partisan L.A. crowd is so ardently vocal and supportive that some say it gives the Dodgers the equivalent advantage of a 10th player on the diamond. It was in that white-and-Dodger-blue edifice—surrounded by giant palms, eucalyptus trees, and a variety of other verdant tropical growths—that local fans like Frank Sinatra, Johnny Carson, Cary Grant, Jackie Gleason, Toni Tennille, Dean Martin, Jonathan Winters, Telly Savalas, Dinah Shore, and myriad other celebrities often gathered to cheer for the hometown boys.

And it was there that the Dodgers did indeed resurrect their offense, and quickly, too—much to the chagrin of the Astros. In the first inning at Los Angeles, Dusty Baker doubled to left-center to drive in Davey Lopes, then moments later came home himself ahead of Steve Garvey, who smashed his second home run of the series, ringing up a 3–0 lead at the end of one inning. Before the day was over the Dodgers nicked four Astros pitchers for 10 hits and sent six players across the plate. Right-hander Burt Hooton allowed only three hits

and a single run in seven innings, and the Dodgers bullpen redeemed itself by not allowing a run or a hit in the last two innings. The 6–1 win brought the Dodgers within a game of the Astros. Still, they had to win two more, and the pitcher waiting for them in the last meeting would be none other than Nolan Ryan, "if it goes that far," Astros manager Bill Virdon announced.

Tommy Lasorda did not have the luxury of holding back his gemstone, Fernando Valenzuela. In the next game, before 55,983 fans, the largest non–World Series crowd in Dodger Stadium history, the youngster from Navajoa, Sonora, Mexico,

Everyone was after this Astros pop-up at Dodger Stadium, but Bill Russell (left) got his glove on it and held on. That's Dusty Baker (foreground) and Ken Landreaux also in pursuit of the ball.

set down the first 13 Astros in order before giving up a hit to Cesar Cedeno, whom he then promptly picked off first base. In the Dodgers' half of the fifth inning, third baseman Pedro Guerrero put the home team on the scoreboard with a home run. That and a run in the seventh when shortstop Bill Russell laced a single to right to drive in Steve Garvey, along with Valenzuela's mastery on the mound, were enough to give the Dodgers a 2–1 win and bring the miniplayoffs to a climactic showdown the next afternoon at Dodger Stadium.

Jerry Reuss opposed Nolan Ryan, and it figured to be another Dodgers-Astros hurling duel before a capacity crowd. As expected, the pitchers dueled for five scoreless innings. By the bottom of the sixth, only Davey Lopes had managed to get a hit off Nolan Ryan. In the two previous games against Ryan—18 full innings—the Dodgers had gotten only two hits and scored nary a run. Now the fans in Dodger Stadium were beginning to ask with legitimate reason if they would *ever again* score a run off the Astros ace. They also must have been wondering if Reuss was ill-fated enough to hold the Astros scoreless through another nine-inning game only to see it all go down the drain as Dodgers batters proved powerless against Ryan's blinding fastballs and sharp-breaking curves.

Nolan Ryan was not invincible, however. His fall began in the sixth inning with a walk to Dusty Baker. A single by Steve Garvey sent Baker to third. Then Rick Monday lined a single to right and Baker scored. That alone would have been enough, as it turned out, because Jerry Reuss did not give up a single run that day. Still, the sixth-inning bonanza

Ken Landreaux makes a diving catch of a short Astros fly ball at Dodger Stadium to stifle a Houston threat. Dodgers fielding and a sudden burst of hitting at home reversed the momentum of the series to decide the winner of the NL West for 1981. Landreaux had come to the Dodgers just before the start of the season from the Minnesota Twins and hit .251 during the regular season.

Pedro Guerrero returns to the Dodgers dugout in triumph after breaking a 0–0 tie with a home run in the fifth inning of Game 4 of the miniseries. The Dodgers went on to win the game 2–1 and tie the Astros at two games apiece.

was not over, and catcher Mike Scioscia singled to drive in Garvey and scored shortly thereafter on an Astros error. Steve Garvey iced the proverbial cake the following inning with a triple to drive in L.A.'s fourth run of the day. Jerry Reuss got the win with an impeccable performance, giving up only five hits in the 4–0 shutout. The Dodgers, in search of their offense and a three-game sweep, had found both that day in Dodger Stadium.

Phil Hersh, a *Chicago Sun-Times* writer, described the aftermath:

The celebration was worthy of a prize much larger than the championship of the National League West divisional playoffs. The Dodger clubhouse was off-bounds only to those who chose to avoid a drenching with Hans Korbell champagne. The prudent were few, the prurient many. . . . Ron Cey, who hadn't even played in the series, turned an indomitable woman reporter's interview into a wet T-shirt contest. An infant was being bottle-fed champagne. He appeared to

Fernando Valenzuela went the distance in Game 4 of the series against the Astros and accepts a high five from Ron Cey for his 2–1 victory. It was a pleasant sort of revenge for the loss Valenzuela suffered in Game 1 of the series. The catcher is Mike Scioscia.

LANGUAGE BARRIER

From the *Los Angeles Times:* "TV viewers may have been surprised Monday when the camera zoomed in on Dodger pitcher Fernando Valenzuela and Manager Tommy Lasorda on the mound in the bottom of the ninth inning of the National League playoff decider against the Expos. Lasorda brought in Bob Welch and Valenzuela started laughing . . . because when Lasorda reached the mound he said, in Spanish, 'It's time for a fresh horse.'"

be the only one actually drinking the stuff. Pitcher Bob Welch was pouring a bottle over his own head. "And this is only Friday," said a bemused Sandy Koufax, putting the triumph in terms of a weekend binge. It was a scene the ex-Dodger great had seen only at the end of a World Series.

Act II got under way after a one-day intermission. It brought a new cast to Los Angeles, all the way from Montreal. The Expos had knocked off the Philadelphia Phillies to earn the National League East crown, and they had to play the first two games of the standard best-of-five National League playoffs at Dodger Stadium. It was not the most encouraging of situations for Montreal because in the arena of the 10th player, the Expos had lost not only 9 straight games but also 18 of their last 19. On the other hand, the warm-weather Dodgers were not especially looking forward to the consequence of having to finish out the series up in Canada where mid-October temperatures are often in the forties, sometimes in the thirties, and snow is not considered out of the question.

The adrenaline in the Dodgers' veins was still flowing like the torrents of spring when the north-landers came down to southern California. Burt Hooton, pegged for the first game, quickly convinced everybody of the depth of the Dodgers starting pitcher corps by hurling seven and one-third scoreless innings. On offense, Ron Cey, back in a game for the first time since breaking a bone in his arm five weeks earlier, drove in Steve Garvey with a double and scored himself on a squeeze bunt by Bill Russell in the second inning. Then in the eighth, with two outs, Cey produced

Davey Lopes leaps high for a throw from the outfield in the postseason confrontation between the Dodgers and the Expos in Montreal. The Dodgers took two out of three up in the cold climes of Canada, and with it the National League pennant for 1981.

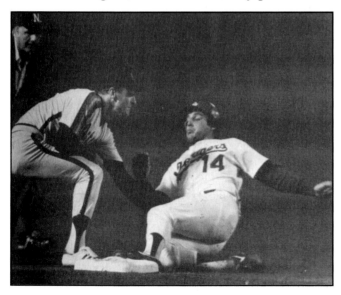

Dodgers catcher Mike Scioscia is almost caught off first base here, but the tag from Astros first baseman Art Howe is just a moment too late.

his second hit of the day, and Pedro Guerrero and Mike Scioscia obliged Dodgers fans everywhere with back-to-back home runs. Dodgers relievers Bob Welch and Steve Howe allowed the Expos only three hits and a solitary run in the one and two-thirds innings they toiled. It was the Dodgers' fourth straight playoff win at home, and the Expos' 10th straight loss in Dodger Stadium. When it was over, Montreal catcher Gary Carter shrugged and

There were two outs in the ninth inning of the final game of the NL championship series in Montreal when Rick Monday stepped into this pitch from Expos reliever Steve Rogers and sent the ball soaring into the right-center-field seats. The Dodgers won it 2–1 and clinched the National League pennant. The Dodgers first-base coach is Manny Mota, and the Expos catcher is Gary Carter.

Burt Hooton, hurling here against the Montreal Expos in Game 1 of the 1981 National League championship series, went on to win that game, and also Game 5, to help the Dodgers cop the pennant. He was named the series' Most Valuable Player. During the regular season, Hooton had the club's best (and his career best) ERA (2.28), while posting a record of 11–6. His most productive year as a Dodger was 1978, when he won 19 and lost only 10.

said: "I guess it must be Dodger magic. . . . We are aware we have been stinking here."

The stench wore off the next day, however. Fernando Valenzuela, with only three days' rest, went to the mound for the Dodgers. He had trimmed the Expos in both of his regular season starts against them. But he was weary that night in L.A., and that was apparent in the early going. In the second inning the Expos got to him for two runs and then added a security score in the sixth. It was a 3–0 shutout, and a five-hitter for Expos pitcher Ray Burris. So, with the series tied at 1–1, the Dodgers packed their long underwear and headed north.

Predictably, it was cold up there for Game 3, a windy 42 degrees. The Dodgers were just as cold: they could only come up with a single run, driven

in by the well-healed Ron Cey. The Expos tied it, then blew the game apart in the bottom of the sixth when Jerry White tagged Dodgers starter Jerry Reuss for a three-run homer. It gave the Expos a 4–1 win and forced the Dodgers into another desperate, back-to-the-wall situation.

The Dodgers, who had produced only one run in two games, had lost their hitting momentum. And they had to find it immediately or the next night they would be flying back south along with the migrating Canadian geese, and their only contact with the World Series would be as television viewers.

But just as they had with Houston, the Dodgers found their bats when they needed them. And again the catalyst was the ever-reliable Steve Garvey. With the score tied 1–1 in the top of the eighth, Garvey came up with Dusty Baker on first after a leadoff single and drove the first pitch from Bill Gullickson out of the park, a 380-foot blast. The floodgates were open, and the Dodgers added four more runs in the ninth to devastate the Expos 7–1. Burt Hooton, who had baffled the Expos for seven and one-third innings and allowed them only five hits, merited the win. And the scene was set for another showdown; everything—the pennant and the right to go to New York to face the Yankees, who had just added another to their immense collection of American League flags—was riding on one last game.

The Expos had Ray Burris ready, with glittering memories of his five-hit win over the Dodgers several days earlier. Tommy Lasorda announced that Fernando Valenzuela would pitch for the Dodgers, again with only three days rest. The weather forecast was for a high in the upper thirties and an 80 percent chance of rain or snow.

It did not snow in Montreal that Monday afternoon. It had rained earlier in the day, however, and the tarp stayed on the infield at Olympic Stadium until 30 minutes after the game was scheduled to start. When it was finally rolled up, the thermometer outside the press booth registered a nippy 41 degrees. Decked out in a variety of mufflers, ear muffs, and stocking caps were 36,491 fans who cheered, sang, stomped their feet, and jumped around for the dual purpose of spurring on their Expos and keeping their own bodies warm.

After the Dodgers clinched the NL pennant in Montreal, the traditional champagne showers flowed. Above left are Jay Johnstone and Steve Howe (No. 57). Below, Steve Yeager aims his spray on that day's winning pitcher, Fernando Valenzuela.

Just about everybody on the field was a little stiff in the first inning, except for Dodgers shortstop Bill Russell, who tripled. However, all the other Dodgers stranded him there. And Valenzuela had some problems of his own when he took to the mound in the bottom of the inning. Tim Raines slashed a double, and then the speedster raced to third on a sacrifice, his headfirst slide beating the throw from Valenzuela. Then Raines scored the game's first run when teammate Andre Dawson bounced into a double play.

It took the Dodgers four more innings to get that run back. In the top of the fifth Rick Monday singled and advanced to third when Pedro Guerrero got a hit. Valenzuela came up with the opportunity to help his cause, and he did, sending a grounder to the right side of the infield, which enabled Monday to score.

Valenzuela had also been aiding his cause from the mound. After that shaky first inning, he retired 18 of the next 19 Expos batters and gave up no other hits until the bottom of the seventh, and no other runs as the game went into the ninth tied at 1–1. Expos ace, Steve Rogers, who had won Game 3 on Friday with a complete game, replaced Ray Burris for that inning, although the starter had only allowed the Dodgers five hits all day. Rogers got the first two outs, sending Steve Garvey and Ron Cey back to the Dodgers dugout. Then, with the count 3–1 on Rick Monday, Rogers made a fatal mistake. He blazed a fastball down the middle, and Monday met it with a little touch of thunder. Monday was already around first base when the towering fly ball finally dropped into the seats in right-center field, some 400 feet from home plate. As it did, he threw a triumphal punch into the air, and the Dodgers dugout erupted into a frenzy.

Valenzuela held on in the ninth, receiving help for the last out from reliever Bob Welch. The final score was 2–1. The Dodgers had done it again. Just as they had with Houston, they had come from behind to whip the Expos—and this time they had done it in a hostile ballpark. They had the National League pennant, their seventh since moving to Los Angeles in 1958, and now they would go to the World Series for the 17th time since that classic began back in 1903.

CHAPTER 19

WORLD CHAMPIONS

Before the 1981 World Series, two who had been there several times before pose together: the Dodgers' Steve Garvey and the Yankees' Reggie Jackson. "Mr. October" is the nickname Jackson earned with his always-phenomenal World Series play. Garvey would prove equally adept in the autumn of 1981.

HOLLYWOOD COULD NOT HAVE set the stage better for the drama that was to become the 78th World Series: the Yankees and the Dodgers—two of the game's most fabled names, two organizations rich with heritage, harboring a feud both heated and long-standing. The mere thought of the confrontation stirred the great clouds of nostalgia that forever drifted from the Bronx down the East River to Flatbush. As Maury Allen observed in the *New York Post*:

Seems like old times. Bedford Avenue and Sullivan Place, salami sandwiches from Mom's brown bag at the first light of day. Ebbets Field. The first peek of the stadium as the el ran out of the dark tunnel. The memories of a misspent October youth, the Bums and the Yankees, Ebbets Field and Yankee Stadium, Dixie Walker and Joe DiMaggio, Jackie Robinson and that nasty kid second baseman of the Yankees. All of that is rushing back this day. For the 11th time, they will be out there again, preordained, of course, in this lost summer of 1981, the Dodgers and the Yankees, the way it always has to be.

And if the staging was right out of Tinseltown, the casting for the epic must have been handled by Cecil B. DeMille himself. Here were teams and organizations as totally different in nature as the two cities they represented—sunny Los Angeles, with its Porsches racing along broad freeways; leisure suits; movie stars; tank-topped roller skaters; and a creamy Burt Bacharach ballad in the background; and grayed New York, with its honking taxicabs on shadowy, narrow streets; Brooks Brothers suits; hustling, bustling commuters; shrill accents; all set to the music of *West Side Story*. The teams were as different from each other as their owners were: the winsome Dodgers as smooth and laid-back as Peter O'Malley, the gruff Yankees as flamboyant and volatile as George Steinbrenner. The Dodgers were a team born and bred in the farm system, not a single free agent in the starting lineup. Six of the nine starters had spent their entire major league careers in Los Angeles, and the infield alone had been together for eight long years. The Yankees were another kind of team, built from the free-agent pool, drawn from the playgrounds of many major league teams, and fueled by mega-million-dollar contracts. Here was Steve Garvey, there was Reggie Jackson.

Because the 1981 baseball season was such an elongated one and its improvised playoff system so confused, and because the games had to be hastened before winter set in up north, the Dodgers did not have a day off between the playoffs and the Series. Less than 24 hours would elapse between the time they trotted off the field at Montreal's Olympic Stadium and onto the field in Yankee Stadium. The Dodgers players had arrived at their hotel in New York at 10:20 Eastern Time Monday night and would be out for batting practice in the Bronx ballpark at 3:00 the next afternoon.

Both teams were far from strangers to baseball's annual ultimate dash. The Yankees had been in 32 World Series and won 22 of them, both major league records. The Dodgers had participated in sixteen, but had won only four. In Brooklyn, they had won only one Series and lost eight; their record in Los Angeles was better, but still short of .500 (3–4). The two teams had faced each other in 10 World Series, and the Yankees had come out on top eight times. And whenever they had gotten together in a World Series, there had always been

WORLD SERIES LINEUPS, 1981

DODGERS	YANKEES
Davey Lopes, 2b	Willie Randolph, 2b
Bill Russell, ss	Jerry Mumphrey, cf
Dusty Baker, lf	Dave Winfield, lf
Steve Garvey, 1b	Lou Piniella, rf
Ron Cey, 3b	Bob Watson, 1b
Pedro Guerrero, cf	Graig Nettles, 3b
Rick Monday, rf	Rick Cerone, c
Steve Yeager, c	Larry Milbourne, ss

STARTING PITCHERS
Game 1: Jerry Reuss, Ron Guidry
Game 2: Burt Hooton, Tommy John
Game 3: Fernando Valenzuela, Dave Righetti
Game 4: Bob Welch, Rick Reuschel
Game 5: Jerry Reuss, Ron Guidry
Game 6: Burt Hooton, Tommy John

an abundance of dramatic moments, unexpected happenings, and spectacular plays.

Eternally etched in World Series lore are events like Mickey Owen's dropped third strike in the ninth inning of the 1941 World Series—it should have been the last out of the game, but instead it allowed Tommy Henrich to get on base and eventually score the game's tying run (the Yankees later won it). Or outfielder Al Gionfriddo's miraculous catch of Joe DiMaggio's 415-foot drive to save a game for the Dodgers in 1947. Or Tommy Henrich's storybook home run in the bottom of the ninth to break Don Newcombe's shutout and give the Yanks a win in Game 1 of the 1949 Series. Or the three clutch home runs from 39-year-old Johnny Mize and the two from 20-year-old Mickey Mantle, which enabled the Yankees to come from behind and cop the 1952 Series. Or Carl "Oisk" Erskine's 14 strikeouts in the 1953 Series to set a postseason record. Or Duke Snider's four homers in 1955 to lead the Dodgers to their first Series conquest of the Yankees. Or Don Larsen's perfect game in 1956. Or the incredible four-game sweep by the Dodgers in 1963 on the arms of Sandy Koufax, Don Drysdale, and Johnny Podres. Or Reggie Jackson's five home runs in the 1977 Series, three in a single game. Or Graig Nettles' dazzling display with his gifted glove in 1978.

In 1981 the setting was there, so was the unique cast of characters; all that remained to be seen was the scenario that the two teams would write during the final days of the Series. Pearl Bailey launched it with a lilting rendition of the "Star Spangled Banner" before a crowd of 56,470 at Yankee Stadium. Joe DiMaggio emerged from the Yankees dugout to toss the ceremonial first pitch to catcher Rick Cerone. (George Steinbrenner had asked 82-year-old Jimmy Cagney, a longtime Yankees fan, to toss it, but baseball commissioner Bowie Kuhn had cited an existing rule that prohibits such ceremonial pitches to be thrown by show business personalities or politicians.)

Pulled off the bag by a wide throw, Steve Garvey tries to put a tag on Yankee Bob Watson. The Yankees slugger claimed he had some evening up to do with Tommy Lasorda because long ago the Dodgers manager, then a scout, had snubbed him. Watson did have a fine Series, batting .318 and hitting two home runs. Garvey would do better, however, hitting .417 and collecting more hits (10) than anyone on either team.

Ron Guidry, the Yankees ace who had won 11 games that year, then walked to the mound and threw a strike past Davey Lopes to get the 1981 World Series underway.

The tone of the game was set with the very first batter. Lopes turned Guidry's fourth pitch into a sizzling grounder down the third-base line. Graig Nettles dove as if he were sliding headfirst into the bag and somehow managed to knock the ball down. He grabbed for it frantically, clambered out of the dust cloud he had stirred up, and fired to first base. The umpire called Lopes out and suddenly memories of the 1978 Series, when Nettles' brilliant fielding had sunk a younger Dodgers team, flashed eerily in the minds of Los Angeles fans everywhere. The next two batters went down in order.

The Dodgers must have been worn down from the two sets of nerve-frazzling playoffs they had just battled through, and the lack of a day's R & R. But the Yankees had some problems of their own. Shortstop Bucky Dent was lost for the Series with a torn ligament in his hand. And the October superstar, Reggie Jackson, was out of the lineup with a pulled leg muscle.

The five-day rest the Yankees had after winning the AL pennant seemed an obvious advantage. And the Yankees stepped out smartly in their first turn at bat. Jerry Mumphrey got the first hit off Dodgers starter Jerry Reuss with one out, and went to third when Lou Piniella cracked a ground-rule double that bounced into the right-field stands. There were two outs by the time first baseman Bob Watson came to the plate. He had said that he was aching to get back at Tommy Lasorda who had spurned him, he claimed, 17 years earlier when Watson was a high school player whom Lasorda had scouted but declined to sign. And he reaped revenge that evening in Yankee Stadium, sending a Reuss fastball into the right-center-field stands to give the Yanks a three-run lead in the first inning. Besides the sweet smell of vengeance, Watson could also enjoy the fact that it was a record-tying event: along with 16 other major league players in history, he could now claim a home run in his first at-bat in a World Series.

In the third inning, Mumphrey singled again, stole second, and scored when Lou Piniella came through with his second hit of the game. That was all for Jerry Reuss. Lasorda brought in Bobby Castillo from the Dodgers bullpen, but Castillo apparently had left his control there, because in the fourth inning he walked three Yankees to load the bases and gave up another base on balls to Dave Winfield to walk in the Yankees' fifth run. Castillo promptly departed for what would become a string of Dodgers relievers: Dave Goltz, Tom Niedenfuer, and Dave Stewart.

The Dodgers got one run back in the top of the fifth when Steve Yeager clobbered a Guidry pitch into the right-field seats. It looked like they might be on the way to more in the seventh when Ron Cey slashed a hit into the left-field corner and raced around first toward second. The ball took a bounce right to Dave Winfield who threw a strike to Willie Randolph. Cey dove headfirst and had his hand on the bag but was called out. Protest and pleading, of course, produced nothing. (Later, TV replays showed not only that he had been safe, but that Davey Lopes had beaten Graig Nettles' throw in the first inning. Neither, of course, mattered in the final analysis—the players had been called out, and out they would remain.)

After seven innings, Guidry had given up only four hits to the Dodgers, but he was beginning to show signs of wearying. One of the two Yankees ace relievers, Ron Davis, was brought on in the eighth, but after walking pinch-hitter Derrel Thomas and Davey Lopes, he was yanked by manager Bob Lemon. Goose Gossage replaced Davis, and Jay Johnstone nicked him for a pinch-hit single to score one run and move Lopes to third. Dusty Baker then brought Lopes in with a sacrifice fly, and the Dodgers, having narrowed the gap to 5–3, were making a game of it.

Steve Garvey came to the plate. There were two outs, and with Johnstone on base Garvey represented the tying run. With the count at 3–1, Garvey drilled a shot down the third-base line, a blistering line drive that gave every indication it would go screaming into the left-field corner for extra bases. But there again was a diving Graig Nettles, his body parallel to the ground, his back-handed glove stretched out to its absolute limit, and suddenly there in the outer strand of its webbing was the ball. Nettles went skidding into the dust again but the ball stayed in his glove, and a disenchanted Garvey was tagged with the third out instead of a game-changing hit. The play not only ended the eighth inning rally, but it took the heart out of the Dodgers. Goose Gossage had no trouble setting them down in the ninth, and the Yankees had a one-game edge in the Series.

The next day, the *Los Angeles Herald Examiner* ran the exact same headline it had on October 14, 1978: WIN TO GUIDRY, SAVE TO NETTLES, and the *Los Angeles Times* bannered its story of the game with: SOME DAY, NETTLES WILL BE BRONZED. Tommy

Lasorda shook his head in the dressing room after the game and said, "It makes you sick to your stomach, watching that guy make that play. It looks like he goes to bed hoping and praying he can kill you with that glove."

The next evening at Yankee Stadium the pregame show was more elaborate than opening night. Robert Merrill, baritone of Metropolitan Opera fame, sang the national anthem, at the end of which one of the U.S. Army's Golden Knights, dressed in a gold jumpsuit and carrying the American flag, parachuted onto the playing field. And Jimmy Cagney, wearing a Yankees baseball cap, was escorted out on the field and, this time, *did* toss the ceremonial ball—Bowie Kuhn had had a change of heart and made an exception to the rule because Cagney was, in Kuhn's words, not just an actor but a "national treasure."

Tommy John, 38, was slated to pitch for the Yankees that night. But Los Angeles fans perhaps best remembered him as one of the last of *their* pitchers to beat the Yankees in the World Series— the first of the Dodgers' two wins in 1978—and as a pitcher who had won 87 games for them from 1972 through 1978. Now he was opposing his old teammates for the first time. Facing the Yankees would be Burt Hooton, 31, who was the only other Dodger to beat the Yankees in the 1978 World Series. The two veterans brought with them impressive career records: Tommy John 223–159 (.584) and Burt Hooton 130–107 (.549).

It was to be Tommy John's night, perhaps a little reminder to the Dodgers of what they had given up three seasons earlier. During the first four innings, John retired 12 Dodgers in order. In the fifth, Steve Garvey punctured John's perfect game with a single, then went to second on a ground-out by Ron Cey. He moved again when Pedro Guerrero hit another grounder and Yankees shortstop Larry Milbourne tried unsuccessfully to cut Cey down at third. But John bailed himself out by fanning Ken Landreaux and then knocking down a sharp drive from the bat of Steve Yeager and throwing him out at first.

Dodgers legend Walt Alston, comfortable in the surroundings of a World Series after managing the Dodgers in seven of them, tosses the ceremonial ball to launch Game 4 of the 1981 postseason classic. He brought his old ballclub some good fortune as they overcame the Yankees 8–7 that afternoon to even the Series at two games apiece.

The Yankees got an unearned run in the bottom of the fifth: Willie Randolph got on when Davey Lopes dropped his ground ball, and eventually scored when Larry Milbourne lashed a double to left. The Dodgers offense, on the other hand, was stagnant. When Tommy John left the game after seven full innings he had not allowed a single run and had only given up three hits. But Yankees manager Bob Lemon felt John was tiring, and

Ron Cey took Goose Gossage's fastball flush on the side of his head, but thanks to the protective helmet, he suffered a minor concussion instead of what could have been a tragic, if not fatal, injury. It occurred in Game 5 at Dodger Stadium, but Cey would be back for at least part of the final game at Yankee Stadium.

Lemon wanted to take no chances. So, in came Goose Gossage and his blazing fastball. He had little trouble with the Dodgers in the last two innings, ceding just one hit, one base on balls, and completing the shutout.

The single, unearned run in the fifth would have been enough that night, but the Yankees added two more for good measure in the bottom of the eighth, driven in by Bob Watson and Willie Randolph. Burt Hooton had pitched a fine game for the Dodgers; he gave up only three hits and that unearned run in the six innings he pitched, but it was not enough, and the Dodgers now trailed the Yankees by two games.

Being "down but not out" was hardly alien to the Dodgers of 1981; after all, they had just come from behind in two similar series to get themselves into the World Series. But this situation was different—the wily veteran New York Yankees had an unparalleled tradition of postseason excellence. And there was *another* very disconcerting statistic facing the Dodgers: only seven times in the preceding 77 years of World Series play had a team come back from 0–2 to win the major league

crown—the last team, ironically enough, was the 1978 Yankees, who snatched the world championship from the Los Angeles Dodgers.

As the Dodgers prepared to return home to a stadium that was notoriously more friendly, a sportswriter asked Steve Garvey how he felt about going back on the wrong end of an 0–2 standing. A true back-to-the-wall boy, Garvey said, "We've got 'em just where we want them." Tommy Lasorda took a slightly different tack when another reporter mentioned the possibility of a Yankees sweep. "Sweep?" Lasorda bellowed. "My rear end, that's what they'll sweep."

The Yankees got a slug of bad news as they prepared to fly out to Los Angeles. Graig Nettles had jammed his thumb in Game 2 while making one of his familiar diving stabs, this time for a Bill Russell ground ball. Swollen, painful, and wrapped in a large white bandage, Nettles' thumb was injured severely enough to keep him out of the lineup, perhaps for the remainder of the Series, the Yankee's team physician said. Reggie Jackson would not be on the field either. Bob Lemon said the Yankee star's leg was better, but still he did not plan to start the left-handed batter—who had been out of action for so long—against a left-handed pitcher as deft as Fernando Valenzuela.

California offered the Yankees its own brand of pregame show—two mild earthquakes, which registered 4.5 on the Richter scale, in the early morning hours before Game 3. They were centered about 45 miles southwest of Santa Monica, but were felt in Los Angeles. More pleasantly, the temperature stood at a balmy 71 degrees at game time, delightfully comfortable for the sellout crowd. Tickets for all three games scheduled for Dodger Stadium had been sold out practically from the moment Los Angeles had won the NL pennant—forty-one thousand went to season-ticket holders; the others were sold to the public through a mail lottery and distributed to the Yankees, other major league clubs, and the media. Scalpers were offering the ducats at $50 to $100 each before Game 3; after that contest the price soared to $200 apiece.

As the Dodgers sent Fernando Valenzuela to the mound and the Yankees opposed him with 23-year-old Dave Righetti, it marked only the fourth time in 78 years of World Series play that two rookie pitchers were pitted against each other as starters. The only others were Gene Bearden (Cleveland Indians) vs. Vern Bickford (Boston Braves) in 1948; Whitey Ford (New York Yankees) vs. Bob Miller (Philadelphia Phillies) in 1950; and Gary Waslewski (Boston Red Sox) vs. Dick Hughes (St. Louis Cardinals) in 1967.

The sun and the sway of the palm trees and the thunderous noise from the hometown faithful in Dodger Stadium again served as inspiration to the Dodgers offense. Just as they had done when they returned to Los Angeles down two games to nothing to the Houston Astros, the Dodgers roared back in the first inning at Dodger Stadium. Valenzuela had not given up a run or a hit in the top of the inning, and Davey Lopes led off for the Dodgers with a double. Bill Russell laid down a bunt and beat it out for a hit, as Lopes scampered easily to third. Righetti then got both Dusty Baker and Steve Garvey, but he could not handle Ron Cey. "The Penguin," as he is affectionately known, waited until the count was 3–2, then sent a deep scare through young Righetti when he smashed a drive that pulled just to the wrong side of the left-field foul pole. The scare for Righetti turned to rueful reality on the next pitch. Cey drove this one straighter, and the ball dropped 400 feet away into the left-center-field seats. Just as they had done to the hapless Astros, the Dodgers built a 3–0 lead in the first inning.

Unlike the Astros, however, the Yankees stormed back immediately. A still-vengeful Bob Watson led off the second inning with his second home run of the series. Rick Cerone followed with a double and eventually scored on Larry Milbourne's single. In the third, the Yankees chopped the legs out from under the Dodgers lead. Lou Piniella, ably filling in for Reggie Jackson, got his fourth hit of the Series, a single, and then scored ahead of Rick Cerone, who boomed a home run into the center-field stands. The Yankees led 4–3.

Many in the press box surmised that that would be all for Valenzuela, who clearly had not exhibited his usual poise that night. But it wasn't: he got out of the inning and stayed around to set the Yankees down without a run and with only one hit through the top of the fifth. The Dodgers' fate in this crucial game and their hopes for another comeback would be determined by their performance in the bottom of that inning, along with a little ironic twist.

Steve Garvey hit a high bounder off the hard turf of the Dodger Stadium infield, lofty enough for him

NOTES AND QUOTES DURING THE WORLD SERIES, 1981

Reggie Jackson: "We've got to know this is going to be a tough Series. I'm just leery because we've beaten them, the Dodgers, twice, and it's tough to beat a good team three times." And a week later, "We coulda, shoulda, oughta, mighta . . . but that doesn't mean a damn."

Tommy Lasorda (on Graig Nettles): "I don't understand it. I was asked to a banquet in Anaheim last winter to give him an award of some kind. I sat and stared at him for two hours and he dropped his fork three times. I don't know why he can't drop a ball for us once in a while."

Senators Daniel Moynihan (New York) and **S. I. Hayakawa** (California) got into the spirit of things and told the media they had wagered a case of wine on the outcome of the Series. If the Dodgers lost, Hayakawa said he would send a case of Napa Valley wine to his colleague; Moynihan, on a Yankees loss, would send one of New York's "wide variety of vintages." Both agreed on a formal presentation after the Series, followed by a ceremonial sipping. "And a drunken brawl," Hayakawa added.

Yogi Berra (on the mild earthquake in L.A. prior to Game 3): "I didn't feel it. It must have bypassed me."

Peter O'Malley: "Al Campanis, Lasorda, myself—none of us have our own World Series rings. The ones we do have were earned by my dad, Alston, and Buzzy Bavasi. I think it's about time we get our own."

to beat it out for a hit. Ron Cey managed to draw a base on balls, and Pedro Guerrero then hit another high chopper down the third-base line. It bounced over Aurelio Rodriguez's head and into left field for a double, enabling Garvey to score the tying run.

At that point Tommy Lasorda summoned his Spanish fluency and told Valenzuela, "If we don't get the go-ahead run here, you're gone." Rick Monday was walked intentionally and the bases were loaded with no one out. The play brought up catcher Mike Scioscia, who had come in earlier to replace Steve Yeager. Valenzuela watched as Lasorda sent Reggie Smith into the on-deck circle, apparently to pinch hit for him. As it turned out, Smith wasn't needed. Scioscia hit a grounder between short and second, and Ron Cey raced in with the lead run as Willie Randolph executed a

double play. Reggie Smith went back to the dugout as Valenzuela went back to the pitcher's mound. As Ron Fimrite observed in *Sports Illustrated*, "By both killing a rally and winning the game, Scioscia in effect saved his pitcher from being removed for a pinch-hitter."

"Once he got the scent of that one-run lead," Tommy Lasorda said of Valenzuela after the game, "he had one of the greatest closing acts you'll ever see." That was certainly true; Valenzuela shut the Yankees out during the next four innings, giving up only two hits and one base on balls.

Only once was there a flickering threat. With Yankees on first and second in the eighth inning, Bobby Murcer came in to pinch hit for pitcher Rudy May. He bunted, but it was a soft line drive angling out over the third-base line. Cey went after

The last out of the 1981 World Series has just been registered, and Tommy Lasorda erupts from the dugout on his way to hug and kiss any Dodger within reach. It was Lasorda's first world championship, but his third trip to the World Series in his five years at the Dodgers helm.

it and—in the style of Graig Nettles—dove and caught it. He leaped to his feet, saw Milbourne halfway to second, and fired to Steve Garvey for a double play.

The final score was 5–4, and Cey and Valenzuela were the heroes of the day. Valenzuela had gone the distance and thrown 145 pitches, a prodigious amount for any pitcher; he gave up nine hits and seven walks (two intentional). And Cey, with his bat and his glove, had sparked the entire team.

Tommy Lasorda, needless to say, was jubilant. George Steinbrenner was furious: "It's like playing on a Ping-Pong table—they got some chicken hits," he said in reference to Dodger Stadium and the high hoppers of Garvey and Guerrero in the fifth inning. He was unhappy with the performances of some of his ballplayers, too, and said so publicly. The next day he would be given the opportunity to become much angrier.

Reggie Jackson was back in the Yankees outfield for Game 4, but Graig Nettles was still sidelined. Jerry Mumphrey was benched and no one was saying why, although it was common knowledge that owner Steinbrenner was highly unhappy about his performance in games past. Both teams had to reach rather deeply into their store of pitchers for starters, the Yankees coming up with 10-year (9 with the Chicago Cubs) veteran Rick Reuschel, who had had a 4–4 season in 1981, and the Dodgers choosing Bob Welch, 9–5 that season. Neither lasted very long in a game that employed 36 players, including 10 pitchers.

The game would be an explosive one, suspenseful on one hand, sloppy on the other, but overall wacky, entertaining, and ultimately exciting. The Yankees kicked it off in the first inning when leadoff batter Willie Randolph tripled. Larry Milbourne followed with a double, scoring Randolph. Dave Winfield walked, and the Yankees' own Oktoberfest, Reggie Jackson, singled to load the bases. Bob Welch departed for the day. Bob Watson then drove in the game's second run with a sacrifice fly off Dave Goltz.

WINNING IT ALL

Tommy Lasorda: "Please don't blame the Yankees. Credit the Dodgers. . . . I'm the happiest sonofabitch in the world."

George Steinbrenner: "I want to sincerely apologize to the people of New York and to fans of the New York Yankees everywhere for the performance of the Yankee team in the World Series."

L.A. Mayor Tom Bradley: "This is a team with a lot of character. They did what many people thought was impossible, and we in Los Angeles are very, very proud of them."

Frank Sinatra: "I knew it. I knew it. I knew it."

Jerry Reuss: "If we knew it would be this much fun, we'd have done it a lot sooner."

The Yankees added another run in the second inning on a Willie Randolph homer, and Rick Cerone drove in still another in the third. With the score 4–0, things did not look especially bright for the Dodgers, but this was no ordinary game. In the bottom of the third, the Dodgers got on the scoreboard when pinch-hitter Ken Landreaux came through with a double and scored on Davey Lopes' single. Lopes then stole second, went to third on a Steve Garvey infield hit, and scored on Ron Cey's infield bouncer. In the fifth, the Dodgers cut the Yankees' lead to a single run. Once again it was due to the clutch-hitting of Steve Garvey, who doubled and scored on a Ron Cey single.

But the Yankees came right back. Willie Randolph got on base as a result of a throwing error by Bill Russell and eventually scored on an Oscar Gamble hit. Reggie Jackson drew a walk, and he scored on a hit by Bob Watson, who was having a marvelous time at bat in his first World Series.

The entertainment was far from over—now it was the Dodgers' turn. In their half of the sixth, Mike Scioscia got on with a walk after one out. Jay Johnstone, the team's resident practical joker, who, *Los Angeles Times* columnist Jim Murray said,

The long-awaited spoil of victory, the World Series championship trophy. It takes four sets of hands to handle it: (from the left) Al Campanis, Bowie Kuhn, Peter O'Malley, and Tommy Lasorda. It was the Dodgers' first world championship since 1965.

"would really rather be tying shoelaces together or doing impersonations of the manager with a pillow in his stomach," was called on to pinch hit. And this time the butt of the joke was Yankees relief pitcher Ron Davis. Johnstone lofted a two-run homer into the right-center-field seats. If that was not enough to dishearten the New Yorkers, the next batter, Davey Lopes, popped one to right field, a seemingly easy out. Reggie Jackson came in

for it, running in a strange zigzag sort of pattern; he had lost the ball in the sun, and it bounced off his left collarbone and onto the ground. Lopes raced to second, then stole third, and scored when Bill Russell singled to left. At the end of six innings, the game was tied at six runs apiece.

The Dodgers took the lead for the first time that day in the seventh inning when pinch-hitter Steve Yeager hit a sacrifice fly that sent Dusty

Baker across home plate. Minutes later Davey Lopes singled Rick Monday home. The Yankees picked up a run in the eighth when Reggie Jackson powered a homer into right-center (his 10th career World Series round-tripper). But that was it for the day. The Dodgers were winners, 8–7, and had tied the Series at two games each. Afterward there were wide-ranging comments about the day's events.

Tommy Lasorda: "What a game. . . . Oh, boy! It was the most exciting game I've ever been involved in."

Bob Lemon: "It was exciting as hell when we were ahead."

Jim Murray in the *Los Angeles Times:* "The last time I saw a game like this, the teams didn't have matching uniforms. And there was a beer keg on third—Peerless Hot Laundry vs. The Fourth Street Crushers."

Goose Gossage: "We stunk."

George Steinbrenner: "I'm not lambasting anyone. It was there for 70 million people to see. Our pitching was lousy . . . no excuse for what we did on defense . . . our base running, I don't know when we're going to learn . . . I also didn't like the way our pinch-hitters were used."

Rick Monday: "It wasn't your basic Picasso."

Jay Johnstone: "I'd like to sign a $25-million contract with the Dodgers."

The game certainly had its ragged edges, and there were some awful performances, more appropriate to a mid-March spring-training game. "Goats became heroes, and heroes became goats," is the way it was described in *Sports Illustrated*. It was just that kind of game. A total of 22 runners had been left on base. And pitchers came and went as if they were fashion-modeling uniforms for the more than fifty-six thousand spectators at Dodger Stadium that day. After starter Bob Welch was knocked out, the Dodgers sent up Dave Goltz, Terry Forster, Tom Niedenfuer, and Steve Howe, in that order. Yankees starter Rick Reuschel, who lasted three innings longer than Welch, was sequentially replaced by Rudy May, Ron Davis,

RECORDS BROKEN OR TIED IN 1981 WORLD SERIES:

BATTING
Career slugging average: Reggie Jackson, .755
Most stolen bases, six-game Series: Davey Lopes, 4
Most walks, six-game Series: Willie Randolph, 9
Most times reached base safely, game (tied):
    Reggie Jackson, 5
Home run hit in first Series at-bat (tied): Bob Watson

PITCHING
Most saves, six-game Series (tied): Goose Gossage, 2
Most losses (tied): George Frazier, 3

FIELDING
Most errors, second baseman: Davey Lopes, 6
Most errors in a game (tied): Davey Lopes, 3
Most errors in an inning, second baseman (tied):
    Davey Lopes, 2

TEAM
Most walks received, six-game Series, both teams: 53
Most walks received, six-game Series, one team: Yankees, 33
Most men left on base, six-game Series: Yankees, 55
Most walks, one inning, both clubs: 6
Most pitchers used, six-game Series, one club: Dodgers, 10
Fewest double plays, six-game Series, one club: Yankees, 2

A jubilant Jay Johnstone is congratulated after his clutch pinch-hit home run in Game 4 of the 1981 World Series. The Dodgers went on to win the game that day at Dodger Stadium, 8–7, and even the Series at two games apiece. Johnstone got two hits in his three pinch-hit appearances in the Series and drove in three runs.

George Frazier, and Tommy John. Frazier got his second loss in two days, a World Series mark that had not been achieved in 40 years. (In 1941 the Dodgers' Hugh Casey went down twice in two days to—you might have guessed—the Yankees.)

After four games, there were some definite heroes and bums in the 1981 World Series. For the Dodgers, Steve Garvey was hitting .500 (8 for 16),

and Ron Cey was batting .333 (5 for 15) with five runs batted in. On the other hand, Dusty Baker, batting third in the line-up, had only two hits in 15 trips to the plate for an average of .133, and Pedro Guerrero had struck out five times in 13 at-bats. For the Yankees, Reggie Jackson was batting 1.000 (3 for 3), Bob Watson .500 (7 for 14), and Lou Piniella .364 (4 for 11). But the multimillion-dollar "property,"

Pedro Guerrero (No. 28) earns a high-five from the Dodgers batboy and fellow outfielder Ken Landreaux after clouting a homer in Game 6 of the 1981 World Series. It was his fifth RBI of the day and his seventh of the Series. Guerrero shared the Series MVP honors with Ron Cey and Steve Yeager. The Yankees catcher is Rick Cerone.

Dave Winfield, had an average of .000, hitless in 14 at-bats. Willie Randolph was batting .167 (2 for 12), but his two hits were a home run and a triple.

The aces, Jerry Reuss and Ron Guidry, were back for Game 5, rested and ready, they said. Both teams wanted this game and the tremendous advantage of going up 3–2 in the Series. The Dodgers especially wanted it because they knew that after that game the journey was back to Yankee Stadium, where they had lost six straight World Series games—two in 1981, three in 1978, and one in 1977. There would be no 70-degree weather or friendly fans in that Yankees bastion.

The television cameras panned the enormous audience that had assembled in Dodger Stadium that Sunday afternoon just before the game started. Frank Sinatra and Johnny Carson were there, as were Magic Johnson and Kareem Abdul-Jabbar, the L.A. Lakers' multimillionaire cagers. Howard Cosell, up in the press box, had comments about all of them. There was even a fan perched near the top of one of the palm trees just outside the park, held in place by a telephone lineman's harness—a rather unique method of watching the game without a ticket.

When Jerry Reuss took the mound to start the game, Dodgers fans began making their 10th man noises, which grew in volume and intensity as the day moved on. There were also some ominous rumblings in the Yankees dugout and in George Steinbrenner's booth when Reuss set the first three Yanks down in a row. In the second, however, the autumnally omnipotent Reggie Jackson, determined to maintain his awesome postseason reputation, led off with a double. Not too many moments later, he came trotting across home plate after Lou Piniella slashed a single to left. The Yankees had the lead early.

The game was pegged as a pitchers' duel, and both Reuss and Ron Guidry looked very impressive through the first three innings. A run or two might well decide this game, predicted many in the press booth.

Bob Watson led off the Yankees side of the fourth with a walk, followed by Davey Lopes'

moment of ignominy: Lou Piniella hit a ground ball to the Dodgers second baseman, who fumbled it, finally picked it up, and then threw it into the Yankees dugout. Lopes was cited with two errors on the play; those, along with an error he had made in the second inning, enabled him to go into the World Series record book as one of eight players who had made three errors in a single game. Lopes now had five errors, another record—the most for any second baseman in World Series history. As a result, Watson went to third and Piniella to second, and there was nobody out.

The bases eventually filled, but miraculously, Reuss got himself out of the inning without allowing a run. Everyone breathed a sigh of relief. Davey Lopes' reaction was a little different, as Lyle Spencer reported in the *Los Angeles Herald Examiner:* "As he ran off the field . . . Lopes went directly through the dugout and runway without a word, disappearing into the sanctuary of the clubhouse. There he sat, alone with his thoughts, at his locker." Asked after the game about his fielding faux pas, Lopes said, "If we'd lost the game, I probably would have blown my brains out."

During the inning, at the height of the Dodgers threat, Howard Cosell had said, "If Reuss gets them out of this, it will have a big effect on the Yankees, leaving three men stranded again—not on the scoreboard immediately, but it will affect them." He was so very right.

Reuss and Guidry continued to duel through the next few innings. Neither gave up a run until the bottom of the seventh. In fact, the only interesting offensive moment was Dave Winfield's single in the fifth inning—it was his first hit in 17 at-bats in the World Series. What came after was perfectly chronicled by two *Los Angeles Herald Examiner* writers: Melvin Durslag wrote "Finally purchasing a hit—a lollipop to left . . . he did an extraordinary thing. He stopped the game and asked to be given the ball, which he must have pictured as a collector's item." And Allan Malamud added, "The sad thing about Dave

Winfield calling for the baseball after his first World Series hit is that he wasn't kidding."

The pitchers' duel ended in the bottom of the seventh when Pedro Guerrero came to bat. He took a Guidry fastball and nailed it; at the crack of the bat everyone in Dodger Stadium knew the ball would not land inside the ballpark. Guerrero gracefully circled the base path, and the game was tied. Steve Yeager came up next, and he did the exact same thing; after back-to-back home runs, the Dodgers were suddenly in front 2–1. On only eight other occasions had back-to-back home runs been hit in a World Series game, the most recent by Yankees sluggers Thurman Munson and Reggie Jackson against the Dodgers in 1977.

The game was returned to Jerry Reuss to maintain or lose. In the Yankees half of the eighth, he set Milbourne, Winfield, and Jackson down in order. Only an inning to go. Goose Gossage came on for the Yankees in the bottom of the eighth and gave up a walk to Davey Lopes, then got Bill Russell and Steve Garvey.

The pitch Gossage threw to Ron Cey was timed by the radar gun at 94 miles per hour. It started straight, then veered and hit the Dodgers third baseman square on the left side of the helmet. Cey went down as if he had been shot. The sound of the impact was awful, and after it there was almost total silence from the fifty-six thousand fans in Dodger Stadium. But Cey stirred, and in a few minutes was helped to his feet and walked unsteadily to the dugout. He was all right, and he did come back to play in the next game of the Series two days later. But, as team physician Dr. Frank Jobe said later, judging from the speed of the pitch and where it had hit Cey, if he had not been wearing a helmet, he would have been killed.

Gossage managed to get out of the inning, but he had certainly been disturbed by the pitch that had gotten away from him. He would later reflect, "All I could say was, 'Get up, get up.' There was nothing more I could do."

The Yankees had one more chance, but Jerry Reuss was not about to give it to them. He did get

nicked by Lou Piniella for a single, but that was all. The Yankees lost that day in Los Angeles, 2–1, and the Dodgers had swept their three-game homestand.

The team, now so notorious for coming back when the situation seemed hopeless, needed only one win in the next two games to complete one of the most remarkable series of comebacks in the history of major league baseball. But if they were to do it, the deed would have to be done in Yankee Stadium. And that famous arena had hardly been hospitable to them in the past. As George Steinbrenner said (among other things) after his team's third loss: "I want them back in New York, back in the Bronx, back in front of our fans. Playing in Yankee Stadium can be an intimidating thing, but the Dodgers know that already. They're coming there and we're gonna beat them."

For nostalgic Dodgers fans, there was a bit of sad news shared on the sports pages along with talk of Game 5 of the World Series. "Pistol" Pete Reiser, who had played for the Dodgers for six years during the forties, had died at age 62. The great hustler and superb batsman had a marvelous career derailed in 1942 when he ran headlong into the center-field wall and fractured his skull while he was chasing a fly ball. He never played to his full potential afterward. Still, Reiser had always been one of the great favorites at Ebbets Field.

There would be a day, night, and day of rest before Game 6 got underway in New York. The slumping Yankees certainly needed it. So did the overworked Dodgers; they had had only one day off since flying up to Montreal, which now seemed like ages ago.

Everyone except Bucky Dent was back for Game 6. Graig Nettles would be at third, and Jerry Mumphrey was going to be playing center field, the Yankees announced. The Dodgers said Ron Cey would start at third. Coming off his relief performance of a few nights earlier, Tommy John was Bob Lemon's choice to start for the Yankees. Burt Hooton, who had had such a fine postseason against the Astros and the Expos but had been

The morning after: a victory parade in downtown Los Angeles. Here, Al Campanis (left) and Tommy Lasorda flank Los Angeles mayor Tom Bradley, as eighty thousand Los Angelenos turn out to welcome home their triumphant Dodgers.

tripped up by the Yankees earlier in the Series, started for Tommy Lasorda.

Steve Garvey got the first hit of the game, building up what would be the best individual Dodgers batting average of the Series. Ron Cey was next, and he received a fine ovation from the Yankees fans on his return. They were perhaps not so thrilled with him moments later when he sliced a single to left.

The game's first run, however, did not come until the third inning, and it was scored by the Yankees. With two outs, Willie Randolph blasted his second home run of the Series. But the Dodgers got the run back the next inning. Dusty Baker finally got a single, only his third hit in 21 at-bats. Rick Monday then got a hit, and Baker advanced and finally scored when Steve Yeager added a clutch single to left.

In the bottom of the fourth, with two outs and runners on first and second (the result of a double by Graig Nettles and an intentional walk to Larry Milbourne), Yankees manager Bob Lemon, no doubt grieving the absence of the designated hitter, opted to take Tommy John out of the game for a pinch-hitter. It was a decision he would come to regret before the night was over. Bobby Murcer went to the plate in lieu of John and flied out to right to end the inning. George Frazier took the mound for the Yankees in relief.

And then the fun started, at least for Dodgers fans. Davey Lopes led off with a single and was sacrificed to second by Bill Russell. Ron Cey, substantiating the proof he'd offered in the first inning that the beaning had not intimidated his batting, singled to center to score Lopes and break the tie. Dusty Baker followed with another single, and then Pedro Guerrero tripled to drive in both Cey and Baker. At the end of the fifth, the Dodgers had a comfortable 4–1 lead.

But they were not satisfied. Ron Davis, who was brought in to face them in the sixth, struck Steve Yeager out, but that was the only high point of his appearance that night. He then walked pitcher Burt Hooton and Davey Lopes. Bill Russell singled to left and one run scored. Rick Reuschel was then brought in, and Davis was sent to the proverbial showers. Lopes and Russell immediately stole third and second, respectively, the first double steal in the Series. Then Reuschel intentionally walked Steve Garvey to load the bases. Derrel Thomas came to bat for Ron Cey, who had asked to be taken out of the lineup because he had begun to experience some lightheadedness. Thomas hit a ground ball to force Russell at third, but Davey Lopes scored on the play. Then it finally happened—the spell was broken and Tommy Lasorda's mind was suddenly boggled with surprise and subsequently glee. Graig Nettles made an error at third on a ground ball hit by Dusty Baker. Once again the bases were loaded. Pedro Guerrero, coming out of a Series hitting slump, admirably sent a sharp hit to center, driving in two more runs. The score was now 8–1.

For all practical purposes the game might as well have ended at that point—the Dodgers were soaring so loftily they were untouchable, and the Yankees were beleaguered and spiritless. They did

stage a brief threat by loading the bases in the bottom of the sixth. It caused the removal of Hooton from the game and the entrance of Steve Howe from the Dodgers bullpen. Lou Piniella drove in a run with a single, but that was it for the inning and the game. The Dodgers added another run in the eighth when Pedro Guerrero racked up his fifth RBI of the game by homering into the left-field seats. The final score was 9–2. The loss went to George Frazier, his third of the Series. Only one other time in major league history had a pitcher been credited with three losses in a World Series: Lefty Williams, one of the scandalous seven "Black Sox" who threw the 1919 Series. However,

Williams' three losses occurred over the span of eight games (the major leagues at the time were experimenting with a World Series based on the best of nine games).

The back-to-the-wall boys had done it again. And this time with a flair that no one was likely to forget for quite a while—four straight wins over the so-often-invincible Yankees, the last of which broke that horrible jinx that Yankee Stadium had held for them. It was Los Angeles' first world championship in baseball since the Dodgers of 1965. Tommy Lasorda was everywhere, jumping up and down, kissing everyone in sight, including Peter O'Malley. In the clubhouse there were the traditional champagne showers. There was bedlam and joy, and Dodger Blue had a special incandescence that night.

The Series' Most Valuable Player was an award three Dodgers would have to share in 1981—Ron Cey (.350, one home run, six RBIs), Steve Yeager (.364, two home runs, four RBIs), and Pedro Guerrero (.333, two home runs, seven RBIs). But there was also Steve Garvey, who batted .417 (10 for 24) and made so many great saves of in-the-dirt throws to him at first base. And Jay Johnstone's three very important RBIs. And Davey Lopes' four stolen bases. And, of course, the pitching of Fernando Valenzuela, Jerry Reuss, and Burt Hooton, and the clutch relief performances of Steve Howe.

For the Yankees, there had been good hitting from Lou Piniella (.438), Aurelio Rodriguez (.417), Graig Nettles (.400), Reggie Jackson (.333), and Bob Watson (.318), and stellar fielding from Nettles and Willie Randolph. There had also been fine pitching from Tommy John, Ron Guidry, and Goose Gossage.

But it was the Dodgers who went home with the elaborate trophy that commissioner Bowie Kuhn awarded to them in the winner's clubhouse. They went home to a happy city, where eighty thousand of its citizens turned out the next day to rain confetti on the returning heroes' parade down Broadway and to watch the Dodgers flag raised at city hall. And the Dodgers had plenty of reason to be pleased—besides winning a world championship, they had ended a ruptured baseball season with a surprise three-act drama, filled with suspense that released into a most happy climax, at least from the Los Angelenos' point of view.

CHAPTER 20

A ROLLER-COASTER RIDE TO ANOTHER CHAMPIONSHIP

Gone from the 1981 champion Dodgers was second baseman Davey Lopes, who in 1982 was ably succeeded by Rookie of the Year Steve Sax, shown here scoring against the Giants. Photo courtesy of Getty Images.

TO DODGERS FANS' DISMAY, the glory of 1981 was to be short-lived, the door to the World Series destined to remain shut to Los Angeles through seven exciting but frustrating seasons. The 1982 season seemed to offer such promise, but it began badly and went from dismal to exhilarating to disappointing, culminating with the hopes for another postseason appearance being dashed on the last day of the season.

The world champs of 1981 were pretty much intact, the only departure of note being second baseman Davey Lopes, and he was ably replaced

Fernando Valenzuela had another All-Star season in 1986 and recorded five straight strikeouts in his spectacular appearance in that year's midsummer classic. Photo courtesy of AP/Wide World Photos.

by 22-year-old Steve Sax, who would go on to earn Rookie of the Year honors. Left-handers Fernando Valenzuela and Jerry Reuss headed the pitching staff with right-handers Bob Welch and Dave Stewart rounding out the rotation, a most impressive corps to say the least. But the Dodgers hardly looked like reigning champions. By late July they were 10½ games behind the seemingly indomitable Atlanta Braves. Under new manager Joe Torre, the Braves had won their first 13 games of the season in a row, and, behind the power hitting of Dale Murphy and Bob Horner and the pitching of Phil Niekro, they appeared to be gliding unhindered into the playoffs.

The transition from dismal to exhilarating, however, took place down in Atlanta, where the Dodgers traveled for a crucial four-game series. And in that inhospitable environment, the Dodgers swept the Braves and were suddenly just six and one-half games out. A week later, Atlanta came to Chavez Ravine for another four-game confrontation, and the Dodgers swept them again. In 12 playing days, the Dodgers managed to gain 11 games on Atlanta and take over first place. It was truly one of the more remarkable turnarounds in major league annals.

The race for the West Division title continued neck-and-neck, and it all came down to the last week of the season. With just two games remaining, the Braves led the Dodgers by a single game and the San Francisco Giants by two, all three teams with a shot at the division title. Then Los Angeles eliminated the Giants on the next to last day, humiliated them, actually, by a score of 15–2, while the Braves slipped past the San Diego Padres 4–2. A victory on the final day of the season for the Dodgers would force a playoff with Atlanta, who lost their game at San Diego that day, but the Giants were laying in wait up in San Francisco, bent on revenge for the previous day's embarrassment. And spoilers they proved to be when Joe Morgan drove a three-run homer into the seats in the seventh inning to provide the winning margin in a 5–3 defeat of the Dodgers, the result giving the Braves first place in the NL West.

Pedro Guerrero proved to be the most productive hitter that year, leading the team in batting average (.304), home runs (32), and RBIs (100). Dusty Baker hit .300 with 23 homers, while Ron Cey contributed another 24. Fernando Valenzuela won 19 and lost 13 with a 2.87 ERA; Jerry Reuss was 18–11 with a 3.11 ERA; and Bob Welch was 16–11, an ERA of 3.26.

A big shake-up in the lineup followed. Dodgers stalwarts Steve Garvey and Ron Cey departed before the 1983 season, Garvey going to the San Diego Padres and Cey to the Chicago Cubs.

Guerrero was moved to third base, a position he was unsuited for as it turned out, and Greg Brock replaced Garvey at first base.

Despite the departure of the great Dodgers infield of 1981 (all but shortstop Bill Russell were now gone), Los Angeles managed to post its best season record since 1980, winning 91 games against 71 losses and taking the National League West title by three games over the ever pesky Atlanta Braves. Yet, as in the year before, with July coming to an end, the Dodgers found themselves trailing the Braves, this time by six and one-half games. But this time Tommy Lasorda was not only able to rally his team, highlighted by an eight-game win streak in August, but to maintain the rally through the remainder of the season. They ended up in first place, three games ahead of the Braves, at the end of the regular season.

With the division title safely in tow, only the Philadelphia Phillies stood between the Dodgers and the National League pennant. The Phillies, managed by Paul Owens, had won the NL East by six games (90–72). They were paced by third base-man Mike Schmidt, who hit 40 home runs and drove in 109 runs in 1983, and a pitching staff that featured Steve Carlton and John Denny. Their roster also included the productive bats of Pete Rose (although he was 42 years old in 1983), Joe Morgan (who was 39), and Gary Matthews.

Los Angeles sent Jerry Reuss against Carlton in the opener at Dodger Stadium. Reuss gave up only five hits, but Carlton prevailed, 1–0, in a classic pitchers' duel, the sole run coming on a homer by Schmidt in the first inning. In the second game Fernando Valenzuela also held the Phillies to a single run, but this time the Dodgers backed him up with four runs of their own to tie the series before moving on to Pennsylvania's largest city, which would prove to be less than cordial. There, over the next two days, the Phillies routed the Dodgers by identical scores of 7–2. In taking Game 3, Charlie Hudson hurled a five-hitter and went the distance for Philadelphia, while Dodgers

starter Bob Welch gave up two runs in the second inning and then departed the game. Jerry Reuss yielded three runs in the first inning of the fourth and final game, one in which the Dodgers never really got into contention.

Los Angeles was represented in the 1983 All-Star Game by Valenzuela, Pedro Guerrero, and Steve Sax, along with Tommy Lasorda as a coach. Valenzuela turned in another good season, 15–10 with a 3.75 ERA; Bob Welch won 15 games against 12 losses with a team-best ERA of 2.65; and Jerry Reuss and Alejandro Pena contributed 12 wins apiece. Guerrero again led the team in three categories with a .298 average, 32 home runs, and 103 RBIs. Tommy Lasorda was named the National League Manager of the Year. And his predecessor, Walt Alston, the winningest manager in Dodgers history, became only the second Dodgers pilot to be honored with election to the Hall of Fame (the other, Wilbert Robinson in 1945). Still, the Phillies made it a disappointing postseason.

There was no division title race for the Dodgers—much less a playoff berth—in 1984. For the first time since 1979, Los Angeles ended the season with a losing record, landing in fourth

NO-HITTERS

Dodger pitchers have hurled 26 no-hitters since the first was recorded by Sam Kimber back when the team was known as the Brooklyn Grays, playing in the American Association; he held the Toledo Blue Stockings hitless through 10 innings before the 0–0 game was called because of darkness. The most recent no-hitter was Hideo Nomo's, a 9–0 victory over the Colorado Rockies on September 17, 1996, at Coors Field in Denver.

Sandy Koufax is credited with the most no-hitters (four), one each year between 1962 and 1965, against the New York Mets, San Francisco Giants, Philadelphia Phillies, and Chicago Cubs, respectively.

Carl Erskine pitched two, one in 1952 against the Cubs and another in 1956 against the New York Giants; William "Adonis" Terry also posted two, the first when facing the St. Louis Browns in 1886 and the second against the Louisville Colonels in 1888.

place in the NL West, 13 games behind the San Diego Padres, a lackluster record of 79–83. No Dodgers pitcher recorded more wins than Bob Welch's 13, and he lost 13 as well. Only Pedro Guerrero batted above .300 (.303), but his home run output was down to a mere 16.

On the more positive side in 1984, Dodgers greats Pee Wee Reese and Don Drysdale were inducted into the Hall of Fame in Cooperstown. They became the ninth and tenth players who spent most, if not all, of their careers with the Dodgers to be so honored. Both players' numbers—Reese, 1, and Drysdale, 53—were retired by the Dodgers that year.

But 1985 was a different story altogether, although it did not look like that when the season got underway. A dismal April was followed by a lusterless May and an uneventful June; by July 4 the Dodgers were five games behind the Padres. It was Dodgers pitching, however, that kept the team from slipping much farther down the NL West ladder. Valenzuela had set a major league record for the most consecutive innings at the start of a season without allowing an earned run (41), yet he only had a record of 2–3 after his first five games. Orel Hershiser, then in his third season in the major leagues, was, to Dodgers fans' glee, in the process of establishing himself as one of the game's best pitchers. Welch and Reuss rounded out the rotation, with Tom Niedenfuer and Ken Howell providing the bullpen help.

The summer winds, however, triggered a change. Suddenly the Dodgers bats came alive. Especially Pedro Guerrero's: he set a club record by hitting 15 home runs in the month of June, followed by a batting average of .460 in July. The team that had struggled through most of the first half of the season surged to the top of the division by mid-July. And they never relinquished the lead. The reigning-champion Padres collapsed, and by season's end Los Angeles was five and one-half games ahead of the second-place Cincinnati Reds and twelve ahead of the Padres and the Houston

Astros. Hershiser ended his first truly noteworthy year as a Dodger with a record of 19–3 and an ERA of 2.03; Valenzuela was 17–10, while Reuss and Welch each won 14 games. Guerrero was the team's top batsman with a .320 average—his slugging average of .577 was the league high—and he also hit 33 homers. Mike Marshall whacked another 28 home runs and led the club with 95 RBIs.

In the National League East, the St. Louis Cardinals battled the New York Mets all the way to the final days of the season before securing the title with a record of 101–61. Under the tutelage of Whitey Herzog, the Cards rode along on the league-high hitting of Willie McGee (.353), the pitching of John Tudor and Joaquin Andujar, both of whom won 21 games, and of Danny Cox, who was credited with another 18. They also had some amazing base path numbers: as a team they stole a league-high 310 bases with rookie outfielder Vince Coleman accounting for 110 of them. The Cards were a force to be reckoned with.

The championship series, extended for the first time in 1985 to a best-of-seven series, opened in Los Angeles with Fernando Valenzuela facing John Tudor. Valenzuela and Tom Niedenfuer, who came on in relief in the seventh inning, allowed only one run, and the Dodgers coasted to an easy 4–1

HITTING FOR THE CYCLE

Only seven Dodgers have hit for the cycle (a home run, triple, double, and single in the same game), and none since 1970. Babe Herman remarkably did it twice. The memorable seven and the days they made their marks in Dodgers lore:

Tom Burns: August 1, 1890
James Johnston: May 25, 1922
Babe Herman: May 18, 1931
Babe Herman: July 24, 1931
Dixie Walker: September 2, 1944
Jackie Robinson: August 29, 1948
Gil Hodges: June 25, 1949
Wes Parker: May 7, 1970

victory. The next day Orel Hershiser went the entire nine innings, giving up only two runs and eight hits, while the Los Angeles offense erupted; three runs in the third inning and another two in the fourth were more than enough, but before the game was over the Dodgers had added another three runs for a final of 8–2.

But after leaving the friendly confines of Dodger Stadium for Busch Stadium in St. Louis with a two-game-to-zip advantage, catastrophe lay in wait. In the first meeting at Busch Stadium, the four runs scored by the Cards in the first two innings were enough to rout Bob Welch and enough to win the game, the final score 4–2. The following day was much worse, a 12–2 drubbing in which starter Jerry Reuss and three Dodgers relief pitchers gave up 15 hits. Then, on the final day in St. Louis, the score tied 2–2 in the bottom of the ninth, Tom Niedenfuer came on in relief for Valenzuela, who had given up only four hits in the previous eight innings. He faced the Cards' Ozzie Smith—who had hit only six home runs all year—but the little shortstop drove one out of the park to give St. Louis a 3–2 victory and a 3–2 edge in the championship series.

The next day, back in L.A. after that heartbreaking loss, it appeared the Dodgers were going to take advantage of their home field . . . for a while, anyway. They jumped out to a 2–0 lead after two innings, then stretched that to a 4–1 margin by the end of the fifth, and Orel Hershiser was looking like the dominating hurler he had been all year. But in the top of the seventh, St. Louis exploded with three runs to tie the game. Hershiser was replaced by Tom Niedenfuer, the goat of the previous game. The Dodgers regained the lead in the bottom of the eighth, however, when Mike Marshall blasted a home run into the right-field seats. In the ninth inning, however, disaster struck again; with two men on base and two outs, Jack Clark homered off Niedenfuer. That was it, the Dodgers could not get anything going in the bottom of the ninth, and the game ended, 7–5. The first-ever best-of-seven

Orel Hershiser was an established ace by 1988, when he went on one of the most memorable runs of all time to end the season.
Photo courtesy of AP/Wide World Photos.

championship series was over with the Dodgers on the short end, four games to two.

Continuing what was now beginning to resemble a roller-coaster ride, the Dodgers plummeted in 1986, dropping from NL West champs to a fifth place finish (73–89) and turning in their worst season since 1967, when they had an identical record. With Pedro Guerrero missing most of the season due to a knee injury and only Steve Sax hitting above .300 (.322), the Dodgers were never in contention. Perhaps the only highlight of the year was the performance of Valenzuela, who racked up his first—and only—20-win season; his 21 victories were the most in the league that year, against only 11 defeats (including 20 complete games), and he recorded a club-best ERA of 3.14.

Unfortunately for Los Angeles fans, the roller coaster stayed at the bottom in 1987, and for the second consecutive year Lasorda's Dodgers posted only 73 wins, this time finishing in fourth place in the NL West, 17 games behind the division-champion Giants. Pedro Guerrero was back in form, and he batted .338 with 27 home runs and 89 RBIs. Pitching was still respectable: Hershiser was 16–16 with a 3.06 ERA; Welsh, 15–9 with an ERA of 3.22; and Valenzuela, 14–14 with a 3.98 ERA.

Then the roller coaster headed back uphill. Dramatically. Nineteen eighty-eight would indeed stand as a year to remember.

It all began in the spring. The Dodgers signed free-agent outfielder Kirk Gibson, and the acquisition would prove monumental in the months to come. A nine-year veteran who spent all those years in the American League with the Detroit Tigers, he was destined to have perhaps his finest year ever in 1988. And Orel Hershiser came to

One of the greatest moments in Dodgers history—and one of the most memorable images in all of sports—was Kirk Gibson's pinch-hit home run to beat the A's in Game 1 of the 1988 World Series. Photo courtesy of AP/Wide World Photos.

spring training with the stated intention of posting his first season as a 20-game winner. Both players would prove to be the decisive factors in the fate of the L.A. franchise that year.

Gibson was not the only acquisition. General manager Fred Claire added outfielder Mike Davis, outfielder and sometime-infielder Mickey Hatcher, pitcher Tim Belcher, reliever Jay Howell, shortstop Alfredo Griffin, and catcher Rick Dempsey. Gone, however, was hurler Bob Welch after 10 seasons with the Dodgers.

Los Angeles, a team with a definite new look, started strong in 1988. On May 26 they settled into first place, and by mid-July they were eight games ahead of their closest rival for the NL West crown. But it was not all smooth sailing off the field of play. Around that time, Pedro Guerrero and Kirk Gibson, both short-fused, fiery competitors, had a confrontation in the clubhouse after one game that almost came to blows; a few days later, Guerrero's 10½-year career with the Dodgers ended when he was traded to the Cardinals for 34-year-old pitcher John Tudor. On the field, however, the Dodgers were a sleek ship sailing smoothly toward a division championship. They never left first place after staking it in May.

Orel Hershiser became the talk of the league. He had won his first five games with ease; by late August he was truly at the top of his form. On August 30, Hershiser began a major league record streak, pitching 59 consecutive scoreless innings. He ended the season with six straight shutouts. His 23 wins and eight shutouts that year were league highs; he lost only eight games and had a 2.26 ERA. It was enough to earn him the Cy Young Award for 1988.

Kirk Gibson proved to be such a contributor to Los Angeles' success that he won the league's Most Valuable Player award, the first time a Dodger had been so honored since Steve Garvey in 1974. Gibson batted .290, hit a club-high 25 home runs, scored 106 runs, and drove in another 76.

The New York Mets, who many touted as the best team in major league baseball that year, won

---

WORLD SERIES LINEUPS, 1988

DODGERS	A'S
Steve Sax, 2b	Carney Lansford, 3b
Franklin Stubbs, 1b	Dave Henderson, cf
Mickey Hatcher, lf	Jose Canseco, rf
Mike Marshall, rf	Dave Parker, lf
John Shelby, cf	Mark McGwire, 1b
Mike Scioscia, c	Terry Steinbach, c
Jeff Hamilton, 3b	Glenn Hubbard, 2b
Alfredo Griffin, ss	Walt Weiss, ss

STARTING PITCHERS
Game 1: Tim Belcher, Dave Stewart
Game 2: Orel Hershiser, Storm Davis
Game 3: John Tudor, Bob Welch
Game 4: Tim Belcher, Dave Stewart
Game 5: Orel Hershiser, Storm Davis

---

the NL East by 15 games. Managed by Davey Johnson, the Mets sported an offense with such productive hitters as Keith Hernandez, Gary Carter, Darryl Strawberry, Lenny Dykstra, and Mookie Wilson. Their pitching staff was highlighted by David Cone (20–3 and a 2.22 ERA), Dwight Gooden (18–9), and Ron Darling (17–9), and backed by bullpen aces Randy Myers and Roger McDowell. The Mets were 100–60 in 1988, and they had defeated the Dodgers in 10 of the 11 games in which they faced each other during that year. The oddsmakers considered New York a decided—if not prohibitive—favorite to take the National League pennant.

Tommy Lasorda chose his ace, Orel Hershiser, to face the Mets in Game 1 at Dodger Stadium; New York decided on Dwight Gooden. It was a good choice on Lasorda's part, at least through eight innings. Hershiser held the Mets scoreless until the ninth inning, extending his scoreless pitching run to 67 innings. But then fans in Dodger Stadium watched as a 2–0 lead turned into a 3–2 defeat. With a man on base, Darryl Strawberry doubled to drive him in, and Hershiser's streak came to an end. Jay Howell came on in relief, walked one batter, and allowed Gary Carter to hit a double that drove in the two base runners. Los Angeles failed to score in the bottom half of the ninth, and the Mets had a one-game lead in the playoff series.

Mets ace David Cone was up for Game 2 at Dodger Stadium, but he made a big mistake before ever taking the mound. After the previous day's game he made a comment to the press that Dodgers reliever Jay Howell reminded him of "a high school pitcher." Lasorda plastered the article all over the Dodgers clubhouse; it fueled the Dodgers' fire. "Let's kill this guy," Kirk Gibson suggested in the clubhouse. From the start of the game, the Dodgers shouted their feelings from the dugout at Cone. And Cone heard them. He also heard their bats, five runs in the first two innings before he headed for the showers. Los Angeles added another run and won 6–3. Tim Belcher went eight and one-third innings and struck out 10 Mets.

Three days later, in New York, Hershiser was back on the mound for the Dodgers. He gave up three runs in the first seven innings, but Los Angeles drove home four. Then things turned sour. Jay Howell came on in relief, only to be thrown out of the game after the home-plate umpire discovered pine tar in his glove (he also received a three-game suspension from National League president Bart Giamatti). The Mets erupted for five runs during that hectic inning and won the game by a

score of 8–4. But the next day it was the Mets' turn to experience a reversal: up 4–2 in the ninth inning with Gooden on the mound, catcher Mike Scioscia hit a two-run homer to tie the score and send the game into extra innings. With Roger McDowell in relief for the Mets in the twelfth inning, the New Yorkers watched helplessly as what proved to be the game-winning home run came off the bat of Kirk Gibson. The 5–4 victory tied the championship series at two games apiece.

The final game in New York was all Los Angeles. The Dodgers built a 6–0 lead by the end of five innings, highlighted by a three-run homer by Gibson, and hung on to win it 7–4. Back in L.A. for Game 6 with Cone pitching for New York—and far less riled than he was after his ill-advised comment before Game 2—the Mets took the lead early and held it. This time Cone went the distance, allowing the Dodgers only five hits. The final score: Mets 5, Dodgers 1.

And so the 1988 National League championship series came down to a final, seventh game. Hershiser was Lasorda's choice, although he was coming off only three days rest. It proved to be an excellent choice; the sensational right-hander hurled a five-hit shutout. And the Dodgers offense contributed six runs in the first two innings, and that was the final score, 6–0. The Dodgers were World Series–bound, the first time since 1981.

Awaiting them were the Oakland A's. The A's, managed by Tony LaRussa, had breezed through the regular season, winning the AL West by 13 games with a record of 104–58. Oakland was a true powerhouse: Jose Canseco, the American League's MVP that year, led both leagues in home runs with 42, while Mark McGwire slammed 32 and Dave Henderson another 24. And Canseco's 124 RBIs were another major league high that year. The A's pitching staff was steady and productive; former Dodger Dave Stewart led it with a record of 21–12, followed most notably by another former Dodger, Bob Welch (17–9), and also by Storm Davis (16–7). Reliever Dennis Eckersley recorded 45 saves,

Franklin Stubbs (left) and Mickey Hatcher congratulate Mike Marshall (center) on his three-run, third-inning home run in Game 2 of the 1988 World Series. Photo courtesy of AP/Wide World Photos.

another major league high for 1988. In the AL championship series, Oakland swept the Boston Red Sox with two one-run victories in Boston and two far more lopsided wins at home in Oakland.

Like the Mets in the NL championship series, Oakland was the oddsmakers' favorite in the World Series. The Game 1 confrontation was at Dodger Stadium—Oakland ace Stewart against

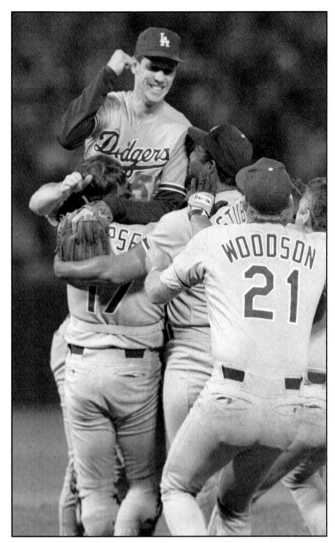

Orel Hershiser (top) fittingly finished off the A's with a 5–2 victory in Game 5 and then was named World Series Most Valuable Player. Photo courtesy of AP/Wide World Photos.

Dodger Belcher. But it was power that decided the game that day. Mickey Hatcher, playing in place of the injured Kirk Gibson (hamstring pull), drove a two-run homer into the left-field seats in the bottom of the first inning. In the top of the next inning, with the bases loaded, Canseco countered with a home run of his own, and Oakland then had a 4–2 lead. The Dodgers got a run back in the sixth inning and set the scene for one of the most dramatic home runs in Brooklyn or Los Angeles

Dodgers history. With the score 4–3 in the bottom of the ninth, two outs, and Eckersley on the mound for Oakland, things did not look good. Lasorda sent Mike Davis up to pinch hit and he drew a walk. Dave Anderson, another pinch-hitter, had been in the on-deck circle, but as Davis trotted down to first base, Anderson turned and trotted back to the dugout—a decoy, Lasorda later explained. And a gimpy Kirk Gibson limped out toward home plate. It was clear he was in pain, and his movement was hobbled. Two pitches from the best relief pitcher in baseball, two swings by Gibson, and he was 0–2. Then a ball, the count was now 1–2. Eckersley chose a slider to string out Gibson, who, forgetting about his pain-filled leg, smashed the ball into the right-field seats.

And so the Dodgers took the first game of the 1988 World Series. For the next encounter they had Orel Hershiser in waiting. Proving once again his unbeatability—a word specially coined for him that year—he shut down the Oakland powerhouse, hurling a three-hit shutout. A five-run third inning for Los Angeles and another run added in the following frame were more than enough, the final: 6–0.

In Oakland for Game 3, Tony LaRussa brought out Bob Welch, and he proved to be far from friendly to his former team, holding them to a single run through nine innings. The Dodgers hurlers—starter John Tudor and relievers Tim Leary and Alejandro Pena—limited the A's to a single run as well, but only through eight innings. In the bottom of the ninth inning, with the score tied at 1–1, Lasorda brought in ace relief pitcher Jay Howell, who led the team with 21 saves during the regular season. Unfortunately for Dodgers fans, it was not his destiny to shine that day; it was instead Oakland slugger Mark McGwire's turn. He sent a Jay Howell fastball deep into the left-field seats to end the game.

With the Dodgers leading the series two games to one but playing in hostile Oakland, the youthful Tim Belcher got the call for Game 4, and Dave Stewart took the mound for Oakland. Los Angeles

Manager Tommy Lasorda (above at right) hoists the World Series trophy with Dodgers vice president Fred Claire after the Game 5 win, then does a little dance (below) for the hometown fans during the team's celebration in downtown Los Angeles. Photo courtesy of AP/Wide World Photos.

jumped to a 2–0 lead in the first inning, but Oakland narrowed it to one run when they scored in the bottom of that inning. Two more runs from the Dodgers and another by Oakland sent the game into the bottom of the seventh inning with the Dodgers ahead by a single run. With the heart of the Oakland batting order up again, it began to look like another nightmare might be developing for the Dodgers; with the bases loaded and two outs, Mark McGwire stepped into the batter's box to face

Howell, who had just replaced Belcher, recreating the same disastrous confrontation that had decided the game the day before. This time, however, Howell got him to pop up. Later, in the ninth inning with the score still 4–3, but the tying run on base and only one out, Howell retired two of Oakland's most dangerous hitters, Jose Canseco and Dave Parker, and the game ended, a 2–1 victory for the Dodgers. With the Dodgers ahead now in the series three games to one, they prepared for another game in Oakland.

Hershiser was ready. He was in the full glory of a truly magnificent season and postseason, and now had just one more game to punctuate it with an exclamation point. Mickey Hatcher hit a two-run homer in the first inning to get it started for the Dodgers; Mike Davis added another two-run round-tripper in the fourth inning. Rick Dempsey drove in another run in the sixth inning. Meanwhile Hershiser indeed proved unbeatable, going the distance again, giving up just two runs and four hits. And with that 5–2 victory, the Dodgers were once again World Champions, the sixth time they could lay claim to that illustrious and coveted distinction.

Orel Hershiser had allowed only two runs and seven hits in the 18 innings he pitched during the 1988 World Series, and he struck out 17 Oakland batters. It was no surprise when he was voted the Series MVP. Mickey Hatcher batted .368 in the Series, his seven hits, five runs scored, two home runs, and five RBIs all club highs. Steve Sax batted .300, contributing six hits and three runs scored.

It had truly been a delicious year for Dodgers fans. The taste of it, however, was going to have to last for a long time.

CHAPTER 21

AN ERA OF ALSO-RANS

The team landed big-name free agents Darryl Strawberry (left) and Eric Davis in the early nineties, but in a miserable 1992 campaign neither slugging outfielder could keep the Dodgers out of the cellar (this being the first time they had landed there since 1905). Photo courtesy of AP/Wide World Photos.

A LONG DRY SPELL IN DODGERS annals was about to begin. There would be changes galore—on the field, in the dugout, and behind the doors of the front office—but the effects would be negligible. The next 15 years in Dodgers history would come to be known as the Era of Also-Rans.

The world-champion Los Angeles Dodgers did not play like world champions in 1989, but rather launched another roller-coaster ride into the nineties that was as frustrating to fans as it was disappointing. As manager, Tommy Lasorda was riding the crest of his career. He had just pulled off

The decade of the nineties opened with 22-year-old Ramon Martinez becoming the youngest Dodger since Ralph Branca in 1947 to win 20 games, going 20–6 with a 2.92 ERA. Photo courtesy of AP/Wide World Photos.

one of the most surprising upsets in World Series history, earning for himself and his Dodgers their second set of championship rings in the eighties. He signed a three-year contract extension to continue bleeding Dodger Blue.

But 1989 was not to be like 1988. Orel Hershiser was not the same Orel Hershiser who won the Cy Young Award and pitched the Dodgers to the World Series and then triumphantly through it; stellar Steve Sax, a free agent, left for George Steinbrenner's high-paying Yankees; and Kirk Gibson and Mike Marshall were troubled with injuries through much of the year. No one batted over .300, and only two (Marshall and the newly acquired Willie Randolph) hit higher than .250. At season's end, Los Angeles, 14 games out of first place, dwelt in fourth place in the NL West behind the Giants, Padres, and Astros.

The year 1990 marked the 100th anniversary of the Dodgers' membership in the National League. During that century of play, they had appeared in eighteen World Series, nine of them while in Los Angeles; the Dodgers won six altogether, and five of those came after the move to California.

The Dodgers began the nineties by heading back uphill on the figurative rollercoaster. Hershiser missed practically the entire season after having shoulder surgery. But another young pitching star emerged: right-hander Ramon Martinez. The 22-year-old took charge and established himself as the team's most productive and reliable hurler, winning 20 games against only 6 losses and posting a 2.92 ERA. (He was the youngest Dodgers pitcher to have won 20 games since 21-year-old Ralph Branca did it back in 1947.) Martinez also tied Sandy Koufax's record of 18 strikeouts in a single game when he hog-tied the Braves on June 4 at Dodger Stadium. Also that year, Fernando Valenzuela made a comeback of sorts, and pitched his first and only major league no-hitter in a game against the Cardinals; he also proved to be the club's second winningest pitcher (13–13).

Los Angeles battled the Cincinnati Reds for the NL West title, but fell five games short. The second-place finish was an improvement over the previous year, and so was the Dodgers performance at the plate. After the weak sticks of 1989, the acquisition of first baseman Eddie Murray, who had had a fine 12-year career with the Baltimore Orioles, was most welcome. He batted .330, hit 26 home runs, and drove in 95 runs. Outfielder Kal Daniels led the team with 27 homers in 1990.

The most dramatic addition to the Dodgers in 1991 was the exceptionally talented but often troubled Darryl Strawberry. The hard-hitting outfielder was lured from the Mets, where he had starred for eight years (in 1990 he batted .277, hit 37 homers, and drove in 108 runs), by a five-year Dodgers contract worth more than $20 million. In the early months of the season, it certainly looked like a bum deal, though; his bat was weak, and his contribution to the team was essentially nonexistent. But all that changed as the Dodgers made a concerted run for the NL West title, battling the Atlanta Braves down to the wire. The lead changed hands several times in the final six weeks of the season, and neither team ever held a lead of more than two games. The crown was decided on the next-to-last game of the season; that day Atlanta topped Houston and the Dodgers fell to the Giants. With a record of 93–69 and one game behind the Braves, Los Angeles had to settle for another second-place finish in the NL West.

Encouraging, however, was the rebound of Strawberry in the second half of the season. At the All-Star Game break he had accounted for only eight home runs; by season's end, however, he had contributed 28 and driven in a club-high 99 runs. Eddie Murray, who also had a disappointing first half, rallied as well and ended up with 19 homers and 96 RBIs. Center fielder Brett Butler, who had left the San Francisco Giants to join Los Angeles before the start of the season, led the National League in runs scored (112) and bases on balls (108); he also batted a team-high .296. Ramon Martinez headed the pitching staff with a record of 17–13; Mike Morgan was 14–10; Bob Ojeda, 12–9; and both Tim Belcher and Kevin Gross won 10 games for the Dodgers. Orel Hershiser, injury-free in 1991, posted a record of 7–2 and sparked at least a little hope for a return to the glorious performance he gave Dodgers fans in 1988.

Then the roller coaster plummeted. And no one foresaw how deep the plummet would be.

The Dodgers brought aboard outfielder Eric Davis, who had spent the previous eight years with Cincinnati. Jose Offerman replaced Alfredo Griffin at shortstop. Ten-year veteran right-handed knuckleballer Tom Candiotti, who had spent most of his career with the Cleveland Indians, was added to the pitching rotation. However, what would prove to be the biggest and most enduring addition was rookie first baseman Eric Karros; he would, in fact, become the only glimmer of light in an otherwise very dark season.

Everything went wrong. There was sloppy fielding (the team's 169 errors were the most in the majors that year, and shortstop Offerman made 42 of them). Darryl Strawberry played in only 43 games because of a back injury. And nobody seemed to be able to hit the ball, with the single exception of rookie Karros, who contributed 20 home runs, 30 doubles, and 88 RBIs and was named NL Rookie of the Year.

When the season mercifully came to an end, the Dodgers languished in last place in the NL West with a record of 63–99, 35 games out of first place. It was the first time in 87 years that a Dodgers team had ended up in the cellar (the last time was back

Eric Karros was the lone bright spot of the last-place finish in 1992, belting 20 homers, collecting 88 RBIs, and garnering the Rookie of the Year award. Photo courtesy of AP/Wide World Photos.

Mike Piazza was an unheralded late-round draft pick who turned in an outstanding Rookie of the Year season in 1993 and has since become one of the greatest catchers of all time.
Photo courtesy of AP/Wide World Photos.

in 1905 when they were 48–104 and 56½ games out of first). It was truly a season to forget.

For 1993, once again, the best news was the arrival of another rookie of distinction. Twenty-four-year-old catcher Mike Piazza joined the team. His explosive bat would soon bring some real excitement in a time when there was not a lot else to cheer about in Dodger Stadium. Darryl Strawberry, however, still had not recovered from his back problem or the ensuing surgery, and to these problems he added a major drug-and-alcohol-abuse issue. Strawberry would appear in only 32 games that year and bat .140.

Although they were never in the race for the division title in 1993, Los Angeles did improve to .500, ending up 81–81, in fourth place, and a distant 23 games behind the first-place Atlanta Braves. Piazza, everybody's choice for Rookie of the Year, led the team in practically every batting category. His 35 home runs and 112 RBIs were rookie records; he also batted .318 and led the team in runs (81), hits (174), doubles (24), and slugging average (.561). Eric Karros added another 23 homers and knocked in 80 runs. Second-year right-hander Pedro Astacio led the pitching staff with a record of 14–9. The roller coaster appeared to be headed back uphill.

The year 1994 in major league baseball was at once controversial, and before it was over the greed exhibited by the players became an embarrassment to the sport and a source of disenchantment for fans. Before the season began, the major leagues were realigned, then on August 11 they shut down. In the new alignment, the two divisions in each league were reconfigured into three: East, Central, and West. The playoffs were scheduled to include the winner of each division and a wild card team, turning it into a two-round event. There was a lot

THE LONGEST BLOWS

In the nearly half century that the Dodgers have been in Los Angeles, only four players have hit a home run that traveled out of the ballpark:

PLAYER	TEAM	DISTANCE	LOCATION	DATE
Willie Stargell	Pittsburgh	506½ feet	right field	Aug. 5, 1969
Willie Stargell	Pittsburgh	470 feet	right field	May 8, 1973
Mike Piazza	Los Angeles	478 feet	left field	Sept. 21, 1997
Mark McGwire	St. Louis	483 feet	left-center field	May 22, 1999

of controversy; people said it would dilute the quality of the playoffs because a team undeserving of them might win an easy division. Others felt that the new system was unfair because a second-place team would be rewarded the same as a division champion. As it turned out that first year of the new system, the skeptics were correct; in the American League West the Texas Rangers took the division crown with the awful record of 52–62, while runners-up in the other two divisions had substantially better records: the Baltimore Orioles in the East were 63–49, and the Cleveland Indians in the Central were 66–47. In fact, third-place Kansas City in the Central was 64–51.

In the National League, the Dodgers, remaining in the West Division along with the Giants, Padres,

By batting .306 during the strike-shortened 1994 season, Raul Mondesi became the third straight Dodger to win top rookie honors. Photo courtesy of AP/Wide World Photos.

and Colorado Rockies, just barely came in above .500 with a record of 58–56. But it was enough to earn them the division title, while the runner-up in the East, the Atlanta Braves, was 68–46, and the second-place Houston Astros in the Central were 66–49.

But, as it turned out, none of it mattered because when the last pitch was thrown and the last bat swung on August 11, the labor dispute between players and owners erupted into a shutdown that would bring the season to an inglorious end. No playoffs. No World Series—the first time since 1904 that there would not be one.

For the Dodgers, Darryl Strawberry was gone before Opening Day; battling his addiction problem, he entered a rehab facility, was placed on injured reserve, and would not return to Los Angeles. On the brighter side, another rookie took the limelight, outfielder Raul Mondesi lit up Dodger Stadium by hitting .306, a slugging average of .516 along with 16 homers and 56 RBIs in the shortened season. He became the third successive Dodger to earn Rookie of the Year honors. Second-year backstop Mike Piazza led the team with a .319 average, 24 home runs, and 92 runs batted in. Thirty-seven-year-old Brett Butler hit .314. Ramon Martinez led the hurling staff with a record of 12–7, and reliever Todd Worrell chalked up 11 saves.

Baseball's labor problems carried over into the 1995 season. As spring training commenced, there was still no resolution, and the prospect of ballclubs fielding teams made up of what were termed "replacement" players was hardly something that would bring the fans back into the ballparks. The great American pastime had reached perhaps the lowest point in the history of the game, the Black Sox scandal of 1919 notwithstanding. The day before the season was to start, however, the players returned and the crisis came to an end. To accommodate them and their lack of spring training, the season's start was delayed three weeks and the season itself shortened to 144 games instead of the regulation 162.

Hideo Nomo kept the string of Dodgers Rookies of the Year alive in 1995, arriving from Japan and creating the phenomenon known as "Nomomania." Photo courtesy of AP/Wide World Photos.

The fans were not mollified—and justly so—and legions of them stayed away from the ballparks, although Dodgers fans were more forgiving than most as more than 2.7 million passed through the turnstiles at Dodger Stadium that year. And they were rewarded; they were treated to a down-and-out divisional race that was not decided until the last day of the season. And to almost everyone's surprise, the stretch-runner that hounded the Dodgers was the Colorado Rockies, who that year counted four .300-plus hitters in the lineup, including Dante Bichette, who batted .340 and led the National League in three categories with his 40 home runs, 128 runs batted in, and a .620 slugging average. But Los Angeles prevailed at season's end, their record of 78–66 just edging out Colorado (77–67).

For the Dodgers, Mike Piazza again paced the offensive attack, hitting .346 with 32 homers and 93 runs batted in. Eric Karros contributed another 32 four-baggers and 105 RBIs along with a batting average of .298. And Raul Mondesi proved more than a rookie-year wonder by hitting 26 home runs and driving in 88 runs in his sophomore season. Again Ramon Martinez headed the pitching staff with a record of 17–7, and he was bolstered by the arrival of rookie Hideo Nomo from Japan, who was 13–6 and carried the team-best ERA of 2.54—it was enough to earn him the distinction of being the fourth consecutive Rookie of the Year produced by the Dodgers.

Facing Los Angeles in the first round of the playoffs were the Cincinnati Reds, who took the NL Central title with a record of 85–59 and were nine games ahead of their closest competitor. The Reds' record was a clear illustration of just how good the Cincinnatians were. They were paced by outfielders Reggie Sanders, who batted .306 with 28 homers and 99 RBIs, and Ron Gant, who belted 29 home runs and drove in 88 runs. Left-hander Pete Schourek headed the pitching staff with a record of 18–7, and reliever Jeff Brantley saved 28 games. They even had on the roster outfielder "Neon" Deion Sanders, but the man better known as a football star, who had been acquired from Atlanta, was hampered by an ankle injury and, in the 33 games he appeared, batted just .240. Cincinnati was good enough to dispatch the Dodgers in three straight: defeating them 7–2 and 5–4 in Los Angeles, and then with great authority, 10–1, back in Ohio.

The most notable addition to the 1996 Dodgers was 23-year-old outfielder Todd Hollandsworth, who would become the fifth consecutive Dodgers newcomer to be named National League Rookie of the Year. But even more notable was the departure of 68-year-old Tommy Lasorda from the Dodgers dugout. In June of his 20th year as manager of his beloved Dodgers, Lasorda suffered a heart attack and was hospitalized. He was replaced on an interim basis by coach and former Dodgers shortstop Bill Russell. A little more than a month after Lasorda was stricken, he called a press conference and announced that he was stepping away from managing the team for good and when he was fully recovered would move to a vice president job in the front office. Certainly the most colorful manager in Dodgers history, Lasorda ended his career with 1,599 wins, second only to the 2,042 racked up by Walt Alston in his 23 years as a Dodgers pilot. The following year he would enter the Hall of Fame in Cooperstown, New York, and his No. 2 would be retired by the Dodgers organization.

Whether Los Angeles would have fared better in 1996 had Lasorda's health not failed him is a question that can never be answered. As it was, they battled down to the wire for the division title, winning 90 games against 71 defeats, but ended up a game behind the San Diego Padres. It was good enough, however, for a berth in the playoffs as that year's National League wild-card.

Through the season, the Dodgers had shown impressive power: Mike Piazza clubbed 36 home runs, Eric Karros 34, Raul Mondesi 24, and rookie Hollandsworth 12. Hideo Nomo topped the rotation with a record of 16–11, and both Ramon Martinez (despite a nagging groin injury) and Ismael Valdez contributed 15 wins. And Todd Worrell had a National League–high 44 saves.

Los Angeles hosted the first two games of the 1996 playoffs, meeting the East champion Atlanta Braves, who were also the reigning world champions, having beaten the Cleveland Indians in six games in the 1995 World Series. Managed by Bobby Cox, Atlanta had easily won its division with a record of 96–66. If the Dodgers had exhibited some power in 1996, the Braves, it could be said, had showcased it: Ryan Klesko belted 34 homers, Chipper Jones, 30; Fred McGriff, 28; and Marquis Grissom and Javy Lopez, 23 each. Right-hander John Smoltz won a league-high 24 games against only 8 losses, and Tom Glavine and Greg Maddux won 15 games apiece. Mark Wohlers headed the Atlanta bullpen, saving 39 games, second best in the league that year after the Dodgers' Worrell.

Unfortunately for Los Angeles, the postseason would turn out to have the same three-game scenario as the year before. At home for Game 1, Ramon Martinez got the call, but the Dodgers could only come up with five hits and a single run all day. The one run was enough, however, to send the game into extra innings. But in the top of the tenth, relief pitcher Antonio Osuna served up a home-run ball to Atlanta's Javy Lopez for a 2–1 Braves victory. The next day Los Angeles could only muster three hits off Greg Maddux, and their two runs were one shy of Atlanta's three. L.A. held a 2–1 lead into the seventh inning, but in that inning, starter Ismael Valdes gave up back-to-back home runs to Fred McGriff and Jermaine Dye. So the Dodgers headed to the southeast, down two games to nothing. It was the fourth inning in Atlanta that did in the Dodgers in Game 3. Hideo Nomo gave up four runs, those and a single run ceded in the first were more than enough. The Dodgers managed a run in the seventh and another in the eighth inning, but the final score was a definitive 5–2, and Los Angeles, unfortunately, became just another also-ran in the 1996 baseball season. Even more unfortunately, it would prove to be the last postseason appearance by a Dodgers team until the year 2004.

On January 6, 1997, a blockbuster of a shocker hit Los Angeles Dodgers fans. Owner Peter O'Malley, after 27 years of leading the franchise left to him by legendary owner and baseball executive Walter O'Malley, told the press, media, and fans that he was planning to sell the team, although no buyer was yet announced.

And on that note the 1997 season began. Bill Russell was retained as manager. And the Dodgers again tried to make a season of it. They stayed in the race throughout the year and in fact had a two and one-half game lead over the pressing San Francisco Giants in early September. But they slipped into a terrible slump as the season moved to its conclusion in the final month. Losing 11 of 15 games, they cut themselves out of contention; their final record of 88–74 left them two full games behind the Giants and was not good enough to earn them a wild-card bid to the playoffs.

ROOKIE OF THE YEAR

During the nineties, Los Angeles established a major league standard when five Dodgers consecutively won National League Rookie of the Year honors: Eric Karros (1992), Mike Piazza (1993), Raul Mondesi (1994), Hideo Nomo (1995), and Todd Hollandsworth (1996).

A little more than a decade earlier, Dodgers rookies had taken the award in four consecutive years: Rick Sutcliffe (1979), Steve Howe (1980), Fernando Valenzuela (1981), and Steve Sax (1982).

Highlights of the year were Mike Piazza's batting average of .362, his 40 home runs, and 101 RBIs. Eric Karros hit 31 homers and drove in 104 runs, while Todd Zeile hit another 31 and Raul Mondesi 30. Chan Ho Park, the first South Korean–born player to pitch in the major leagues, turned in a record of 14–8, while Hideo Nomo was 14–12. Todd Worrell accounted for 38 saves.

On March 19, 1998, the sale of the Dodgers franchise, replete with Dodger Stadium and the team's training facilities in Vero Beach, Florida, to Rupert Murdoch's FOX Entertainment Group (a media empire that included the FOX television network, several newspapers, magazines, and book publishers, as well as the 20th Century FOX motion picture company) was formalized. The sale price of $311 million was the most ever paid for a major league baseball franchise up to that time. And so the O'Malley era, which began when Walter took over the presidency in 1950 and passed it to his son Peter in 1970, was over.

Also in 1998, what had been a gentle decline in the Dodgers' roller-coaster ride turned into a full-fledged nosedive. It was fueled in part by the discontent of the Dodgers' (and one of the major league's) best hitter, catcher Mike Piazza. He was looking for a contract extension: the Dodgers' new owners offered a record $80 million over six years; Piazza turned it down. He wanted to become the first in major league baseball to walk away with a $100 million contract. Contract extension negotiations then came to a halt, and Piazza entered the last season before he could enter the free agency market being paid a Dodgers-record-high salary of $8 million for the year.

Piazza would not have to test the free agency market, however, because in mid-May the Dodgers traded him to the Florida Marlins (who would in turn send him to the New York Mets). The trade was an enormous one; along with Piazza, Los Angeles sent Todd Zeile to Florida and in return got high-powered outfielder Gary Sheffield, third baseman/outfielder Bobby Bonilla, and catcher Charles Johnson.

Gary Sheffield, shown hitting a two-run home run off of Randy Johnson in 1999, joined the team as part of the blockbuster 1998 deal that sent Mike Piazza—albeit briefly—to the Florida Marlins. Photo courtesy of AP/Wide World Photos.

None of it helped the Dodgers, however. They got off to a rocky start, and things never got much better. Near the midpoint of the season, and with the Dodgers playing below .500 (36–38), the new ownership decided to dump both manager Bill Russell and general manager Fred Claire, and, on an interim basis, handed the on-field reins to Glenn Hoffman, a manager in the Dodgers farm system. Tommy Lasorda was moved into the general manager slot.

It did not matter much. San Diego was close to invincible in the NL West in 1998; the Dodgers could only manage a third-place finish behind them and the Giants. Their record was above .500 (83–79), but they were 15 games out at season's end. Newcomer Sheffield was the only player to hit above .300 (.316), and Johnson batted only .217, Bonilla just .237. Mondesi hit 30 homers, Karros, 23, and Sheffield, 16. Chan Ho Park turned in a respectable pitching record of 15–9, and Ismael Valdes was 11–10.

Although 1998 was a disappointing year for the team, one of their own was highly honored. Don Sutton joined Dodgers hurlers Burleigh Grimes, Dazzy Vance, Sandy Koufax, and Don Drysdale in the National Baseball Hall of Fame. His induction was accompanied that year by the retirement of his No. 20, as he became the 11th Dodger to be so honored by the organization.

For the last season of the 20th century, the Dodgers brought in highly regarded Davey Johnson to manage the team. Johnson had managed the Mets to a world championship in 1986 and a division title in 1988 (where they lost in the playoffs to the Dodgers). Kevin Malone was hired as the new general manger, and Lasorda resumed his vice presidential duties in the front office. One of Malone's first actions on behalf of Los Angeles was to acquire pitching ace Kevin Brown, who had headed the staff of the 1998 pennant-winning San Diego Padres (he was 18–7 with a 2.38 ERA), and previously had shone for the Florida Marlins, where he won 17 games in 1996 and 16 in 1997. The Dodgers signed him for what was then the largest amount of money for a player in the history of baseball: $105 million for seven years, $15 million per year.

Despite posting a record of 18–9 with a 3.00 ERA, Brown's presence was not enough to curb the Dodgers' descent, not even enough to slow it to a gentler decline. Los Angeles finished below .500 for the first time since 1994; their record of 77–85, although good enough for a second-place finish in the NL West, left them 23 games behind the divisional champion San Francisco Giants. Shortstop Mark Grudzielanek led all hitters with an average of .326; Eric Karros batted .304 and co-led the team

with 34 homers and 112 RBIs. Gary Sheffield hit another 34 four-baggers and drove in 101 runs, while Raul Mondesi homered 33 times and Todd Hundley hit another 24. Both Chan Ho Park and Darren Dreifort won 13 games for the Dodgers, and Jeff Shaw saved 34. Despite the Dodgers' lackluster performance in 1999, the fans did come out to support them. And on April 30 of that year, the Dodgers reached a milestone. While hosting the Atlanta Braves, they surpassed the 100 million mark in home attendance since Dodger Stadium opened in 1962.

There were some major changes in the Dodgers organization to launch the new century. In the front office, the FOX Entertainment Group sold 5 percent of the franchise to motion picture executive Robert Daly and named him chairman and chief executive officer of the organization. Daly, a lifelong Dodgers fan (he was born and raised in Brooklyn), had been chairman and co-chief executive officer of Warner Brothers and before that a top executive at CBS. And so in the year 2000 he turned his talents from show biz to baseball.

Another new addition whose impact would be immediate was outfielder Shawn Green, whose arrival was the result of a trade that sent Raul Mondesi and pitcher Pedro Borbon to Toronto. The power-hitting Green had belted 45 home runs and driven in 123 runs in 1998. He had spent his entire seven years in the majors up in Toronto, and now he signed a six-year contract with the Dodgers for $14 million per year. With one of the two highest payrolls in baseball, Los Angeles moved warily into the 21st century. And the decline subsided, although to the discontent of Dodgers fans everywhere it only leveled off instead of heading back to the relative highs the team enjoyed in the mid-nineties.

San Francisco still ruled the NL West, winning the division by 11 games; the second-place Dodgers at least reversed directions in the won-lost column and came in above .500 with a record of 86–76, but that was still not sufficient to win a wild-card berth in the playoffs. Green had been a disappointment;

Kevin Brown lived up to his $105-million billing by going 18–9 with a 3.00 ERA in his Dodgers debut season of 1999, but it wasn't enough to keep the club from slipping below .500 for the first time in five years. Photo courtesy of AP/Wide World Photos.

his output was down considerably, only 24 home runs, 99 RBIs, and a batting average of .269. Kevin Brown, the other newly signed multimillionaire, was also down, winning just 13 games. Chan Ho Park headed the rotation with a record of 18–10, while Gary Sheffield proved to be far and away the top batsman, hitting .325 with 43 home runs and 109 RBIs (his 43 homers tied the Dodgers record set by Duke Snider back in 1956).

The front office showed its discontent by replacing the veteran Davey Johnson with a major

league managerial rookie, Jim Tracy. He had been Johnson's bench coach the two preceding seasons and had served in the same capacity with the Montreal Expos before that.

Kevin Brown was troubled with an elbow injury, and his contribution in 2001 therefore was small (10–4), but Shawn Green proved to be the hitter the Dodgers had paid all that money for—he broke the club home-run record by banging out 49 and driving in 125 runs. Catcher and sometime first baseman Paul Lo Duca hit a team-high .320 with 25 homers and 90 RBIs, while Gary Sheffield batted .311 and added another 36 homers and 100 RBIs. And Chan Ho Park again was the mainstay of the pitching staff (15–11 and a 3.50 ERA). Jeff Shaw's 43 saves brought his Dodgers total to 129, then a club record.

The Dodgers ended the season with a record identical to that of the year before, 86–76; only this time they languished in third place in the NL West, but only six games out, five games closer than the year before. If it was a consolation, the Arizona Diamondbacks, who won the NL West, went on to win that year's World Series, defeating the Yankees in seven games.

In 2002, the Dodgers improved their record substantially, winning six more games than they had in the previous two seasons; their record of 92–70, however, was still only good enough for a third-place finish in the NL West, six games behind the reigning world champion Diamondbacks and three and one-half in back of that year's wild-card entry, the Giants.

Gary Sheffield had moved to Atlanta, and closer Jeff Shaw was gone, but he was ably replaced by Eric Gagne, a 6'2", 235-pound right-hander, who had seen only limited duty with the Dodgers in the preceding three seasons. Gagne, a native of Montreal, Canada, was brought up to the major leagues as a Dodger in 1999. He made his debut on September 7 of that year against the Florida Marlins and posted his first career win on October 1 over the Houston Astros. He would not record his first save until April 7, 2002, when he preserved a win over the Colorado Rockies. Then, in that same year, Gagne went on to save a club-record 52 games, which also tied the National League record. He had an ERA of 1.97 in 2002 as well.

Hideo Nomo returned to form and led the regular rotation with 16 wins against 6 losses, while Odalis Perez won 15 games and Kazuhisa Ishii another 14. Shawn Green continued to power from the plate, this time whacking 42 homers and driving in 114 runs. He became the first Dodger ever to have back-to-back seasons of 40-plus home runs. And he also came up with the single most productive day at the plate for any Dodger in history. On May 23, 2002, in a game against the Brewers in Milwaukee, Green hit four home runs (the only other Dodger ever to accomplish that feat was Gil Hodges back in 1950) and set club records with 19 total bases and six runs scored and tied the record for hits with six. The following day Green belted another homer to tie the major league record of five home runs in two consecutive games, and along with two singles that day, he matched still another major league record with 25 total bases in back-to-back games. Then, the day after that, Green walloped two more homers to set a new major league record of seven home runs in three consecutive games.

Another memorable day from 2002 in Dodgers lore was September 2; on that day Dodgers bats accounted for 24 hits to tie the club record in a 19–1 victory over the Arizona Diamondbacks. With such a positive record in 2002, the emergence of Eric Gagne as the game's premier closer, the awesome power of Shawn Green at the plate, and a solid pitching rotation, Dodgers fans had good reason to look for a return in 2003 to postseason baseball in Los Angeles.

Gagne certainly lived up to expectations. He broke his own record for saves by totaling 55 in

TRIVIA

The most home runs hit by the Dodgers in a single game at Dodger Stadium remains seven, hammered out on May 25, 1979, against the Cincinnati Reds. The seven round-trippers were contributed by Dusty Baker, Rick Sutcliffe, Steve Garvey, Gary Thomasson, Joe Ferguson, Derrel Thomas, and Davey Lopes.

2003—not just 55 saves, but 55 saves in 55 chances. His perfect record and a 1.20 ERA earned him that year's Cy Young Award, the first time a Dodger had been so honored since Orel Hershiser back in the world championship year of 1988. Gagne became only the seventh Dodgers hurler in team history to win the Cy Young Award.

Slugger Shawn Green did not fare as well, however, as his home-run output plummeted to 19 from the 42 he had hit the season before and he accounted for only 85 RBIs. Third baseman Adrian Beltre hit the most home runs (23), and no batter hit above .300. One highlight, however, was that Paul Lo Duca hit safely in 25 consecutive games, the second longest streak since the team moved to Los Angeles (shared with Steve Sax and Willie Davis, the longest streak being Davis' 31 back in 1969). From the mound, Hideo Nomo won 16 while losing 13, and Kevin Brown posted a record of 14–9.

It all added up to another mediocre season. Los Angeles ended in second place with a record of 85–77, 15½ games behind the Giants. And another year without postseason play, another season in the era of also-rans, went down in the Dodgers history books.

But finally, in 2004, the disappointing Dodgers of the late nineties and the early 2000s, were about to change direction, and the thrills of victory were poised to return to Dodger Stadium.

CHAPTER 22

BACK TO POSTSEASON PLAY IN 2004

New owner Frank McCourt, shown speaking to the media with his wife Jamie two days after purchasing controlling interest in the Dodgers, took over the ballclub in January 2004. Photo courtesy of AP/Wide World Photos.

ON JANUARY 29, 2004, Frank McCourt and his wife Jamie purchased a controlling interest in the Dodgers from the FOX Entertainment Group and Robert Daly. McCourt assumed the role of chairman and his wife that of vice chairman; two weeks later the McCourts hired Paul DePodesta to replace Dan Evans as general manager. In the dugout Jim Tracy was retained as manager. And the Dodgers were positioned to enter another new era.

The season opened at Dodger Stadium on April 5 against the San Diego Padres, who had occupied the cellar of the NL West in 2003. Shawn Green

OPENING DAY LINEUP, 2004

Dave Roberts, lf
Cesar Izturis, ss
Milton Bradley, cf
Shawn Green, 1b
Paul Lo Duca, c
Juan Encarnacion, rf
Adrian Beltre, 3b
Alex Cora, 2b
Hideo Nomo, p

had moved to first base to accommodate the often volatile center fielder Milton Bradley, who had been with the Cleveland Indians in the American League the season before. Hideo Nomo, who was coming off shoulder surgery, was on the mound for the Dodgers. It was not a pleasant Opening Day. The Padres took the lead in the third inning and then exploded for six more runs in the fifth. Green solo-homered for the Dodgers and Cesar Izturis drove in another run, but the Dodgers left eight men on base in the first three innings alone and could only score two runs on the 15 hits they got that day. The final was Padres 8, Dodgers 2. An inauspicious start, to say the least.

But it was going to get much better. Los Angeles followed the opener with a four-game

Shawn Green's 28 home runs in 2004 were the second most for the team that year, behind Adrian Beltre (48). Photo courtesy of AP/Wide World Photos.

win-streak, and by May 1, with a record of 15–8, held first place by a few percentage points ahead of the resurgent San Diego Padres. The Dodgers ran neck-and-neck with the Padres through the next month and by June 1, having won 27 games while losing 23, remained in first place, ahead by less than a game. But by July 1, the Dodgers, suffering an early summer swoon, dropped to third place in the NL West. Suddenly the surging San Francisco Giants had taken the lead, the Padres were in second place, and Los Angeles, with a record of 40–36, was languishing in third, two and one-half games behind the leader.

Perhaps the most noteworthy news, on an individual basis, was the fact that Eric Gagne had continued to save every game he was brought in to save. By early July he had extended his streak to 84 consecutive saves, a blockbuster of a major league record. The streak came to an end, however, on the evening of July 5 against the Arizona Diamondbacks when he relinquished a 5–3 lead in the ninth inning of a game the Dodgers lost in the tenth. Despite the loss, Gagne received a standing ovation when he left the field that night. The consummate closer had not blown a save since August 22, 2002 (coincidentally enough against the Diamondbacks). The new record of 84 straight saves was 30 more than the previous major league record held by Tom Gordon of the Boston Red Sox. What Gagne had to say about it when it was finally over: "I never really thought about the streak at all. I'm not really relieved about it, but it was so much fun to be a part of it."

Gagne, unsurprisingly, was selected for the 2004 All-Star Game, as was his battery-mate Paul Lo Duca (as a reserve), who was batting .313 at the All-Star break. By the end of July, however, Lo Duca, to many fans' chagrin, would be gone, traded along with outfielder Juan Encarnacion and relief pitcher Guillermo Mota to the Florida Marlins for first baseman Hee Seop Choi and right-handed pitcher Brad Penny. The Dodgers also acquired outfielder Steve Finley, a four-time Gold

Relief pitcher Eric Gagne burst onto the scene with a Cy Young Award campaign in 2003 and then took his consecutive-saves streak of 84 into July 2004. Photo courtesy of AP/Wide World Photos.

Glove winner, and catcher Brent Mayne from Arizona, then sent Dave Roberts to the Red Sox for several minor league players.

All the trades came at the end of a glorious month for Los Angeles. The team was 20–7 during July, catapulting them back into first place by August 1, then two and one-half games ahead of San Diego and four and one-half in front of the Giants. Their record stood at 60–43.

At that point in the season, third baseman Adrian Beltre had belted 29 home runs, the second most in the major leagues (and more than he had hit in any full season so far in his six-year Dodgers career), and had driven in 74 runs, fourth highest in the National League. Beltre, at 5'11" and 220 pounds, batting right-handed, and a native of Santo

Domingo, Dominican Republic, had joined the Dodgers in 1998. In his debut performance that year on June 24 against the Angels, he doubled in his first at-bat. Beltre cracked his first home run six days later in a game against Texas. By 2004, at age 24, he was truly coming into his own. After three years in which he hit just 13, 21, and 23 home runs and never batted above .265, he was leading both leagues in home runs and was among the top hitters in the National League with an average of .330.

Beltre, needless to say, was the Dodgers' top batter at that point in the season. Cesar Izturis was the only other .300 hitter (.305), but Jayson Werth and Alex Cora were very close to the .300 mark. Gagne had recorded 30 saves, and reliever Guillermo Mota had the best ERA in the National League (2.14), although he was, at that August date, putting on a Florida Marlins uniform. Kazuhisa Ishii had won 11 games against 5 losses, and Jose Lima was 9–3.

August proved to be an equally satisfying month for the Dodgers, who never gave up or shared the divisional lead. By September 1, Los Angeles boasted a record of 76–64 (.585) and led both the Padres and the Giants by five and one-half games. Their record at home was 39–25 and on the road 37–29. Adrian Beltre led both leagues in home runs, his total now up to 42, and his batting average had increased to .342, the third highest in the National League. His 164 hits were the third most in the NL, and his 98 RBIs ranked fourth. Eric Gagne had toted up 36 saves, ranking fourth in the National League.

The Dodgers were flying high as autumn approached. And they continued that flight through September, although they were not flying as high as some fans would have liked and did swoop once or twice. Still, they never let go of the National League West lead. By the end of the month, however, Eric Gagne, their Cy Young closer, was out with mild tendinitis in his shoulder, and cantankerous outfielder Milton Bradley was serving a four-game suspension after throwing

a plastic bottle, which had been thrown onto the field, into the box seats. On the brighter side, Adrian Beltre collected his 200th hit, joining an elite group of only five other L.A. Dodgers to record that many in a season, and still led both leagues in home runs with 48 (also a Dodgers record for a right-handed batter).

It would not be until the next-to-last game of the season, however, that the Dodgers would clinch the division title. On that Saturday afternoon at Dodger Stadium, the San Francisco Giants were just two games behind in the division standings and held a 3–0 lead over the Dodgers in the ninth inning. If that lead were to hold up, it would leave San Francisco just a game out and give them the chance the following day to tie for the divisional title and force a playoff. But the come-from-behind Dodgers lived up to their reputation—they had already set a franchise record for comeback victories in 2004 (53)—and pulled off the win in a most dramatic fashion: a seven-run, bottom-of-the-ninth explosion.

Not without a little help from the Giants, however. San Francisco closer Dustin Hermanson walked three batters, the last forcing in a run. An error allowed another run to score, and then Jayson Werth tied the score with a single to right field. Steve Finley, who had been acquired from the Diamondbacks at the trading deadline earlier in the summer, came to the plate with one out and the bases loaded, then sent a towering drive into the right-field bleachers—the grand-slam homer gave the Dodgers a 7–3 victory and the NL West divisional championship.

Finley explained after the game, "I was dreaming about it, and it happened. I knew I was going to get it done. When I walked to the plate, I knew the game was over. I even had a smile on my face." And closer Eric Gagne added, "We do it the Hollywood way, that's for sure. It's amazing."

And so, after an eight-year drought, the Dodgers were heading into postseason play. Their opponent for the first-round of the playoffs was the

St. Louis Cardinals, a team that easily won the NL Central with a major-league-best record of 105–57, 13 games ahead of their closest rival, the Houston Astros. The Cardinals were a true powerhouse: first baseman Albert Pujols hit 46 homers, second only in the majors to the Dodgers' Adrian Beltre that year, and Jim Edmonds contributed another 42, Scott Rolen 34, and Reggie Sanders 22. Pujols also batted .330, drove in 123 runs, led the National League in total bases with 389, and had the second-highest slugging percentage, .657. Jeff Suppan led the pitching staff with a record of 16–9, while Matt Morris, Jason Marquis, and Chris Carpenter each won 15 games; Jason Isringhausen contributed 47 saves, tying for the most in the National League in 2004.

The Cardinals earned home-field advantage, and it proved to be just that. The Dodgers lost both games at Busch Stadium by identical scores of 8–3. There was now the discomforting fear that the Dodgers were on the brink of being swept as they had been by the Cincinnati Reds in 1995 and the Atlanta Braves in 1996—with these two failures in St. Louis, the Dodgers had now lost eight playoff games in a row. Returning to the friendlier climate of Los Angeles, however, the Dodgers hoped to once again summon that mystical force that had enabled them to come from behind and triumph so many times during the regular season.

For Game 3 Jose Lima got the call to try to shut down the Cardinals' offensive powerhouse, which had produced 16 runs in the first two games of the playoff series. Lima, a right-hander signed as a free agent that year, was 13–5 during the regular season; he proved he was up to the task, hurling a five-hit shutout. Two solo home runs by Shawn Green and a double by Steve Finley that drove in another two runs were enough; the 4–0 win brought Los Angeles within a game of tying the playoff series. It was the Dodgers' first postseason victory in 16 years.

Odalis Perez, taking the mound for Game 4, was not so successful. He lasted only two and one-

Third baseman Adrian Beltre, at the tender age of 24, had a breakout season in 2004 and established himself as one of the game's superstars. Photo courtesy of AP/Wide World Photos.

third innings, giving up two runs and three hits. Five ensuing relievers did not do much better. They gave up another four runs. Two hits and four RBIs from Albert Pujols were more than enough to give the St. Louis Cardinals a 6–2 victory and a pass to play for the National League pennant. And for the Dodgers, playing that day before the largest crowd in the 43-year history of Dodger Stadium, 56,268, it signaled the end of the most exciting season in years.

"The ending was as unpredictably classy as the journey," Bill Plaschke wrote the next day in the *Los Angeles Times*. "First, the Dodgers congratulated the St. Louis Cardinals, jogging onto the field to shake hands for what may be the first time in

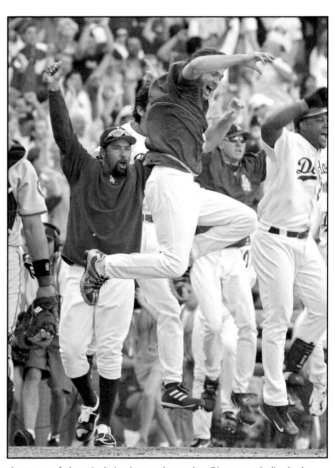

No home run in 2004 was bigger than Steve Finley's grand slam in the bottom of the ninth inning to beat the Giants and clinch the NL West on October 2. At left, Robin Ventura (No. 23) and Jayson Werth celebrate as they score on the play, while the dugout erupts into cheers. Photos courtesy of AP/Wide World Photos.

baseball history. Then, the Dodgers congratulated their fans, clapping at them, waving to them, showering them with wristbands and batting gloves and caps."

Adrian Beltre turned in the best stats of his entire career. Besides setting the Dodgers' home-run mark for right-handed batters, his 48 tied Hall of Famer Mike Schmidt for the most ever hit by a third baseman in the major leagues. He also led the team with a batting average of .334, 200 hits, 121 RBIs, and 104 runs scored. Steve Finley belted 36 home runs (13 after joining the Dodgers), Shawn Green 28, and Milton Bradley 19.

Eric Gagne's 45 saves ranked third in the National League. Jose Lima, Kazuhisa Ishii, and Jeff Weaver accounted for 13 wins apiece.

Outfielder Steve Finley won a Gold Glove award, his career fifth, and shortstop Cesar Izturis was awarded his first. Adrian Beltre won the Silver Slugger award for being the best-hitting third baseman in the National League.

All told, it had been a fulfilling year of baseball excitement for Dodgers fans: a divisional title and a postseason appearance. In the exuberance after the final game of the 2004 divisional championship series, when the Dodgers, in an unprecedented show of grace and sportsmanship, congratulated the Cardinals and the record-breaking crowd in Dodger Stadium, consummate closer Eric Gagne said it all for the team and the fans alike: "I wanted to tell the fans that next year, when we start over, we want to keep this same feeling."

Indeed.

HALL OF FAME

Zack Wheat

Wilbert Robinson

Burleigh Grimes

Dazzy Vance

Jackie Robinson

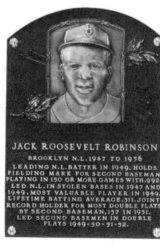

Roy Campanella

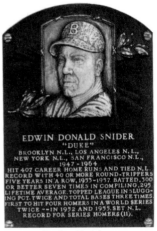

Duke Snider

Sandy Koufax

Don Drysdale

Pee Wee Reese

Don Sutton

Walt Alston

Tommy Lasorda

UNIFORM NUMBERS RETIRED

No. 1	Pee Wee Reese	No. 24	Walt Alston
No. 2	Tommy Lasorda	No. 32	Sandy Koufax
No. 4	Duke Snider	No. 39	Roy Campanella
No. 19	Junior Gilliam	No. 42	Jackie Robinson
No. 20	Don Sutton	No. 53	Don Drysdale

AWARD WINNERS

PLAYER OF THE DECADE (1960–1969)

Sandy Koufax

MOST VALUABLE PLAYER

Jake Daubert, 1913
Dazzy Vance, 1924
Dolph Camilli, 1941
Jackie Robinson, 1949
Roy Campanella, 1951, 1953, 1955
Don Newcombe, 1956
Maury Wills, 1962
Sandy Koufax, 1963
Steve Garvey, 1974
Kirk Gibson, 1988

CY YOUNG AWARD

Don Newcombe, 1956
Don Drysdale, 1962
Sandy Koufax, 1963, 1965, 1966
Mike Marshall, 1974
Fernando Valenzuela, 1981
Orel Hershiser, 1988
Eric Gagne, 2003

ROOKIE OF THE YEAR

Jackie Robinson, 1947
Don Newcombe, 1949
Joe Black, 1952
Junior Gilliam, 1953
Frank Howard, 1960
Jim Lefebvre, 1965
Ted Sizemore, 1969
Rick Sutcliffe, 1979
Steve Howe, 1980
Fernando Valenzuela, 1981
Steve Sax, 1982
Eric Karros, 1992
Mike Piazza, 1993
Raul Mondesi, 1994
Hideo Nomo, 1995
Todd Hollandsworth, 1996

GOLD GLOVE

Gil Hodges, 1957, 1958, 1959
Charlie Neal, 1959
Wally Moon, 1960
John Roseboro, 1961, 1966
Maury Wills, 1961, 1962
Wes Parker, 1967, 1968, 1969, 1970, 1971, 1972
Willie Davis, 1971, 1972, 1973
Steve Garvey, 1974, 1975, 1976, 1977
Andy Messersmith, 1974, 1975
Davey Lopes, 1978
Dusty Baker, 1981
Fernando Valenzuela, 1986
Orel Hershiser, 1988
Raul Mondesi, 1995, 1997
Charles Johnson, 1998
Cesar Izturis, 2004
Steve Finley, 2004

COMEBACK PLAYER OF THE YEAR

Phil Regan, 1966
Al Downing, 1971
Jimmy Wynn, 1974
Tommy John, 1976
Jerry Reuss, 1980
Pedro Guerrero, 1987
Tim Leary, 1988
Orel Hershiser, 1991
Tim Wallach, 1994

LEAGUE LEADERS

HITTING

BATTING AVERAGE

Jake Daubert	1913	.350
Jake Daubert	1914	.329
Zack Wheat	1918	.335
Lefty O'Doul	1932	.368
Pete Reiser	1941	.343
Dixie Walker	1944	.357
Jackie Robinson	1949	.342
Carl Furillo	1953	.344
Tommy Davis	1962	.346
Tommy Davis	1963	.326

HOME RUNS

Jim Sheckard	1903	9
Harry Lumley	1904	9
Tim Jordan	1906	12
Tim Jordan	1908	12
Jack Fournier	1924	27
Dolph Camilli	1941	34
Duke Snider	1956	43
Adrian Beltre	2004	48

RBIs

Hy Myers	1919	72
Dolph Camilli	1941	120
Dixie Walker	1945	124
Roy Campanella	1953	142
Duke Snider	1955	136
Tommy Davis	1962	153

RUNS SCORED

Pete Reiser	1941	117
Arky Vaughan	1943	112
Eddie Stanky	1945	128
Pee Wee Reese	1949	132
Duke Snider	1953	132
Duke Snider	1954	120*
Duke Snider	1955	126

HITS

Wee Willie Keeler	1900	208
Ivy Olson	1919	164
Duke Snider	1950	199
Tommy Davis	1962	230
Steve Garvey	1978	202
Steve Garvey	1980	200

TRIPLES

Jim Sheckard	1901	21
Harry Lumley	1904	18
Whitey Alperman	1907	16*
Jake Daubert	1918	15
Hy Myers	1919	14*
Hy Myers	1920	22
Pete Reiser	1941	17
Luis Olmo	1945	13
Junior Gilliam	1953	17
Wally Moon	1959	11*
Charlie Neal	1959	11*
Willie Davis	1962	10*
Maury Wills	1962	10*
Willie Davis	1970	16

DOUBLES

James Carlisle "Red" Smith	1913	40
John Frederick	1929	52
Pete Reiser	1941	39*
Wes Parker	1970	47

SLUGGING AVERAGE

Jim Sheckard	1901	.536
Harry Lumley	1906	.477
Zack Wheat	1916	.461
Hy Myers	1919	.436
Pete Reiser	1941	.558
Duke Snider	1953	.627
Duke Snider	1956	.598

BASES ON BALLS

Jack Fournier	1925	86
Dolph Camilli	1938	119
Dolph Camilli	1939	110
August Galan	1943	103
August Galan	1944	101
Eddie Stanky	1945	148
Eddie Stanky	1946	137
Pee Wee Reese	1947	104*
Duke Snider	1956	99
Junior Gilliam	1959	96

STOLEN BASES

Jim Sheckard	1903	67*
Pete Reiser	1942	20
Arky Vaughan	1943	20
Pete Reiser	1946	34
Jackie Robinson	1947	29
Jackie Robinson	1949	37

*Tied for the league lead.

Pee Wee Reese	1952	30	
Maury Wills	1960	50	
Maury Wills	1961	35	
Maury Wills	1962	104	
Maury Wills	1963	40	
Maury Wills	1964	53	
Maury Wills	1965	94	
Davey Lopes	1975	77	
Davey Lopes	1976	63	

PITCHING

WINNING PERCENTAGE

Joe McGinnity	1900	.763	29–9
Burleigh Grimes	1920	.676	23–11
Fred Fitzsimmons	1940	.889	16–2
Larry French	1942	.789	15–4
Preacher Roe	1949	.714	15–6
Preacher Roe	1951	.880	22–3
Carl Erskine	1953	.769	20–6
Don Newcombe	1955	.800	20–5
Don Newcombe	1956	.794	27–7
Johnny Podres	1961	.783	18–5
Ron Perranoski	1963	.842	16–3
Sandy Koufax	1964	.792	19–5
Sandy Koufax	1965	.765	26–8
Phil Regan	1966	.933	14–1
Tommy John	1973	.696	16–7
Tommy John	1974	.813	13–3
Rick Rhoden	1976	.800	12–3
Orel Hershiser	1985	.864	19–3

ERA

Dazzy Vance	1924	2.16
Dazzy Vance	1928	2.09
Dazzy Vance	1930	2.61
Johnny Podres	1957	2.66
Sandy Koufax	1962	2.54
Sandy Koufax	1963	1.88
Sandy Koufax	1964	1.74
Sandy Koufax	1965	2.04
Sandy Koufax	1966	1.73
Don Sutton	1980	2.21
Alejandro Pena	1984	2.48
Kevin Brown	2000	2.58

STRIKEOUTS

Burleigh Grimes	1921	136
Dazzy Vance	1922	134
Dazzy Vance	1923	197
Dazzy Vance	1924	262
Dazzy Vance	1925	221
Dazzy Vance	1926	140
Dazzy Vance	1927	184
Dazzy Vance	1928	200
Van Lingle Mungo	1936	238
Don Newcombe	1951	164*
Don Drysdale	1959	242
Don Drysdale	1960	246
Sandy Koufax	1961	269
Don Drysdale	1962	232
Sandy Koufax	1963	306
Sandy Koufax	1965	382
Sandy Koufax	1966	317
Fernando Valenzuela	1981	180
Hideo Nomo	1995	236

SHUTOUTS

Nap Rucker	1912	6
Clarence Mitchell	1921	3*
Dazzy Vance	1928	4*
Douglas McWeeny	1928	4*
Dazzy Vance	1930	4*
Van Lingle Mungo	1935	4*
J. Whitlow Wyatt	1940	5*
J. Whitlow Wyatt	1941	7
Don Newcombe	1949	5*
Johnny Podres	1957	6
Roger Craig	1959	4*
Don Drysdale	1959	4*
Sandy Koufax	1963	11
Sandy Koufax	1964	7
Sandy Koufax	1966	5*
Al Downing	1971	5*
Don Sutton	1972	9
Andy Messersmith	1975	7
Jerry Reuss	1980	6
Fernando Valenzuela	1981	8
Orel Hershiser	1988	8
Tim Belcher	1989	9
Ramon Martinez	1994	3
Hideo Nomo	1995	3*

*Tied for the league lead.

ALL-TIME DODGERS LEADERS

HITTING

GAMES

Wheat, Zack	2,322
Russell, Bill	2,181
Reese, Pee Wee	2,166
Hodges, Gil	2,006
Gilliam, Junior	1,956
Davis, Willie	1,952
Snider, Duke	1,923
Furillo, Carl	1,806
Garvey, Steve	1,727
Karros, Eric	1,601

AT-BATS

Wheat, Zack	8,859
Reese, Pee Wee	8,058
Davis, Willie	7,495
Russell, Bill	7,318
Gilliam, Junior	7,119
Hodges, Gil	6,881
Snider, Duke	6,640
Garvey, Steve	6,543
Furillo, Carl	6,378
Wills, Maury	6,156

RUNS

Reese, Pee Wee	1,338
Wheat, Zack	1,255
Snider, Duke	1,199
Gilliam, Junior	1,163
Hodges, Gil	1,088
Davis, Willie	1,004
Robinson, Jackie	947
Furillo, Carl	895
Griffin, Mike	882
Wills, Maury	876

HITS

Wheat, Zack	2,804
Reese, Pee Wee	2,170
Davis, Willie	2,091
Snider, Duke	1,995
Garvey, Steve	1,968
Russell, Bill	1,926
Furillo, Carl	1,910
Gilliam, Junior	1,889
Hodges, Gil	1,884
Wills, Maury	1,732

RUNS BATTED IN

Snider, Duke	1,271
Hodges, Gil	1,254
Wheat, Zack	1,223
Furillo, Carl	1,058
Garvey, Steve	992
Karros, Eric	976
Reese, Pee Wee	885
Campanella, Roy	856
Davis, Willie	849
Cey, Ron	842

STOLEN BASES

Wills, Maury	490
Lopes, Davey	418
Davis, Willie	335
Daly, Tom	298
Sax, Steve	290
Pinkney, George	280
O'Brien, Darby	272
Griffin, Mike	264
Foutz, Dave	241
Reese, Pee Wee	232

DOUBLES

Wheat, Zack	464
Snider, Duke	343
Garvey, Steve	333
Reese, Pee Wee	330
Furillo, Carl	324
Davis, Willie	321
Gilliam, Junior	304
Karros, Eric	302
Hodges, Gil	294
Russell, Bill	293

TRIPLES

Wheat, Zack	171
Davis, Willie	110
Myers, Hy	97
Daubert, Jake	87
Burns, Oyster	85
Hummel, John	82
Snider, Duke	82
Reese, Pee Wee	80
Sheckard, Jim	76
Daly, Tom	76

HOME RUNS

Snider, Duke	389
Hodges, Gil	361
Karros, Eric	270
Campanella, Roy	242
Cey, Ron	228
Garvey, Steve	211
Furillo, Carl	192
Piazza, Mike	177
Guerrero, Pedro	171
Mondesi, Raul	163

TOTAL BASES

Wheat, Zack	4,003
Snider, Duke	3,669
Hodges, Gil	3,357
Davis, Willie	3,094
Reese, Pee Wee	3,038
Garvey, Steve	3,004
Furillo, Carl	2,922
Karros, Eric	2,740
Gilliam, Junior	2,530
Russell, Bill	2,471

EXTRA-BASE HITS

Snider, Duke	814
Wheat, Zack	766
Hodges, Gil	703
Davis, Willie	585
Karros, Eric	582
Garvey, Steve	579
Furillo, Carl	572
Reese, Pee Wee	536
Cey, Ron	469
Robinson, Jackie	464

BATTING AVERAGE

Keeler, Wee Willie	.360
Herman, Babe	.339
Fournier, Jack	.337
Piazza, Mike	.331
Wheat, Zack	.317
Mota, Manny	.315
Jones, Fielder	.313
Sheffield, Gary	.312
Robinson, Jackie	.311
Walker, Dixie	.311

PITCHING

WINS

Sutton, Don	230
Drysdale, Don	209
Vance, Dazzy	190
Kennedy, Brickyard	176
Koufax, Sandy	165
Grimes, Burleigh	158
Osteen, Claude	147
Valenzuela, Fernando	141
Podres, Johnny	136
Hershiser, Orel	135
Rucker, Nap	135

GAMES

Sutton, Don	534
Drysdale, Don	518
Brewer, Jim	474
Perranoski, Ron	457
Labine, Clem	425
Hough, Charlie	401
Koufax, Sandy	397
Kennedy, Brickyard	381
Vance, Dazzy	378
Podres, Johnny	366

GAMES STARTED

Sutton, Don	517
Drysdale, Don	465
Osteen, Claude	335
Kennedy, Brickyard	332
Vance, Dazzy	326
Valenzuela, Fernando	320
Koufax, Sandy	314
Podres, Johnny	310
Hershiser, Orel	309
Grimes, Burleigh	285

STRIKEOUTS

Sutton, Don	2,652
Drysdale, Don	2,486
Koufax, Sandy	2,396
Vance, Dazzy	1,918
Valenzuela, Fernando	1,759
Hershiser, Orel	1,456
Podres, Johnny	1,331
Martinez, Ramon	1,314
Welch, Bob	1,292
Rucker, Nap	1,217

SAVES

Gagne, Eric	152
Shaw, Jeff	129
Worrell, Todd	127
Brewer, Jim	125
Perranoski, Ron	101
Howell, Jay	85
Labine, Clem	83
Niedenfuer, Tom	64
Hough, Charlie	60
Howe, Steve	59

COMPLETE GAMES

Kennedy, Brickyard	279
Terry, Adonis	255
Vance, Dazzy	212
Grimes, Burleigh	205
Rucker, Nap	186
Drysdale, Don	167
Pfeffer, Jeff	157
Sutton, Don	156
Caruthers, Bob	147
Porter, Henry	139

INNINGS PITCHED

Sutton, Don	3,728
Drysdale, Don	3,432
Kennedy, Brickyard	2,857
Vance, Dazzy	2,758
Grimes, Burleigh	2,426
Osteen, Claude	2,397
Terry, Adonis	2,376
Rucker, Nap	2,375
Valenzuela, Fernando	2,348
Koufax, Sandy	2,324

WALKS

Kennedy, Brickyard	1,128
Sutton, Don	966
Valenzuela, Fernando	915
Drysdale, Don	855
Koufax, Sandy	817
Vance, Dazzy	764
Grimes, Burleigh	744
Terry, Adonis	734
Martinez, Ramon	704
Rucker, Nap	701

SHUTOUTS

Sutton, Don	52
Drysdale, Don	49
Koufax, Sandy	40
Rucker, Nap	38
Osteen, Claude	34
Vance, Dazzy	29
Valenzuela, Fernando	29
Pfeffer, Jeff	25
Hershiser, Orel	24
Podres, Johnny	23

EARNED RUN AVERAGE
(2,000 OR MORE INNINGS)

Pfeffer, Jeff	2.31
Rucker, Nap	2.42
Koufax, Sandy	2.76
Smith, Sherry	2.91
Caruthers, Bob	2.92
Drysdale, Don	2.95
Scanlan, Doc	2.96
John, Tommy	2.97
Singer, Bill	3.03
Sutton, Don	3.09
Osteen, Claude	3.09

SINGLE-SEASON RECORDS

(SINCE 1890)

HITTING

Batting average: .393, Babe Herman, 1930
Slugging average: .678, Babe Herman, 1930
On-base percentage: .455, Babe Herman, 1930
At-bats: 695, Maury Wills, 1962
Runs: 148, Hub Collins, 1890
Hits: 241, Babe Herman, 1930
Singles: 187, Wee Willie Keeler, 1899
Doubles: 52, John Frederick, 1929
Triples: 26, George Treadway, 1894
Home runs, right-handed batter: 48,
    Adrian Beltre, 2004
Home runs, left-handed batter: 49,
    Shawn Green, 2001
Home runs in one month: 15,
    Duke Snider, August 1953
    Pedro Guerrero, June 1985
Home runs, rookie: 35, Mike Piazza, 1993
Grand-slam home runs: 3,
    Kal Daniels, 1990
    Mike Piazza, 1998
Extra-base hits: 94, Babe Herman, 1930
Total bases: 416, Babe Herman, 1930
Runs batted in: 153, Tommy Davis, 1962
Bases on 0: 148, Eddie Stanky, 1945
Stolen bases: 104, Maury Wills, 1962
Pinch-hits: 18, Dave Hansen, 1993
Pinch-hit home runs: 7, Dave Hansen, 2000

SINCE MOVING TO LOS ANGELES, 1958

Batting average: .362, Mike Piazza, 1997
Slugging average: .643, Gary Sheffield, 2000
On-base percentage, .438,
    Wally Moon, 1960
    Gary Sheffield, 2000
At-bats: 695, Maury Wills, 1962
Runs: 130, Maury Wills, 1962
Hits: 230, Tommy Davis, 1962
Singles: 179, Maury Wills, 1962
Doubles: 49, Shawn Green, 2003
Triples: 16, Willie Davis, 1970
Home runs, right-handed batter: 48,
    Adrian Beltre, 2004

Home runs, left-handed batter: 49,
    Shawn Green, 2001
Home runs, in one month: 15,
    Pedro Guerrero, June 1985
Home runs, rookie: 35, Mike Piazza, 1993
Grand-slam home runs: 3,
    Kal Daniels, 1990
    Mike Piazza, 1998
Extra-base hits: 77, Raul Mondesi, 1997
Total bases: 370, Shawn Green, 2001
Runs batted in: 153, Tommy Davis, 1962
Bases on balls: 110, Jimmy Wynn, 1975
Stolen bases: 104, Maury Wills, 1962
Pinch-hits: 18, Dave Hansen, 1993
Pinch-hit home runs: 7, Dave Hansen, 2000

PITCHING (SINCE 1890)

Wins, right-hander: 30, Tom Lovett, 1890
Wins, left-hander: 29, Joe McGinnity, 1900
Win percentage: .933 (14–1), Phil Regan, 1956
Win percentage, 20-game winner: .880 (22–3),
    Preacher Roe, 1951
ERA: 1.58, Rube Marquard, 1916
Games lost: 27, George Bell, 1910
Games: 106, Mike Marshall, 1974
Games started: 44, Bill Terry, 1890
    George Haddock, 1892
    Brickyard Kennedy, 1893
Complete games: 40, Brickyard Kennedy, 1893
Innings pitched: 382.2, Brickyard Kennedy, 1893
Innings pitched, reliever: 208, Mike Marshall, 1974
Saves: 55, Eric Gagne, 2003
Save percentage: 1.000, Eric Gagne, 2003
Strikeouts: 382, Sandy Koufax, 1965
Bases on balls: 151, Bill Donovan, 1901
Hit batsmen: 41, Joe McGinnity, 1900
Wild pitches: 17, Sandy Koufax, 1958
    Darren Dreifort, 2000
Shutouts, right-hander: 9, Don Sutton, 1972
Shutouts, left-hander: 11, Sandy Koufax, 1963

SINCE MOVING TO LOS ANGELES, 1958

Wins, right-hander: 25, Don Drysdale, 1962
Wins, left-hander: 27, Sandy Koufax, 1966
Wins, reliever: 16, Ron Perranoski, 1963
Win percentage: .933 (14–1), Phil Regan, 1966
ERA: 1.73, Sandy Koufax, 1966

Losses: 18, Claude Osteen, 1968
    Don Sutton, 1969
Games: 106, Mike Marshall, 1974
Games started: 42, Don Drysdale, 1963, 1965
Complete games: 27, Sandy Koufax, 1965, 1966
Innings pitched: 335.2, Sandy Koufax, 1965
Innings pitched, reliever: 208, Mike Marshall, 1974
Saves: 55, Eric Gagne, 2003
Save percentage: 1.000, Eric Gagne, 2003
Strikeouts, right-hander: 251, Don Drysdale, 1963
Strikeouts, left-hander: 382, Sandy Koufax, 1965
Bases on balls: 124, Fernando Valenzuela, 1987
    Chan Ho Park, 2000
Hit batsmen: 20, Don Drysdale, 1961
    Chan Ho Park, 2001
Wild pitches: 17, Sandy Koufax, 1958
    Darren Dreifort, 2000
Shutouts, right-hander: 9, Don Sutton, 1972
Shutouts, left-hander: 11, Sandy Koufax, 1963

Bases on balls: 5,
    Greg Brock, 5/17/1983
    Gene Hermanski, 9/22/1949
Stolen bases: 5, Davey Lopes, 8/24/1974

PITCHING

Strikeouts: 18,
    Ramon Martinez, 6/4/1990
    Sandy Koufax, 4/24/1962, 8/31/1959
Innings pitched: 26, Leon Cadore, 5/1/1920
Hits allowed: 23, Jeff Pfeffer, 6/1/1919
Home runs allowed: 6, Hollis Thurston, 8/13/1932
Walks allowed: 11,
    Hal Gregg, 6/15/1944
    Van Lingle Mungo, 6/9/1932
    Sandy Burk, 9/23/1910
    Harry McIntyre, 8/9/1906
Wild pitches: 5, Larry Cheney, 7/9/1918

GAME RECORDS

HITTING

Runs: 6, Shawn Green, 5/23/2002
Hits: 6,
    Paul Lo Duca, 5/28/2002
    Shawn Green, 5/23/2002
    Willie Davis, 5/24/1973
    Cookie Lavagetto, 9/23/1939
    Walter Gilbert, 5/30/1931
    Hank DeBerry, 6/23/1929
    Jack Fournier, 6/29/1923
    George Cutshaw, 8/9/1915
Reached first base safely, nine-inning game: 7,
    Cookie Lavagetto, 9/23/1939
Singles: 6, Willie Davis, 5/24/1973
Doubles: 3, by many, last: Chad Kreuter, 6/3/2001
Triples: 3, Jim Sheckard, 4/18/1901
Home runs: 4, Shawn Green, 5/23/2002
    Gil Hodges, 8/31/1950
Consecutive home runs: 3,
    Shawn Green, 5/23/2002
    Duke Snider, 5/30/1950
    Gene Hermanski, 8/5/1948
Total bases: 9, Shawn Green, 5/23/2002
Runs batted in: 9, Gil Hodges, 8/31/1950